143

D1260956

CRITICAL GENEALOGIES
Historical Situations for Postmodern Literary Studies

THE SOCIAL FOUNDATIONS OF AESTHETIC FORMS
EDWARD W. SAID, EDITOR

CRITICAL GENEALOGIES:

Historical Situations
for
Postmodern Literary Studies

JONATHAN ARAC

New York Columbia University Press *1987*

Library of Congress Cataloging-in-Publication Data

Arac, Jonathan, 1945–
  Critical genealogies.

  Bibliography: p.
  Includes index.
    1. Criticism—History—20th century.   2. Criticism—
History—19th century.   3. Literature, Modern—19th
century—History and criticism.   I. Title.
PN94.A7   1987   801′.95′09   86-26894
ISBN 0–231–06254–0

Columbia University Press
New York   Guildford, Surrey
Copyright © 1987 Columbia University Press
All rights reserved

Printed in the United States of America

This book is Smyth-sewn.

CONTENTS

Acknowledgments

Parts of chapter 1 appeared in "The Criticism of Harold Bloom: Judgment and History," *Centrum* (1978), 6(1):32–42; "Afterword," in *The Yale Critics: Deconstruction in America* (Minneapolis: University of Minnesota Press, 1983), which I edited with Wlad Godzich and Wallace Martin, pp. 176–99; review-essay on criticism of Wordsworth, in *Studies in Romanticism* (1983), 22:136–46.

A first version of chapter 2 appeared in *boundary 2* (1979), 7(3):31–48; and its last section draws on a review-essay from *The Wordsworth Circle* (1982), 13:147–49.

A first version of chapter 3 appeared in *boundary 2* (1979), 8(1):261–73.

A first version of chapter 4 appeared in *boundary 2* (1980), 8(3):241–57.

Parts of chapter 5 appeared in *boundary 2* (1984), 12(3)–13(1):143–55.

A first version of chapter 7 appeared in Walter Benn Michaels and Donald E. Pease, eds., *The American Renaissance Reconsidered* (Baltimore: Johns Hopkins University Press, 1985), pp. 90–112.

Part of chapter 8 first appeared in *boundary 2* (1980), 9(1):75–90.

A first version of chapter 9 appeared in *Salmagundi* (Winter 1982), no. 55, pp. 135–55.

A first version of chapter 10 appeared in *boundary 2* (1981), 9(3)–10(1):437–54.

Part of chapter 11 first appeared in *Union Seminary Quarterly Review* (1983), 37:273–81.

A first version of chapter 12 appeared as the introduction to *Postmodernism and Politics* (Minneapolis: University of Minnesota Press, 1986), which I edited, pp. ix–xliii.

I would like to thank those who gave permission for the use of material they were first to publish.

Acknowledgments

Since I have tried to make documentation as brief as possible in this book, the first versions of these chapters in all cases contain references that may well interest readers but proved inessential to my overall argument here.

I am especially grateful to those whose invitations, commissions, or suggestions provoked portions of this work: Paul A. Bové, David Bromwich, Marshall Brown, Peter K. Garrett, Wlad Godzich, Kathleen Hulley, Lawrence I. Lipking, Marie-Rose Logan, Wallace Martin, Daniel T. O'Hara, Donald E. Pease, Bruce Robbins, Gene Ruoff, Edward W. Said, Samuel Schulman, Patricia Harkin, W. V. Spanos, Cornel West.

My thanks go also to those institutions that aided various aspects of this undertaking: the University of Illinois at Chicago for sabbatical and research leaves, and for much else; Princeton University, Columbia University, and the University of Pittsburgh for typing assistance; and the American Council of Learned Societies for a year's fellowship, intended for another project, that made possible many of the explorations which led to this book.

My greatest professional debt and pleasure is spread among the editorial group of *boundary* 2, for nearly a decade of provocation, comradeship, and criticism. For even longer, I have enjoyed the loving dialogue of Carol Kay.

CRITICAL GENEALOGIES
Historical Situations for Postmodern Literary Studies

Introduction

THIS BOOK has two major goals: to add to our substantive knowledge of the history of literary criticism, and to contribute to a new practice of writing literary history. The project springs from an anomaly of current intellectual life. In the 1960s and early 1970s, literary studies dissipated its disciplinary identity by pursuing "theory" in such diverse areas as linguistics, psychoanalysis, anthropology, and phenomenology. In the last decade, however, the very willingness of literary studies to compound and then cope with this hybrid mixture has made it a resource, a transfer point for renewal across a wide range of disciplines. Important historians of European intellectual culture such as Hayden White and Dominick La Capra, students of American politics such as Michael Paul Rogin, critics of the global politics of scholarship and journalism such as Edward W. Said, critically oriented art historians so different as Michael Fried and Svetlana Alpers, philosophers against the grain of Anglo-American analysis such as Richard Rorty and Alasdair MacIntyre, and Marxist theorists such as Fredric Jameson have all either based themselves in or allied themselves with literary studies in their procedures or their audiences. Yet these same years have also registered a baffling disappointment. A major impetus to the boom in American theory was the hope for a "new literary history" (the journal of that name was founded by Ralph Cohen in 1969). Yet no accomplished projects have been widely recognized as fulfilling that hope. My first chapter lays out this problem in more detail through analyzing the works of two figures closely associated with the project of "new literary history": Harold Bloom and Geoffrey Hartman.

The weight of my undertaking falls on recent literary studies—figures and concerns that come after the terminal date of 1950 René Wellek set for his *History of Modern Criticism*. Thus very literally my subject is "postmodern," a topic addressed more fully in the last chapter. Wellek himself has avowed despair at making his multi-volume study (in progress since the 1940s) anything more than a series of essays on individual critics. I believe, to the contrary, that a fresh exploration of recent criticism's problems with history can help to resolve these problems not only conceptually but in practice, by itself exemplifying a new kind of history writing.

My concern with these matters stems from my studies in the history of the novel. My first book, *Commissioned Spirits: The Shaping of Social Motion in Dickens, Carlyle, Melville, and Hawthorne*, aimed to be a work of "new literary history." In taking both English and American writers, it forced inquiry to issues more fundamental than emerge in the usual nationalist discourse. It drew upon current means of close textual analysis for its readings, while articulating history in two directions: within literary history it looked back to romanticism and forward toward modernism, while it also joined the literary history of the mid-nineteenth century to the social, political, and economic history of the time.

In a related book nearing completion, *Rhetoric and Realism in Nineteenth-Century Fiction*, I treat Goethe, Hawthorne, Flaubert, George Eliot, and Henry James. The scope has expanded chronologically and geographically to allow for a more fully detailed argument on the passages between romanticism and modernism. But in shifting my analytic focus from matters of plot and narrative stance in *Commissioned Spirits* to stylistic texture, I encountered difficulties. To try to help myself work through them, I began probing recent criticism of poetry, which more closely approached the stylistic history I was attempting. These inquiries led to a series of essays on the relations among romanticism, modernism, and current theory, which form the basis for this book.

These explorations point to the problems of our current attempts at histories of criticism. Wellek's hope for an all-embracing completeness doomed his project; my enterprise strives to situate itself specifically in relation to contemporary issues. It aims to excavate the past that is necessary to account for how we got here and the past that is useful for conceiving alternatives to our present condition. (For the moment, take this as what I mean by "genealogy"; later chapters will discuss the notion in Nietzsche and Foucault.) In *The Republic of Letters*, Grant Webster's model from Thomas

Introduction

Kuhn's history of science overemphasized the separation of one critical movement or moment from another. It failed to acknowledge the persistence of both critical institutions (so different yet significant as journals, departments, and classrooms) and literary objects. (I do not deny that a critical revolution can change the object of literary study, but this has happened nowhere near so frequently as Webster's model requires.) In *Criticism in the Wilderness* Geoffrey Hartman and in *After the New Criticism* Frank Lentricchia, for all their differences, both overemphasized philosophy: "too much Kant," said one; "too little Hegel," the other. They thus failed to acknowledge the specificity of criticism. But from Hartman, as from earlier work by Frank Kermode and Paul de Man, I take the valuable reminder that the history of criticism is itself part of the history of literature. Therefore, my chapters include close attention to poems and novels as well as to essays and books of criticism; in this respect I differ from works otherwise so different from each other as those by Lentricchia, Wellek, and Webster. This book is, I believe, unique as a study of the history of criticism in relation to the literary practices and the literary institutions of the last two centuries.

The heart of my historical argument is the claim that to read contemporary criticism requires recognizing the interrelations of at least three layers, like geological strata. Coleridge's romantic metaphysics of symbol and imagination; Arnold's Victorian stance of disinterested, yet worldly, discrimination; and modernist, technical specifications of professional critical tasks together form the ground that current literary study has begun to shift.

First, contemporary criticism is still significantly determined by its romantic beginnings. From T. S. Eliot and I. A. Richards in the 1920s and 1930s, to Cleanth Brooks, Robert Penn Warren, and F. O. Matthiessen in the 1930s and 1940s, to M. H. Abrams and Paul de Man since the 1950s, one crucial axis of modern criticism is a series of rereadings in Coleridge. In order to displace this Coleridgean fascination, I focus especially on Wordsworth. For Wordsworth did more than anyone else to establish the vocation of literature in relation to which Coleridge's, and our own culture's, idea of the literary critic took shape. Yet as a critic, and self-critic, Wordsworth opposed Coleridge. I also counterpose to Coleridge Hazlitt (who reached an understanding of Wordsworth no less powerful than Coleridge's but decisively different) and Shelley (whose impas-

3

sioned skepticism modulated both Coleridge's idealism and Hazlitt's progressive politics). Recent work on Hazlitt by David Bromwich and on Shelley by Paul Fry and Jerrold Hogle permits my treatments of these figures to remain brief.

In a gesture that established the second layer, Matthew Arnold rejected the romantics (they "did not know enough") in theory, while in fact continuing to elaborate Coleridgean positions that made possible the institution of criticism as we have known it. Then in the twentieth century, Arnold was rejected and Coleridge rediscovered. I argue, however, that a "Victorian" stratum still decisively determines our criticism, and not only among those who follow Lionel Trilling in continuing to admire Arnold. It is important to recognize alternatives to Arnold among his contemporaries such as Emerson in America, Nietzsche in Germany, and Pater in England (all of whom I draw on, but again briefly, thanks to work by Daniel O'Hara). It is also important, however, to recognize an alternative within Arnold himself. In the witty mockery of his prose that infuriated his sober opponents, in his concern with the most advanced French and German theory as a goad to the empirical complacency of England, and in his dismantling of the traditional sanctities that had guided the reading of the Bible, Arnold prefigured a wide range of current American advanced criticism, which will continue to occupy a false position until it comes to terms with its embarrassingly respectable ancestor.

The modern stratum of contemporary criticism (roughly 1920–1960) has been intensively studied, for my purposes especially by Paul Bové. But primary attention has gone to New Criticism, which focused on individual poems without special regard to the historical relations that bore on their production, reception, and transmission. I displace New Criticism through attention to D. H. Lawrence, a great modern theorist who renewed Shelleyan rather than Coleridgean motifs. Moreover, I pose a fresh question about the age of New Criticism: what had New Criticism to do with the relatively novel kind of literary history that coexisted with it, the "period study"? Here I emphasize M. H. Abrams (widely considered the preeminent postwar American historical critic) and F. O. Matthiessen, whose *American Renaissance* (1941) made possible the American study of American literature as Arnold's work had the English and American study of English literature. In Matthiessen's career I find again an

4

interaction of strata, for he turned from the Victorian Arnold to the modernist Eliot, and correlatively within romanticism from Shelley to Coleridge.

In the context of the "period study" and modernist criticism, I also examine the work on Baudelaire by the German critic Walter Benjamin (d. 1940), who has been vigorously rediscovered since the 1960s and often seems like one of the answers to how a "new literary history" should be done. For his utopian strain emphasized the role of criticism in helping to make a future, while his materialist concern with the study of reception emphasized the consequentiality of our decisions as to what portions of the past we preserve as "ours." All this and more from Benjamin has been essential to my orientation in this book, yet I try to treat Benjamin's work as seriously as if he were still alive, rather than allowing him to figure with the privilege of a marginal redeemer, a role his work threatens to occupy in much recent criticism.

The "postmodern," which I address as a specific topic in the last chapter, in contemporary criticism seems less a stratum than a de-stratification, for its characteristic gesture is unsettlement, "crisis" as set to work by Paul de Man and Frank Kermode in the middle 1960s. Through the recovery of Nietzsche by Jacques Derrida and Michel Foucault in France, and through new readings in Marx after Althusser, we reach the problem of how to conceptualize a "discontinuous history," an especially rich problem in Fredric Jameson's work. For Jameson insists on the incoherence and gaps that fissure any work, while at the same time he insists on holding our thought to the standard of "totality" and proclaims the necessity to think historically. The dominant tradition in literary theory, however, has emphasized the wholeness of the work and a correlative continuity in history. Aristotle, Coleridge, Arnold, Georg Lukács—Greek, Christian, humanist, Marxist—could all agree on this. The problem of discontinuous history has provoked fresh attention recently to theorists with more complex or disruptive models of the work and of history: Longinus in classical criticism, Shelley among the romantics; Pater, Lawrence, and Benjamin as Victorian and modern. This makes possible the point of view from which my project begins, though I hope I have also remained critical concerning the problems and limitations within this body of work.

To preview what only the chapters to follow can begin to substantiate, I find through these studies that the urgency of relationship between the particular present moment of literary historical writing and the particular past moment(s) being studied contrasts both to the continuous linear sequence of traditional narrative time and to the equally continuous homogeneity of modernist myth. It produces a discontinuous, textured, historical temporality. One consequence of this model for my practice has been the overlay and recurrence that mark my chapters: Wordsworth occurs in many places; Paul de Man receives extensive treatment early and late, as does Nietzsche; Conrad is discussed in relation to Benjamin, to Kermode, and to Jameson; the Bible in relation to Coleridge, to Arnold, and to Kermode. Chronological sequence is not essential for this kind of historiographic attempt; in fact, density of correlation may clarify, rather than mask, historical differences.

Beyond these chronological discontinuities, my procedures also produce gaps in "coverage." Not only compared with Wellek, but even compared with Raymond Williams' *Culture and Society*, this work lacks "totality," an issue I address more fully in the last chapter. Here I will reiterate the lesson of Wellek's failure as well as of Erich Auerbach's *Mimesis*: too great a hope for completeness ruins the comprehensiveness it wished to make possible. Only by determining not to do everything could I accomplish whatever I have. Benjamin's thoughts on "constellating" moments of the past into a shape with present meaning seem to me of particular methodological use. This book, then, is shaped to cope with problems of postwar American literary studies as they have been refocused in the last fifteen years. Despite much recent clamor about theory, the basic concerns extend a good way back.

"Few facts about the life of our culture are more striking than the recent growth of literary criticism in both extent and prestige." It has become "fiercely professional, an 'institution' as well as a discipline, a self-contained world as well as a secondary branch of humane letters." When Irving Howe wrote this in 1958 ("Modern Criticism" 1), the end seemed near to what Randall Jarrell had called "The Age of Criticism." M. D. Zabel noted in 1962 "the effect of self-cancellation which a large part of contemporary critical writing conveys." Yet to mark this effect, Zabel reached back four decades to H. M. Mencken's mockery of "criticism of criticism of criticism" (xix). This triplication defines an uneasy, self-enclosed

6

vitality. Criticism is literary writing that begins from previous literary writing, and it thus questions that literature is limited by
canons of "imitation" of the world or "expression" of an author,
by the exigencies of conventional form or the growth of organic
form. In the isolation of such freedom, writing and readers prolif-
erate but are restricted to an ever more marginal coterie. This is
how Swift and Pope portrayed early eighteenth-century Grub Street.
Since then, the publics for literature have grown, but other technical skills have proved more socially powerful than the mastery of
words as codified in rhetoric. Proliferation inseparable from marginality remains the paradox of literature in consumer democracy, only
more visibly exacerbated in the case of criticism.

May a margin function as a leading edge? Those who came to
intellectual maturity in the shadow of modernism, in "The Age of
Criticism," recall excitedly running to their little-magazine shop to
get the new issue with its Blackmur essay. But those joys are past:
"The most intense moment in the history of modern criticism, the
moment of its greatest hold upon the imagination of serious young
people, has probably just come to an end," declared Howe in 1958
("Modern Criticism" 8). To an older generation nostalgic for the
great days of *Partisan Review* and the old *Kenyon Review*, the current scene is debased parody, a frivolous reenactment, because it is
not grounded in the "overwhelming power" once possessed by "the
avant-garde experience" (Litz 74). Despite the problems I find in
contemporary criticism and theory, I cannot agree with this fundamental dismissal. There need not be a literary avant-garde for
criticism to flourish; in some cases criticism itself plays a leading
cultural role.

In the first chapter I further address relations of criticism and an
avant-garde, but here I must insist that the very particular circumstances of the earlier twentieth century should not establish a
dogma. In the careers of Paul Valéry, T. S. Eliot, Walter Benjamin,
Roman Jakobson, there existed a close link between literary innovation and what we judge the best criticism, theoretical as well as
practical. Nonetheless, in the history of criticism in English, it is
not clear that this model prevails. Sir Philip Sidney wrote his *Apology for Poetry* before the great writing of the Elizabethan age; Ben
Jonson devoted little of his *Timber* to his own time, and his most
generous estimate of Shakespeare came only after his rival's death;

Dryden's intense poetic engagement with Milton had little place in his best critical prose; and Samuel Johnson's greatest critical performances treated Shakespeare and Pope (dead over thirty years when Johnson wrote his life). The dogma of the necessary subordination of criticism to the advanced literature of its time has distorted our understanding of Coleridge's *Biographia Literaria*, causing neglect of its first half. Even more damagingly, this dogma has granted us an easy sense of superiority over Matthew Arnold, and this lets us hide from ourselves the extent to which our critical institutions remain Arnoldian, as I shall argue repeatedly, beginning from the first chapter.

PART ONE
THE HISTORY OF ROMANTICISM IN CONTEMPORARY CRITICISM

Chapter 1
The Impasse of American New Literary History

MUCH DEBATE over the last fifteen years has addressed the "theory boom" in American literary studies, which may be located in relation to various possible starting points: E. D. Hirsch's *Validity in Interpretation* (1967), the arrival of Hillis Miller and Paul de Man from Johns Hopkins to join Harold Bloom and Geoffrey Hartman at Yale, the founding of *Diacritics* at Cornell. I would choose rather Ralph Cohen's journal *New Literary History* (1969), based in a department of which Hirsch was chair and in its first years publishing all the Yale critics as rapidly as did *Diacritics*.

HAROLD BLOOM: JUDGMENT AND HISTORY

The most securely canonized critic to emerge from this boom has been Harold Bloom, author of more books in the seventies than any other major critic and singled out by A. Walton Litz in his essay on "Literary Criticism" in the *Harvard Guide to Contemporary American Writing* and by Frank Lentricchia to give the first Wellek Library Lectures. I shall be addressing the relevance of Bloom's criticism to the questions a new literary history might face, and I shall be demonstrating that Bloom's turn to his characteristic stance of "revisionism" involved a reversal of his views on Matthew Arnold, turning from dismissal to emulation.

Of the critics who defined their identities in the postwar years, Harold Bloom was one of the most useful. He taught us much about reading romantic and more recent poems, but such individual readings only extended New Criticism, which Bloom in other ways reached beyond. Northrop Frye's archetypal criticism made the totality of literature, rather than the individual poem, the unit of effective wholeness, but Bloom challenged both Frye and New Criticism in opening for exploration a middle range, a human scale: individual poets rather than single poems or all poetry. For understanding the dynamics of literary careers, his work and Edward Said's *Beginnings* have been exemplary, and for thinking about literary history as made by writers' responses to earlier writers, Bloom on the last two centuries and Reuben Brower on Pope and on Shakespeare have offered the most concrete instances. Bloom's work, however, still lacks any single achievement comparable to *The Mirror and the Lamp, Anatomy of Criticism, John Keats* by W. J. Bate, or *Wordsworth's Poetry* by Geoffrey Hartman. Bloom's work is hard to grasp because it is not systematized. After discovering through Blake how it might be possible to read all literature, Northrop Frye produced a series of exploratory essays, publishing *Anatomy of Criticism* ten years after *Fearful Symmetry*. Bloom similarly found through Yeats his fundamental insight into the revisionary process, but the result was a flurry of books, each both amplifying and modifying what came before.

Bloom's concerns and gestures participate in the continuing contests of literary criticism, extending from the current scene and the recent past a long way back. By looking at Bloom's early work for his starting points and by relating these points to the larger history of criticism, I hope to show of Bloom what he has shown of Shelley: the irrelevance of the esoteric. Like Blake, like Frye, Bloom scorned mystery. To place him in his own tradition, as he did Yeats and Frye did Blake, helps us both to use and to judge Bloom. I therefore avoid his intricate schemes and terms. For the six "revisionary ratios," after being kabbalistically elaborated, appeared in *Wallace Stevens* as transformations of the classical rhetorical "places." The way lay open for Bloom to prove his "mappings" no more outlandish than the Renaissance studies of Rosemund Tuve or Louis Martz. It is a loss for literary history that no one has pursued this path.

To point to a possible absurdity, or self-contradiction, and walk away smiling and wiping one's hands is the privilege of the press consultant. Once works have appeared and had an impact, it seems necessary to suggest their appeal, their use, and their growing points. The typical attraction of Bloom's writing is assertiveness, the powerful phrase that makes him so fine a writer of introductions as well as of polemics: for example, the summary interpretation of Blake's "London" as "a Jonah's desperation at knowing he is not an Ezekiel" (*Poetry* 44). Following analysis of the poem's figures and movement in relation to a passage from Ezekiel, this phrase moved out from the poem to a sense of a man and a history, the history not only of prophetic poetry but also of the English 1790s, when the French Revolution awakened both apocalyptic hopes and the repression that made it worth a person's life to voice those hopes. Blake abandoned voice for the silence and cunning of his art in an internal exile whose cost he felt and that long kept his work from any place in the public life of English poetry. Here I run ahead both of Bloom and of my exposition, because Bloom does make you run ahead. I will consider these issues later in analyzing Bloom's impasse as a historian.

Bloom is a fine reader of poems but does not grind them into bits; rather, he finds just the right passage to persuade you of the excellence of a writer or work. Bloom's power of quotation suggests that he is haunted by phrases from his reading and keeps trying to make a context that will give them the full weight he feels they contain. Thus in *Fearful Symmetry*, Frye mentioned Lucretian *clinamen* to characterize the fall of Los, which swerves into creation (257). Years later, this term appeared as the cornerstone of Bloom's revisionism. Sometimes, however, the assimilation is less complete and yields dismal pastiche: a full paragraph about Bloom's changed views on Keats wears the language of Wordsworth's "Elegiac Stanzas" (*Poetry* 115). It's like *Play It Again, Sam*: the greatest success is suddenly to be in the position to repeat words you have long hallowed. For a critic, such abdication is costly, but I suspect that thinking about his own need to do this aided Bloom's perceptions about influence.

Such compositional problems, like the boulders from Freud or Nietzsche that often necessitate detours, all suggest a great virtue: Bloom's "brooding." He is a rethinker. He will not rest with achieved positions but is always ready to return upon himself. One fascinating movement in Bloom was the drama of reduction, as a Shelleyan skepticism drove him to question, and abandon, his cherished earlier positions. How much can you give up and still have something? Bloom gave up the imagination: from the apocalyptic autonomy of Blake, it became an effect of repression or an illusion,

Hobbesian "decaying sense" (*Map* 165). So Blake, prophet of the future, yielded as the father of modern poetry to Wordsworth with his Freudian sense of the past. Bloom once found in Keats and Stevens a naturalistic acceptance of death but then lost this consolation. Death is all we have, immortality all we want, and this split is our life. Finally Bloom also gave up the idea that a poem can fulfill an earlier poem or tradition; it can only revise it (*Poetry* 88, 95). Therefore poetry always declines. Only this cost could buy assurance of poetry's continuation. Culminations exhaust poetic lines, but while falling, one can keep swerving.

What did Bloom keep? In exchange for his losses, Bloom grasped the *self*. Revisionism brought "the man who suffers" back into relation with the poem, from which Eliot and Frye alike had barred him. Despite many qualifications ("To be a poet is to be an inter-poet," *Kabbalah*, 114), this notion remains fundamental. The self, the natural, embodied person, once Blake's Spectre of Urthona, became for Bloom the only defense against two sets of enemies: spiritualists, whose totalized view of tradition would murder all desire by showing a culture complete without us into which we mysteriously fit; mechanists, who would disintegrate us into shards of language. Bloom's second position, maintained even longer, is Abrams' "heterocosm," the assurance that literature enjoys autonomy as a world elsewhere (*Mirror* 272–84). These two premises keep Bloom in touch with humanistic traditions and account for much of his appeal. For he thereby neutralizes the Nietzschean and Freudian challenges to the unity of the self and resists the growing necessity to link literature to the histories we live in the world.

From this overview, I turn to the historical situation. Bloom enjoyed a privileged place in the major critical change of the postwar period, the precondition of the "theory boom": the revival of romanticism and the displacement of New Criticism, a process encapsulated in the books by Frye, Abrams, Bate, and Hartman cited earlier. Bloom studied with Abrams at Cornell, worked with Hartman at Yale, was among the first reviewers of Frye's *Anatomy*, and carried on in print a dialogue with Bate's work on Keats and on the burden of the past. Bloom also had to reach terms with New Haven formalism, most formidably embodied in W. K. Wimsatt, and this necessity may account for Bloom's attention to "reading" individual poems in his first three books. The effectiveness of these books as teacherly commentary established the goodwill and authority that made Bloom's voice heard when he launched the revisionary series.

How did Bloom see the critical situation when he began? It was an "odd and unnatural . . . time": "A formidable array of minor poets-turned-critics convinced the academies that twentieth-century verse had somehow repudiated its immediate heritage, and mysteriously found its true parentage in the seventeenth century." Only Yvor Winters had the "descriptive accuracy" to recognize that "almost all poetry written in English since the age of sensibility . . . was inescapably Romantic," but Winters saw only to condemn (*Ringers* 219). In a pattern of repetition on which I will comment further, however, Bloom's own later revisionism found the true parentage of the romantics in the seventeenth century (Milton) rather than in their immediate heritage from the eighteenth century.

Bloom's earliest significant collected essays engaged at once with this condition. In "Lawrence, Eliot, Blackmur, and the Tortoise" (1958), Bloom set Frye against the principles and judgments of New Criticism. Through the critique of evaluation in the *Anatomy*, Bloom exposed the "social . . . dialectic" informing R. P. Blackmur's dismissal of Lawrence's poetry (*Ringers* 198). That dialectic systematically excluded the "Protestant, romantic, radical" (*Ringers* 204). By inverting Eliot's triad of Catholic, classic, and monarchist, Frye had offered a new tradition to oppose that established by the New Critics: prophecy and romance against wit ("Blake After Two Centuries" [1957], in *Fables* 149). Bloom could thereby rescue not only Lawrence but also Yeats and Stevens from New-Critical standards and join them to the romantic tradition.

Three further issues of continuing importance emerge, the first of which is evaluation. From Frye's position, Bloom could scorn Blackmur as "a judicial critic" who "approximates the Arnold of our day" and "ranks poets" into a "new scriptural canon" (*Ringers* 197). The need for a canon, for rank and exclusion, motivated Bloom's later break with Frye, after which Bloom called Frye "the Arnold of our day" (*Anxiety* 31). Our second issue, then, is "Why Arnold?" which also means "What about the touchstones?" The third issue comes in a question, asked rhetorically, which still awaits Bloom's real answer: "Why should the order of institutions be more valid for

15

poetry than the order of a gifted individual?" (*Ringers* 198). At the time of asking, the answer was, it should not be and is not. By now for Bloom, "the gifted individual" is involved with other individuals, but the question remains how institutions operate in the canon formation at which his theory increasingly aims.

I begin, however, with Arnold. To define his significance as a bogey will clarify some of Bloom's premises about literary history. Arnold manifested for Bloom a process that began with Coleridge and ran through Eliot and Blackmur: defeated poets propounding a view of literature that stifled the radical extremities of romanticism, the individuality of Protestantism. Arnold's career moved in three phases that marked a retreat first from romantic poetry, then from any poetry. His 1853 "Preface" tried to correct the practice of poetry. A poet speaking to poets and reviewers polemically sacrificed his major work and called upon his fellows to join him in preferring their art to themselves. Such sacrifice only brought further retrenchment in "The Function of Criticism at the Present Time" (1864). Arnold spoke as a critic who by sacrificing the practice of poetry altogether hoped to establish the preconditions for a future poetry written not out of romantic, individual ignorance but from common knowledge. In "The Study of Poetry" (1880) the writing of poetry disappeared. The "future" of poetry was immense, but only as *read*. The notorious touchstones aimed to free the reader from personal or historical bias by showing the perfect adequacy of Shakespeare and Milton. Arnold's career thus showed that to give up romanticism was to give up the self and to give up any future writing of poetry.

Arnold repeated Coleridge's idolatry of the great dead and his turn to public cultivation. The great lost word for Bloom was Shelley's; his "Defence" is "the most profound discourse on poetry in the language" (*Blake's Apocalypse* 334). Strikingly, Bloom's scattered references to the "Defence" bear on time, the future, the process of history, not the "platonic" immutability usually associated with Shelley. Shelley offered, indeed, a basis for the "catastrophe theory of creativity" that Bloom turned to in the 1980s (beginning with "Freud and the Sublime"). Poetry in Shelley entailed recreative discontinuity: we build our "paradise . . . out of the wrecks of Eden." There is no creation, only transformative perception. The poet always comes after; we compose only when the breeze has already

16

departed, the coal is fading. If Dante formed a "bridge" between ancient and modern poetry, the crossing was strangely discontinuous, for he was also a "Lucifer" whose every "burning atom" bore an even more disruptive "lightning." Shelley hoped for a progressive poetic history, in which all poets contribute to one "great poem," but he feared that the first poem already contains all that poetry offers. Only the endless unveilings of interpretation could make it differ from itself over time (493–500). From this aspect of Shelley's theory, which follows from the impossibility of creation, Earl Wasserman concluded, as did Bloom, that poetry is only possible if every poem reconstellates previous poetry.

In contrast to Shelley, the criticism of Northrop Frye lacked bite. There was no negative moment in his understanding of literature. Frye held that poetry, like dreams, worked through the dialectic of desire and repugnance, but the repugnance was inessential. It only produced the displacements that criticism must undo in order to reveal the total form of literature as fulfilling desire. Frye was like the early Freud who found no "no" in the unconscious, only an erotic will to union. But Freud's later instinctual dualism made aggression as fundamental as eros and thus explains competition and aggression, the world of Bloom's later work.

Now why did touchstones so worry Bloom? In one of the latest essays in his first collection, he cited several passages beside some lines from Ammons but warned that this was "not to play at touchstones, in the manner of Arnold or of Blackmur" (*Ringers* 280). Subsequently, however, Bloom self-consciously yielded. To illustrate Stevens' greatness as a poet of sublimity, he offered some "Arnoldian or Blackmurian touchstones" (*Poetry* 282). Why the fuss? This issue marked Bloom's break with Frye and Frye's optimistic view of human nature. Arnold took his touchstones from the *paragoni* of Italian Renaissance criticism, set pieces of comparison that readily became rivalry (*paragone*, from Greek *parakone*, "touchstone," confused with *agon*, "struggle" or "competition.") Touchstones set poetry against poetry rather than like Frye integrating poetry with poetry. Furthermore, citation of short passages out of context *fragments* the unity of a work, violating principles on which Wimsatt and Frye could both agree with Aristotle.

The classical source for literature as fragmentary and competitive is Longinus *On the Sublime*. Longinus helped extricate the romantics from the dilemmas of eighteenth-century poetry and was crucial to Bloom's new romantic criticism. Longinus is extravagant and difficult, and since Bloom rarely cited him, many readers have not appreciated his place in Bloom's work. Longinus held that the sublime was disjunctive, a power that "scatters everything before it like a thunderbolt," in a moment. This power derived from the grandeur of the human mind, "the echo of a great soul," and was freed from any natural mimesis. It offered a theory of inspiration that depended on no divinity. Men became gods to one another, as the "effluences" of past greatness filled the young writer. To achieve full power, however, one must leave such passive receptivity and emulatively combat one's predecessor, as Plato did Homer, "entering the lists like a young champion matched against the man whom all admire." Thus Bloom's agonistic metaphors joined a tradition of discourse. Likewise, another of Bloom's important, apparently idiosyncratic notions: the Scene of Instruction. To achieve the sublime, one may conjure up the great past writers as judges and exemplars: the "ordeal" of this ghostly "tribunal" will yield us the power to immortalize ourselves, or else it will quell us if our spirits are inadequate (*On the Sublime* 1.4, 9.2, 13.2, 13.4, 14.2).

For Longinus the eternity of literature was not dead monuments, empty pyramids that testify to the vain hunger of the imagination; it was human encounter, both pedagogic and competitive, that mysteriously bridged time. Bloom found the sublime an archaic mode that was nonetheless "always available to us again, provided a survivor of the old line comes to us" (*Figures* 246). Thus the sublime is associated not only with demonization, repression, and hyperbole, but also with the final position in Bloom's map: return of the dead and transumption. This context defined one of Bloom's most provocative undertakings toward a new literary history. His analysis of "transumptive allusion" in *Paradise Lost* attempted a precise rhetorical explanation of the eternity-effect of great literature, since classical times a puzzle more invoked than explored. The romantic theory of the symbol, and its New-Critical inheritors, could only explain this effect metaphysically, through the participation of a temporal part in an eternal whole. Transumption, however, "murders time" only "figuratively." It is only "troping on a trope" and enforces a "state of rhetoricity" at the expense of the "presentness of the present," in contrast to the presence necessary to the symbol

(*Map* 138, 142). The rhetoric of sublimity allowed Bloom to evade the critical line from Coleridge to Blackmur, from which his thought took its oppositional beginning.

Within the Longinian tradition, it is worth noting, the *Conjectures on Original Composition* by Edward Young (1759) offered precedent for other Bloomisms. On the trope of self-begetting: "As Tacitus says of Curtius Rufus, an original author is born of himself, is his own progenitor." On metaleptic reversal in temporality: "Suppose you was to change place in time with Homer; then, if you write naturally, you might as well charge Homer with imitation of you." On the modern poet as satanic: Young lamented the "fall" from Homer to Pope, but claimed of Pope that "in his fall, he is still great,"

> Nor appears
> Less than archangel ruin'd, and the excess
> Of glory obscur'd
> (*Paradise Lost* 1:592–94; Young 370, 362, 367–68)

This last point may remind us how completely Bloom neglected Pope, who nonetheless seems crucial for any thorough understanding of the strengths and weaknesses of English poetry since Milton.

From this historical view, I turn to Bloom's own career. Read now, his first book, *Shelley's Mythmaking*, proves astonishingly at one with revisionism in its concerns, though not in its positions. The basis from which Bloom defined and analyzed Shelley's myths, the Buberian personalism of "I-Thou" confrontation, persisted and informed the dialectical "subject-centered . . . person to person" relations of influence, defending against both linguistic reduction (it-it) and the oppressions of tradition (I-it). The Shelley book already emphasized the "corrective competition" between Shelley and Milton, and Bloom heard the uncanny echoing between "The Witch of Atlas" and Yeats' "Byzantium" years before the ratio of apophrades could account for it.

Even problems of method in reading emerge reflectively. Yeats' observations on Demogorgon on *Prometheus Unbound* suggested that the "misunderstandings of one great poet by another" are valuable. Wilson Knight exemplified the danger that criticism might become "independent vision," an "individual and inferior poetry" (123, 196). The term "misreading" occurred often in *Shelley's Myth-making*, always negatively. Nonetheless, Earl Wasserman's review of the book charged that Bloom himself "repeatedly misread" and damaged his case by insisting that his misreadings "are the *opus ipsum* [work itself]" and "disclaiming that he is offering *creative* interpretations" (611). As if taking advice from Wasserman, *The Visionary Company*, Bloom's next book, began a self-revision toward "the necessity of misreading." Robert Graves was "the most persuasive of modern misreaders," "more imaginative" than other critics on Keats' "La Belle Dame sans Merci" (403).

Bloom's first three books maintained his loyalty to Frye, but his break began late in the third book, *Blake's Apocalypse*: "I don't believe that Blake's reading of the Bible was as imaginatively liberated as Frye takes it to have been" (392). Since Frye had begun our whole current attention to "reading" by defining the key to Blake as his reading of the Bible (*Fearful Symmetry* 11), this disagreement was fundamental. Bloom could not accept Blake's Christian understanding of the so-called "New Testament" as completing and purifying the "Old Testament" (an important issue for Frank Kermode too, in chapter 9). From this refusal followed the general impossibility of "fulfillment" in literary tradition, the recognition that fulfillment involved invidious judgments, that Frye's criticism depended on decisively evaluating the relation of the Hebrew Bible to the Christian Bible. Thus Frye proved a canonizer, another Matthew Arnold.

Yeats, which occupied Bloom through most of the sixties, marked his crisis. He had to recognize his own activity in making the canons of literature. He too was ranking, making judgments, invoking romantic tradition in order to diminish Yeats by it. His earlier work could be seen as wholly positive (though it also had its polemic), offering only descriptive appreciation of misunderstood works. But now, like any Leavis—or Arnold—he was engaged in "scrutinoid" revaluation (*Shelley's Mythmaking* 125), performing acts not only of love but also of aggression toward poetry, undoing much of Yeats in order to clear a view of the romantics. Revisionism was the means to comprehend and justify the double process by which Bloom discovered what Yeats had done to Blake and Shelley and what he himself was doing to Yeats. Reflection upon this experience would suggest literary history as an activity simultaneously individual and exclusive, competitive and delusive. Elaborating these qualities would produce the apparatus of precursor and canon, Freudian psychology and Nietzschean rhetoric.

Leaving Coleridgean formalism and the archetypes of Frye, Bloom turned source study "inside out" (*Figures* 9), humanizing it as Frye's Blake had humanized nature. The "organic analogue" yielded to the "human analogue": "To say that a poem is about itself is killing, but to say that it is about another poem is to go out into the world where we live" (*Map* 198). But what is this "world" like, and what are its relations to history, exclusion, and power, the very concerns that motivate Bloom's theory?

No sooner did Bloom offer engagement with the world than he retracted it: "Mature creation, for a poet, rises directly from an error about poetry rather than . . . about life" (*Figures* 175). Some indirect process of relation between poetry and the world might be of interest, but not to Bloom. So far is poetry from the world that it "transcend[s] mimesis"; poets confront "not the universe, but the precursors" (*Kabbalah* 82). Bloom's promised "literary-history as canon-formation" (*Kabbalah* 63) can never be achieved, given his positions that erode this goal: "There is no literary history . . . only biography," individual "defensive misreadings" (*Kabbalah* 106). No dialectic of "art and society" but only of "art and art" fuels the process of poetry (*Anxiety* 99). This is a major impasse in the quest for a new literary history.

Such unwillingness to come to disciplined terms with the world produced the extreme variation of Bloom's claims for the applicability of his theory. At first it was scrupulously limited to post-Enlightenment poetry. So Shakespeare was exempt by living in "the giant age before the flood" (*Anxiety* 11). Bloom here echoed Dryden's poetic idealization (an epigraph to the first chapter of W. J. Bate's *The Burden of the Past*), but such a dualism of before and after is obviously mythical, not historical. Discovering the dialectic of influence in earlier contexts forced the alternative, equally unhistorical, assertion of universality (*Map* 77). Only precise attention to the place of poetry in society—the opportunities offered for voice, script, and instruction, by whom, to whom, and for what purposes—will allow the nuance, detail, and differentiation that make a history and set proper limits to a theory.

Bloom, however, denied himself the means needed for this end. He abandoned many idealizations but still maintained that "canon-formation is not an arbitrary process" and therefore "not, for more than a generation or two, socially or politically determined" (*Map* 200). This is still faith in the mystic agency of Shelley's "redeemer and mediator, Time." What Bloom posited as inevitable, Walter Benjamin set rather as a task for human agency, "a revolutionary chance in the fight for the oppressed past" (*Illuminations* 263). Benjamin's "redemption" of the past so that it "becomes citable in all its moments" required struggle as did Bloom's version of history: "In every era the attempt must be made anew to wrest tradition away from a conformism that is about to overpower it" (*Illuminations* 254–55). For Benjamin, however, the struggle required cooperation; it must draw strength from, while also helping to illuminate, the hitherto "anonymous toil" of those overshadowed by solitary Bloomian "great minds and talents" (*Illuminations* 256).

Yet Bloom's assertion that "poets survive because of inherent strength" neglected his own insight into the subordination of the Old Testament to the New, the centuries-long suppression of the Gnostics and the Kabbalists, Blake's lament "I am hid." Against such social, political, and ideological repression, Bloom insisted upon the psychological: "A strong reading is the only poetic fact, the only revenge against time that endures" (*Poetry* 6). But what of the material basis of such facts? How do I enforce my reading? Such questions fell outside Bloom's thought: "The idea of a 'finished' poem . . . depends upon the absurd, hidden notion that reifies poems from relationships into entities" (*Poetry* 99). But what if we replace "finished" with "published"? Isn't such reification exactly what publication performs and what we value it for? Replace "finished" with "censored"; the purity of relationship is compromised by the material vulnerability of the poem's existence. Replace "finished" with "vanished." If its reified traces disappear, we have no relationship at all, except in a Blakean imagination that lets no act of humanity perish. My treatment of Benjamin and Dickinson focuses on a poet and a critic both of whom are still far from having assumed their full places in our culture precisely because of the extreme material vulnerability of their works, and even of their lives. Jerome McGann has begun a post-Bloomian revisionism that acknowledges the social and physical materiality of poetic texts.

Bloom's position lacked any imaginative form for organizing what he knew about poetry in the world. For psychology he had Freud as precursor, Lacan as transatlantic contemporary, and Geoffrey Hartman as colleague; for rhetoric, Nietzsche as precursor, Derrida as transatlantic contemporary, and Paul de Man as colleague; for history, Marx and Foucault would have made a start. I have suggested the relevance of Benjamin and must also mention E. P. Thompson. Thompson's *Making of the English Working Class* sought to "rescue" the early industrial revolution from anonymous toil by its passionate citation of arguments and struggles long hidden by the "enormous condescension of posterity" (Thompson 12). In this task, the book is crucially articulated—at beginnings and ends of the major sections—around moments from the work of William Blake (15, 446, 832). From their different sides, Thompson and Benjamin both testified to the possibilities of literature in history. To take on one more reduction, to give up at last the heterocosmic autonomy of literature, will enrich and complicate Bloom's new literary history and join it fully to the world where we live.

GEOFFREY HARTMAN: HISTORY AND INDETERMINACY

In this analytic survey of Harold Bloom's work, I have begun to elucidate the most fundamental challenge of the "theory boom" to our ways of literary study. This challenge falls within the interlinked topics of romanticism, narrative, and the question of writing in criticism, history, philosophy. Bloom wrote a history of romanticism as a falling from Milton and what follows as a falling from romanticism; and J. Hillis Miller wrote such probing essays as "Tradition and Difference," which posed Nietzschean deconstruction against the historiography of M. H. Abrams in *Natural Supernaturalism*, and "Narrative and History," which brought together George Eliot's *Middlemarch* and Walter Benjamin's "Theses on the Philosophy of History." But more ominous than either of these were the unwritten histories of romanticism by Paul de Man and Geoffrey

23

Hartman. Their rigor of renunciation counted for more than end-lessly successful revisionist or deconstructive readings in affecting our thought about literary history, and literary study at large. This further impasse I shall analyze here with particular regard to Hart-man; de Man figures especially in chapters 4 and 10.

Against the New-Critical, modernist devaluation of romanticism, there seemed an easy historical response, to join Northrop Frye, Frank Kermode, Raymond Williams, and others in establishing the significant continuities that link modernism to romanticism. This move, however, was vulnerable to the arguments of Gerald Graff, who revived Irving Babbitt's and Yvor Winters' condemnations of modernist literature as itself merely romantic. Such a double con-demnation was well established in Germany, de Man observed in "Literary History and Literary Modernity" (*Blindness* 144). But the continuity between romanticism, modernism, even postmodernism, that Graff specified—the fetishism of the "symbol" and the "self-sufficient" artwork leading both "formalist" critics like Cleanth Brooks and "visionary" critics like Frye to unite in adoring the "fu-sion of dancer and dance," relativistically denying the possibility of "error," in defiance of reason or logic (*Literature* 48, 13, 136, 62)—all these de Man had already castigated as misreadings of roman-ticism, beginning from his review of Anglo-American neoformalism in the 1950s, continuing through his review of Bloom's *The Vision-ary Company* in the early 1960s, "The Rhetoric of Temporality" in the late 1960s, and "Semiology and Rhetoric" in 1973. By arguing that allegory projects as narrative the contradiction that ironically rends any moment; by arguing that allegory represents an unreach-able, barren, painful anteriority; and by finding such allegory in Rousseau, Wordsworth, and Hölderlin, de Man protected romanti-cism against any attack it has yet faced in America. But he also assaulted the "false historicism" and utopian formalism that made possible any narrative romantic history (*Blindness* 241). At mo-ments de Man idealized this condition as perfect lucidity and thus fell into a romantic myth of reflexivity. But his last decade avoided this temptation.

The real but imperfect self-consciousness of romanticism Hartman associated with experimental prose forms that mingle literary the-ory and practice with the writing of philosophy. Hartman took Ar-nold's charge against the romantics that they did not know enough as meaning that they failed to agree with Arnold that self-consciousness is paralyzing. What Hartman called the "Arnoldian Concordat" (*Criticism* 6) thus preserved criticism by subordinating it to literature and separating both from philosophy. For Arnold, to recognize philosophy as writing would diminish its conceptual force, while to recognize criticism as writing would compromise the aesthetic form of literature. My chapter on Arnold will suggest how little I can accept these claims, but for Hartman they explained the basis from which Arnold could then narrate a history of the development from romantic ignorance of these imperatives to a later and more perfect understanding. "Romanticism" thus emerged as the name in our culture for the entanglement that joins the philosophy of history with the history of philosophy with the theory of narrative.

The fullest engagement with these matters came in Hartman's recent books, which proclaimed the revaluation of romanticism and consequent "rethinking of literary history" (*Criticism* 44). Hartman turned to de Man for aid in his "effort to overcome falsely progressive (Hegelian and dialectical) theories of art" (*Criticism* 107). Theories of loss and gain, or even of transformation, are all suspect, even when used in defense of romanticism, for "at its most radical" the project of contemporary criticism—what Hartman called "Revisionism"—"challenges all historic explanation" insofar as such explanation is based on "concepts of fall, secularization, restoration, etc.," that forge a drama in which the "natural supernaturalism of art" regains "something 'divine' that is lost" (*Criticism* 180). (Hartman alluded to *Natural Supernaturalism* by M. H. Abrams, who had been a teacher of Harold Bloom and senior colleague to de Man and Hartman at Cornell.) According to Hartman, such myths of progress and loss comprised a "historicism" that is "monumentalizing" (*Criticism* 110) and therefore deadening and oppressive. Hartman parallels Nietzsche's critique of monumental history and critical history: there is danger to life in overvaluing the past no less than the present.

The same "hygiene" that should sanitize our dealings with history or a career guided the "hermeneutics of indeterminacy" that Hartman proposed for reading a poem. We must avoid the masterful temptations of "technocratic, predictive, and authoritarian formulas" (*Criticism* 41). Rather than judgment, true criticism instead is "suspensive discourse," less cognition than commemoration. Engaged with a poem, we should feel responsible to "hold it in mind" rather than to "resolve it into available meanings" (*Criticism* 274). Heidegger's critique of technology and insistence on "letting be" echo here, as in Hartman's resolve not to "coerce the future" by prediction (*Criticism* 162). Even more than Heidegger, however, Hartman echoed the Wordsworth he so long and lovingly held in mind. In resisting the theory of progress, Hartman could find his emblem in the "halted traveller" of *Wordsworth's Poetry*: as Wordsworth confronted his imagination in book 6 of *The Prelude*, he was "lost / Halted without an effort to break through." The theorist of "suspensive discourse" echoes the poet who made a signature of the word "hang," not only in his poetry (cf. 1850 *Prelude* 1:330; 5:381, 392) but also in discussing the imagination in the preface to his 1815 collected volume. Hartman's fear of preemptive closure shared Wordsworth's aspiration toward "something evermore about to be" (*Prelude* 6:608). Thus, romanticism properly read would save us from all that the misunderstanding of romanticism had cost. The critic should "accept" rather than "subvert or overlook" the "language of great writers" (*Saving* xv).

Yet to accept the language of a great writer may give results very different from what Hartman seemed to expect. According to Wordsworth, unprecedented "national events" in politics, the "increasing accumulation of men in cities," and in work a new "uniformity in their occupations," while the growth of mass media facilitated "rapid communication"—all together threatened to "blunt the discriminating powers of the mind," making the humanities marginal or degraded. Therefore the preface to *Lyrical Ballads*, from which I have been quoting, proclaimed the need for sober and serious opposition to what Pope and Swift had dismissed with satiric scorn. Arnold, Eliot, and Leavis subsequently accepted this call. In going behind Arnold to Wordsworth, therefore, Hartman preserved deep concerns, and he also challenged our current institution of literary study by questioning Arnold's modest prose-pose. For Hartman knew that such modesty was politically significant (*Criticism* 50), and he also knew that Wordsworth never renounced the immodest energy of "Hannibal among the Alps" (a figure I return to in chapter 8), yet Hartman did not want to cause trouble.

Hartman defused the political implications of his institutional challenge by removing the threat of avant-garde coerciveness, refusing to join Wordsworth in sometimes traveling "before." Bloom, for all his problems, helped mobilize a new literary history by his turn to Arnoldian judgment; Hartman, for all his richness, helped obstruct a new literary history by refusing judgment and choosing indeterminacy. Arnold had seen critics as avant-garde, perishing in the wilderness while pointing the way to a promised land for poetry; but Hartman insisted, "This wilderness is all we have" (*Criticism* 15). Hartman likewise revised Georg Lukács's definition of the essayist as a John the Baptist preaching "in the wilderness," the "pure type of the precursor," a road needing its end to be complete (*Soul and Form* 16–17). He suggested rather that as critics "we are forerunners to ourselves" (*Criticism* 15). Hartman here was also opposing the reading of Abrams in *Natural Supernaturalism*, which found in romanticism, and in Wordsworth above all, a completed pattern of journeying. In my next chapter, I too criticize Abrams, but here I would insist that even if "the artist is surely the liminal or threshold person par excellence" (Hartman, *Fate* 109), one need not require the critic to be so. The comforting persistence of critical identity ("Where they are, there I shall be") Hartman finds in self-precursiveness may cover the line Carlyle-Ruskin-Pater, yet in the relations Carlyle-Dickens, Ruskin-Proust, Pater-Joyce, I find distinctions between precursor and after-runner larger than Hartman's formula would suggest. His denial of closure threatens a coercive denial of difference.

Let us, therefore, think again through Hartman's argument. He wanted a history that does not become "monumental and preemptive." Critics must "avoid historicism," that is, the "staging of history as a drama in which epiphanic raptures are replaced by epistemic ruptures [a witty parody of secularization models], coupures as decisive as Hellene and Hebrew, or Hegel and Marx" (*Saving* xx). The pointedly contrasted parallels in Hartman's prose foreground stylistics. The prose of "History-Writing as Answerable Style" (*Fate* 101–13) should resemble what Hartman found in Wordsworth's poetry: unpointed yet finely nuanced, a medium that preserves the archaic while gently purifying it and allowing it to mingle with a popular, everyday influx. (Reading "Nutting" in the next section of this chapter, I find something fiercer and more decisive.)

According to Hartman, "Perhaps the only true literary history we have" is Auerbach's *Mimesis* (*Criticism* 235), devoted to the mingling that overcame—at certain moments—the classical separation of stylistic levels. Yet even as I thus summarize Auerbach, a "drama" begins that caused Auerbach uncertainty and aroused criticism. For he expressed second thoughts about his fundamental contrast between Homer and the Bible ("Epilegomena"), while E. R. Curtius argued that more flexibility existed among stylistic levels than Auerbach's story allowed for ("Lehre"). Nonetheless, Auerbach went on in his final book toward the goal of disclosing a whole that "takes on the character of a dialectical unity, of a drama, or as Vico once said, of a serious poem" (*Literary Language* 7). He saw this book as "a kind of drama which advances no theory but only sketches a certain pattern of human destiny. The subject of this drama is Europe" (21). The "Hegelian and dialectical" prove hard to leave behind, and could they be left behind that would in itself provide a plot of progress.

Consider Hartman's own story in *Criticism in the Wilderness*. It ran from the Arnoldian Concordat through the New-Critical Reduction to the Revisionist Reversal. This is so bald a version of loss and gain that it signals parodic self-deprecation, yet it was also meant to work. And when Hartman feared "the Critic become Commissar" (*Criticism* 162), we feel the alliterative point dotted full seriously. Matters of practical, even capital, concern—defining one's own place among the critics, protecting the freedom to write—enforce the need for historical differentiation. Hartman's practice, against his theory, confirms Benjamin's claim that history-writing "means to seize hold of a memory as it flashes up at a moment of danger" (*Illuminations* 255).

Consider another invocation of history as a matter of real interest, of "saving the text" by bringing the philosophic vocabulary of Derrida's deconstruction over into literary studies. Since "dissemination" is "what does not return to the father," Hartman linked Derrida's term to the interplay in the Middle Ages and Renaissance between the authoritatively learned, classical, patriarchal language (*sermo patrius*) and the naturally imbibed, vernacular, mother tongue (*lingua materna*) (*Criticism* 88; *Saving* 154). In using deconstructive semantic play to enrich Auerbach's analysis of tensions between classical and Christian, Hartman *combined* the two tendencies in current criticism—Auerbachian spiritualizing and Derridian mechanizing—that Harold Bloom (as I noted earlier) had hoped to stay *between* (*Map* 79). By this means, Hartman aimed to save literary "deconstructive" practice from being what Rodolphe Gasché called "a mechanical exercise similar to academic thematism or formalism." Hartman wished to avoid the "abstract and monotonous vigor of its application to this or that slice of text" (*Saving* 49). To prevent this deathly repetition required placing "dissemination" in a "differentiated series" of stylistic practices including "imitation, translation, contamination, secularization, and (sacred) parody." In his own need for differentiation, Hartman referred to the "evolution" of language and charged that Derrida "fails to provide a history that charts the path from 'imitation' to 'dissemination'" (*Saving* 49). Hartman's language thus rejoined Arnold and Lukács; rather than resting in the wilderness with Derrida, it followed the road to a new end, apparently against the writer's will.

Hartman wanted history-writing to shun "historicism" while preserving the truly "historical," which pertains to our "mortal" being and "threatens lasting monuments or totalizing mind" (*Criticism* 110). This evokes the project of a Heideggerian literary history, echoed in Bové's *Destructive Poetics*, a project made arduous because there may be "no indication that Heidegger thinks poetry has a history" (Rorty, *Consequences*, 47). The conjunction of history with mortality again links history to our interests. Yet I find a monumentalizing that deadened Hartman's own historical prose. He wrote that "political and economic unrest" in the 1930s "made it important to protect art from imperious demands of an ideological nature, emanating from politics" (*Criticism* 284). Perhaps historical sentences need not have human agents, but to avoid the monumental, they must at least have interested parties. To whom was it important? Certainly Walter Benjamin never gave up on the political project of rescuing art from fascism and using it against fascism; George Orwell was willing to declare that "all art is propaganda" (1:492); and Kenneth Burke recollected, "When the Leftists first began to move onto the scene, I began to fear that they were dishonoring Shakespeare. For a couple of years there, I took all sorts of notes for articles in defense of Shakespeare. Then all of a sudden I made the discovery: Look, this fellow has been taking care of himself for a long time. . . . From that time on, at least that much of my puzzle was resolved" (Aaron et al 500).

Hartman's theoretical unease with history damaged his practice when he, inevitably yet as if inadvertently, wrote historically. His sentences became indistinguishable from those of Gerald Graff, an anti-indeterminist for whom history was in theory no problem: "As the growth of class-consciousness threatened the stability of the established order, reason was associated with a blind fanaticism" (*Literature* 41). Again, to whom was this association significant? Graff shared with Hartman a fear of coercing reality. He insisted on our knowing the object as in itself it really is "before leaping in with our value judgments" (86). Here too a hermeneutics of indeterminacy operated, despite Graff's intention to oppose such positions. We must be responsible for the whole being, rather than focusing only on what touches us, for "the existing order . . . has to be understood as it is before it can be altered" (27). This statement is false: we have yet to understand the Third Reich or the slave system of the American South, yet those existing orders were decisively altered. If Graff meant an order *should* be understood before altered, I wonder who will define the object. The debate on the standard of living in nineteenth-century England still persists among historians. Should a worker unemployed by the new industrial "order" have waited for our results before breaking frames? Even if the overall standard rose, there were moments, places, persons, for whom it did not. Human interests differ, and only in a radically different society would a community of interest make possible consensually shared knowledge in the most urgent matters. This is the point of Foucault's hyperbolic equation of speech with war, and the problem with Habermas' invocation of the ideal speech-situation (as I have discussed in "The Function of Foucault").

We are limited beings, yet a hermeneutics of indeterminacy refuses to accept our determinations, actively resists our ends, and thus contradicts what Hartman considered the necessary "historical" concern with mortality. A valuable openness may become a fearful refusal. Hartman's sense of reading in "How to Reap a Page" (in *Saving*) might take as emblem Cleopatra's dream of Antony:

> For his bounty
> There was no winter in't; an autumn 'twas
> That grew the more by reaping.
> (*Antony and Cleopatra* 5.2.86–88)

The dream defies the reality of Antony's death, even as the accepted editorial emendation of the Folio reading "an Antony it was" into "an autumn 'twas" displaces the mortal human name by the natural force of the season. In refusing to look ahead with Arnold or Lukács to the end of the road, the promised land, Hartman instead undertook to make the wilderness blossom:

> Roses are planted where thorns grow,
> And on the barren heath
> Sing the honey bees.
> (Blake, *The Marriage of Heaven and Hell*, plate 2)

He exchanged the future-orientation of Shelley's "Ode to the West Wind"—which sees autumnal destruction but looks ahead to the promise of spring—for the presentness of Keats' "To Autumn." The difference between seasons deferred to the dilation of a moment. Yet as William Empson objected at the 1976 MLA Convention, Hartman's own brilliant reading of Keats' ode (in *The Fate of Reading*) elided any consciousness that Keats wrote it with the knowledge that he would soon die. To move from Yeats' "Byzantium" to Keats' "Autumn" makes gentler the wish to be invulnerable to time, yet "suspensive" criticism here resembles the hovering of New-Critical ironic disinterest. Hartman's endless "hesitation" repeats I. A. Richards on the tragic "attitude" in *Principles of Literary Criticism*, a frozen readiness that never commits itself, a monument of "patience" (*Fate* 109).

When Keats gloried in the "energies" of a "quarrel in the streets" (2:80), it would be priggish to demand that he abandon his spectatorship and join in, or try to stop it. Yet in writing history, such Burckhardtian aestheticism joins with cynical pessimism about the future, as Hayden White has argued in *Metahistory*. Fredric Jameson tried, however, to integrate an aesthetic moment with a more positive orientation to the future. To complement the necessary cynicism of ideological analysis, he urged a utopian, "anticipatory" analysis that finds figures for what will be fully realized only when all human beings can act and speak freely together as equals (*Political Unconscious* 296). Social conflicts bring together even those most committed to atomic individualism and unite them in larger, common purposes. Ideological analysis criticizes the purpose; anticipatory criticism appreciates the union. Thus the solidarity of mill owners conspiring to blacklist dissident workers prefigures what we may enjoy in a "finer tone" (Keats, 1:185) in an imagined end to history. Our judgments of present interest are suspended, but only for a moment, as part of moving toward a new goal. In chapter 11, I shall raise problems with Jameson's position, but against Hartman I wish now to emphasize that in its isolating an energy, in breaking the frame of value, overturning our moral conceptions, such a moment is Nietzschean, as is Derrida when he sets in play the deconstructive energies within the monuments of logocentrism. Such attempts aid rather than hinder the search for a new literary history.

Yet Hartman feared the "abstract and monotonous vigor," the deadly repetition-compulsion in Derrida, and he feared also utopian avant-gardism like Jameson's. The history of terms meaning "avant-garde" is not encouraging. When Keats' Coelus assured Hyperion that his "ethereal presence" would allow him to be "in the van of circumstance" (1:34–44), Hyperion launched himself only into his own fall. In the first figurative adaptation to cultural matters of the military term "vanguard," Carlyle wrote that "at length Germany and Weissnichtwo were . . . in the vanguard of the world" (*Sartor Resartus* 1:3), but this mocked the establishment of a "Professorship of Things in General" (*Allerley-Wissenschaft*) that lacked both teaching responsibilities and pay. This commitment to "Affirmation and Reconstruction" was in "Name merely." Hartman, and in their different ways the other Yale critics, preferred not to "travel before" with Wordsworth but to walk alongside of received opinion, a paradoxical sidling that supported what it somehow also stood apart from. By the logic that Sacvan Bercovitch has analyzed in *The American Jeremiad*, the very crisis provoked by the Yale critics— their "un-Americanness"—set to work a process that reaffirmed the solidarity of what it enclosed. In shunning the purposiveness of "ideological criticism" and preferring a "deliberately relaxed style" in essays that are "digressive yet powerfully recursive," Hartman himself followed the model he discerned in Lionel Trilling, and

Hartman bid to succeed Trilling as "Man in the Middle" (*Fate* 294–97). We remain suspended always on the threshold of a change that never occurs. Returning to Trilling, in the last chapter I argue that one change we should acknowledge is the historical delimitation of the "Stalinist" threat in the United States: Stalinism is alive neither as an option nor a danger for those of us whose consciousness has been formed since the McCarthy era. Making this judgment lessens the attraction of politically self-protective indeterminacy.

The Yale critics manifested a timidity that still threatens to make literary studies "merely the name . . . for an academic department where memories of youthful hope are cherished, and wistful yearnings for recapturing past glories" (Rorty, *Consequences*, 147, on philosophy). As readers we need less of Hartman's hesitant "patience"; in contrast, despite problems that I address in chapter 9, I recommend more confidence in what Frank Kermode called the "patience" of great literature, or what Kenneth Burke might have called Shakespeare's self-reliance. We must not fear that if we make interpretive decisions rather than indeterminations—and thus try to make literature part of our future as well as our present—we will thereby destroy or violate the works we care for. Despite Hartman's critique of the historicism of gain and loss, he feared losing the object. *Saving the Text* had at least this meaning.

Such loss is possible. Hazlitt's prose Immortality Ode "On Reading Old Books" lamented the vanishing of privileged early moments of literary experience. Hazlitt's long love for Wordsworth diminished his response to Keats: "The sharp luscious flavor, the fine *aroma* is fled. . . . But it was not always so. There was a time when . . . every word was a flower" (12:225). Emerson's "Experience" of reading charted a series of lost objects: "Once I took such delight in Montaigne, that I thought I should not need any other book; before that in Shakespeare; then in Plutarch; at one time in Bacon; afterwards in Goethe; even in Bettine, but now I turn the pages . . . languidly." Of paintings, he continued, "How strongly I have felt . . . that when you have seen one well, you must take your leave of it; you shall never see it again" (476). Such loss is possible, but it is not the end. The object remains, but no longer ours. We go on.

Emerson and Foucault defined a relation to history different from any that has supported the institutions of reading which Hartman, and even Derrida, function within. I mean more than the term "power" Hazlitt and Emerson shared with Foucault. This distrust of the ingenuities needed to startle familiar texts into fresh life made attractive Foucault's archival research that continued to find materials bearing on our interests. Even Emerson's notorious disappointment that Shakespeare used his genius only as "master of the revels to mankind" (725) joins an analysis of literature as social power in a leading text of American "new historicism": "Where Montaigne withdrew to his study, Shakespeare became the presiding genius of a popular, urban art form with the capacity to foster psychic mobility in the service of Elizabethan power" (Greenblatt 253). Such a view avoids the antithesis between Shakespeare and the mass media that culture critics from Wordsworth and Leavis to the present have maintained, and instead it emphasizes important similarities.

I do not think such revisions are violations or that they will lose utterly Shakespeare or anything else we value. I agree that artworks are not there for us to use in any way we want. The world of nature, however, is even less there for us to use, yet our lives depend on taking the chance that we may find a proper use. I must resist the rhetoric of tactful purism that Hartman proposes. As teachers we must not try to deny our students the experiences that have brought us our deepest conviction. The voice of criticism need not be the voice of caution.

As an experiment in interpretive reading that acknowledges but challenges a "hermeneutics of indeterminacy," I turn now to a poem of Wordsworth's that has already been important for the movement toward a new literary history that began in the 1960s, a movement that has by now, I have argued, reached an impasse. I hope in this reading to indicate some of the further directions needed to renew the project of new literary history.

WORDSWORTH'S "NUTTING": SUSPENSION AND DECISION

"Nutting" was published by Wordsworth in his 1800 *Lyrical Ballads* but was begun while he and his sister Dorothy were in Germany in 1798. It arose in close conjunction with the first work toward *The*

Prelude and then for two years passed through considerable draft work, although as published it did not greatly differ from the version already reached in a letter of Dorothy's to Coleridge late in 1798. Both its separation from *The Prelude* and the unsuccessful attempts to change its character suggest a combination of intractability and disturbance about the poem that has made it rewarding to investigate for a number of critics since David Perkins and David Ferry brought it to attention over twenty-five years ago. I use here the text in its finally revised form of 1845; the revisions strengthen the contours of the poem but do not significantly affect the historical argument with which I am concerned. In the next chapter, Wordsworth's revisionary practice will receive special attention.

Here is the poem:

> ——————————————It seems a day
> (I speak of one from many singled out)
> One of those heavenly days that cannot die;
> When, in the eagerness of boyish hope,
> I left our cottage-threshold, sallying forth   (5)
> With a huge wallet o'er my shoulders slung,
> A nutting-crook in hand; and turned my steps
> Tow'rd some far-distant wood, a Figure quaint,
> Trick'd out in proud disguise of cast-off weeds
> Which for that service had been husbanded,   (10)
> By exhortation of my frugal Dame—
> Motley accoutrement, of power to smile
> At thorns, and brakes, and brambles,—and, in truth,
> More ragged than need was! O'er pathless rocks,
> Through beds of matted fern, and tangled thickets,   (15)
> Forcing my way, I came to one dear nook
> Unvisited, where not a broken bough
> Drooped with its withered leaves, ungracious sign
> Of devastation; but the hazels rose
> Tall and erect, with tempting clusters hung,   (20)
> A virgin scene!—A little while I stood,
> Breathing with such suppression of the heart
> As joy delights in; and, with wise restraint
> Voluptuous, fearless of a rival, eyed
> The banquet;—or beneath the trees I sate   (25)
> Among the flowers, and with the flowers I played;
> A temper known to those who, after long

And weary expectation, have been blest
With sudden happiness beyond all hope.
Perhaps it was a bower beneath whose leaves   (30)
The violets of five seasons re-appear
And fade, unseen by any human eye;
Where fairy water-breaks do murmur on
For ever; and I saw the sparkling foam,
And—with my cheek on one of those green stones   (35)
That, fleeced with moss, under the shady trees,
Lay round me, scattered like a flock of sheep—
I heard the murmur and the murmuring sound,
In that sweet mood when pleasure loves to pay
Tribute to ease; and of its joy secure,   (40)
The heart luxuriates with indifferent things,
Wasting its kindliness on stocks and stones,
And on the vacant air. Then up I rose,
And dragged to earth both branch and bough, with crash
And merciless ravage: and the shady nook   (45)
Of hazels, and the green and mossy bower,
Deformed and sullied, patiently gave up
Their quiet being: and unless I now
Confound my present feelings with the past,
Ere from the mutilated bower I turned   (50)
Exulting, rich beyond the wealth of kings,
I felt a sense of pain when I beheld
The silent trees, and saw the intruding sky.—
Then, dearest Maiden, move along these shades
In gentleness of heart; with gentle hand   (55)
Touch—for there is a spirit in the woods.

The work of Harold Bloom, Geoffrey Hartman, and Paul de Man has been indispensable in starting me toward a reading that satisfies, but I find that their emphases remain too strongly internal to language. We must also read poems as actions, and events. The ultimate question, then, will be "What happens in, and through, 'Nutting'?" Bloom's theory that poets in unconscious oedipal rivalry revise the work of precursors proves helpful in understanding what "Nutting" does to Milton's *Paradise Lost*, but it does nothing to help think about the social exercise of power in the poem, the commands given to the "Maiden" of the last lines. This ending leaves intra-masculine struggle and enters cross-gender relations, while shifting temporal orientation from the past toward the future. Hartman once fruitfully suggested that the poem marked "close to a turning-point in English poetry" (*Wordsworth's Poetry* 73), but his recent "psychoesthetics" leads insistently to a "hermeneutics of indeterminacy" ("Touching" 358). This position only exacerbates the dubiety of his early claim ("close to"), and it forbids readers and critics the decisiveness of the poem's speaker, consigning us to the maiden's gentleness. One need not credit the literal referentiality of a literary representation in order to see that such representation has effects; a psychoanalytic understanding somewhat different from Hartman's or Bloom's will be relevant here. De Man searchingly analyzed the dilemma of literary modernity as a wish to escape history that continually finds itself enmeshed again by its own efforts ("Literary History and Literary Modernity," in *Blindness*). Yet this analysis treats as universal what may itself be historicized, not as the essence of literature but as the conditions of a certain kind of writing at a certain time, under certain circumstances. As opposed to the Yale critics, then, I hope by my conclusion to suggest some of the ways that both past literature and present literary study arise from, and exercise, ideological power in history.

I will start by singling out a phrase from the poem, "indifferent things" (line 41). In its literal denial of difference, in attenuating any distinction, this phrase provokes discomforting doubts, while in most of Wordsworth's great work, the word "things" instead comfortingly transcends difference. The nuance between transcending and denying difference separates a culturally valued sublimation from a more dubious fetishism, but our inquiry may finally suggest that they are separated only as two sides of one coin.

The word "thing" or "things" figured prominently, and positively, in some of Wordsworth's most memorable lines, as from "Tintern Abbey": "we see into the life of things"; "a motion and a spirit . . . that rolls through all things." His very use of the word helps to define his place in literary history. The statistical tables in Josephine Miles' *Eras and Modes in English Poetry*, supplemented by concordances, show that the word occurred frequently in almost all English poets until the mid-seventeenth century, but it was prominent in only five of fifteen poets in the seventeenth century born after Dryden, and in only one of twenty-five poets born in the eighteenth century before or contemporary with Wordsworth. In him, however, it was prominent, and with Browning and Arnold became general in Victorian poetry, through Yeats; after D. H. Lawrence it again receded.

Wordsworth, then, reinaugurated the poetic prominence of the word "thing" through the First World War. It was a part of his modernity but not of ours. Within Wordsworth's oeuvre, the word appeared only as he achieved his distinctive way of writing. Going through his poems chronologically by composition, one finds the word only once in 125 pages (in the Hayden edition) of apprentice work. The word appeared frequently first in his verse-drama of 1796–97 *The Borderers* and appeared again and again in the great poetry of 1798, as in my earlier quotations from "Tintern Abbey." Consider also this important MS passage from "The Ruined Cottage," the poem in which he began the psychological speculation that led to *The Prelude*:

> Was it ever meant
> That this majestic imagery . . .
> Should lie a barren picture on the mind?
> . . . Let us rise
> From this oblivious sleep, these fretful dreams
> Of feverish nothingness. Thus disciplined
> All things shall live in us and we shall live
> In all things that surround us.
> ("*Ruined Cottage*," pp. 269–71)

To write about "things" in this way brought Wordsworth close to the sense of the "one life" articulated in this same year by Coleridge. The phrase "living thing" appeared importantly in both writers in 1797–98. "Nutting," however, reads "indifferent things." The locution is no more or less precise or concrete than "all things"; both gesture toward an unknown, and yet a world of feeling lies between them.

"Nutting" further claims attention because it poses a problem of representation not only with respect to "things," but also at once in relation to temporality. The beginning of the poem is puzzling: "It seems a day" (line 1) seems to promise a descriptive poem (like the 1798 lyrical ballad "It is the first mild day of March"), but the intrusive parenthesis complicates our understanding: "(I speak of one from many singled out)" (line 2). Even while its singularity is emphasized, the day is placed among many; it loses individuality; it is generalized: "One of those heavenly days that cannot die" (line 3). Here, as often, Wordsworth singles out a beginning, one of the "spots" that focus a life, but usually (as in the passage I emphasize in the next chapter) such spotting leads to a knotting, joining it to the present and the future. Here there is no such clear temporal trajectory. The beginning remains in suspension, and the poem becomes a narrative of the past. The present tense of the opening is only rationalized in the poem's last lines of address to the "maiden" (line 54). The poem, then, seems a mimetic representation. It brings into the present a duplication of a past day and its events, reproducing a previous experience.

This combination of temporal complexity plus representative narrative counted importantly for Geoffrey Hartman's crucial analysis of "Nutting." Hartman proposed the poem's "mutilated bower" as an emblem for his whole book on Wordsworth, and he defined its subject as "the emergence of a modern imagination" (*Wordsworth's Poetry* 73) through a dialectical process of regression and purification. In "Nutting," Hartman argued, this process occurred through Wordsworth's relation to the poetry of romance. Wordsworth leapt over the Enlightenment to recover romance (just as I have suggested that his use of "things" allied him to Elizabethan poetry), but then he criticized and left behind what he had recovered.

In "Tintern Abbey" the problems seem less: things are more reassuring, and the past of memory and culture may be preserved without negation. In that poem the "burden of the mystery" is lightened, our bodily life is "almost suspended," and "we see into the life of things" (lines 38–49). This echoes King Lear's prison speech to Cordelia. In a similar visionary renunciation of activity, the older man and the younger girl, like "god's spies," "Take upon's the mystery of things" (5.3.16–17). So too the motion and spirit in "Tintern Abbey" that "rolls through all things" (line 102) comes to its climax in a phrase ("all things") that occurred nearly fifty times in *Paradise Lost*. Wordsworth's recovery here of older verbal modes for new purposes seems effortless. But "Nutting" suffers the tensions we have remarked, perhaps because unlike "Tintern Abbey" the poem did not lay claim to the traditional elevation of the ode and therefore had more difficulty assimilating epic or tragedy.

Instead, Wordsworth had to worry about how—in Henry James' phrase from the preface to *The Portrait of a Lady*—to "orchestrate an ado" about nutting. The narrative begins with bare registration of homely circumstance: the cottage (line 5), wallet (line 6), and nutting-crook (line 7). Already some comic condescension marks "the eagerness of boyish hope" (line 4), a remarkable contrast to the moving line already drafted for the 1799 *Prelude*, "the eagerness of infantine desire" (2:25). As the language of "Nutting" rises to-ward that of chivalric adventure—"sallying forth" (line 5), the gen-erality and extremity of "some far-distant wood" (line 8), the "Dame" (line 11)—the humor of mock-romance becomes stronger. Yet under the defense of comedy, the language asserts larger claims for the importance of the action. To the boy there was romantic excitement; to the poet something else must give significance.

"Trick'd out in proud disguise of cast-off weeds" (line 9) precisely catches the literary mode here. The poem is still dressed up as ro-mance, using the old garments saved by that frugal dame, the muse of romance. Modernity demands something sterner. In his critical writing, Wordsworth frequently and consistently contrasted the false garment of style to the "nakedness" of true poetry. For Pope, true wit was "Nature to advantage dressed" (*Essay on Criticism*, line 298), but Wordsworth in explicit contrast warned that lan-guage must be the "incarnation" of its thought. If it is only the "clothing," it will act like the shirt of Nessus that maddened and wasted its wearer (*Prose* 2:84).

After the bathos of "in truth, / More ragged than need was!" (line 14), the verse suddenly gains power:

> O'er pathless rocks,
> Through beds of matted fern, and tangled thickets,
> Forcing my way, I came to one dear nook
> Unvisited (14–17)

The reversed stress in the initial "Forcing" and the enjambed, post-poned "Unvisited" signal Milton, and this note continues:

> where not a broken bough
> Drooped with its withered leaves, ungracious sign
> Of devastation; but the hazels rose

> Tall and erect, with tempting clusters hung,
> A Virgin scene! (17–21)

That summarizing conclusion unmistakably echoes "A sylvan scene" in Milton's Eden as first approached by Satan, while making explicit the sexual suggestion many readers have found in Milton:

> As with a rural mound the champaign head
> Of a steep wilderness, whose hairy sides
> With thicket overgrown . . .
> Access denied.
> (*Paradise Lost* 4:134–38)

The next twenty lines disperse the energy the poem has gained. While the boy is still, the poem wanders: "A little while I stood" (line 21); "or beneath the trees I sate" (line 25); "Perhaps it was a bower" (line 30). The rhetorical scheme of dreamy alternatives recalls what Hartman characterized as the romantic "surmise," as in Keats' dark garden of the nightingale ode; more precisely and traditionally it may be called "alloiosis," the offering of alternatives. As possibilities multiply, however, the basic figure proves "dubitatio," what Puttenham called "the doubter," or in Greek, "aporia." The narrative reaches an impasse. After eagerly leaving the "cottage-threshold" (line 5), the speaker now seems stuck in liminality, and we may reflect on Freud's analysis of doubt as a mode of defense. Yet this very condition is the goal toward which much current critical theory seems to urge us. Although I find some use for Geoffrey Hartman and Paul de Man in my arguments here, I do not share de Man's commitment to aporia, and I oppose Hartman's "hermeneutics of indeterminacy."

As the poem's action stalls, its tone and stance also waver. Alongside the consciousness of the boy runs the moral generalization associated with maturity: "Such suppression of the heart / As joy delights in" (lines 22–23); "A temper known to those who, after long / And weary expectation, have been blest / With sudden happiness" (lines 27–29); "In that sweet mood when pleasure loves to pay / Tribute to ease" (lines 39–40). The first glimpse of the bower already proleptically showed its "devastation" (line 19), though under negation. Here too the goal seems already reached; "joy"

41

(line 23) and "happiness" (line 29) and "pleasure" (line 39) seem present "for ever" (line 34) without needing completion in action. A sense of perversity emerges in "wise restraint / Voluptuous" (line 24), and it becomes strangely polymorphous yet self-denying in "eyed / The banquet" (lines 25–26). Eating with the eyes satisfies the wrong organ, and running over its proper line end, the virgin scene shockingly becomes a "banquet," expropriatively reduced by desire out of phase with nature. It is hard to feel any charming innocence in this childishness.

Literary fictionality suffuses the scene in the predominant pastoral topoi, like the obtrusively developed metaphor of the "green stones . . . fleeced with moss . . . scattered like a flock of sheep" (lines 35–37), and even more in the homogenization of sound that brings those lines under the domination of long ee. If sense yields to the play of signifiers, the result is not the verbal anarchy sought by *Tel Quel* theorists, but rather to suggest the effect of Augustan couplets, as the lines end with "foam" and "stones"; "trees" and "sheep" (lines 34–37).

Here occurs the anomalous usage of "things," with which I began my observations:

> of its joy secure,
> The heart luxuriates with indifferent things,
> Wasting its kindliness on stocks and stones,
> And on the vacant air. (40–43)

In anticipatory contemplation, delighting in pastoral fiction, the mind sinks into itself and gradually empties out nature, leaving only "vacant air." By a strange path, we have reached a Wordsworthian commonplace: the interruption of a quest causes the mind to feel its power over things. The most familiar example is the moment in book 6 of *The Prelude* when Wordsworth realized that he had already crossed the Alps and, feeling still the wish for more, recognized the power of his imagination. As opposed to the exaltation of that moment, here the feeling is acutely uncomfortable and demands a new relation to things. If the "hazels rose" (line 19) in the first positive assertion of the scene, a vigorous riposte is required:

> Then up I rose,
> And dragged to earth both branch and bough, with crash
> And merciless ravage. (lines 43–45)

This pattern in "Nutting" closely corresponds to that registered in Wordsworth's note to the "Immortality Ode": "I was often unable to think of external things as having external existence, and I communed with all I saw as something not apart from, but inherent in, my own immaterial nature. Many times while going to school have I *grasped* at a wall or tree to recall myself from the abyss of idealism to the reality. At that time I was afraid of such processes" (*Poems* 1:978). Only later did he come to value the "Fallings from us, vanishings" that accompany life in "worlds not realised" ("Ode," lines 142–46). The adult finds compensation in what the child found intolerable.

The dragging to earth with crash, enacted in the heavy monosyllabic line and overrun, reestablishes relationship. It fights the fear of the vacancy that things take on in their indifference, the "dreams of feverish nothingness," when the heart is too secure. The otherness of things, their "quiet being" (line 48), revealed through our action upon them, becomes a positive value against solipsistic doubts and the literarization of the world. This action, then, restored the otherness of things and rescued the boy from fiction. It was an act of modernity; it stripped away old clothes; restored us "to earth" like the giant Antaeus whom Hazlitt took as a figure for true poetry. It let light into the enclosure of the bower ("Come forth into the light of things / Let Nature be your teacher"—"The Tables Turned," lines 15–16).

We have now worked through the narrated action of the poem. I will go on to define the relation between that action and the social transaction at the poem's end, the address to the maiden. Here certain resources of psychoanalysis will prove useful. Until now I have treated the poem as mimetically representing a past event. Even if there was modernity then, now is only its duplication. But Wordsworth questions, "Unless I now / Confound my present feelings with the past." Did modernity happen then, or is it now in the poem? Doubt baffles Wordsworth's unwelcome recognition, but we have already noted the poem's doubleness, the adult coloring spread over what might have been the boy's experiences. Even more doubt of the poem's precise status comes from Wordsworth's note: "Like most of my schoolfellows I was an impassioned nutter. . . . These verses arose out of the remembrance of feelings I had often had when a boy, and particularly in the extensive woods that still stretch from the side of Esthwaite Lake" (*Poems* 1:956–57).

This marks the poem's narrative as a fiction. There is no particular "mutilated bower"; the woods "still stretch"; there was no event that corresponds to the feelings, even though readers so antimimetic as Geoffrey Hartman and Leslie Brisman refer to "the event recorded" (*Wordsworth's Poetry* 73), the "event and the retelling of it" (Brisman 299). In his programmatic preface to the 1800 volume in which "Nutting" first appeared, Wordsworth emphasized that what made these poems *lyrical* ballads was that feeling predominated over action and situation. Readers' sense of an epochal moment in the dragging down of the boughs comes wholly through the poem's fabrication, which has stretched out sequentially the feelings of the "impassioned nutter" Wordsworth recalled, or of the recollecting poet, or perhaps of some third thing that emerges between them. So the very moment of modernity in tearing down the boughs rejoins fiction. The frugal dame of romance has her due again.

What feelings do we read in the play between the poet trying to break away from romance into modernity and the boy whose quest he projected, trying to grasp the being of nature? The poem's evident sexuality—specifically a sense of the boy's action as rape—helped in the fifties to gain it critical attention and is still acknowledged, though with some embarrassment. But wouldn't the boy's "feelings" of which Wordsworth spoke be less those of adult heterosexuality than are the feelings on the surface of the poem? It makes sense to invoke here the model analysis Freud offered of "Screen Memories." These are memories "relating to" childhood that work like dreams or symptoms to disguise fantasies from either earlier or later than the childhood moment evoked, and they may be recognized by the contrast they offer "between the acting and the recollecting ego," that is, by their objectifying the child in the viewpoint of an external "observer" (3:321–22). Clearly such is the case here, as in our remarks contrasting the boy's and the narrator's perspectives. Moreover, since the work is a poem, no matter how "naked" in certain respects, we can readily accept Freud's insistence on the multilayered composition of "screen memories."

We might then speculate that by the turn to female sexualization composing the scene, the poem displaced youthful autoerotic fantasies, the symbolic masturbation Freud recognized in what Americans would call "jerking off" branches (3:319). But to follow this lead and emphasize the hazels as "tall and erect" (line 20) produces an even more shocking scene. For if the feminized landscape is also phallic, as theorists of the pre-oedipal suggest that in that stage we attribute both sexes to the mother, then the boy's action could read as castrating the mother. This does not actually define Wordsworth's boyish feelings, only exposes the degree of linguistic figuration that arose from them in his writing. Representation here is not mimetic but allegorical. Through the compromise-formation of the text, we find something with no natural existence, an act which could not occur. Freud identified the maternal phallus with the fetish, the shard one grasps in order to deny a terrifying differentiation (21:152–53), and Julia Kristeva argued that such fetishization forms the basis for aestheticism, that is for the ideology of art's autonomy (64; 45–48, 463).

That fantastic act of castrating the mother, moreover, is originative. By it the father establishes his dominion over what Lacan called the realm of the symbolic (roughly, that of language), in founding by violence the difference between the sexes. The poet thus put himself in the father's place, made himself truly modern, revenging himself on the frugal dame, usurping the law as his own. In an essay on Mary Wollstonecraft, Carol Kay has characterized a general process of "remasculinization" in the culture of the 1790s, which bears on Wordsworth's position. This new authority accounts for the last lines of the poem; they are so puzzling and antipathetic to modern readers that they usually receive only the most idealizing comment if any, although Margaret Homans forcibly applied them to the curtailment of Dorothy Wordsworth's poetic vocation (54). Rich beyond the wealth of kings through having textually achieved an impossible desire, the speaker has power to lay down the law to the "dearest maiden." Here we see that an action with no referent may nonetheless have an effect. He, and he alone, has had the experience, but his modernity becomes her tradition. She must believe on faith alone that there is spirit in the woods, and not find out for herself. Wordsworth's modernity, again, is not ours. If his heavenly day never dies, we will never have light of our own.

We may cast further light on the procedure here by recognizing that the poem narrates an activity with important ritual antecedents. In a work Wordsworth owned (Shaver and Shaver 48–49), old Roman Cato described the appropriate procedure to placate the spirits when opening up an untouched grove. (The Latin phrase is "lucum conlucare"; the verb *conlucare* means to let light in, and the noun is famous for its etymology in Quintilian, "lucus a non lucendo": "lucus from not being lighted.") I have no time here to pursue the possibilities this opens up for the "Lucy" poems, which are related to "Nutting" both in time of composition and through a draft in which the "dearest maiden" is called "Lucy" (*Poetical Works* 2:504–6). However, it is worth knowing that the ritual included a prayer and the sacrifice of an animal. In "Nutting" the speaker's last lines function as a prayer, but it seems the maiden must be the sacrifice. Enlightenment has eliminated blood ritual, but the line between humans and animals is now redrawn between men and women.

Within the world of poetry, the lines that establish Wordsworth's modernity and authority are:

> I felt a sense of pain when I beheld
> The silent trees, and saw the intruding sky. (52–53)

Compare a phrase from the passage of pastoral reverie, "I saw the sparkling foam" (line 34). "Saw" seems to promise the Wordsworthian magic of perception, but "sparkling foam" is cliché, cast-off weeds. "The intruding sky" in contrast is extraordinary: for its condensation (the sky should not be there and would not be except for my act of violation); its displacement (I didn't let the sky in; it just broke in); its substantiality (like a rock extruding from earth into air, the sky intrudes toward earth); and its personification, like Donne's "unruly sun."

Yet if I just compared it with Donne, is it truly free from literariness? I find in fact that its special power arises from Wordsworth's revision of Milton. Wordsworth's bower echoed the language of Milton's Eden, and that language returns now reversed. When Eve picked the fruit, "Earth felt the wound" (*Paradise Lost* 9:782), and when Adam took his turn:

> Nature gave a second groan,
> Sky loured and muttering thunder, some sad drops
> Wept. (9:1001–3)

In Wordsworth, however, it is "I" who "felt a sense of pain," and the "silent trees" become noteworthy in contrast to nature's noisiness at the fall. The "intruding sky" is free from tears. In the 1815 preface to his poems, Wordsworth cited these lines from *Paradise Lost* in contrast to verses by Lord Chesterfield that used a similar figure. Against the social triviality of Chesterfield, Wordsworth judged the fall of mankind sufficiently "momentous that the mind acknowledges the justice and reasonableness of the sympathy in nature so manifested" (*Prose* 3:37). But in "Nutting" Wordsworth absolutely did without Milton's supernatural fictions, as in the 1800 preface he insisted that poetry does not shed "tears 'such as Angels weep,'" another Miltonic figure (*Prose* 1:135). In a draft associated with "Nutting," Wordsworth praised the person "Whose feelings do not need the gross appeal / Of tears and of articulate sounds" (de Selincourt 613). In this argumentative context, then, Milton is cast among the "gross and violent stimulants" denounced in the 1800 preface, even though that very passage in the preface preferred Milton over the "frantic novels, sickly and stupid German Tragedies, and . . . idle and extravagant stories in verse" (*Prose* 1:129) that marked the current age. Wordsworth's modernity, thus, first rejected its own moment by contrast to past greatness but then went beyond even that past in its boldness. Milton had dismissed classical epic and chivalric romance for their focus upon externalities, against "the better fortitude / Of patience" (*Paradise Lost* 9:31–32) manifest in Christianity. Wordsworth found patience in trees yet advised the "maiden" not to test it further. The modernity of his poetic act forms a parenthesis, a suspension within tradition, like the fictional action of "Nutting," suspended within the address to the maiden.

I have suggested earlier that de Man's analysis of modernity required further specification, rather than being allowed to cover all "literature." Wordsworth stands at a very special place in history, which might arguably be called the "end of English poetry" and the "beginning of English literature." Recall that in the 1800 preface Wordsworth abjured the "phrases and figures of speech which from father to son have long been regarded as the common inheritance of poets," the "family language" belonging to poets by Burkean "prescription," he added in 1802 (*Prose* 1:131–33). Moreover, the generic uncertainties we have seen in "Nutting" participate in Wordsworth's larger programmatic innovation. The terminological shift from "poetry" to "literature" was not yet complete, but the institutional and ideological developments were in place. For historians so different from each other as Raymond Williams and Michel Foucault have in quite different ways that nonetheless converge showed that only around 1800 did there come into being the notion of "literature" as we have since known it, as part of what Paul O. Kristeller defined as "the modern system of the arts." The insights of Margaret Homans and Julia Kristeva, emerging from current feminist commitments, help us to see that the erection of literary autonomy was accompanied both by the exclusion of women from the experience that makes literature possible and by the assumption of universality that fetishistically treats sexual differences as "indifferent things." (We now have both sides of the promised coin.) Wordsworth offered the poet as "the rock of defence for human nature" (*Prose* 1:141), yet he was "a man speaking to men" (1:138), or even to women, as in the address to the maiden, who emphatically asserted the right to talk about women and for women.

Wordsworth heroically, ascetically, did without the traditional supports of poetry and still achieved literary greatness. He rejected both poetic tradition and the social status with which it had come to be associated: in sending the 1800 *Lyrical Ballads* to the leader of the political opposition, Charles James Fox, he emphasized works "written with a view to shew that men who do not wear fine cloaths can feel deeply" (*Letters* 315). We recall here the "cast-off weeds" of "Nutting"; in 1800 the phrase actually read "Beggar's weeds." Through the fiction of "Nutting," as in his other most powerful moments, Wordsworth attained an originality that was radically archaic, that took the "common-place" things of life and made them new. In the "Essays Upon Epitaphs" he characterized this accomplishment; it is as if one had "mounted to the sources of things [note the word!], penetrated the dark cavern from which the River that murmurs in everyone's ear has flowed from generation to generation" (*Prose* 2:78–79). By that return to the source, in this case we have argued the phallic mother, he acquired authority on primeval ground. Once poetic authority was lost, once the previously existing social demand for poetry had been transformed, once the writer was no longer producing on direct demand by patrons, or even subscribers, but was isolated in the marketplace producing for unknown readers whose taste could not be predicted but might with luck be formed, once, in other words, a certain condition of alienation prevailed, then the possibility of literary autonomy also came into existence. The process of internalization by which Wordsworth not only defended but also formed a new, literary human nature—the human nature that makes psychoanalysis possible—cannot be understood apart from such externalities. The example of "Nutting" has suggested, moreover, that this literary possibility came only at the cost of reasserting an inequality between the sexes, a form of domination even more fundamental than those of social class and cultural tradition. To answer my beginning question, then, what happened in "Nutting" was the psycho-social construction of literary authority.

A new literary history must heed the warning of Walter Benjamin, written just after the outbreak of the Second World War, and acknowledge that our "cultural treasures" (*Illuminations* 256) are documents not only of civilization but also of barbarism; to the extent that we revere those treasures, we carry on the barbarism. Our task demands "detachment," even from what we have loved. But Benjamin's dialectic goes both ways; it requires also resisting modes of analysis and reception that cover over live elements. I want then to conclude this chapter by detaching myself more extensively from recent criticism: it is not exclusively criticism with theoretical ambitions that accounts for the impasse of a new literary history.

WORDSWORTH AS PSYCHOLOGIST AND SOCIALIST

The last twenty years have marked an industrial revolution in the American academic study of Wordsworth. The challenging books by David Ferry and David Perkins, working out of New Criticism and a more traditional humanism, did not quite, but the European perspectives of *Wordsworth's Poetry* by Geoffrey Hartman did succeed in making Wordsworth a center of American critical activity. This in itself, even in "an age of criticism," would not make an industry, were it not conjoined with the rich scholarship that followed Helen Darbishire's revision of de Selincourt's *Prelude*: Mark Reed's chronology, the Prose edited by Smyser and Owen, and finally the Cornell Edition. The powerful interplay of this fresh critical orientation and scholarly documentation emerged in a great array of representative work since the later 1970s.

This scholarly accumulation makes possible for Wordsworth as for few other authors the practice of genetic criticism as "inside narrative." At a time when the traditional practice of literary history is at least under suspicion and perhaps in crisis, such scholarship has allowed more traditional scholars an equivalent to the textualization of literary history associated with the Yale critics. Equally relevant is the theoretical impasse posed by Paul de Man in his "inability to progress" from "reading" to a larger history of romanticism (preface to *Allegories of Reading*). De Man articulated a bafflement many share. One response to this blockage has been the Cornell Edition itself, which in producing new "original" texts rewrites history by editorial positivism, when other interpretive approaches seem unavailable.

The buzz of this new industry has silenced the problematic dialogue of Wordsworth studies with modern humanism. David Perkins' neglected *Wordsworth and the Poetry of Sincerity* (1964) marks an important road that must be taken again, for the great issues posed about Wordsworth in the nineteenth century remain unresolved. I mean above all the issues between Hazlitt and Coleridge as to which was the appropriate totality that defined Wordsworth's poetry: social or metaphysical, Hazlitt's "spirit of the age" or Coleridge's "shaping spirit" of imagination. In its Coleridgean concern with metaphysical categories, much recent criticism has disconnected Wordsworth's writing from its affiliations in life: traditionalism reaches the same impasse as revisionism.

So in a highly professional recent work by John Hodgson, *Wordsworth's Philosophical Poetry*, the close genetic attention by which he textualized literary history led to extraordinary omissions. He

50

never investigated why Wordsworth decided to leave certain projects fragmentary and others, apparently completed, unpublished; he presupposed that the words a poet wrote at a given time fully and clearly reveal the philosophic position the poet held at that time. Yet any work we may expect to be "dialogic" in the sense Mikhail Bakhtin defined; even unpublished work articulates a relation with the internalized literary public implicated in stylistic and thematic choices, as I try to specify in my chapter on *The Prelude*. So too, more specific issues connecting Wordsworth's life to his works were passed over. Although *The Borderers*, the unpublished drama of 1796–97, presented a crucial step in Hodgson's arguments for Wordsworth's development (as it does for most such explorations), he did not even cite the evidence connecting the drama to Wordsworth's "long residence in France" (*Poems* 939) and the ethical problems of revolution. In accepting the "tripartite process of development" (Hodgson 31) sketched in "Tintern Abbey," Hodgson passed over Wordsworth's sense of "flying from something that he dreads" (line 71) and did not question Wordsworth's *need* to forge a smooth continuity between 1793 and 1798, thus obviating the crisis of the mid 1790s.

In contrast, *Wordsworth's Second Nature* by James Chandler, while exemplary in its "dialogic" attention, foundered on a fundamental incoherence. Chandler ignored recent work like that of Derrida and de Man that would discredit any simple dichotomy between Rousseau and Burke, evidently because he preferred to use "Rousseau" and "Burke" as they figured in the polemics of the 1790s. (Even in the 1790s, Mary Wollstonecraft's Rousseau is more complex, as Carol Kay has reminded us.) But the Wordsworth presented is wholly a creation of modern scholarly criticism, requiring access to materials that Wordsworth kept in manuscript. This figure, therefore, has no relation to the "Wordsworth" who figured in the arguments or perceptions of his contemporaries. The paradox is rich to meditation: Wordsworth's own contemporaries did not know his place in the political debates of the age. But the problem of historiographic method remains: Wordsworth is the only figure to be treated from the inside, rather than primarily as a figure in public debate. To bridge the gap from text to text, Hodgson too fabricated an inside narrative: "By late 1798, Wordsworth was coming to regard his belief in the one life as simply inadequate to sustain and console him" (49). Despite all the mastered minutiae of Hodgson's powerful scholarship, he had no warrant for such a statement; it was as sheer and risky an interpretation as any could be that did not hope to rest on the security of editorial positivism.

Even a book that worked hard at contextualizing Wordsworth in relation to the literary history of the Sentimental movement, the "Age of Sensibility" in which he came of age, James Averill's *Wordsworth and the Poetry of Human Suffering*, at every point elided the relevance for Wordsworth's poetry of the social and political upheavals of the 1790s. In focusing on the "betrayed women, beggars, maniacs, discharged soldiers, and decrepit old men" (10) of Wordsworth's early poetry, Averill did not recognize in this "mixed rabble" the "female vagrants, gipsies . . . ideot boys and mad mothers" that, for William Hazlitt, marked Wordsworth's allegiance to the "sentiments and opinions" of the French Revolution (5:161–63). Helen Maria Williams, whose sentimental verse elicited Wordsworth's first published poem, became known a few years later for her adherence to the revolutionary cause. In citing the 1800 preface to *Lyrical Ballads*, Averill quoted Wordsworth on the "multitude of causes" producing a craving for "gross and violent stimulants" (182). These causes for Wordsworth began from political crisis, "the great national events which are daily taking place"; but Averill's commentary, no less than Hartman's discussed earlier, wholly passed over the complex of politics, urbanization, economics, and mass communications that Wordsworth specified.

All this might be insignificant did it not lead Averill to ignore the clear persistence in the revolutionary books of *The Prelude* of the problematic that his study has so effectively focused on: the "Wordsworthian spectator," obliquely engaged by the sufferings of others. In order to justify his right to address an English audience in 1798 or 1800 or 1805, Wordsworth showed that the isolation from his audience that he wished to heal corresponded to his solitude even amid his revolutionary comrades and went back to the beginnings of his life. Wordsworth's encounter with the "dead man" drowned at Esthwaite placed human suffering at the start of his relations with other people in the 1799 version of *The Prelude* (1:177). By the revision of 1805, his experience of literature intervenes to complicate his response. Because the revolutionary books have no direct counterpart in 1799, they tend to be ignored by those who rely upon the new textual scholarship, but again and again in the revolutionary books this same pattern recurs: cultural givens skew what one might expect to be a simple, sympathetic moment of human solidarity. Wordsworth's feeling is represented as always strangely elsewhere. Space prohibits my working through in full the set of such "spots." (This key term emerges in the 1850 text of the "dead man" episode and also in the 1850 text of Wordsworth's encounter with a site of revolutionary massacre. See 1850, 5:444 and 10:58.) Take one instance for its symmetrically inverted relation to the encounter with "the dead man." At Esthwaite, "terror" at the sight of the corpse was mitigated by earlier reading (1850, 5:451–59); in France, the scene of revolutionary terror ("the dead, upon the dying heaped") failed to move Wordsworth because he "cannot read" its signs (1850, 10:56–63). Only after a sleepless night spent "reading" did images "from tragic fictions or true history" (1850, 10:71, 76) overwhelm him with anxiety. My excitement with this topic arises from Averill's work, but his failure to note it himself marks a symptom of current critical difficulties.

I conclude with some larger reflections on how our new genetic criticism works within the history of our reading Wordsworth. In the continuing delayed action of his work, Wordsworth has achieved the fortune of an "untimely" writer, such as Nietzsche considered himself and found exemplified in Stendhal. A curious instance of that untimeliness shows in the first responses to the publication of *The Prelude* in 1850. The terms used to characterize Wordsworth mark him precisely as having been ahead of his time, for the terms came into English only well after *The Prelude* was already in progress. One reviewer found the essential character of the poem "psychological" (*Prelude* 553). This term fails to surprise us, yet the word is first registered in the *OED* only in 1812, and the next citation is from Coleridge (1818). The word "psychological" itself is part of the history that Wordsworth and his fellows were making in the mind of England.

A second characterization is more surprising. Macaulay found the poem "to the last degree Jacobinical, indeed Socialist" (560). "Socialist" had only come into use in the 1830s, connected with the works and projects of Robert Owen, at about the same time it appeared in France. It helps us understand the remark to learn that by the 1820s "Jacobinical" was used to describe "every political objector," anyone who wished "any internal reforms" (*OED*). Nonetheless, its application to *The Prelude* still shocks us, for we are so used to finding in the poem only Wordsworth's turn in horror from the French Revolution that we do not notice so sensitively as Macaulay did Wordsworth's refusal to abandon the principles of democracy and equality that had animated his commitment to the revolution. More crucially, however, we accept "psychological" and reject "socialist" as descriptions of *The Prelude* because for us the psychological and the political have become much further separated than they were for Wordsworth. Part of the fascination of the genetic study of *The Prelude* is that through it we can follow Wordsworth's work as he began to establish that separation which has become second nature to us.

In response to the failure of his hopes for the revolution in France and its impact on Britain, Wordsworth found it necessary to make a self that could cope with the new conditions of his life. That making of the self and the making of the text of *The Prelude* are thoroughly correlative. In "Freud and the Scene of Writing," Jacques Derrida asked, "What must a psyche be if it can be represented by a text?" for Freud recurred to psychic models that are textual. Wordsworth's was one of the first selves to which we can securely ascribe this textual quality that a century later Freud could expect to find anywhere. Wordsworth's textual self-making enacted what Louis Althusser defined as the function of ideology, to represent an "imaginary" relationship to the "real" conditions of life, and this is no less the case if the ideology is "counterpolitical," to use Carl Schorske's term for Freud.

After their withdrawal from the French Revolution, Wordsworth and Coleridge alike laid the grounds for a new specification of the self in the nineteenth century, Wordsworth through the poetic psychology he elaborated, Coleridge notably through the path he opened to the psychological analysis of Shakespeare's characters. Recall, for instance, that in his exemplary, profoundly influential interpretation of Hamlet, Coleridge quoted from Wordsworth's unpublished *The Borderers* lines proclaiming that "action is transitory," and contrasting it to the inward permanence of "suffering." The inward self, whether that of *The Prelude* or Hamlet, entails a paradox, for in making this self one makes something that (as my next chapter details) is perceived as having no origin, that recedes further the more you press it (e.g., 1799 *Prelude* 2:242–67). This is not closure in the usual sense, this Derridian "always already" of a receding origin, but at least it defended against the threat of traumatic change. It offered an individual equivalent to the Burkean state, which also required both the veiling of origins and the possibility of always going further back. This inward self, like Hamlet to his interpreters or Wordsworth to himself in *The Prelude*, invited but resisted the final shaping that would give the finishing touch. The principle is like that which Michel Foucault studied in the establishment, at about the same time, of a less introspective psychology that also contributed to what in *Discipline and Punish* he called the "post-Christian soul." By the process of inquiry in prisons and *The Prelude* the self was not found but made.

In the mode of Hamlet or Wordsworth there are dangers to such exacerbated self-consciousness, but there was also the great attraction of holding off as long as possible when the only paths in sight appeared either suicidal impossibilities or demoralizing compromises. In Wordsworth's time, it was socially possible to live through this dilemma as a poet. From the position of poet, Wordsworth could make a version of his self available in less agonized form, and it had an extraordinary impact on the lives of his younger contemporaries. John Stuart Mill's *Autobiography* and Matthew Arnold's "Memorial Verses" testified to the resource the great Victorians found in the Wordsworthian depth of feeling. That deep, inward self became representative and formative for other selves not by action but by feeling (the formula for "lyrical ballads"); it was typical not in what it did but in its formation.

In a usage that philosophers took up in the 1830s, to define something by describing the manner of its formation is to offer a "genetic" definition. That is to say, the very matter of recent "genetic' criticism into which we are inquiring is itself a product of the same historical transformation as Wordsworth's self-composition. What Carlyle wrote of Teufelsdröckh in *Sartor Resartus* (in the first *OED* citation for the term) we might well say of the twenty manuscripts of *The Prelude*: "A complete picture and Genetical History of the man and his spiritual Endeavour lie before you." Although there long existed a politically subversive practice of "genealogy," and Nietzsche returned that term to a severely critical sense important for this book, the "genetic" inquiry of the earlier English nineteenth century was more Burkean and appreciative—in Mill's terms more a Coleridgean than a Benthamite activity, rather a mode of legitimation than of undermining. Thus Wordsworth's self-genetic inquiry into the growth of his own mind aimed to validate his practice and position as a poet. It was above all necessary for him to prove—at least to himself, Coleridge, and Dorothy—that his poetry did not, as Hazlitt would later so memorably and persuasively argue, come from the French Revolution but was instead continuous with all that he had earlier and always been. He had the further task of defining his relation to his public, the community of England, for his actual function as a poet was more entrepreneurial than artisanal, producing for a market rather than upon commission, having to call into existence needs of which their possessors were unaware rather than serving known needs in a customary way.

Our current genetic criticism elides the political aspect of his work that Wordsworth segregated but did not repress or exclude after the 1799 text of *The Prelude*. It seems that adding that early text to our canon has confirmed a shift in the emphasis of our criticism from the "socialist" to the "psychological." A clear pattern emerges: Wordsworth's social and political concerns in *The Prelude*, which made so acute a bourgeois apologist as Macaulay call him a "socialist," even on the evidence of the piously revised text of 1850, no longer engage our best critical attention, which has been fascinated by the explorations provoked by the interaction of positivism and nihilism, the resonance of editorial with deconstructive rigor in our new literary genetics. I have been attempting to reestablish connections that must be maintained if a new literary history is to avoid textualist isolation. Marilyn Butler's important new initiatives have as yet had little resonance for Americans raised in two generations of New Haven close reading, but the various forms of "new historicism" may usefully join the modes of close analysis that continue to define the American profession of literary study.

Chapter 2
The Prelude and Critical Revision:
Bounding Lines

THIS CHAPTER addresses the process of rewriting *The Prelude*, begun by Wordsworth in 1798, protracted through his lifetime, and continuing posthumously in the work of critics and editors, culminating in the remarkable efforts of the Cornell Edition to create, at last, the "original text" (Parrish, vii). It thus continues the inquiry of the previous chapter, establishing the relations of historical scholarship to criticism while further elaborating the particular role Wordsworth has played in defining the contours of recent literary study.

Even a century now after Walter Pater suggested it, Wordsworth remains exemplary for the "initiation" he offers into "reading between the lines" (*Appreciations* 40). But what should we make of our interlinear relationship? We might try to hold the lines ever more closely together through adding our presence to them, engage in a glossing that knits parts into a comprehensive totality. Such a reading of *The Prelude* would find example in the expansion from two parts in 1798–99 to five and then thirteen books in 1805. In spinning out more and more material to stand between parts that were originally compacted together, Wordsworth suggests an interlinear glossing comparable to Coleridge's marginal revision of "The Rime of the Ancient Mariner" (which I discuss in the next chapter). Such inscription of part into whole would return to romantic principles, the literary symbol and the philosophical dialectic. It would find in *The Prelude* what Coleridge sought in *The Recluse*, "a redemptive process in operation," an "idea" that "reconciled all the anomalies and promised future glory and restoration" (*Complete Works* 6:404).

Instead, however, we might recognize that Wordsworth never wrote *The Recluse* and was dissatisfied by *The Prelude*. He had looked forward to the day of its completion "as a most happy one," but he found it "not a happy day": "I was dejected on many accounts; when I looked back upon the performance it seemed to have a dead weight about it, the reality so far short of the expectation. . . . The doubt whether I should ever live to write the Recluse and the sense which I had of this Poem being so far below what I seem'd capable of executing, depressed me much" (*Letters* 594). For its force to be felt, this must be set beside the closing lines:

> The mind of man becomes
> A thousand times more beautiful than the earth
> On which he dwells, above this frame of things
> . . . .
> In beauty exalted, as it is itself
> In substance and of fabric more divine.
>   (1805, 13:446–52)

To contrast this elation to the dejection of the letter is to pose starkly the problems of disjunction between the empirical self and the poetic self.

An alternative position "between the lines" might try thinking through the relations of these two selves in *The Prelude*. Such a reading might open the spaces between parts of the poem, perhaps by noting that *The Prelude* is less a fixed text than a poem in process for some forty years (1798–1839). The differences that emerge between an "original" line (whether in the text of 1799 or 1805) and its ultimate successor (1850 text) might point toward problems within any state of the text, lines that run in different directions to form a "palimpsest" (Smith 156). Varieties of such "reading asunder," of *The Prelude* as of all Wordsworth's poetry, characterized A. C. Bradley and Matthew Arnold no less than Pater. Each of these great Victorian critics strove to discriminate the essential Wordsworth, the true virtue that remained when "the electric thread untwined" (Pater 41) lay before us. They renewed motifs from Longinus on the sublime in their concern with the great moment, their reliance upon touchstones, and their concern for finding and sharing the greatness of the poet's mind.

The Prelude *and Critical Revision*

In 1850 Wordsworth's poem was published as *The Prelude, or Growth of a Poet's Mind*; de Selincourt reproduced the 1850 title page with this subtitle (de Selincourt 1), which the Norton editors made it almost impossible to discover, in their vendetta against Victorian "alterations and intrusions" (xii). In the poem these great Victorian readers sought the mind. New Criticism, however, owed more to Aristotle than to Longinus, attended more to poems than to poets, downplayed the violence of separation to emphasize the harmony of integration, the totality that results from organic "growth." In *The Mirror and the Lamp*, M. H. Abrams greatly clarified the differences between these two positions (22), but his own practice in *Natural Supernaturalism* sided with Aristotle. He flexibly cast aside strict New-Critical distinctions of intrinsic versus extrinsic ("Rationality" 461), but only in order to understand *The Prelude* as an even grander "heterocosm." In the middle of *The Prelude*, Abrams found a world he shared, and offered us to share, with the poet, whose scene articulated "a truth about . . . the ineluctable contraries that make up our human existence" (*Natural Supernaturalism* 107). But this world changed. Finally by book 14 Wordsworth "progressed" in his fiction to a "higher realization" (112), now "collects and resolves the contrary qualities" (111), and, transforming his "life into a landscape" from the "high perspective" of "metaphoric flight" can "discern that all its parts are centered in love" (114). Such discernment has cognitive value not as a view of the world but only as a reading of *The Prelude* as a world apart, a "heterocosm" (*Mirror* 272). Even that value, however, is severely limited if we recall that shortly before the passage Abrams emphasized (*Prelude* 14:381–89), Wordsworth had, with equal authority, claimed that love is inseparably linked to imagination, the "feeding source" of the poem (14:189–94). Thus he preemptively displaced the centrality of love. Wordsworth himself wanted a reading of *The Prelude* that bound together all the parts, eclipsing imagination with love, but he could not in fact achieve it, and it is not clear that we should.

We do ourselves little good as readers if we allow our pleasure in a new relation to *The Prelude*, our recent conviction of its crucial greatness, to mask the problems posed between its lines. Attention to these problems will be more productive than hyperbolic acclaim for success. *Natural Supernaturalism* most distinguishedly represents the danger I am posing. In contrast to Miller's important critique ("Tradition") of Abrams' premises, I focus on theoretical issues that emerge from Abrams' actual reading of *The Prelude*. The massive learning, the cogent shaping of rich materials, the compositional finesse of the work, all lent authority to its arguments that in *The Prelude* Wordsworth achieved a "circular shape" (*Natural Supernaturalism* 79) "centered in love," a romantic version of Christian and Neoplatonic commonplaces that figured the progress of the soul as a journey leading through a circuitous path to home (chs. 3–5, especially pp. 278–92). I recognize the wish of Wordsworth's that this reading fulfilled, but I find in *The Prelude* discrepancies from such a pattern, crevices that interrupt the smooth path around. If "circular shape" suggests a satisfying, compensatory return, circles may also figure a lack or an excess. Thus Emerson wrote, "Our life is an apprenticeship to the truth, that around every circle another can be drawn; that there is no end in nature, but every end is a beginning; that there is always another dawn risen on mid-noon, and under every deep a lower deep opens" (403). Emerson opened up the circle in two respects: it may be a limit rather than a fulfillment; it is liable to internal rupture. He jammed together two contradictory moments from *Paradise Lost*, Raphael's appearance in Eden (5:310–11) and Satan's sense of having "no place," for "in the lowest deep a lower deep / Still threat'ning to devour me opens wide" (4:76–77). This astonishing juxtaposition suggests the double pull that spoils Wordsworth's circle—the expansion of its end into "something ever more" and the recession of its origin.

The boat-stealing episode provides focus for these issues:

> It was an act of stealth
> And troubled pleasure, nor without the voice
> Of mountain-echoes did my boat move on;
> Leaving behind her still on either side,
> Small circles glittering idly in the moon,   (365)
> Until they melted all into one track
> Of sparkling light. But now, like one who rows,
> Proud of his skill, to reach a chosen point
> With an unswerving line, I fixed my view
> Upon the summit of a craggy ridge,   (370)
> The horizon's utmost boundary; for above
> Was nothing but the stars and the grey sky.

She was an elfin pinnace; lustily
I dipped my oars into the silent lake,
And, as I rose upon the stroke, my boat   (375)
Went heaving through the water like a swan;
When, from behind that craggy steep till then
The horizon's bound, a huge peak, black and huge,
As if with voluntary power instinct
Upreared its head. I struck and struck again.   (380)
And growing still in stature the grim shape
Towered up between me and the stars, and still,
For so it seemed, with purpose of its own
And measured motion like a living thing,
Strode after me. With trembling oars I turned,   (385)
And through the silent water stole my way
Back to the covert of the willow tree;
There in her mooring-place I left my bark,—
And through the meadows homeward went, in grave
And serious mood; but after I had seen   (390)
That spectacle, for many days, my brain
Worked with a dim and undetermined sense
Of unknown modes of being; o'er my thoughts
There hung a darkness, call it solitude
Or blank desertion.   (395)
   (1850, 1:361–95)

This sequence represents several crucial elements of *The Prelude*. As in rowing one strives to "reach a chosen point" by looking backward, so *The Prelude* by retrospective inquiry aimed to project the poet forward into *The Recluse*, for which *The Prelude* was "preparatory" (*Prose* 3:5). *The Prelude* tried to integrate "spots of time" into the consecutive history of a life project, just as each of the single "small circles" made by the fall of the oar, each new trace of energy, finally "melted all into one track." Wordsworth was trying to open circles to achieve an "unswerving line." But this typical spotting and knotting, doubling back to single out moments that can be joined each to each to define a direction for the present, is interrupted. The outer circle, which was to contain the projected line, fails to hold. The "huge peak" breaks open "the horizon's utmost boundary," supplanting the "summit" which was to serve as point of reference for the line. The terror of disruptive recession at the origin precludes the goal. The return "back to the covert" marks a frustration, a triumph of anxiety to make a closure against both the yawning backward abysm and the unspecified and unreachable goal. If end and origin fall away, the starting point at least remains.

In *The Prelude*, by 1850 if not in 1805, Wordsworth's return to his own imaginative starting point comforted the double failure to achieve *The Recluse* and to find the origin. Whatever his wishes, Wordsworth could no more write *The Recluse* than he could keep ascending after he had reached the highest point of his journey in the Alps. That Alpine experience of crossing limits repeats the characteristic movement of *The Prelude*. A compromise is suddenly resolved into its conflicting components: the solid ground opens downward into the "mind's abyss," outward into "something evermore about to be," and upward into the rising of imaginative "Power" (6:591–608).

In revising the boat-stealing sequence between 1805 and 1850, Wordsworth made a number of changes that suggest his own "reading asunder." He tried to clarify ambivalence by reducing blurring and blending, creating stronger points in textually distancing from each other elements that once fell together. Through adding "to reach a chosen point / With an unswerving line" (lines 368–69), Wordsworth highlighted the fact of interruption by introducing the goal and emphasizing the direction of will toward it. Furthermore, Wordsworth reinforced with a superlative the apparent firmness of the origin: "The horizon's utmost boundary" (line 371) replaced "the bound of the horizon" (1805, line 399). Similarly, "above" (line 371) replaced "behind" (1805, line 399), because to mention a "behind" already weakens a "bound" by extending it. Such a pairing of "bound" and "behind" in 1805 proleptically figured the later usurpation of "bound" by "behind" (lines 377–78). Instead of reserving the thrust of the peak for a sudden point of emergence as in 1850, the prolepsis spread over the whole scene the rising power of imagination. Likewise in establishing the surroundings, Wordsworth deleted "A rocky steep uprose / Above the cavern of the willow-tree" (1805, lines 394–95). He thereby preserved for its punctual presence the sudden verticality of the "grim shape" (line 381).

Yet however carefully he read between his lines and wrote out the differences produced, Wordsworth never wholly untangled the elements of the scene. If the "steep uprose" (1805, line 394) was deleted, in its place stood "one who rows" (line 367). The nonsense of homophony (rose-rows) reasserts the imaginative disruption. Wordsworth no doubt heard this problem in writing that the peak "towered" (line 382), replacing "rose" (1805, line 410), but this attempt at discrimination only blurred the point anew in losing the precise identity between how "I rose" (line 375) and how the cliff did, and in displacing from a privileged spot one of Wordsworth's characteristic words of imaginative activity. Finally, the crucial word "bound" (line 378) resounds disturbingly; it already contains within itself the discrepant elements of the episode. The word suggests not only limitation and geographical fixity (its literal function in the passage), not only integration ("my days . . . bound each to each"—from "My Heart Leaps Up") and obligation, but also directed mobility. To summarize: while the rower is outward bound, a shape bounds up beyond the bounds of the horizon, and he feels bound to return.

This episode suggests both the failure of Wordsworth's career to reach its goal and its correlative fascination with origins. The revision sharply illuminates this line, suggesting Wordsworth's own awareness of it. The message sounds throughout the rest of *The Prelude* and of Wordsworth's other writings: let the interruption be the end; overlook nothing that comes athwart your path. Such dislocations from the expected circuit are the true reward. The Boy of Winander episode, bound up in the early MS JJ with the boat stealing (see Parrish 84–89), amplified upon this pattern. Calling out to the owls, the boy awaited a response from them. Sometimes they responded with "concourse wild / Of jocund din," but at other times:

> When a lengthened pause
> Of silence came and baffled his best skill,
> Then sometimes, in that silence while he hung
> Listening, a gentle shock of mild surprise
> Has carried far into his heart the voice
> Of mountain torrents; or the visible scene
> Would enter unawares into his mind,
> With all its solemn imagery, its rocks,
> Its woods, and that uncertain heaven, received
> Into the bosom of the steady lake. (1850, 5:379–88)

The suspended middle state, in which the boy "hung" while the goal of owl sound was held off, allowed for the "gentle shock of mild surprise," the taking in of voice and scene that replaced the anticipated hoots. In 1805 the first lines of this passage read, "When it chanced / That pauses of deep silence mocked his skill" (lines 404–5). The major effect of the revision is to lengthen the pause by adjective ("lengthened"), by singularizing it, and by placing it at the line's end. This transformation of the pause and the antithetical balancing in revision of the beginnings of lines 379 ("Of jocund din") and 380 ("Of silence") combined to sufficiently "deepen" the silence without further need for the adjective. Just as in revising the boat stealing Wordsworth drew special attention to the frustration of the goal, the truncation of the proposed journey, so here too the weight fell increasingly on the length of the intermediate state. In revision, the poet holding vigil over the boy's grave stood "mute," like the boy, "a long half hour" (line 396), replacing "a full half-hour" (1805, line 421). The boy's time was thus explicitly paralleled to the poet's ("lengthened"—"long"), and the time was emptied ("full" yields to "long"). It was a time of receptivity, of potential only.

I read in these revisions Wordsworth's increasingly active grappling with the change that had come over *The Prelude* between its first completion and its final revision. We ourselves hardly have the concepts to disentangle so complex a knot of intention, text, and history. One easy gauge, however, is to recognize in *The Prelude* of 1805 "the poem to Coleridge," as it was regularly called in the Wordsworth household (*Prelude* 529, 530, 535). (It is not clear from the evidence in the Norton *Prelude* [531–33], however, that Wordsworth "always" [ix] thought of it in these terms.) The addresses to Coleridge in the poem were at first no literary fiction; even when written in his absence they solicited his return, and Coleridge's "To William Wordsworth" responded in kind to *The Prelude* when it finally reached its destination. By the final revision, Coleridge was dead. What had at first been addresses to the reader turn to apostrophes.

The whole question of Wordsworth's relations to his hearers and readers requires much more study. Bateson examined the significance of Wordsworth's addressing his intimates rather than the public (187–97), but confusion has often arisen. So Abrams cited a passage from *The Prelude* of 1805 to show "the deliberately . . . affirmative stance" the romantics adopted when "they undertook to speak with an authoritative public voice" ("Rationality" 462–63), but only a New-Critical refusal of history can grant "public voice" to a work that its author never published and never spoke save to a few intimates. Abrams deprecated the "ingenious exegetic" (*Natural Supernaturalism* 446) of those who find self-division in Wordsworth's "stance," or alienation in the privacy of his "public voice," but he did not acknowledge the processes that produce his own reading or the historical transformations that redefine the status of Wordsworth's text. In this instance, after Coleridge's death the decorum shifts from epistolary (address) to lyrical (apostrophe), intimate to monumental; the poem gains at once a dimension of fiction.

The relation *The Prelude* bears to *The Recluse* resembles its relation to Coleridge, whose pet project was *The Recluse*. Just as *The Prelude* was intended to reach Coleridge, so it was "subsidiary" to *The Recluse* (*Prose* 3:5). But in the final revisions the means became the end, no longer a stage to pass through in life but a posthumous life, the "poem on his own life" (*Prelude* 535–36) to be given to the world when he was dead. In both of the relations—to Coleridge and to *The Recluse*—*The Prelude* moved from transitivity to intransitivity; it became that aesthetically self-focused message that Jakobson defined as fundamentally poetic ("Linguistics" 356). The poem ran the danger of yielding to a nostalgic wish to annihilate half a lifetime and of becoming purely recollective—not of the earlier self remembered in 1805 but of the younger poetic self *writing* in 1805.

Yet to recall what Coleridge awaited, required, in *The Recluse* makes even the dangers of *The Prelude* a good alternative. Wordsworth was to "assume the station of a man in mental repose . . . whose principles were made up . . . prepared to deliver upon authority a system of philosophy" (*Complete Works* 6:403). Even Wordsworth was never so perfect a *"Spectator ab extra"* as to arrogate this "position." Wordsworth never achieved such grounding and was therefore unwilling to "assume" it. He recognized that his life as a poet depended upon disturbance, "shock" and "surprise," however gentle and mild. If he could speak "upon authority," it was derived not from the stability of truth but from the lability of moments in which the world slipped away as a shape rose from behind the bound, or in which one felt "the sentiment of being spread / O'er all" (1805, 2:420–21).

I have earlier attended to the archaically repressive, patriarchal Wordsworth of "Nutting" and to the doubly anticipatory character of *The Prelude* as "psychological" and "socialist." Here I emphasize its value as aesthetic space and echo themes familiar from Geoffrey Hartman, but I pose them as a determinate interpretive construction of Wordsworth's situation. There is a humane liberation in letting go—even with indecision, anxiety, and guilt—such a project as *The Recluse*, in deferring the end, keeping suspended in receptivity like the Boy of Winander. There is reward too in replacing the end, letting the interruption stand for the achievement, the wandering for the goal: "something evermore about to be" (6:608), "The budding rose above the rose full blown" (11:121). The revisions to *The Prelude* demonstrate the continuing liveliness of response in Wordsworth, his continuing power to find between the lines of the earlier text places where imagination would come to him. Even in first composing the childhood scenes of *The Prelude*, Wordsworth relied not on "naked recollection of the past" but instead imaginatively produced memories through "after-meditation" (3:614–16). So in revising, he did not merely recollect a younger self writing, he repeated that writing and made it different.

The situation of the spectator *ab intra*, the man poised between an origin that bounds up always just beyond grasp and an ever more excessive goal, recalls Wordsworth's definition of the writer of epitaphs. The writer of epitaphs occupies a "midway point" between the contrasting views of humankind as spirit and humankind as embodied (*Prose* 2:53). Although deduced from the "consciousness of . . . immortality" (2:50), the desires epitaphs serve begin from the fact of human finitude, in attempting "to preserve the memory of the dead, as a tribute due to his individual worth, for a satisfaction to the sorrowing hearts of the survivors, and for the common benefit of the living" (2:53). As a further figure of the writer's attempt to negotiate extremes, Wordsworth offered the circle. He declared that views which "seem opposite to each other" (humankind as spirit, humankind as body) have "a finer connection than that of contrast.—It is a connection formed through the subtle progress by which . . . qualities pass insensibly into their contraries, and things revolve upon each other." The analogy is then developed to a "voyage . . . sailing upon the orb of this planet" (2:53). But such a fidelity to the surface of earth immediately suggests the circle as a figure of human limitation, rather than of triumphant completion as in Abrams. Compare the answer Wordsworth suggested to a child wondering about the origin and tendency of a stream: "The spirit of the answer must have been, though the word might be sea or ocean, accompanied perhaps with an image gathered from a map, or from the real object in nature—these might have been the *letter*, but the *spirit* of the answer must have been . . . a receptacle without bounds or dimensions;—nothing less than infinity" (2:51). Only through a spiritual gloss can we make our parts whole. Since we cannot achieve the boundlessness of pure origin or ultimate end, we rest in between closed into a circle by the failure of our line to extend itself infinitely, "our little life rounded."

Such observations elucidate *The Prelude* better than does Abrams' ingenious exegetic thrust toward infinity. Not only do they echo the boat stealing, where the circle defines limitation in the face of the unbounded surroundings, but they clarify a puzzle from the ending. Throughout *The Prelude*, origins, as in the boat stealing, have receded. For each initiatory attempt of the "blest . . . infant Babe" an answering "already" is there before him (2:232–51), and not just phenomenologically, Wordsworth would have it, but logically as well: "in the words of Reason deeply weighed," each thought "hath no beginning" (2:228–32). The "native rock" that had been "goal / Or centre" of childhood activity is "gone," and "in its place / A smart Assembly-room usurped the ground." The disconnection from origins figured here is so intense that Wordsworth felt "Two consciousnesses, conscious of myself / And of some other Being" (2:32–39). The revision once again makes the point. In 1805 the stone was "split, and gone to build / A smart Assembly-room" (2:38–39), a process that however violent still preserves a continuity between a native single wholeness and the "assembly-room" where differences meet and crowd together in shifting combinations.

Just as the origin recedes, the hope to "reach a chosen point" is repeatedly frustrated. "The story of my life" failed to remain a "theme / Single and of determined bounds" for which the "road lies plain before me" (1:639–41). This problem stemmed less from the "broken windings" (2:274) than from a growing fear of the path's end. Such windings become not obstacles but devices serving a wish never to end, a fear of the unbounded goal that turns one back:

> Even as a river,—partly (it might seem)
> Yielding to old remembrances, and swayed
> In part by fear to shape a way direct,
> That would engulph him soon in the ravenous sea—
> Turns, and will measure back his course, far back,
> Seeking the very regions which he crossed
> In his first outset; so have we, my Friend!
> Turned and returned with intricate delay.
>   (1850, 9:1–8)

We recognize the Freudian circuitous path, the "intricate delay" that knots our life together, delaying death. In 1805 this moment was followed by its opposite, "An impulse to precipitate my verse" (9:9–10), the wish for total expenditure that hastens the end and undoes the bindings of economy. Wordsworth reconsidered the dangers of urging on too rapidly the end of the story of one's own life. The root sense of "precipitate" is "headlong, head over heels" (perhaps too, "verse" echoes French *verser*, "to pour out, overturn"), and Wordsworth revised this dangerous plummet with an image of overview, the retrospect of "a traveller, who has gained the brow / Of some aerial Down" (9:9–10). The dangers of the end fuel a wish for transcendence, a safe height (an "aerial Down" names the danger of descent while sublimating it upward). Paths attract Wordsworth not by reaching a goal, but to the extent that a "disappearing line" is like "an invitation into space / Boundless" (13:146–51). Just as in the "Essays Upon Epitaphs" "origin and tendency are . . . inseparably co-relative" (*Prose* 2:51), so in *The Prelude* too the infinite distancing of one answers to that of the other.

But if the poem is to reach any conclusion, some halt must be called to this double regress, and in the last book Wordsworth arbitrarily did so. He could only make the poem end by declaring that the origin had been found. Declaring imagination the "moving soul" of the work, Wordsworth wrote in 1805:

> we have traced the stream
> From darkness, and the very place of birth

> In its blind cavern, whence is faintly heard
> The sound of waters
>   (1805, 13:172–75)

But this attempt at grounding an end did not work. The poem was not finished; it did not prepare for *The Recluse,* and Wordsworth continued for the rest of his poetic life to wander within it: "Along the mazes of this song I go. / . . . Thus do I urge a never-ending way / Year after year" ("Fragments . . . akin to *The Prelude,*" in *Poetical Works,* 5:347). While still in revision retaining the terminal gesture, Wordsworth significantly attenuated it:

> we have traced the stream
> From the blind cavern whence is faintly heard
> Its natal murmur (14:194–96)

The promised end, prefigured in the apocalyptic "sound of waters," vanishes with the "natal murmur"—a phrase that returns to beginnings yet asserts them much less emphatically than "the very place of birth." The effect is like that described by Lamb many years earlier: "Here the mind knowingly passes a fiction upon herself . . . and, in the same breath detecting the fallacy, will not part with the wish" (1:265). Specific place yields to murmur, eye to ear, letter to spirit, as in the "Essays Upon Epitaphs."

Similar compromises determined the major intellectual issue of *The Prelude.* A pure naturalism would be as untenable as engulfment in the "ravenous sea," and a pure assertion of imagination as impossible as enclosure in the "blind cavern." So the mind was proclaimed "lord and master" (12:222) and countered with the claim "From Nature doth emotion come" (13:1), and the formula of "ennobling interchange" (13:375) attempted to harmonize them. Such a resolution of radically discordant elements, however, decomposed constantly; the resultant is resolved back into its component forces. The circle figured a wish to deny the opposition of extremes, and in the "Essays Upon Epitaphs" the master trope of *Natural Supernaturalism,* "life as a journey," stood as a consolatory commonplace (*Prose* 2:54). If *The Prelude* fulfilled the ambition it expressed, it was not because it reached its goal, but rather because interrupting accident had intervened, because the means had become the end, as for the Boy, as in the boat stealing.

In the "Essays Upon Epitaphs" Wordsworth considered the relation of means and ends—life and death—and found in immortality the figure necessary to relate the two. Otherwise, "such a hollowness would pervade the whole system of things, such a want of correspondence and consistency, a disproportion so astounding between means and ends, that there could be no repose, no joy" (*Prose* 2:52). The trope of immortality ("death *is* eternal life") established the desired relation between means and ends, truncation and infinitude, just as the imagination did in *The Prelude*. Or in *The Prelude* was it love that centered the system, or nature, or the interaction among various of these elements? *The Prelude* offered "several frames of things," and their relations vary. They may be "mutually indebted" or instead "half lost / Each in the other's blaze" (8:481–84). The process may transform from a totalizing "swallowing up of lesser things in great" to a disruptive "change of them into their contraries" (11:179–80). Wordsworth's terms cut the kind of figures around each other that such crucial notions of Neoplatonic art theory as "idea" and "nature" did. They hold what Erwin Panofsky anticipating Jacques Derrida called "a peculiar relation of mutual supplementation" (*eigentümlich wechselseitige Suppletivverhältnis*), in which the terms do not oppose each other but "correspond" to each other, "completing or even replacing each other" (*ergänzend oder sogar stellvertretend*) (35).

I have tried to suggest ways of reading the circle, the journey, *The Prelude* itself, that differ from those of *Natural Supernaturalism* not only to further an understanding of Wordsworth that I find more humane, although less grand, but also because the recent criticism of Wordsworth engages fundamentals of critical practice and principle. This is even clearer now in the later 1980s than in 1978 when I first wrote this essay. The issue I shall arrive at is the critique of "spatial form," crucial for Frank Kermode and Paul de Man, and the starting point for Derrida's reach from philosophy toward literature in "Force and Signification" and for W. V. Spanos in defining the postmodernism of *boundary 2*.

Our current context for understanding *The Prelude* is still defined by the appearance almost twenty-five years ago of works by Herbert Lindenberger, M. H. Abrams ("English Romanticism," the first ma-

The Prelude *and Critical Revision*

jor step toward *Natural Supernaturalism*), and Geoffrey Hartman. Despite notable British essays by Leavis, Knight, and Empson, American New Criticism had not much attended to *The Prelude*, and these works of the early 1960s looked beyond new criticism in important respects. They have so thoroughly reoriented Wordsworth criticism as to overshadow the books of David Perkins and David Ferry, which hinted at a valuable turning toward *The Prelude* within the American academy as redefined by New Criticism.

Our new way with Wordsworth came under the sign of comparative literature, engaging emphases at once more theoretical, more international, and more historical than those associated with New Criticism. Our wish for a "new literary history" and our current concern with methods of "critical inquiry" are both prefigured in this eruption within the criticism of Wordsworth. As is so often the case with critical revision, this innovation came through looking back, from engagement with the nineteenth-century German tradition of Romance philology. Hartman dedicated his book to the memory of Erich Auerbach; Abrams' essay drew on Auerbach for its climactic argument; and Lindenberger related *The Prelude* to topoi studied by E. R. Curtius. All three located Wordsworth in the history of European rhetoric (as did the early work of Paul de Man, although its influence was not felt until later). Hartman began by isolating the romantic figure of "surmise," derived from the classical "*fallor . . . an*" construction. Lindenberger devoted his first chapter to "*The Prelude* and the Older Rhetoric" and went on to define Wordsworth's new "rhetoric of interaction." Abrams connected the sublime to the matter-of-fact in Wordsworth through the Christian rhetoric of *sermo humilis*, derived from the low style in which the Bible set forth the greatest matters.

These new emphases altered the tradition of criticism of Wordsworth. Through their relations to these new studies, several older essays came into new prominence: those by A. C. Bradley, Matthew Arnold, and Walter Pater, all English critics who worked in their differing ways at joining the new thought and writing of Germany to native concerns. Arnold and Bradley have been accepted as the two poles of Wordsworthian criticism (Abrams, "Introduction," 2–4), and Abrams and Hartman as their heirs. Bradley's darkly philosophical, brooding poet, hostile to "sense" and verging on apocalypse (130–34), has an affinity to Hartman's Wordsworth that is well

71

known because Hartman himself noted it. Rejecting Wordsworth's "philosophy," Arnold in contrast looked back to Wordsworth for a consoling joy that forecast Abrams' argument. In considering the necessity for poetry to engage with "*life*" and not rest in mere formalism, Arnold drew a figure from Epictetus. Perfection of form bears the same relation to life that "inns bear to home": "As if a man, journeying home, and finding a nice inn on the road . . . were to stay forever." Against this negative prototype of the "halted traveler" (Hartman), Arnold inveighed, "Man, thou hast forgotten thine object; thy journey was not *to* this, but *through* this." In contrast, "a poet like Wordsworth," Arnold concluded, "prosecutes his journey home" by choosing to sing "Of truth, of grandeur, beauty, love, and hope. . . . Of joy in widest commonalty spread" (*Complete Prose* 9:46–47). Arnold prefigured Abrams' master figure of the journey homeward and his central focus on the "Prospectus" to *The Recluse*. Arnold did not, however, claim that Wordsworth actually reached home, only that he was en route, and I take this as a critical judgment, not merely as Arnold's writing before the publication of "Home at Grasmere," on which Abrams relied to supplement *The Prelude*.

Pater has had less impact because he did not fix an image of Wordsworth. Likewise the multiple approaches of Lindenberger's book have prevented it from consolidating a clear position in the critical tradition. But iconoclasm may help evade the impasse of strongly etched but opposite images. Can we set such images into an active relation with each other that is not merely synthetic? Just as Lindenberger followed one strand at a time of *The Prelude* and did not strive for a coherent picture, so Pater emphasized that "sometimes" Wordsworth felt a pure, imaginative solipsism, in which "the actual world would, as it were, dissolve and detach itself, flake by flake." "At other times," however, he felt a pantheistic "spirit of life in outward things, a single, all-pervading mind in them, of which . . . even the poet's imaginative energ[ies] are but moments" (*Appreciations* 54–55). Pater presented the variety and mobility of writing in *The Prelude* without, like Abrams, demanding a harmonious resolution to a triumphant plot, and without, like Hartman, insisting upon a fierce, debilitatingly self-conflicting struggle. At best, such a strategy of reading encourages a fresh sensitivity to more of the poem than would a strategy prepared to find only a single story. Such sensitivity, I have been arguing, is required if we are to respect and analyze the poem's historical complexity, rather than freezing it into an idealized emblem.

Yet how can we read the work as a whole without fixing an image? This is a version of the problem of "totality" and "representation" that has provoked such controversy in the last decade across the humanities and social sciences, and to which I return in the last chapter. Within literary study this problem vexes the reading of nineteenth-century novels as well as poetry. For realistic fiction works by eroding conventional forms, which are set up only to be undermined. If one "stands at a distance" from such a work, it seems the very image of what it is attacking. Apart from local texture, *Don Quixote* looks like a heroic romance, *Madame Bovary* like a love story. The issue becomes even more difficult when the technique of realism is less ironic than these and more allegorical, depending like Thackeray or George Eliot on the sequence of larger units, so that any portion of such a plural work may show only one emphasis. Nonetheless, attention to rhetoric (in its largest sense of how words work to different effects from those of grammar or logic) offers some resistance to fascination by the image. This is the problem area of my own "Rhetoric and Realism" and for much of the work of Paul de Man, which I address later.

Pater implied one rhetorical reading of *The Prelude* in analyzing the problems of means and ends (which have already engaged us in thinking through the relations between *The Prelude* and *The Recluse* and then in following Wordsworth's meditations on epitaphs). Pater suggested that the way we relate means to ends is the "type or figure under which we represent our lives to ourselves." He offered three instances: that which subordinates means to end, "a figure, reducing all things to machinery"; that which justifies the end by the means—"whatever may become of the fruit, make sure of the flowers and the leaves"; that in which "means and end are identified" (60–62). These figures correspond to metonymy, synecdoche, and metaphor, as elaborated by Hayden White from Kenneth Burke and Vico. They offer rhetorical models for the major intellectual elements of *The Prelude*: the metonymic "reducing" of associational psychology ("An unrelenting agency / Did bind my feelings even as in a chain" [3:168–69]); the synecdochic organicism

73

of pantheistic totality (that "grows / Like harmony in music" and "reconciles / Discordant elements" [1:340–43]); the metaphoric leap of pure imagination that achieves identity without mediation ("the light of sense / Goes out, but with a flash" [6:600–1]).

These rhetorical models support Lindenberger's reading of *The Prelude* in terms of three separate organizing principles: a memoir of facts in order (a metonymic reading Lindenberger ascribed to the nineteenth century); the principle of which "Wordsworth himself was most aware . . . the threefold pattern of early vision, loss, and restoration," modeled on the "traditional cycle of paradise, fall, and redemption" (Abrams' synecdochic, Hegelian reading); and a third principle that "stands at odds with the other two, for . . . it recognizes no beginning, middle, or end" (190–91). This third principle, metaphoric, in its eclipse of mediation, Lindenberger calls "repetition," drawing from Kierkegaard's critique of Hegel (196–97). A fourth principle might be adduced (tropologically, a type of irony) on the model of Derrida's *différance*. It would find an unbridgeable gap between means and end. Neither the end nor the origin would exist, but our consciousness of their absence would nonetheless define our life as medial. I have tried reading *The Prelude* along this line, to challenge the dominance of the second.

Even if rhetorical analysis helps prevent fixation on an image, the German philological tradition that made rhetoric available to us for the study of Wordsworth has problems of its own. Although from our distance they are both German Romanists, Auerbach and Curtius significantly diverged, as R. P. Blackmur recognized at the first Princeton Seminars in Criticism (Fitzgerald 38–39). Auerbach's admiring reviews nonetheless criticized Curtius' *European Literature and the Latin Middle Ages* for its fundamentally unhistorical method, for neglecting Christian innovations and choosing a topical, synoptic emphasis on classical continuity. This criticism bore directly on the opposing positions of the two men toward literary modernism. Auerbach was strongly disturbed by modernism, despite his acute comments on it in *Mimesis* and his recognition that his own method bore the marks of modernity. Curtius, however, wrote early defenses and interpretations of Joyce, Eliot, and others. As early as 1929 he adumbrated Joseph Frank's analysis of "spatial form": "In order really to understand *Ulysses* one would have to have the entire work present in one's mind at every sentence" (*Es-*

says 353). Curtius cast his own *European Literature* into this modernist form, describing it in terms of "aerial photography" (ix) and "spiral ascent" (381). Auerbach's *Mimesis* remained resolutely chronological, yet committed as well to articulate disturbances and breakthroughs. Although Auerbach's crucial conception of "figuralism" showed a resemblance to spatial form (according to Frank 237), Christian figuralism was only a phase in the overall history Auerbach pursued. Abrams' *Natural Supernaturalism* put some of Auerbach's topics to use, but it followed Curtius' organization, deliberately echoing the "spiral form" ("Rationality" 450) it found in romantic writing. By this German route, Abrams arrived at the formalist cancellation of time, along with the New Critics, despite their other differences.

Despite the problems that the previous chapter has shown with Hartman's attempt at an anti-Hegelian historiography, and despite further problems I shall explore in Paul de Man, it still seems possible that a more resolute focus on rhetoric, on language in action, might evade the totalizing, binary opposition of spatial versus temporal. Rhetorical studies such as Miller's "Fiction of Realism" (123–26) have undermined a similar dichotomy, Roman Jakobson's polarizing of metaphor and metonymy, by recalling the necessary interplay between the two in any articulated work (since to rest wholly at one pole is to suffer an aphasia). Is it possible wholly to segregate space and time, any more than Wordsworth's 1850 revision of the boat stealing wholly segregated the elements and eliminated blending? In contrasting Homer to the Bible, the first chapter of Auerbach's *Mimesis* set in motion the terminology of space and time. The "complete externalization" (2) and "foregrounding" in the *Odyssey* create a static icon in which all time is present, while in the Bible, matters of history, formation, and development determine what is presented and how (14–15). Auerbach argued (as later of *Ulysses*) that the *Odyssey* may be analyzed structurally (11, 487), but that only in the Bible is the temporality of interpretation necessary (12). Yet within Auerbach's text, the critical metaphors followed an opposite line as well. Connections in the Bible are "vertical," in Homer horizontal (14). The parts of Homer's world link contiguously, metonymically, as the text moves along the syntagmatic axis that marks the flow of language in time; in the Bible, however, the leap of metaphor relates a human event to its para-

75

digm in divine providence. "History" (15ff.), as in the Bible, is understood from a perspective that lifts up every moment into eternal significance, while the Homeric icon, complete at every moment, from moment to moment metamorphoses. That is, the radical opposition of Homer to the Bible, with which Auerbach (as I noted in chapter 1) acknowledged discomfort ("Epilegomena" 2), proves unstable; the curse of fixity, the privilege of change, pass across the bounding line.

In the palimpsest of our cultural history, the languages of space and time are both inscribed. A purifying revision, or retranscription, that tried to straighten out the tangles of these lines, to free us from our need to read between them, would no doubt like Wordsworth achieve some fresh moments and new emphases. Should it strive to do better? The "peculiar relation of mutual supplementation," by which minor terms become major and opposites complete or replace one another, saved Wordsworth from the complacency of *The Recluse*; his position was never wholly "made up" or composed but always liable to displacement. This is the interest of his situation. Should we strive for the disinterestedness of stepping out from between the lines, into the position of the ideal recluse, released by omitting "all cross currents, all friction . . . everything unresolved, truncated, and uncertain" (*Mimesis* 16)? This would be, in Auerbach's terms, to will ourselves from "history" into "legend," the "homogeneous, empty time" against which Benjamin struggled (*Illuminations* 261).

I have tried to argue against Abrams' legend of Wordsworth and replace it with the "friction" of history, to unfix the firmness of his image. Such a project could undertake much more than I have here. For example, it is remarkable, but I believe previously unremarked, that Wordsworth's three major periods of revisionary labor on *The Prelude* correspond to the major historical crises of post-Napoleonic England in his lifetime: 1816–19, the movement up to Peterloo on which E. P. Thompson has written so powerfully; 1831–32, the period of Reform agitation; and 1838–39, the time of Chartism and the "Condition-of-England Question." So too, one could further historicize the critical revision in our understanding of *The Prelude*, as I begin to in the next section of this chapter.

For now, this beginning has attempted to indicate both that ways of reading associated with "deconstruction" have a history (including figures so different as Pater and Panofsky) and that such ways of reading may help to address matters of history (in this case, the textual status of *The Prelude*) more flexibly and precisely than our established practices of literary history (such as Abrams'), which prove closer to New-Critical ahistoricism than has usually been acknowledged.

In concluding this chapter, I will consider somewhat more closely the intellectual location of M. H. Abrams' work, which has been decisive for American academic criticism of the last three decades. The authority of his two major scholarly works, *The Mirror and the Lamp* (1953) and *Natural Supernaturalism* (1971), made him a weighty contestant against "deconstruction" when he was summoned to the combat by Wayne Booth. Thus in the mid-seventies Abrams contributed three pieces to the new journal of Chicago "pluralism," *Critical Inquiry*. Although Abrams' famous model of four types of critical theories owes a good deal to the modes of analysis associated with R. S. Crane and others of the early "Chicago" group, his power in the American academy can only be understood if his work is also related both to New Criticism (as I have started to do in this chapter) and to his beginnings in what I will call a "Harvard" school of literary history.

To think further for a moment about Abrams and New Criticism, consider his books' titles: *The Mirror and the Lamp: Romantic Theory and the Critical Tradition; Natural Supernaturalism: Tradition and Revolution in Romantic Literature.* Both works were historical, but both titles replaced sequence (contrast *From Classic to Romantic* by W. J. Bate) with paradox, and thus in their rhetorical structures conformed to New Criticism. Abrams' alertness to what was the advanced literary and critical milieu of his youth shone forth in the title of his first book—but also his dissertation of 1940. The play of mirror and lamp came from a phrase in Yeats' Introduction to *The Oxford Book of Modern Verse* (1936). Even now it is rare for a serious scholarly dissertation to take its title from a phrase in an absolutely contemporary work by a poet. The subtitular concern with "tradition" was no less New Critical in its tendency to hypostasize rather than to differentiate. T. S. Eliot's "Tradition and the Individual Talent" struck the keynote, developed in Cleanth Brooks'

Modern Poetry and the Tradition (1939). Abrams' very concern with key "metaphors" as images—mirror, lamp, spiral, journey—was much closer to the visual rhetoric of the New Criticism than either to A. O. Lovejoy's conceptually analyzed "unit ideas" (such as the "principle of plenitude" he constructed to give philosophic substance to the "great chain of being") or to the "starting-points" Erich Auerbach considered fruitful for philological inquiry (a rhetorical figure such as an address to the reader; a phrase like "la cour et la ville"). It was New Criticism and concomitant tendencies in philosophy that reduced all rhetoric to metaphor. Roman Jakobson restored metonymy, and recent work has begun to repluralize the figures, much against the grain of Abrams' work.

It makes sense that a student of I. A. Richards, as Abrams was, should have had a close yet complex relation to New Criticism, yet Abrams' work also opposed the antiromantic tendencies of New Criticism and helped to make romanticism intellectually legitimate again. To unpack these relations further requires establishing the historical context for Abrams that most needs recovery: the 1930s and a "Harvard" school of literary history, against Yale formalism or Chicago pluralism.

What was the critical scene in Cambridge from 1930, when Abrams entered Harvard College, to 1940, when he received his Harvard Ph.D.? Irving Babbitt was retiring: a propagandist for "tradition" whose work had deeply influenced Eliot; a scathing critic of *Rousseau and Romanticism* (1919) for breaking from that tradition; and an acute analyst of *Masters of Modern French Criticism* (1912), against whom he sharpened himself in disagreement. One dimension of Abrams' career, then, may be understood as establishing a paradoxical, rather than sequential and antithetical, relation between two of Babbitt's key terms. I. A. Richards came from Cambridge, England, just at the point that his *Coleridge on the Imagination* (1934) appeared. A. O. Lovejoy's *The Great Chain of Being* appeared in 1936, based on the William James Lectures he had delivered at Harvard in 1933. T. S. Eliot gave new prestige to the study of English criticism with his Norton Lectures published as *The Use of Poetry and the Use of Criticism* (1933). All this was certainly in the air, but perhaps a little stratospheric. What were younger persons doing? Among Harvard's younger faculty were Walter Houghton (who received the Christian Gauss award for *The Vic-*

torian Frame of Mind [1957] three years after Abrams did, the year Frye's *Anatomy of Criticism* appeared), Perry Miller, and F. O. Matthiessen. Miller and Matthiessen have never been associated with Abrams, but not only did they all live and work in the same department for most of the 1930s, but *The New England Mind* (1939) and *American Renaissance* (1941) are among the few academic works that have been in print continuously longer than *The Mirror and the Lamp*. These three works are among the earliest, and definitive, instances of the characteristic genre of modern academic literary history—the "period study." Finally we may note younger contemporaries who received the Ph.D. shortly after Abrams. Jerome Buckley won the Christian Gauss award a few years before Abrams with his period study *The Victorian Temper* (1951); W. J. Bate, who won the first of his Gauss awards the year after Abrams, shares precisely with Abrams a life concern with the space of transition from Johnson to Coleridge.

In trying to evoke an intellectual spirit of the age in Cambridge of the 1930s, I would cite also one of the extremely rare self-references in Abrams' major work. As *Natural Supernaturalism* made its key transition from "Apocalypse by Revolution" to "Apocalypse by Imagination," Abrams cited another Harvard contemporary, Herschel Baker, to claim that *The Prelude* recorded "the spiritual biography of [Wordsworth's] generation." Then Abrams quoted from Auden's *New Year Letter*: "We hoped; we waited for the day . . . That theory promised us would come, / It didn't." Abrams added that "Auden, writing in 1940, reminds us that [Wordsworth's disappointment] also anticipated remarkably the spiritual biography of Auden's own generation, and mine" (*Natural Supernaturalism* 333–34). For Abrams, then, we may surmise a particular urgency in the relation of "theory" to the disappointments of "history." The continued explicit concern with "theory" has kept his work fresh and relevant in our age, while the primary emphasis on "history" gave the work its solid, conservative appeal.

Yet the act of historical connection Abrams made between romanticism and his own time, the refusal to let romanticism be buried by the conquering "golden chain" of Babbitt's "tradition" (244) or by the New-Critical scorn for its adolescent immaturity, may evoke another text from 1940, Benjamin's "Theses on the Philosophy of History." For Benjamin, to "articulate the past historically" meant to "seize hold of a memory as it flashes up at a moment of danger" (*Illuminations* 255). We give more specificity to the motives of literary history if we relate them to the historical moments that move historians to write. In flight after the fall of France, and meditating on the pact between Nazi Germany and the Soviet Union, Benjamin rejected the theory of progress. Belief in progress linked a spectrum from the Communists through the German Social Democrats, the bourgeoisie, and even fascists. Benjamin's critique of progress, however, did not mean giving up the struggle toward a cultural transformation that would exercise "retroactive force" and "constantly call in question every victory, past and present, of the rulers" (*Illuminations* 255). We have already noted the problems with the 1930s in Hartman's work, and I shall address the thirties in more detail when I discuss F. O. Matthiessen and, finally, the New York Intellectuals. Both new Yale "theory" and old Harvard "history" must work through this impasse if we are to achieve a new literary history.

Chapter 3
Coleridge and New Criticism Reconsidered: Repetition and Exclusion

ROBERT PENN WARREN'S "A Poem of Pure Imagination" (1946), his reading of "The Rime of the Ancient Mariner," achieved at once a major statement of New Criticism and a beginning to the still-active revision of Coleridge's romanticism. Through rereading Warren, I will elucidate a problematic fundamental to my larger exploration of history, especially the history of literary reception: the interplay of repetition and exclusion. This activity joins critics with the poet as self-critic, as did the activity of "revision" in my previous chapter. Warren constantly repeats variants of the opposition between too much and too little meaning, while excluding from sight those elements of Coleridge's text that fall through the meshes of this network of oppositions. Those activities of (repetitive) emphasis and (exclusive) selection involved in reading a text pertain to the whole problem of cultural reproduction, the formation of textual canons and institutional elites that determine—both constrain and enable—the critical practices of a given time and place. We attend now to Warren's essay because of his place in New Criticism and our sense of all that we inherit from that way of reading, writing, and teaching: the burden of its repetitive concerns from which we must free ourselves, the absence we wish to make good of texts and methods it excluded. Yet a liberation of poetry and criticism from what we take as excessively limiting in New Criticism cannot come from merely looking *through* New Criticism, poring over its texts so intensively that we see daylight, or the abyss, through the weave, however tight its texture may have been drawn. We have to look *around* it as well. This claim for contextualism over textualism echoes Foucault's critique of Derrida

("My Body"), but in chapter 11 I exercise it against Fredric Jameson as well.

In opposing the views of John Livingston Lowes (author of the extraordinary source study *The Road to Xanadu* [1927]) and Earl Leslie Griggs (already established as the century's major editor of Coleridge's correspondence), Warren's essay was a crucial document in the struggle that allowed criticism to supplant scholarship as the major activity by which even academic teachers and students of literature defined their relations to the texts they read. The victory belonged, however, not simply to criticism, but to New Criticism, and even that of a specific variety. In 1938, when Warren and Cleanth Brooks, both teaching at Louisiana State University, published *Understanding Poetry*, they were far less important representatives of New Criticism than William Empson, Kenneth Burke, or R. P. Blackmur. By twenty-five years later, when I entered college, *Understanding Poetry* was in its third edition, Brooks and Warren had long been at Yale, and their sober, pedagogic effectiveness had displaced the willfulness of Empson, the preciosity of Blackmur, the playfulness of Burke. For the classroom, or even for comfort, those three were too disturbingly brilliant (like the sun in "The Ancient Mariner"). Furthermore, from the thirties to the sixties, Blackmur, Burke, and Empson were all proving themselves ever more clearly critics in the larger, Arnoldian sense (that Edward Said has been instrumental in renewing for our time), while the students and disciples of Brooks and Warren were working to refine a more exclusively *literary* criticism. The rhetorical subtlety of Paul de Man only further narrowed these limits, I shall argue in later chapters. Indeed, literary history, as defined (repeatedly) by de Man—the shift in rhetorical registers within the small space of a short text or few pages of a longer text—seems too exclusive to achieve the larger scope we want, almost a new version of Matthew Arnold's "touchstones." We want both to take in more than a few pages of Rousseau or a sonnet of Mallarmé and to put out more, to write books as well as essays of literary history (as in my current attempt). One such book would be a study of New Criticism that undertook to chart its effect, to place it not only intellectually but also institutionally (in relation to such issues as textbooks, graduate schools, job placement). We also need thoughtful attention to the readers of New Criticism. How did an intellectual movement that received so much bad press, so many serious attacks, as did New Criticism, somehow prevail? (Graff's *Professing Literature* contributes here.)

I begin with Warren's most striking exclusion, which leads to Coleridge and repetition. Despite his wish to show the consistency between his interpretation of "The Ancient Mariner" and Coleridge's "sober prose" (203) (an oddly ironic way of describing Coleridge's theology and metaphysics), Warren mentioned only once, briefly and early, Coleridge's most crucial term, the Reason, the power of transcendent intuition, Coleridge's master word for the unity he so constantly sought, and at which Warren aimed also (210–11). Here is a key definition from around the time that Coleridge was republishing "The Ancient Mariner" with the newly added gloss: "The REASON without being either the SENSE, the UNDERSTANDING or the IMAGINATION contains all three within itself, even as the mind contains its thoughts, and is present in and through them all; or as the expression pervades the different features of an intelligent countenance" (*Collected Works* 6:69–70). Warren instead establishes the imagination, for Coleridge a "mediatory" power, as the dominant operative term of his reading. For Coleridge, the imagination was "the completing power which unites clearness with depth, the plenitude of the sense with the comprehensibility of the understanding," that "reconciling and mediatory power . . . incorporating the Reason in Images of the Sense, and organizing . . . the flux of the Senses by the permanence and self-circling energies of the Reason" (6:69, 29). Warren found in the poem an opposition of moonlight to sunlight, symbolizing the opposition of imagination to understanding. It is hard to establish clearly the relations among Coleridge's major terms. (This is why he is so fruitfully available to some readers and contemptuously dismissable for others.) Nonetheless, there is little warrant in Coleridge for the opposition of understanding to imagination and even less for the alignment of concept with image (the understanding as the sun) that Warren proposed.

In Coleridge's later prose the sun was regularly aligned with the Reason: "Reason and religion are their own evidence. The natural sun is in this respect a symbol of the spiritual" (6:10). Or again, "The light of religion is not that of the moon, light without heat;

but neither is its warmth that of the stove, warmth without light. Religion is the sun whose warmth indeed swells, and stirs, and actuates the life of nature, but who at the same time beholds all the growth of life with a master-eye" (6:48). Ignoring the Reason drove Warren into what seems an unintentional antiphrasis, when he made the sun symbolize the "reflective faculty" (241), although the sun's power is projective. Furthermore, in discussing the symbol by "necessity" (219), the natural symbol, Warren failed to note the natural dependence of the moon, which *is* "reflective," upon the sun for its light. (The imagination does not in Coleridge similarly depend upon the understanding.) For all its attempts to contextualize its reading in terms of Coleridge's "sober prose," Warren's essay actually achieved its reading in a way exemplary of New Criticism, through fidelity to the poem's independent contours, *despite* its difference both from Coleridge's theology and from nature. A distance remains between the poem and the origins with which Warren wished it to be continuous: the world of nature (with which it should be integral by the theory of the symbol) and the poet's prose (with which it should be developmentally coherent [cf. 273]).

What conditions might determine Warren's misreading, his neglect of the Reason and its connection to religion and the sun? First, there is the *problem* of religion. Although Warren importantly renewed our understanding of the theological bases of Coleridge's criticism, he did not acknowledge that for Coleridge's writing religion was not just the base, the point of departure, but was even more the center and ultimate goal. Warren remained far more committed than Coleridge to a separate aesthetic sphere. To recognize this would have raised the question of religion as displacing Coleridge's poetic activity and would have necessitated thinking through the notorious fact that Coleridge's most productive years as a prose writer were extremely lean poetically. To be sure, the revisions of "The Ancient Mariner" for *Sybilline Leaves* (1817) (notably the gloss) were contemporary with his activity in speculative prose and succeeded in "connecting . . . the chief poem of Coleridge with his philosophy" (Pater, *Appreciations* 100). They may well also, however, have afforded a haven from which Coleridge was unwilling or unable to set out again. We may acknowledge the 1817 "Ancient Mariner" as "Coleridge's one great complete work, the one really finished thing, in a life of many beginnings" (Pater 101), and still find this completion the terminal domestication of Coleridge's poetic wanderings, the ultimate correction of error through revision, in contrast to Wordsworth's ceaseless wandering through the mazes of his song. Such considerations would all have compromised Warren's hope for the peaceful coexistence of religion and poetry.

We arrive then at a second area of determination. By ignoring the Reason and its relation to the sun, Warren harmonized poetry and religion but set in opposition imagination and understanding. He thus repeated the characteristic New-Critical dichotomy of poetry and science, echoed at about the same time by Cleanth Brooks in *The Well Wrought Urn.* "Myth is truer than history," explained Brooks in discussing Keats' "sylvan historian," repeating yet another version of this opposition and suggesting some of the function of such oppositions (213). Myth holds together what falls apart into distinction in the harsh sunlight of history or science or understanding.

Within the poem such an archaizing move toward unity and away from history governs the function of the word "cross." In his prose speculations on language, Coleridge noted a historical tendency to "desynonymize" words with multiple meanings (*Collected Works,* 7.1:82). Such words split into different words, each bearing a single meaning of the original plurality. A word like "cross" accordingly takes on different meanings in its historical evolution. But its sequence of uses in "The Ancient Mariner" suggests a unity that overrides any possible historical distinctions or any logic that would analyze the uses as mere homonymity.

The climax of the poem's second section relates the albatross to "cross" in a specifically Christian context:

> Instead of the cross, the Albatross
> About my neck was hung.
> (141–42)

The force of this moment derives in part from two earlier uses of "cross," each of which links "cross," the albatross, and religious language in a way that appears merely casual:

> At length did cross an Albatross,
> Through the fog it came;

85

As if it had been a Christian soul,
We hailed it in God's name.
    (63–66)

"God save thee, ancient Mariner!
From the fiends, that plague thee thus!—
Why looks't thou so?"—With my cross-bow
I shot the ALBATROSS.
    (79–82)

The third instance ("Instead of the cross") reveals the system behind these chance appearances. The arbitrary, metonymic links of poetic syntax prove instead meaningful, metaphoric, paradigmatic. The earlier references to "God" and "Christian" are now packed by implication into the "cross," to which the albatross is shown as equivalent, holding the same place. For Coleridge such unity derives from Reason, but for New Critics like Warren, from experience. In terms of Warren's distinction between two types of symbol, this usage for Coleridge would be of "necessity," from the preexisting divine unity that establishes correspondences in the nature of things, in which words participate. For Warren, however, "cross" would function as a symbol of "congruence," based on our experience of the poem, which succeeds in establishing an order otherwise unavailable (219–20).

I finally find a third area of contradiction that Warren avoided by not recognizing the Coleridgean Reason in its full force and its association with the sun. Warren saved himself from having to puzzle over the negative value he found accorded to the sun in "The Rime of the Ancient Mariner." Such a reversal of values would have forced Warren to question his premise that the poem must be "truly the poet's," that it "expresses him" and therefore "involves his own view of the world" (203). Or if it did not shake this premise, then it would change the "view of the world" ascribed to Coleridge. It would suggest an incoherence in Coleridge's Christianity (and William Empson read the poem in this light) that might in turn lead to the "personal" themes of Kenneth Burke's inquiry, which Warren ruled out of his concern (214–16). Coleridge could no longer have served so effectively as the normative figure of a sensibility unified on the basis of religion.

In pursuing further ramifications of this problem with the sun, I will not myself explore the "personal" but will assume the context of Western religious experience (the wish to mediate the distance from an excessively omnipotent father-divinity) and Western rhetorical practice (the inevitable interruption and displacement of philosophic discourse by metaphoric vehicle, as Derrida argued in "White Mythology"). Indeed, from Derrida's observations on the ship, the sun, and the home as figures of metaphor, one might read "The Ancient Mariner" as the narrativization of a theory of metaphor.

Despite the supreme value accorded to the sun of Reason in Coleridge's prose, the sun characteristically does not, as Warren noted, figure affirmatively in his poetry. The sun's power is too overwhelmingly great. There is no return possible to the sun, no reciprocity. It pours ever forth a light that humanity can only receive; in its immediacy, the sun is blinding, stunning. Coleridge preferred mediated systems that allow the recipient to give something back. Thus we reach the positive function of the moon in Coleridge's poetic world. At night the sun remains a hidden source, known in its deferral, like the divine, creative I AM that we know only through its repetition in our primary imagination. The earth may then further echo the moon, as the secondary imagination the primary. The moon is both mirror and lamp, source and recipient of light, as in the earthlight evoked in the epigraph to "Dejection," as in the echoings of sound and light in "The Nightingale" and the icicles at the end of "Frost at Midnight," "Quietly shining to the quiet moon." In his poetry Coleridge gained intimacy and identity in distancing himself from the direct presence of the origin and symbol of totality. Thus for Coleridge, no less than for Paul de Man, humankind's effective relationship to nature began with a loss of immediacy, the recognition of a power different from the self.

In the terms of Roman Jakobson's communications model, the addresser (the source, God, the sun) is displaced into the message ("Linguistics" 353). So in "Hymn before Sun-Rise in the Vale of Chamouni" all the landscape is called upon to "Utter forth God" (line 69). This ecstasy is summoned, however, only before the sun emerges, while the divine I AM is held off. Appropriately Coleridge wrote this poem as if he had been spectator at a scene he in fact

87

never visited but knew only through the mediation of other literary texts. When Shelley actually visited the scene, "Mont Blanc" enacted a very different experience.

Coleridge was always probing the origin of evil, the question of original sin, the danger of the human I AM as an originating self-will that threatens to usurp the power properly belonging only to the sun or God. He offered a possible aesthetic resolution to this problem in a letter highly relevant to the subject and form of "The Ancient Mariner":

> The common end of all *narrative*, nay, of *all*, Poems is to convert a *series* into a *Whole*: to make those events, which in real or imagined History move on in a *strait* Line, assume to our Understandings a *circular* motion—the snake with it's Tail in it's Mouth. Hence indeed the almost flattering and yet appropriate Term, Poesy—i.e. poiesis = *making*. Doubtless, to *his* eye, which alone comprehends all Past and all Future in one eternal Present, what to our short sight appears strait is but a part of the great Cycle—just as the calm Sea to us *appears* level, tho' it be indeed only a part of a *globe*. Now what the Globe is in geography, *miniaturing* in order to *manifest* the Truth, such is a Poem to that Image of God, which we were created into, and which still seeks that Unity, or Revelation of the *One* in and by the *Many*, which reminds it, that tho' in order to be an individual Being it must go forth *from* God, yet as the *receding from him* is to *Proceed* towards Nothingness and Privation, it must still at every step turn back towards him in order to *be* at all—Now a straight Line, continuously retracted forms of necessity a circular orbit. (*Collected Letters* 4:545)

Coleridge imaged "individual being," human identity, as a suspended fall. One is always falling away from God in order to be differentiated from the totality, yet always falling back toward the source, being held in orbit, in order not to become the satanic reduction of pure self-will that has fallen to the bottom. My I-ness exists in a distanced relation that avoids both the career into outer space of atheism and the engulfment in an undifferentiated source. (See also *Collected Works* 6:60.) This conversion of "a series into a whole" gives a model for the systematization of the "arbitrary," or in Brooks' terms, the transformation of history into myth. This topic is fundamental for the concerns of this book, from Wordsworth's figure of the journey, through Lawrence's critique of the snake with its tail in its mouth, to the problematic of representation and narrative that emerges in the chapter on Shelley and returns in the concluding discussion of postmodernism.

Despite the danger he feared in satanic origination, Coleridge recognized a constant need for a responsive beginning (a proper human I AM). In "To William Wordsworth," Coleridge was at first overwhelmed by hearing *The Prelude* read aloud to him. He found in the poem Wordsworth's "inner Power" (line 16), a solar energy that "streamed from [him], and [his] soul received / The light reflected [i.e., back to him], as a light bestowed [as if from without]." Coleridge recognized in Wordsworth's imagination the "strength of usurpation" (1805 *Prelude* 6:532–33) that made Wordsworth himself the origin, which like a star "shed influence" (line 52). Wordsworth's power, however, aroused in Coleridge only self-regarding pain over his own waste. Finally, Coleridge succeeded in moving out from himself into a state of "prayer" (line 112). He motivated himself by revising his solar, stellar figures for Wordsworth, at the same time revising Wordsworth's poem, repeating it with a difference:

> My soul lay passive, by thy various strain
> Driven as in surges now beneath the stars,
> With momentary stars of my own birth,
> Fair constellated foam, still darting off
> Into the darkness; now a tranquil sea,
> Outspread and bright, yet swelling to the moon.
>   (96–101)

In this scene the vagaries of will are "constellated," given a beautiful order by what they reflect; its "surges" are tranquilized, organized into a totality of response, as the quiet ocean gravitationally swells toward the moon that makes it "bright" (in Coleridge's *Naturphilosophie* gravitation and light are two of the fundamental components). Wordsworth became no longer the sun but the moon, and Coleridge could feel at rest in a "sweet sense of Home" (line 92) rather than in a "coffin" (line 75) as earlier.

This climactic passage in Coleridge's poem echoed and revised the climactic scene of moon and sea at Snowdon in *The Prelude*. And Coleridge fully succeeded in giving something back to Wordsworth, for I find in Wordsworth's own later revision of the Snowdon scene a significant Coleridgeanizing of his experience and comprehension of imagination.

> Meanwhile, the Moon look'd down upon this shew
> In single glory, and we stood, the mist
> Touching our very feet; and from the shore
> At distance not the third part of a mile
> Was a blue chasm; a fracture in the vapour,
> A deep and gloomy breathing-place through which
> Mounted the roar of waters, torrents, streams,
> Innumerable, roaring with one voice.
> The universal spectacle throughout
> Was shaped for admiration and delight,
> Grand in itself alone, but in that breach
> Through which the homeless voice of waters rose,
> That dark deep thoroughfare had Nature lodg'd
> The Soul, the Imagination of the whole.
>   (1805, 13:52–65)

In revision the extremes of power and isolation were moderated; the scene was filled out by the addition of Coleridgean "stars"; and reciprocal interrelations were established. The moon became no longer "single" but "sovereign" (1850, line 54); indeed, the isolation was revised away as if it had been "encroachment" (1850, line 50). As in Coleridge's poem, the moon now gazes on "the billowy ocean" (1850, line 55). The "fracture" and the "homeless voice" are simply excluded, and the scene ascends to be "felt by the starry heavens" (1850, line 62), but without the reiteration of "through" and "thoroughfare" that would emphasize a violent trajectory.

The passage in "To William Wordsworth" that I have argued entered into Wordsworth's revision of Snowdon itself revised a text Coleridge began writing en route to Germany (with Wordsworth) in 1798. While William and Dorothy were "shockingly ill! . . . vomiting & groaning & crying the whole time!" Coleridge was well enough to note, "The Ocean is a noble thing by night— / the foam that dashes against the vessel, beautiful. White clouds of Foam roaring & rushing . . . by the side of the Vessel with multitudes of stars of flame that danced and sparkled" (*Notebooks*, 1, #335). His letters from the same voyage offer a debunking earthly source: "What these

Stars are, I cannot say—the sailors say, that they are the Fish Spawn which is phosphorescent" (*Collected Letters* 1:416).

Through pursuing "response" and revision in this way, we may find "The Ancient Mariner" a figural meditation on reading. The Wedding Guest figures the naïveté of response that can say nothing back and is merely "stunned" by the poem as the Mariner was by the noon sun and Coleridge (at first) by *The Prelude*. Not to be annihilated, to respond, one needs some distance from the object: one must diminish the object, "miniaturing in order to manifest" it. Following Warren's observation that "the poem is the light and not the thing seen by the light" (212), the reader must turn the poem from a sun into a moon, as Coleridge had done with Wordsworth. The gloss he added to the poem in its 1817 publication functions as Coleridge's own, responsive, beginning to the process of diminishing the poem, distancing it into a manageable moon, closing the annihilating gap across which power had first streamed only in one way. In speaking, we sometimes make a "glottal stop," a constriction at the top of the throat by which we prevent hiatus, a choking in order to keep from gaping (as "in the middle of saying 'No' by going *unh-unh*," according to Bloomfield and Newmark 38). We (physically) draw a bar to make a difference. The glottal stop involves a "momentary complete closure" followed by an "explosive release" (*American Heritage Dictionary*). So, as Pater claimed and Lawrence Lipking detailed (613–21), Coleridge's glossal stop makes a whole of the poem by closing it off. Yet that model of reading released all the many further readings of the poem, like Warren's repetitive proliferation of the differentiating closure begun by Coleridge.

A further element of responsibility and imaginative responsiveness joins "The Ancient Mariner" to the tale from the Arabian Nights in the anecdote of Mrs. Barbauld with which Warren began his essay. (Coleridge told Mrs. Barbauld, "As to the want of a moral . . . in my own judgment the poem had too much; and . . . the only or chief fault . . . was the obtrusion of the moral sentiment so openly on the reader as a principle or cause of action in a work of such pure imagination. It ought to have had no more moral than the Arabian Nights' tale of the merchant's sitting down to eat dates by the side of a well, and throwing the shells aside, and lo! a geni starts up, and says he *must* kill the aforesaid merchant, *because* one of the date shells had . . . put out the eye of the geni's son"—*Complete Works* 6:324.) The full version of the tale involves not only a gratuitous act and dreadful consequence, but also a circular journey (the merchant defers his end for a year but must return to pay his penalty to the genie) and a focus on fabulation (the merchant is saved when three mysterious old men buy off the genie with ever more marvelous stories—all of which concern transformations between man and beast, magic versions of the theme of "the one life"). The tale (the very first of the *Arabian Nights*) thus immediately echoes the framing situation of Scheherazade and her life-preserving power of narration. A sufficiently marvelous response may control even the most extravagant arbitrariness.

But we may follow Warren to ask what kind of control we achieve through our response. Warren opened "Pure and Impure Poetry," his most programmatically New-Critical essay, with an analogy that joined criticism to the world of fable: "The poem is like the monstrous Orillo in Boiardo's *Orlando Innamorato*." (Orillo's powers of regeneration resemble those of the hydra.) No critical method, Warren argued, can take care of the poem as dexterously as the hero managed to deal with the monster. For us critics, "there is only one way to conquer the monster: you must eat it, bones, blood, skin, pelt, and gristle." But this strategy limited the mastery of the critic over the poem: "Even then the monster is not dead, for it lives in you, is assimilated into you, and you are different, and somewhat monstrous yourself, for having eaten it" (3). This passage acquired sufficient talismanic force for William Van O'Connor to quote it without further comment as the last words in his survey of American criticism, 1900–1950, as a warning against a "few zealots" who might threaten literature with a "complex edifice composed of interrelated lines of knowledge of philosophy, anthropology, and linguistics" (174–75). Warding off "science," Warren thus recognized the place of repetition in the critical relationship. The principle of contagion Warren figured forth recalls the sober prose of Cleanth Brooks arguing that paraphrase only begins to succeed as it becomes itself poetical (*Well Wrought Urn* 198). There is no metalanguage to criticism, only repetition and variations on the poem. Warren acknowledged, therefore, that the founding criticism of the poem, the gloss itself, hardly did all that one would have hoped. The gloss "should have made the structure of the poem clearer" (262), but it failed to: "Apparently the Gloss needs a gloss" (231). Repetition solicits repetition.

At this point we may leave Warren. He found in the poem "lags and lapses" that blocked its "pervasive logic" (262); he discerned the "meaninglessness" (303), the "over-lays" and "undigested chunks" (288), that are the meat of much modern criticism, but his interest lay elsewhere. One task that still awaits the student of modern criticism is to define that interest, to locate New Criticism from the distance that we now hold from it.

If Warren discovered, but avoided, the impasses many critics now seek, he did not avoid them enough for Elder Olson. In one of the most important early responses to Warren, Olson raised issues that are still very much with us. He defined "The Ancient Mariner" as "one of those poems the interpretations of which have rather illustrated the different methods of interpretation than explained the poem," and he found Warren's essay "valuable principally as exhibiting what happens to poetry in interpretation"—the use we too have made of it. For Olson this was no praise. He dismissed Warren's project as fundamentally flawed: "The words have a meaning; they mean the poem; but why should the poem itself have any further meaning? What sense is there in asking after the meaning of something which is itself a meaning? . . . Shall we not have further meanings still, and so on *ad infinitum*, so that interpretation becomes impossible, as being an infinite process?" (138–39). Forty years ago Olson saw Warren as what we now would call the precursor of Roland Barthes in *S/Z*, opening the abyss of unlimited semiosis that Olson's fellow Chicagoans in *Critical Inquiry* are still trying to cover. Are we then so distant from New Criticism?

Finally I would like to leave the chain of displacements I have been pursuing through Coleridge and his critics, end this cycle of repetition, and ask (again!) after an exclusion. The ideological function of Coleridge for New Criticism has been much studied, but why are we—post–New Critics—still so fascinated by Coleridge as to allow him to dominate our discourse, even if we are speaking of him in order to refute, or expose, him? This is the somewhat different kind of question that arises in thinking of what Michel Foucault called a "discipline": a pattern of practices for which repetition counts more than does what we call "position."

Consider instead for a moment Shelley, a theorist who like Coleridge tried to harmonize Bacon and Plato; who like Coleridge focused on the imagination; indeed, who offers everything Coleridge does except for the theology. Pater defined "two ways of envisaging those aspects of nature which seem to bear the impress of reason or intelligence." One takes them "merely as marks" and "separates" nature from any ultimate source. The other "identifies the two" and "regards nature itself as the living energy of an intelligence" like our own (Pater, *Appreciations* 75). Coleridge took this latter way; his speculative world presented smooth closures, echo and participation. If we cannot be *at* the divine origin, he offered the hope of being *with* it through his systems of mediations and repetition. Shelley instead *opened* gaps: "It is infinitely improbable that the cause of mind . . . is similar to mind" (478). For Shelley, the "footsteps" of imagination "are like those of a wind over a sea, which the coming calm erases, and whose traces remain only as on the wrinkled sand which paves it" (504). This complex process of transmission and inscription makes the source so different as to be unimaginable from its traces. And even if we could think our way back to it, the source would no longer be there. Shelley's history runs forward without return.

For Coleridge it was crucial to correlate language with the energies of nature: "Is *thinking* impossible without arbitrary signs? &— how far is the word 'arbitrary' a misnomer? Are not words &c parts & germinations of the Plant? And what is the Law of their Growth?— In something of this order I would endeavor to destroy the old antithesis of *Words & Things*, elevating, as it were, words into Things, & living Things too" (*Letters* 1:625–26). As opposed to Coleridge's organic notion of language, Shelley considered language not divine, natural, or vital: "Language is arbitrarily produced by the Imagination and has relation to thoughts alone" (Shelley 483). Shelley derived his highest values (love, beauty, truth, virtue) from the fact that people live among other human beings, from the principles by which "the will of a social being is determined to action, inasmuch as he is social" (481).

In the nineteenth century both Coleridge and Shelley were read by poets and those who cared deeply for literature, but there was an instructive divergence in their wider readerships. Coleridge was read by Anglican divines and Tory politicians; Shelley by workers and radicals. New Criticism banished Shelley's poetry and appropriated Coleridge's theory. Only now is Shelley again receiving serious attention as a thinker, even as his poetry is also regaining the attention it deserves; this renewal figures strongly in the search for a new literary history.

Chapter 4
Shelley, Deconstruction, History

ROBERT PENN WARREN was not alone; the first great harvest of American academic literary criticism came after the Second World War and drew on Coleridge. In *The Well Wrought Urn* by Cleanth Brooks (1947), *Theory of Literature* by René Wellek and Austin Warren (1949), *A History of Modern Criticism* by Wellek (1955–), and *Literary Criticism: A Short History* by Brooks and W. K. Wimsatt (1957), a formalism that had begun as polemical opposition reached authoritative maturity. This harvest was gathered, and in the 1960s a belated, apocalyptic time of crisis trampled out the vintage. In the 1970s, that vintage fermented, following a notable effervescence at the decade's beginning—the moment I have defined as that in which the "new literary history" announced its promise. At that moment appeared Paul de Man's *Blindness and Insight* (1971); Harold Bloom began his revisionary labors with *Yeats* (1970). Geoffrey Hartman posed the still-urgent question of what lies *Beyond Formalism* (1970), and Fredric Jameson posed an answer in *Marxism and Form* (1971). Not only *New Literary History* (1969) but also *Diacritics* (1970), *sub-stance* (1971), and *boundary 2* were founded, among other journals closely involved with the "theory boom," and during most of the 1970s such important critics as Hartman, de Man, Jameson, and J. Hillis Miller were publishing essay after essay; only Bloom and Edward W. Said emphasized books. By the end of the decade two collections of essays by many hands offered some chance for assessment of what it had all come to. For since 1980, a new spate of books has begun to redefine our problematic. At the end of the seventies, the collections *Textual Strategies*, edited by Josué Harari, and *Deconstruction and Criticism* (the collective volume by Harold Bloom, Jacques Derrida, Geoffrey Hartman, Paul de Man, and J. Hillis Miller) made clear that the prime issue was deconstruction. After the effervescence, after the fermentation, the end of the 1970s offered a cup that made Shelley again positively relevant, not any longer the whipping boy of New-Critical "maturity":

> I rose; and, bending at her sweet command,
> Touched with faint lips the cup she raised,
> And suddenly my brain became as sand

> Where the first wave had more than half erased
> The track of deer on desert Labrador,
> Whilst the fierce wolf from which they fled amazed

> Leaves his stamp visibly upon the shore
> Until the second bursts—so on my sight
> Burst a new Vision never seen before.—
> (Rousseau, in Shelley's *The Triumph of Life*)

The interest of deconstructive criticism became compelling in the United States in the late 1960s and early 1970s, the Nixon years, a time of sickening knowledge that much had gone wrong in our national life. This atmosphere saturated the opening of "Semiology and Rhetoric" by Paul de Man, the beginning for his work of the seventies, the lead essay in his major completed book, *Allegories of Reading*, reprinted also about the same time in *Textual Strategies* after it had first appeared in *Diacritics* as part of a conference held early in 1973. The essay thus followed the Treaty of Paris ("ending" the war in Vietnam) and fell within the pause between the Watergate break-in and the moment the full scandal "burst."

I cannot gauge de Man's intentions, but I find it certain that much of his essay's impact derived from the figures of politics that moved his text from its beginning. To speak of criticism, he evoked "the spirit of the times," a creature of Hegelian *Geistesgeschichte*. He found that spirit opposed to "formalist and intrinsic criticism" and pushing if not toward "relevance" at least to "reference" and "reality." He summarized this spirit: "With the internal law and order of literature well policed, we can now confidently devote ourselves to the foreign affairs, the external politics of literature" (*Allegories* 3). Who that read de Man at that time, or even now I suspect, would take the side of "law and order," a noxious euphemism for repression? So we joined him in doubting that any such thing had in fact been established; after all, it was the forces of law and order that had ordered and executed the Watergate break-in. Moreover, the turn to "foreign affairs" in Vietnam had first compromised and then devastated the hopes for domestic social and economic well-being. Thus, the "external" move that de Man sensed was doubly associated with imperialist inhumanity. And finally, there had been a massive cover-up, a bad totality that had to be unraveled, whether regarding Watergate or United States aggression against Cambodia, still scarcely suspected in anything like its full dimensions. It was imperative, therefore, to scrutinize as closely as possible the texts of our internal "law and order." It was a *Zeitgeist* worth fighting, and de Man seemed to offer a weapon.

Deconstruction's drive to demystification assuaged as well more local needs provoked by those established academic authorities, at campuses all over the nation, who in the name of "reason" strove to suppress serious questioning of the university's social functions. In the name of reason, and by means of retort, sarcasm, vituperation, misrepresentation, and armed force, these questions were managed. In contrast to such authoritative behavior, deconstruction was intellectually serious. It encouraged questions and urged their pursuit to the limits of possibility.

Deconstruction, moreover, opened historical vistas. Consider Derrida's "The Supplement of Copula" (1971), in *Textual Strategies*. With philosophic moves from Nietzsche and Heidegger, Derrida questioned the linguistic science of Emile Benveniste. Before taking on Benveniste, however, Derrida defined Nietzsche's linguistic critique of philosophy as "inseparable from the development of historical linguistics in the nineteenth century" (an insight available from Foucault's *The Order of Things*, although Derrida did not attribute it to this source). And after his encounter with Benveniste, Derrida inquired whether Heidegger himself had not fallen to the temptation to read the history of being as a fall. Thus Derrida used history to challenge philosophy, and philosophy to challenge science, as well as history to challenge science in his critique of Benveniste: "One cannot . . . use the word 'category' as if it had no history"; it is "historical haste" to ignore the "history that goes under Aristotle's name and 'legacy'" ("Supplement" 91–92). Finally, decisively, in a phrase that joined Derrida with allies so different as Foucault, Ian Hacking, and American pragmatism against the predominant tradition of philosophical analysis, "It would be wrong to believe in the immediate and ahistorical accessibility of a philosophical argument" (97).

Deconstruction, then, offered a history that structuralism and New Criticism both denied. Yet it was also a technique of close reading and therefore attractive and accessible to Americans familiar with New Criticism. Indeed, structuralism as opposed to deconstruction and other forms of poststructuralism has had little direct impact on American criticism because it does not encourage reading. The theory of "literary competence" proposed by Jonathan Culler's *Structuralist Poetics* has had extraordinarily little effect in diminishing the interpretation of individual works, and his *On Deconstruction* points back toward a renewal of readings.

Finally, deconstruction presented a winning ethos in its mixture of rigor and modesty. De Man and Derrida scrupulously, brilliantly, pointed out others' errors and incidentally suggested whole new dimensions of the texts they read. There they stopped, Derrida with a question and beyond that an impasse, de Man with a paradox that rescued him from arrogance: "Literature as well as criticism—the difference between them being delusive—is condemned (or privileged) to be forever the most rigorous and, consequently, the most unreliable" of human discourses. Such tentativeness, refusing to assert grand claims or emphatic closure, attractively rejoined critical writing to one of its beginnings, the form of the essay. I shall return to the questions of rigor, modesty, and history in current deconstructive criticism, but first we need another history.

The romantic poets have figured inescapably in modern American criticism: Keats for the traditional belletristic humanism of Douglas Bush and W. J. Bate, no less than for Charles Olson's radical renewal of humanism; Coleridge for the New Critics, as we have seen particularly with Warren; and in moving from New Criticism, Blake for Northrop Frye and Wordsworth for M. H. Abrams and Geoffrey Hartman, as we have also already explored. Jerome McGann's recent work has begun a criticism that works from the public rhetoric of Byron. The authors of *Deconstruction and Criticism* originally planned their volume as a set of essays on Shelley (Hartman, "Preface," ix), and after C. E. Pulos' recovery of his skepticism, Shelley seemed an appropriate ally for deconstruction.

Shelley's philosophical project, like the deconstructive attempt at "semioclasty" (Harari 30), aimed to free us from "the misuse of words and signs." By signs he meant "almost all familiar objects," which stand "not for themselves but for others, in their capacity for suggesting one thought, which shall lead to a whole train of thoughts. Our whole life is thus an education in error" (Shelley 477). No less than the philosopher, the poet must break up these signs with a violence like the "force" so crucial to deconstruction (Hartman, "Preface," vii). Thus the prose of Bacon "distends, and then bursts the circumference of the hearer's mind" (Shelley 485), and in reading we may reverse the flow of power. If the Middle Ages created "a paradise . . . out of the wrecks of Eden" (Shelley 497), Shelley's own reading of *Paradise Lost* built on what ordinary academic scholars would judge the wreck of Milton's intentions: "Milton's poem contains within itself a philosophical refutation of that system of which, by a strange and natural antithesis, it has been a chief popular support" (498). Shelley thus relied on a deconstructive double reading and even used a rhetorical term ("antithesis") to define the relation between the two readings. The doublet of "strange and natural," moreover, catches the uncanniness that so fascinates deconstruction.

Derrida has defined the "paleonymic" strategy of deconstruction, its hesitation to invent new master terms and its consequent practice of undoing traditional metaphysical oppositions by first reversing and then displacing them ("Signature" 195). So Shelley handled Aeschylus in *Prometheus Unbound*. In the lost conclusion to Aeschylus' trilogy, Zeus finally secures his domination through a compromise with Prometheus. Shelley used the same names but rejected "a catastrophe [i.e., outcome] so feeble as that of reconciling the Champion with the Oppressor of mankind" (133). Shelley's atheistic radicalism demanded a different solution: the hierarchical opposition is reversed (Jupiter is overthrown) and displaced (by the new term of Demogorgon). But Shelley went further; deconstructing one opposition may unlock others. Edward Said has argued that Aeschylus in the *Persae* helped establish the hierarchical domination of "Western" over "Oriental" (*Orientalism* 56–57). Shelley, however, made Asia the vigorous agent who redeemed the passively suffering Prometheus. In the *Oresteia*, moreover, Aeschylus laid a foundation for Western sexism (according to Froma I. Zeitlin), which Shelley transformed in the erotic relations of *Prometheus Unbound*.

No less than might the current practice of deconstruction, Shelley challenged the sovereignty of the subject. In "On Life" he argued that "the words *I* and *you* and *they*" are "merely marks," "grammatical devices . . . totally devoid of the intense and exclusive sense usually attached to them" (Shelley 478). This semiological critique allowed Shelley a conclusion that catches current deconstructive rhetoric right down to the frustrated, self-aware paradox that interrupts it: "The existence of distinct individual minds similar to that which is now employed in questioning its own nature, is likewise found to be a delusion" (477). Yet if these arbitrary differences were erased, sameness fared no better. "On Life" presented the philosophical case against selfhood, but "On Love" struggled with selfhood. Just because it's a "delusion" doesn't make it go away, any more than Christianity disappeared when Nietzsche found its history that of an "error." Love arises from our discovery of "the chasm of an insufficient void" within ourselves and our consequent hopeless attempt to "awaken in all things that are, a community with what we experience within ourselves." That community does not exist; we may not really be individual selves, but we are not all the same either. Shelley could only confess, "I know not the internal constitution of other men." Whenever he thought "to appeal to something in common," he "found [his] language misunderstood" (473).

Shelley's skepticism thus forced him constantly to acknowledge irreconcilable polarities, and his greatest texts inscribe the struggle to keep both poles active, to avoid the monism that would follow either from dialectical reconciliation or from the subordination of one pole to the other. The "Defence of Poetry" opens with a hierarchical opposition between reason and imagination that is classically metaphysical: "Reason is to Imagination as the instrument to the agent, as the body to the spirit, as the shadow to the substance" (480). The basic opposition we read as that of secondary to primary: the mechanical, material, and delusive against the vital, spiritual, and reliable. And this opposition is systematically elaborated. Reason is associated with the narrativity of a "story" concerned with

"time, place, circumstance, cause and effect" (485), while imagination is associated with poetry, which in its "highest" kinds is
wholly indifferent to "the grammatical forms which express the
moods of time, and the difference of persons and the distinction of
place" (483). The ecstasy of inspiration is joined with poetry and
imagination, the rest of life with reason and story. In "Adonais"
Shelley opted out of life; in a sudden transcendent move he chose
the unworldly side of the opposition, which is death but also immortality, undying influence. The "Defence," however, gradually
accumulated positive material on the side of life. For poetry itself
proves secondary and thus crosses over to the side of life: it is an
"expression of the Imagination" (480). The defense of poetry, therefore, necessitates the praise of the secondary: "all language, institution, and form, require not only to be produced but to be
sustained" (492). After inspiration come those who "follow the
footsteps" and "copy the sketches" of poets "into the book of common life." These belated figures establish our human world; "they
make space and give time" (501). If Shelley yearned for an inspired
state in which "time and place and number are not" (483), he nonetheless also cherished "the cyclic poem written by Time upon the
memories of men" (494). As in Derrida's critique of Benveniste,
history challenges metaphysics.

In his first book, as we observed in chapter 1, Harold Bloom chose
Shelley as a figure to lead his break away from New Haven formalism, and beyond Bloom and Pulos, Shelley has found one other decisive modern critic, Earl Wasserman, for many years a colleague
of Hillis Miller and for some of them also of Paul de Man, at Johns
Hopkins. Wasserman was a totalizing hermeneut, master of the heterocosmic reading that revealed each work as a world of its own
rather than sifting through the sedimentations that link it with
other worlds. Yet Wasserman recognized the very activity of reading
as problematic. He observed in his study of Keats, "I have limited
myself to five poems because they are the only five poems of Keats
that I have learned to read to my own satisfaction" (*Finer Tone* 9).
He omitted the Hyperion poems because, as "fragments," they "lack
a total structure, cannot be organic wholes, and therefore cannot
be explicated, in the full sense of that word" (10). One encounters
then with some shock Wasserman's discovery that "in any reading
of the 'Ode to a Nightingale' the turmoil will not down. Forces

contend wildly within the poem, not only without resolution, but without possibility of resolution" (178). Later Wasserman reiterated: the poem "will thwart every effort at reconciliation and leave us no center of reference. Images and statements will alter in value metamorphically before our eyes and turn out to be their own converses as their referents are interchanged. And therefore the best that an explication of these stanzas can do is set in action the bewildering oscillations" (208).

Wasserman wished for a "nice organicism" (207) but had instead to invent a deconstructive rhetoric in order not to falsify what he read. Here was a critic who knew what he meant by "reading," by totality, by explication "in the full sense of the word," yet who let this chapter stand and even gave the privileged name of "reading" to what he did in "set[ting] in action the bewildering oscillations." What then of the deconstructive mystique of the unreadable? Of Shelley's *Triumph of Life*, Hillis Miller claimed (in syntax that mimed its subject), "The poem, like all texts, is 'unreadable' if by 'readable' one means a single, definitive interpretation" ("Critic" 226). Was Miller invoking a standard that even a master of those who read would not have recognized?

Miller's essay, like those of Derrida and de Man, the only others in *Deconstruction and Criticism* to address the original topic of Shelley, did not mention Wasserman's work, nor did any of the three mention Shelley's prose writings. Such omissions marked a change that occurred over the seventies, at least in the American academy. Deconstruction became less modest, no longer so historical, but even more rigorous. Paul de Man ended, we recall, "Semiology and Rhetoric" by linking the rigor of his method to unreliability; he concluded "Shelley Disfigured" by finding a "rigor" that was "more reliable" than traditional methods (*Rhetoric* 123). According to Geoffrey Hartman's preface to the collective volume, all five contributors shared "a new rigor" (*Deconstruction* viii). In Latin, rigor means "numbness, stiffness," and its *OED* senses include "harshness," "hardness of heart," "puritanic severity," as well as "propriety" and "severe exactitude." Why should critics so desire such a thing? I shall return to this master term after exploring further the state of deconstruction in Hillis Miller's "The Critic as Host."

"The Critic as Host" was not, like "Semiology and Rhetoric," a modest proposal. It defended a practice that had already established itself, and it thereby revealed the power of de Man's earlier text. In reading Proust in "Semiology and Rhetoric," de Man found "the same pattern of deconstruction" as in Nietzsche's late critique of metaphysics, and in turn that critique "exactly corresponds" to Nietzsche's earlier analysis of "the structure of the main rhetorical tropes" (*Allegories* 15). Having set so much at one—Proust, late Nietzsche, early Nietzsche—de Man then leapt to the claim that "the whole of literature would respond in similar fashion." He knew "no reason why analyses of the kind suggested here for Proust would not be applicable, with proper modifications of technique," to other major writers. In an Arnoldian gesture, de Man then prophesied, "This will in fact be the task of literary criticism in the coming years" (16–17). The power of de Man's text realized this prophecy; no other critic of the seventies had de Man's magnetic effect on the writing of both his graduate students and his readers.

Miller's essay testified to the effectiveness of the detour de Man established to prevent the move of literary study toward relevance or reference or reality. Miller could already take as established a "regular law" that guaranteed the "self-subversion of all the great texts" ("Critic" 228). De Man had weighed the possibility of "the deconstructive moment as constitutive of all literary language," and Miller found in literature a recurrent "linguistic moment," namely "the moment in a work of literature when its own medium is put in question" ("Critic" 250). Relying less than de Man on insinuation and irony, Miller offered an outright statement of value. He considered it "more flexible, more open to a given work" to look for "heterogeneity" than for organic unity (252). Yet the necessity of this dilemma was nowhere demonstrated. Wasserman found organic unity in one ode by Keats, heterogeneity in another. I judge this even more flexible and open. The language of deconstructive self-defense makes for strange company. When Miller claimed that "though each poet is different, each contains his own form of undecidability" (248), he echoed the theological totalization of Coleridge, by which "each Thing has a Life of its own, & yet they are all one Life" (*Letters* 2:866). Finally, we reach the "ultimate justification for this mode of criticism," which proves wholly pragmatic: "it works" ("Critic" 252). And so it has. Look on your bookshelf, in the journals, in your department.

105

This calm pragmatism somewhat jars with a dominant motif in Miller's analysis of Shelley. Repeatedly, he defined Shelley's poetry as the record of a failed "performative apocalypse" ("Critic" 237), as the "failure" of words to act "as performatives magically transforming the world" (246). From the "failure of these magic performatives," Miller concluded that "words do not make anything happen" (244). It has become common in American deconstructive criticism to attack J. L. Austin's notion of "performative" language, set out in *How to Do Things with Words*, but Austin never claimed that performatives were "magic." He emphasized their subordination to a system of conventional and institutionalized social practice. Full-blown "speech-act philosophy" (now codified by John Searle) depends on intention, and therefore may be deconstructed as metaphysical, as Derrida did in "Signature Event Context." Derrida did not charge "magic," however; he showed that even effective performances are contaminated by the parasitism of fiction. That is, he showed not that there is no power to words, but that even words traditionally considered impotent may be strong. Once Derrida criticized Austin, the American deconstructionists have rallied to the attack, spurred by Searle's continuing offensive dismissals of their critique.

Further ground for deconstructive hostility to speech-act criticism emerged from de Man's comments on Richard Ohmann's venture in this direction. Such work, de Man warned, exemplified the danger of "moral conscience" (*Allegories* 3) that tempts us beyond where we may legitimately venture. Indeed, while deconstruction flourished in the seventies, the radical conscience of Richard Ohmann carried him not to further refinements of speech-act theory but to direct analysis of the institutions of literary study. Ohmann's *English in America* remains the fullest attempt to specify the relations between our words, as teachers and critics, and the world around us, in which things happen not magically but in ways patterned by disciplines, technologies, and policies. Now in the later eighties, such a perspective is gaining vigor. Ohmann's work recalls what I have already suggested. The modesty of "Semiology and Rhetoric" dissembled or ignored or forgot the power of words and practices, even when placed within an undertaking that claimed no relevance or reference or contact with reality.

Shelley, Deconstruction, History

After the detour from history in "Semiology and Rhetoric," Paul de Man's "Shelley Disfigured" staged a history so horrid as to scare us back into the text. Through reading *The Triumph of Life*, de Man argued that we are deluded when we think that events can be linked in historical connection whether narrative or causal or both. For the "decisive textual articulation" of the poem was "its reduction to the status of a fragment brought about by the actual death and subsequent disfigurement of Shelley's body, burned after his boat capsized and he drowned off the coast of Lerici" (*Rhetoric* 120). Moreover, "this mutilated textual model exposes the wound of a fracture that lies hidden in all texts," so that the final test of a reading will be "how one disposes of Shelley's body" (121). The apparent "materialism" here is very different from what Walter Benjamin called "historical materialism"; in his "Theses" even the vision of catastrophic horror witnessed by the "angel of history" solicited redemption, not disposal (*Illuminations* 257–58). Benjamin struggled with the need both to face the worst and to maintain hope. But when de Man claimed for Shelley an exemplary "rigor," above all the stiffness of death was imaged: "*The Triumph of Life* warns us that nothing, whether deed, word, thought or text, ever happens in relation, positive or negative, to anything that precedes, follows, or exists elsewhere, but only as a random event whose power, like the power of death, is due to the randomness of its occurrence" (*Rhetoric* 122). Existentialist contingency becomes the groundless ground of a zero-degree aesthetics, for the deep truth of which Shelley "warns" us is imageless. Yet inevitably we lapse into "recuperation," constructing images or narrative, as did de Man himself in thus figuring disfiguration as a mutilated corpse. But why choose to figure history in the rigor of a corpse? Benjamin, as I show in chapter 8, sought explanation where de Man rested with the figure.

"Semiology and Rhetoric" also figured the fracture of textuality. It illustrated the "rhetorization of grammar" in a rhetorical question asked by Archie Bunker that is laughably, literally, answered by his wife Edith, until Archie explodes. De Man claimed that the "mini-text" of the rhetorical question "holds our attention only as long as it remains suspended," and that this literary interest is dissipated by the "intervention of an extratextual intention, such as Archie Bunker setting his wife straight" (*Allegories* 10). "Extratextual intention," the turn to relevance, reference, or reality, thus figured as a sexist, reactionary false consciousness. If going outside the text joined us with Archie Bunker, we gladly remained in.

According to de Man, Shelley offered, against the horror at the edge of the text, the fascination of a "knot," a "self-effacing" scene that "arrests the process of understanding" as had Archie's rhetorical question. Quite close in structure, though not in feeling, to Hartman's "indeterminacy," such suspension, arrest, freezing, is the focus on the text de Man taught: "The resistance of these passages is such that the reader soon forgets the dramatic situation and is left only with these unresolved riddles to haunt him" (*Rhetoric* 98–99), passages like that which I quoted at the beginning of this chapter. Uncomfortable as haunting may be, it spares us facing directly the "situation," the disfigured corpse, and so we remain bound. Like the "deconstructive" or "linguistic" moments we noted earlier, we might call this the "moment of rigor," when in order to avoid what lies beyond, we fix our gaze on what lies before us. This is the last romantic agony of aesthetic enclosure. To "regress from the rigor" would be to rejoin life, to be liable to naivete, to error, even to death. To share the rigor of Shelley, or of the "bolt-upright" erect corpse of Wordsworth's "dead man" that de Man cited (*Rhetoric* 121, and that I have tried to rejoin with politics in chapter 1) is to choose "numbness, stiffness." One who gazes on the Medusa head does not acknowledge that something he wishes there is missing, but sees instead a tangle so complex that it turns him to stone and thus assures him of a potency that time or chance or malice cannot alter. That is, in the terms of Freud's essay on the Medusa, de Man's textualism would be a form of denying castration, of defensively evading the alterity of the real.

De Man's figure of rigor reinscribed and transvalued characteristic Shelleyan preoccupations. Even the problem of "how one disposes of Shelley's body" echoed a famous anecdote. Shelley once said he would like to swim but instead "lay stretched out on the bottom like a conger eel" until rescued. He explained, "I always find the bottom of the well, and they say Truth lies there. In another minute I should have found it, and you would have found an empty shell. It is an easy way of getting rid of the body" (Trelawny 62–63). De Man, however, did not cite any such intertexts because "in all rigor . . . *The Triumph of Life* can be said to reduce all of Shelley's previous work to nought" (*Rhetoric* 120). In other words, recognizing the claim to "rigor" as the expression of a wish, the power of de Man's reading would be greater if the rest of Shelley's corpus were annihilated. This is an easy way of getting rid of the body. As Earl Wasserman emphasized, however, Shelley resisted solutions and preferred to maintain irreconcilable polarities—if not within every work, then in his larger corpus. Between acts three and four of the "beautiful idealisms" of *Prometheus Unbound* (Shelley 135), Shelley wrote the "sad reality" (133) of *The Cenci*, a tragedy of rape, incest, and parricide. Neither work annihilated the other; they coexist as different, as do "On Life" and "On Love," we noted earlier. Indeed, according to Shelley, not difference but "reiteration" (477) annihilates the world for us, yet it is not right to say that *The Triumph of Life* merely reiterates and so reduces to naught the rest of Shelley's work.

Let me link Shelley's other work to de Man's reading of *The Triumph of Life*. In "On Life" Shelley recognized but shunned what I have called the "moment of rigor." He observed that we typically do not give ourselves over to the "contemplation of life" and argued, "It is well that we are thus shielded by the familiarity of what is at once so certain and so unfathomable from an astonishment which would otherwise absorb and overawe the functions of that which is [its] object" (475). The involuted syntax signals the danger for life in the self-effacing knot of life contemplating life; like Perseus, Shelley acknowledged the medusan potential and preferred to remain shielded.

More crucially, the power beyond image and sequence that de Man called the "positing power of language" (*Rhetoric* 116) occupied the place in his argument that the moment of inspiration did in Shelley's "Defence of Poetry." In the power of the poem's inaugural sunrise to impose itself on earth, de Man saw the "sheer dint of a blind force" (118) that is discontinuous with our existence and that we hide from ourselves by the figurations we ascribe to it. So, for Shelley, inspiration had "no necessary connexion with consciousness or will" (506); consciousness and will are part of human life in time, from which inspiration abstracts us. The famous image of the fading coal caught the discontinuity Shelley posed between the moment of power, of "original purity and force" (504), and whatever else there is. De Man and Shelley both saw a gap between two states, one powerful and timeless, the other human: it is only in the "intervals" between moments of inspiration that "a poet becomes a man" (507). In de Man's argument being a man meant only the possibility of exhibiting an exemplary rigor, while Shelley, as we have seen, hoped for more from human life, at times. De Man did not misread Shelley, but he decisively chose one alternative over the other. Did he choose the more open and flexible?

Alongside "Shelley Disfigured" it is instructive to read a comparably ambitious essay that appeared in *Textual Strategies*, "The Museum's Furnace" by Eugenio Donato. Donato like de Man opposed history by identifying it as "archaeology"—that is, etymologically, the study of origins, and, pejoratively, antiquarianism. This essay displayed a rigor just opposite to de Man's. Chaucer's Franklin observed that patience will win many things that rigor never attains, and "The Museum's Furnace" moved to the kill so impatiently as to suggest how much by the end of the 1970s advanced critics could take for granted in the practice of deconstruction, both assumptions about how things were and judgments of those who took things differently.

Donato first sketched Flaubert's linguistic nihilism, seen through the critique of the *"Library"* in *Bouvard and Pecuchet*; next he argued that even more powerful a model in that novel was the *"Museum,"* the failure of which demonstrated Flaubert's epistemological nihilism; finally, the museum and its delusive archeological temporality yielded to the new science of thermodynamics (the *"Furnace"*), which through the theory of entropy undid all historical models, showing that Flaubert was also a historical nihilist.

Donato defined his reading as "contextual"; he rarely quoted from *Bouvard and Pecuchet*. Instead he located some of its intellectual affiliations, in principle a valuable departure from the textual enclosure we observed in the Shelleyan readings of *Deconstruction and Criticism*. Donato particularly focused on the idea of the museum, which he joined Flaubert in deconstructing. He found that idea silly: "The fiction is that a repeated metonymic displacement of fragment for totality, object to label, series of objects to series of labels, can still produce a representation which is somehow adequate to a nonlinguistic universe" (223). The museum will therefore fail "at reaching the nature and essence of the objects it displays," because, argued Donato, "it tries to understand them in relation to the spectator rather than in relation to the objects themselves" (225).

How does this analysis relate to the texts Donato cited to represent the idea of the museum? (Note that he relied on representation and made archeological use of sources at least to this extent.) These sources clearly show that the museum is not interested in objects in themselves, but they do not say that the museum was believed to reach the "nature and essence" of things. One of the texts begins, "The ideal museum should cover the whole field of human knowledge." The other starts, "In the galleries of these museums are gathered together examples of the art and craftsmanship of man." The human world—of arts and crafts and knowledges—is what museums represent, as I read these documents. The ideology of the museum echoed historistic humanism, such as Vico established in distinguishing between the impossibility of our understanding the world God created and the possibility of our understanding what humankind has made. Thus, in choosing the point of view of the spectator rather than that of "objects themselves," museum makers founded the intelligibility of their undertaking. One might deconstruct this humanism, but Donato did not.

We may ask further why a double metonymic remove should doom representation. Donato noted that objects in a museum are "spatially and temporally detached from their origin and function" (224). Well, so is a lawyer in Washington detached in space, origin, and function from a farmer in Iowa, but is it impossible for a lobbyist to represent farm interests? When representation is held out as something that only a Bouvard or a boobie would credit, I remember what Mencken (or was it Mark Twain) said when asked if he, the notorious freethinker, believed in infant baptism: "Believe, hell, I've seen it." As Hillis Miller claimed of deconstruction, so may we of representation—it works. Moreover, fuller analysis in chapter 12 shows that the "critique of representation" by poststructuralism is hardly what it has been taken for in America.

Representation works because it is not just metaphysical consolation. It is a disciplined cultural practice. Donato ignored this completely: "'Meaning,' the result of metaphoric or metonymic displacements, is anthropomorphic and anthropocentric, and . . .

necessarily doomed to failure. Archeology, ultimately, is not an objective science but a fantasy of the perceiving subject" (225). Foucault, whom Donato dismissed with more rigor than patience, illuminated the limits of possible statements within any discipline. Only certain people can make statements that will be accepted, and not even everything that such people say will be accepted. A discipline reaches far beyond any individual "perceiving subject" into rules of discursive formation and production. The whole idea of "fantasy" on which Donato depended for this claim loses its point if fantasy can be reliably, intersubjectively shared.

Donato quoted Edward Said on the purpose of the museum or philological demonstration being "to exhibit a relationship between the science . . . and the object, not one between the object and nature" (230). Donato concluded, therefore, that "any attempt of ours to reconstruct a history is nothing but vain fabulation" (231). Said's next sentence, not quoted by Donato, insisted that Renan's work was not vain. On the contrary, however much one may oneself oppose it, it was a "fact of power, by which the Orientalist philologist's authority summons out of the library at will examples of man's speech, and ranges them there surrounded by a suave European prose that points out defects, virtues, barbarisms, and shortcomings" (*Orientalism* 142). We are back at the problem of speech acts. Representation is not merely to be judged true or false. It is something that people do, in politics, in constructing knowledge, in works of literature, for purposes and with effects (which are by no means always identical).

In adopting the thermodynamic point of view, Flaubert abandoned the patient particularity that would allow the registration of human facts and chose instead "a notion of history based upon any metaphor that can be read as abolishing differences" (Donato 236)—such as excrement, manure, garbage. Donato's inquiry produces a Flaubert who hated the bourgeoisie more deeply than he understood it, who, rather than analyzing his time, retreated to a point of indifference "at the end of time" (238). That thermodynamic point of maximal entropy gave the "ultimately" from which all human action was vain, naive, deluded. For those living in a local flux of energy, however, as we all do, things are different. Donato accepted the position he attributed to Flaubert. He refused the available deconstructive strategy of dislodging that position by showing the incoherence between "epistemological" nihilism (which criticizes the museum for "homogenizing the diversity of various artifacts") and "historical" nihilism (committed to "abolishing differences"). He refused as well the alternative to deconstruction in Sartre's analysis of Flaubert, which accepted roughly the same characterization of Flaubert as Donato's but criticized it and located its basis in the experience of the French bourgeois class, which Flaubert belonged to as well as hating. In rejecting all alternatives and adopting Flaubert's figures of garbage, excrement, and manure, a certain strain in deconstruction reached the final step in its rejection of history.

PART TWO
THE DISCIPLINE
OF WHOLENESS

Chapter 5
Matthew Arnold and English Studies: The Power of Prophecy

ADDRESSING ARNOLD will quickly return us to the questions of deconstruction that focused the preceding chapter. I begin, however, from the fact, recorded by Lionel Trilling, that Matthew Arnold "established criticism as an intellectual discipline among the peoples of two nations" ("Introduction" 3). I shall return to the world of nations. Now I emphasize only that for American academic students of literature, Arnold is our history: to forget him is to repeat him. Unlike Marx or Freud, Arnold is not an unforgettable founder, an authority to whose resources later inquirers in his tradition necessarily return. In the 1920s he was still visible. Critical controversy raged over clearly identifiable parts of Arnold: impressionists taking his sensibility, humanists his morality, liberals his methodology (Raleigh 149). But then the modernist revolution repressed Arnold. He has ceased to be a focus for any criticism offering itself as innovative. He returns only as reaction or under negation, as the unacceptable half of an antithesis.

Arnold never appears more forgettable than when taking the stance of prophecy, passive before a future on which he relied to validate him. All the future need do is say no, as did two generations of Yale modernist critics. In the mid-fifties, Cleanth Brooks and W. K. Wimsatt denied the "Arnoldian prophecy" that opened "The Study of Poetry" (an essay now just over a century old). Opening the eighties, Geoffrey Hartman, as we have earlier noted, denied Arnold's prophecy at the end of "The Function of Criticism at the Present Time." I shall emphasize not Arnold's weakness but his power, both in those prophetic moments and in the present, for I find that the debate between "Wittgenstein" and "Nietzsche" in current criticism is also the struggle for control over one element in the Arnoldian apparatus.

Brooks and Wimsatt heard in Arnold only a threat of didacticism when he proclaimed, "The future of poetry is immense. . . . Without poetry our science will appear incomplete, and most of what now passes . . . for religion and philosophy will be replaced by poetry." They therefore declared that the counterattack against humanism in 1930—when *Humanism and America* was answered by *Critique of Humanism*—"announced the end" of this threat, which had failed to display "a distinct concern for literature" (451).

One may easily understand the assurance with which Brooks and Wimsatt wrote. Arnold's essay had originally prefaced T. H. Ward's *English Poets*, a four-volume set of excerpts with introductions for use in the schools; by 1938 Cleanth Brooks and Robert Penn Warren had produced in *Understanding Poetry* the most intellectually distinguished poetry textbook since Ward's. Brooks and Warren shifted from the Arnoldian principle of organizing the study of poetry by authors, known by fragmentary touchstone passages (as we observed of Victorian criticism on *The Prelude*), to the study of single works placed in relation to formal or technical problems. Commentary was no longer segregated to the introductory portion of each author's section but instead distributed pervasively throughout the textbook. Moreover, modernist criticism had systematically inverted the Arnoldian canon. Shakespeare was now praised for the unity of his works, not, as in Arnold, suspected for the disintegrative power of individual figures. Donne, ignored by Arnold, had become crucial. Milton was no longer admired above all for his "grand style" but was seen as a danger to all subsequent English poetry precisely for that style. Dryden and Pope were no longer "classics of our prose" but quintessentially poetic for their techniques of wit. Modernist criticism agreed with Arnold in finding the romantics a source of disturbing temptation, but even here changes were instituted. Byron, for Arnold second only to Wordsworth, dropped beneath discussion, while Coleridge, praised by Arnold for his prose works, became a major poet, and Keats rose to the top of the romantics for the integrity of his poetic thought—again, in contrast to Arnold's finding him like Shakespeare too fragmentary.

Nonetheless, the historical fiat of Brooks and Wimsatt could not dissociate New Criticism from Arnold. The epigraph to I. A. Richards' *Science and Poetry* (1926) quoted the "Arnoldian prophecy," and in their pedagogic concerns, the New Critics followed Arnold and the humanists. What marks modern Anglo-American (as opposed, for instance, to French and German) literary study is that the Arnoldian concern for criticism, carried on in differing ways by F. R. Leavis, Richards, Trilling, has so prevailed in the academy. Moreover, the prophecy of literature's triumph over religion, philosophy, science, remains relevant to such important recent work as that of Frank Kermode in hermeneutics (*The Genesis of Secrecy*, 1979), Hayden White in philosophy of history (*Metahistory*, 1973), and Richard Rorty in epistemology (*Philosophy and the Mirror of Nature*, 1979).

After Brooks and Wimsatt, Geoffrey Hartman declared not that Arnold was already dead, but that we must escape him, for he had made us weak. Arnold's distinction between criticism and real literary creation, Hartman argued, ensured the triumph of modest, practical criticism. Hartman took his title of *Criticism in the Wilderness* from Arnold's prophecy that looked ahead to a poetic promised land but declared that we—critics—"shall die in the wilderness." Arnold here revised the imagery of Carlyle's *Heroes and Hero-Worship*, which doomed the modern Man of Letters to failure and marginality, wandering like an "Ishmaelite" (Carlyle 5:159). Arnold made the critic a member of the chosen people rather than a banished outsider, and he even encouraged the identification of the critic with Moses, who saw the land he had led his people to but could not himself enter. From an outlaw to one of the people of the law, the critic in Arnold's prophecy became the Lawgiver himself, the Representative Man of his culture. Self-definition could reach no higher, I would have thought, but Hartman, reading Arnold as weak, tried hyperbolically to overgo him: "This wilderness is all we have" (*Criticism* 15). Criticism thus became the end, but to no end. Against Arnold's gesture of prophecy, Hartman opposed this variant of "rigor."

I would question Hartman's judgment in two respects. First, it is not true that Arnold's time was as universal a literary wilderness as his figure made it. Although he could read Dickens with some pleasure and George Eliot with some respect, only as the novel reached toward religion with Tolstoy or rhapsody with George Sand could he consider it worth writing about, as part of the real life of literature in his time. Yet to us the novel represents the greatest work of his period. Moreover, even in poetry there was more worth his attention than he allowed, even if we grant that Tennyson and Browning had nothing to offer the lover of Wordsworth, Keats, and Shelley. But as he charged against the romantics, Arnold himself did not know enough. Walt Whitman was still not discovered in England, and Emily Dickinson's work, although largely written, was still unknown. The failure of the age was not in the production of great poetry but in the mechanisms of reproduction, distribution, and publicity.

Second, and rather more shocking, Arnold's prophecy was accurate. The line from Arnold to Irving Babbitt is incontestable, and Babbitt's elaboration of the "golden chain" that linked all "masterpieces" into a "single tradition" that seemed the work of "one all-seeing, all-hearing gentleman" (244, in part quoting Emerson) helped to make possible the technique and outlook of the early T. S. Eliot. The line from Arnold to Walter Pater is more contested, but equally real, and Pater's rhapsody on the Mona Lisa formed for Yeats the cornerstone of modern poetry as he defined it in the *Oxford Book of Modern Verse* (1936). Arnold-Babbitt-Eliot; Arnold-Pater-Yeats. Perhaps there really is a promised land; at least there is a posterity, even if they are not so grateful as one had hoped.

How do I situate myself? For Arnold has preempted the available critical stances. To join Hartman and Brooks and Wimsatt in judging Arnold is repetitively to fulfill his injunction: "Literary criticism's most important function is to try books as to the influence which they are calculated to have upon the general culture. . . . Of this culture literary criticism is the appointed guardian" (*Complete Prose* 3:41; henceforth abbreviated *CP*). Writing in the 1860s, Arnold may have usurped the power of appointment, but that function, that obligation of guardianship, of tutorship, has long outlived him. Samuel Johnson, England's previous great judicial critic, had concerned himself with nothing so large and impalpable as "influence." Johnson assessed the quality of the work itself, which might include the damage it threatened the reader with, but he did not look to the impersonal "culture," a notion quite alien to his age. If without judging, I try simply to see Arnold as he was, I only echo his insistence upon seeing the object "as in itself it really is," and should I shun objectivity for the personal, I meet Arnold's praise of Goethe for always asking, "But is it so? is it so to *me*?" (*CP* 3:110). Already in the preface to *The Renaissance* Pater performed this move from

Arnoldian objectivity to Arnoldian naturalism, and for him then it achieved some of the "really subversive" power Arnold found in Goethe's use of it. I doubt that any such virtue still lingers in the position.

I shall ask rather, "How is it for *us?*"—despite Trilling's critique of such communal awareness as conformity (*Beyond* xvi). I want to emphasize that our past is a creation we continually produce for the needs of our present—as we have already seen done by Brooks and Wimsatt and Hartman—just as Arnold produced an Athens "adequate" to the needs of his age, when in his inaugural lecture at Oxford he assessed the "significance for *us*" of Greek literary culture (*CP* 1:31).

Well then, who are we? We are not free-floating intellectuals. We are professionals, joined in associations such as the MLA, founded just over a century ago, the same year that Matthew Arnold was forbidden to speak on the campus of Princeton University (Raleigh 73). We are widely various, yet in the debates of current criticism Arnold is everywhere—though rarely acknowledged. I shall only touch on the more obviously Arnoldian issues raised by critics so different from each other as Edward Said, Gerald Graff, and Frederick Crews, in order then to focus on Arnold in the philosophic debates about what has been called the "Yale School," a debate often cast in the form of Nietzsche versus Wittgenstein.

In "Reflections on American 'Left' Criticism" (in *World*) Edward Said wrote harsh things about Arnold, but in conjuring a better time for criticism than that of the last thirty years, Said's point of departure was an explicitly Arnoldian moment from F. O. Matthiessen's "Responsibilities of the Critic." In urging, moreover, that criticism must move away from enclosure within technical refinement to engage directly the worldly place of both literature and criticism, Said followed Arnold's preface to his *Mixed Essays*—so named because they addressed "Democracy," "Equality," and "Irish Catholicism and British Liberalism," as well as literary topics. Arnold wrote, "Whoever seriously occupies himself with literature will soon perceive its vital connection with other agencies." Literature itself, he argued, was a "powerful agency" that worked upon the world, but one could not understand its effects without taking up its relations to other worldly forces (*CP* 8:370).

Agreeing with Said that current criticism has lost its social bearings in pursuit of useless refinement, and inquiring "Who Killed Criticism?" Gerald Graff located a major failure in our current inability to maintain a critical "point of view." This failure arose because academic criticism "takes on vested interests." Graff contrasted our situation with that of literary journalism in the nineteenth century, when appeal to a general audience was necessary, and disinterested judgment could occur. This is an Arnoldian ideal of criticism, and it is especially interesting to find Graff looking back to Arnold's age for the time when the ideal was realized. (Terry Eagleton in *The Function of Criticism* has more recently tried to find it in the eighteenth century.) As Arnold assessed his age, however, the ideal was far from the case; rather, it defined his hopes for the future. "The Function of Criticism at the Present Time" strikingly surveyed the periodical press of its time and determined that not a single organ existed to which one could turn for disinterested "free play of the mind" (*CP* 3:270).

In a more oblique attack on our current critical condition, Frederick Crews in "Analysis Terminable" listed many Continental thinkers and writers important to advanced literary studies and noted that they all admired and relied upon Freud. To expose them all as obscurantists, Crews then raked Freud's scientific claims over the coals of modern scientific evidence, while noting that such claims persist even in so praised a Freudian revisionist as Heinz Kohut. Replacing psychoanalysis with religion, Crews' tactic was the same as Arnold used in "Bishop Butler and the Zeit-Geist." Faced with claims for the "Newtonian method" practiced in theology by this eighteenth-century divine, Arnold charged that it was impossible to "verify" Butler's "arbitrary and fantastic hypothesis" of a divine plan; likewise Butler's "elaborate psychology" was unsatisfying because of its "radical defectiveness as natural history" (*CP* 8:41). To expose false, or at least untenable, claims to scientificity was Arnold's tactic against theology in *Literature and Dogma* as well. Crews weakened his case because he failed to carry out the other half of what Arnold did with the Bible, that is, raising the question of literature: for the "literary Freud" most lives for many Freudians today. The work of Richard Rorty and Alasdair MacIntyre may suggest, moreover, even within Anglo-American philosophy a shift from scientific to literary models of knowledge. This brings us to the issue of Wittgenstein versus Nietzsche as opposing banners for this shift, alternative guides "beyond epistemology."

Wittgenstein proved crucial to M. H. Abrams, who in "How to Do Thing with Texts" argued that not "rules," or anything so formally specifiable, but practical experience allowed us to legitimate, or condemn, certain ways of reading. Abrams' word for this practical knowledge was "tact" (587)—a term Arnold used some fifteen times in *St. Paul and Protestantism* and *Literature and Dogma*. Tact is at once cognitive and practical: "the power, through reading, to estimate the proportion and relation, in what we read." To avoid the error of insisting on every word a writer wrote, we need "discriminative tact . . . to control what one reads." Tact tells you what to skip, where not to "press," and thus makes an appropriate conservative tool (*CP* 6:153–57). Yet tact is an arbitrary power, which may mean authoritative and may mean random; it may operate either to centralize or to disperse. As Theodor Adorno reflected on the status of "tact" from Goethe to the "administered society," he defined the fundamental historical paradox determining this uncertainty: tact "demanded the reconciliation—actually impossible—between the unauthorized claims of convention and the unruly ones of the individual." In cultural style no less than in neo-Coleridgean literary theory, such hope for reconciliation fossilizes a past historical moment, for "tact" belonged to a brief, transitional phase: "The precondition of tact is convention no longer intact but still present" (*Minima Moralia* 36).

To Arnold's contemporaries, the randomizing force of the unruly individual was strongly felt; "tact" seemed revolutionary. W. J. Courthope attacked the "academic liberalism" he traced from Goethe to Carlyle to Arnold to Pater in a review of *Literature and Dogma* and Pater's *Renaissance*. He found "tact" a key to the "politics of culture" waged by "men of letters," in their "secession" from practical life into a "literary sacerdotalism" that proliferated a "Babel of sects." "Tact" was part of the Protagorean, skeptical sophistry fostered by a new "rhetoric" that in emphasizing "style" rather than truth produced—this was 1874!—"criticism as poetry," the "pure romance" of Pater on the Mona Lisa. The radical unsoundness of the whole method was proved for Courthope by another critic who exercised "tact" to praise as the greatest contemporary poet "an execrable American scribbler, one Walt Whitman." Since 1874, the banalization of tact has made the term commonplace and reversed its valence. Already by the second edition of *Seven Types of Ambiguity*, William Empson could define his "attitude in writing": "An honest man erected the ignorance of 'tact' into a point of honor" (vii). By now conservatives wield the term against those who pursue the values it once stood for.

The new rhetoricians for a while grouped as the "Yale School" exercised tact in Courthope's sense; the link to Arnold was long neglected because they practiced under the sign of Nietzsche. Yet I have demonstrated earlier the large degree to which Harold Bloom's career may be understood as a struggle with Arnold on the issues of judgment, the canon, and touchstones. Hillis Miller's Heideggerian deployment of etymology in "The Critic as Host" and elsewhere might find warrant as well in Arnold's etymological inquiry in *God and the Bible* into the "God of the Metaphysicians." Hartman in *Criticism in the Wilderness* offered the contrast of Nietzsche to Arnold as emblematic of the difference he was trying to define, open up, and valorize. Yet Arnold's work, especially on theology, not only often echoed Nietzsche's but was usually written earlier. Nietzsche dwelt on the "seduction of language" that took "effects as conditioned by . . . a 'subject'" (*Genealogy* 1:13), which was, however, merely a rhetorical superaddition. Likewise Arnold, after his inquiry into the metaphysical vocabulary denoting "being," concluded of these terms, "By a simple figure they declare a perceived energy. . . . Of a subject . . . they tell us nothing." And he recommended *"Power"* as a "better word" than "being," "because it pretends to assert . . . nothing more than effect on us, operation" (*CP* 7:186, 213).

Such rhetorical deconstruction operated throughout Arnold's Bible criticism. He found in the Disciples' relation to Jesus the metaleptic retrospective production of a cause by its effects: "They unconsciously exercised a creative pressure, long after the time when they were going about with Jesus . . . on the sayings and doings of their master: 'When he was risen from the dead . . . *his disciples remembered* that he had said this'" (*CP* 7:318). The relation of science to popular religion could readily be defined as a rhetorical transfer: "For science, the spiritual notion is the real one, the material notion is figurative." Therefore, "what is called 'orthodox

124

divinity' is, in fact, an immense literary misapprehension" (6:55, 276). So in *The Antichrist*, Nietzsche called the "history of Christianity . . . the history of the misunderstanding . . . of an original symbolism" (section 37).

Arnold arrived at formulations of the self-consuming entanglements of meaning and narrative like those Paul de Man later disarticulated as "allegories of reading." The writer of the fourth Gospel, in order to preserve Jesus' sayings, had to construct a narrative to hold them in place, but the result was that they became "the materials out of which was built up a miraculous tale exactly effacing the truth which Jesus wished to convey" (7:351). (Trilling later lamented a similar fate that befell Arnold, "where what he actually said is falsified even when he is correctly quoted" [*Matthew Arnold* 9]—evidently a failure of tact.)

Arnold recognized in the "Jesus" of the New Testament a complex construction, built up out of materials from the Hebrew Bible by a violent "exegetical proceeding" (the insight that Harold Bloom finally reached, against Frye). Arnold went on to reflect, "To us, who have been formed and fashioned by a theology whose set purpose is to efface all the difficulties in such a combination . . . it may appear natural. In itself . . . it cannot but be pronounced violent" (*CP* 7:351). To understand the "natural" as violently produced rather than as already given is to confess the strong side of "discriminative tact."

Arnold helped empower instances of our critical discipline so diverse as Abrams and de Man, but there is no essence that binds them together. Arnold set in process certain practices that have taken different forms over time. I want to beware of subjectifying "Arnold." I ask not *who* was Matthew Arnold to produce such effects; I seek rather to specify the power that operated in such a way and still traverses the texts and procedures of our profession. Arnold himself noted that "it seems lost labor to inquire what a poet's *aim* may have been. . . . For aim, let us read *work*" (*CP* 8:274). Concern with the "who," the psychological subject, led to impasse, even in the work of Arnold's most closely attentive current student, David DeLaura. DeLaura quoted this passage from Arnold's preface to *Merope*, on the effect of tragedy: "This sense of emphatic distinctness in our impressions rises . . . to a lofty sense of the mastery of the human spirit over its own stormiest agitation, and this, again, conduces to a state of feeling which it is the highest aim of tragedy to produce, *a sentiment of sublime acquiescence in the course of fate, and in the dispensations of human life*" (*CP* 1:58–59). DeLaura could only observe, however, that "psychologically, this is an interesting interplay of 'mastery' and 'acquiescence'" (124).

Not by looking psychologically to "who," but by asking "what" is at stake in this passage, it is possible to place Arnold within the practice of "humanism," a matter that still has great concern for us. Foucault's definition of humanism provided terms that respecify the interest of this passage. Humanism, Foucault asserted, was all in our culture that told us, "Even though you don't exercise power, you can still be a ruler." Everything, that is, which told us that "acquiescence" made "mastery" possible (*Language* 221–22). It told us this by establishing a series of "subjected sovereignties," for our subjectivity provided the site through which this subjugation occurred: the soul (over the body, under God), consciousness (rules judgment, under truth), the individual (wields personal rights, under the laws), basic freedom (internally, submitted to destiny). Foucault later decided that his use of "power" in these formulations was too absolute and insufficiently situational. Disciplines are not privative or repressive but are productive—as we already have remarked in the empowering proliferation of activities that emerged from the Arnoldian discipline of criticism. At the same time, disciplinary relations still take the form of "subjected sovereignty," in social roles such as that of the junior faculty (master in class, under tenure), the professor (master of tenure, subject to administration), or the critic (master of readers, subject to the text read).

As Foucault later emphasized, following Nietzsche, self-subjection is empowering; discipline is affirmative; asceticism "strengthening." I find particularly relevant Nietzsche's analysis of the will to power as "self-sacrifice," that is, "self-involvement with a great quantum of power to which one is able to give direction" (section 776). So Arnold avowed the task of criticism as "creating a current of true and fresh ideas" and setting that current to work. Arnold did not always use such active language; he preferred irony, which he defined as "saying rather less than one means" (*CP* 5:414). Unfortunately for our self-understanding as critics, this irony has been read too literally, the characteristic modernist misreading of the Victorians.

126

Arnold's style, the burden of Hartman's complaint in *Criticism in the Wilderness*, has often caused trouble for its understatement. Long before Hartman, in the 1860s, Francis Newman complained of Arnold's stylistic principles for the translation of Homer that such a style "smooths down the stamp of Homer's coin" (Dawson and Pfordresher 80); and in the 1950s, John Holloway found Arnold's use of definitions deliberately "dull" (28) compared with those of Newman or Carlyle. Yet from Arnold's time too readers began to sense that something was happening in those worn-out verbal ruts. The *Westminster Review* observed that Arnold's phrase "intellectual deliverance" was a useful euphemism for so dangerous a term as "free thought" (Dawson and Pfordresher 110). Frederick Harrison, who had early on mocked Arnold's characteristic terminology in "Culture: A Dialogue," lived long enough to acknowledge early in the twentieth century that Arnold's phrases were "generative, efficient, and issue into act." Yet even those on whom they acted most strongly found some embarrassment in the power of such unprepossessing words. The authors of the manifesto *Humanism and America* recurred at climactic moments of their arguments to Arnold, yet to phrases that they felt compelled to deprecate as "well-worn" or "tiresomely familiar" (Foerster 229, 255). I have been suggesting that the history of Arnold's reception shows that the phrases were never new, always already well-worn, phrases that were as Hillis Miller observed "scrupulously empty" (*Disappearance* 265), precisely in the hope that they might thereby be as open as possible to the future.

Arnold's language might be compared with that of the protagonists of Sir Walter Scott's novels, as Judith Wilt has brilliantly explored it. Scott's "wavering" young heroes spoke an empty, compromising "language of carnal reason," in contrast to the rich peasant idiom, or scriptural vigor, or even literary-romantic, high-flown "tushery" of their fellow-characters, and this linguistic weakness set to work the process of passivity that swept them helplessly through the course of action, which they observed but never controlled. They, nonetheless, were the prophetic figures in their books; they were associated with the Unionist hegemony Scott was writing to support; they represented the modernizing forces that were obliterating the Scottish culture which Scott was embalming in his books before it disappeared totally, swept away by the future carried by these helpless young men. Their language expressed the reason-able man's unreasonable desire to be on both sides of every bridge, and the exorbitance of this desire was punished by impotence before being rewarded with victory. Arnold, although he sometimes pre-tended otherwise, knew that no author was responsible for his part, no ultimately reassuring divine "subject" controlling things, at most a "power" that you could hope to locate, join, and direct.

Arnold's bafflingly empty style was one mode of negotiating this situation, but he also at times turned to the oratorical resources of a prophetic mode, as in the passages discussed earlier. At the close of "The Function of Criticism at the Present Time," the eras of Aeschylus and Shakespeare appeared as the "promised land" of the "true life of literature," for which "critical" ages like the present could only be preparatory: "That promised land it will not be ours to enter, and we shall die in the wilderness; but to have desired to enter it, to have saluted it from afar, is already, perhaps, the best distinction among contemporaries; it will certainly be the best title to esteem with posterity." We have already noted Geoffrey Hart-man's critical counterstatement, arguing against Arnold's subordi-nation of critical writing to what Hartman styled "genuine creation" (*Criticism* 6).

Yet Arnold in this very essay, with characteristic irony, had made some very strong claims for criticism. He explicitly opposed the elitism that held only poets as creative:

> The exercise of a creative power . . . is the highest function of man; it is proved to be so by man's finding in it his true happiness. But . . . men may have the sense of exercising this free creative activity in other ways than in producing great works of literature or art; if it were not so, all but a very few men would be shut out from the true happiness of all men. They may have it in well-doing, they may have it in learning, they may even have it in criticising. (*CP* 3:260).

Arnold here sensibly negotiated a moral problem that Coleridge had opened up with his distinction between "primary" and "secondary" imagination, and that the editors of the authoritative Bollingen *Biographia Literaria* believe he resolved on the opposite side from Arnold, holding that only an infinitesimal elite of Miltons and Shakespeares enjoy real human happiness. Whatever dignity the term "criticism" may have acquired, even now the verb "to criticize" still carries the sense of petty fault-finding, and in using this term, Arnold was being deliberately self-deprecatory, precisely because of the seriousness of the claims enacted here and by the essay as a whole.

In a similar way, the virtues he promoted in "On the Literary Influence of Academies" were not those of "genius," but only those of "intelligence." Yet that essay claimed for intelligence the power to provide "discipline" and thereby to acquire transmissibility, the capacity to perpetuate itself, unlike genius, which was isolated and discontinuous. (The issue is very much what we have discussed in Shelley as the relation of the "secondary" reason to imagination.) The future belongs to intelligence, then, and through its practice Arnold achieved what Johnson and Coleridge, those earlier geniuses of English criticism, did not do: he established the terms of a continuing cultural discipline. In the later years of his life, when he produced canonizing volumes of selections from Wordsworth and Byron, and reworked the book of Isaiah as a textbook for literary study, Arnold also produced for the general reader and the classroom a selection from Johnson's *Lives of the Poets*—thus joining criticism to very high canonical company, helping to establish its claims as an integral part of an enduring cultural tradition.

If Arnold often worked under the mask of banality, then, this did not always keep ideologically acute readers from discerning his strategies. Thus, the *Westminster Review* judged the language of *Literature and Dogma* to be itself—as it claimed of the Bible—"literary" language: "It is probable that he speaks of Jesus as the Son of God only by a violent metaphor, inspired by the hope of maintaining the revered names . . . while changing the entire basis of religion, by new definitions of them" (Dawson and Pfordresher 306). Just as Arnold exposed the "violence" of "natural" beliefs, the reviewer showed Arnold trying to exploit that naturality. Criticism works most insidiously when its figurative violence is not recognized.

The processes by which we shape our history were crucial in Arnold's reflections: "Many of us have a kind of centre-point in the far past to which we make things converge. . . . Our education is such that we are strongly led to take this centre-point in the history of Greece or Rome, but it may be doubted whether one who took the conquest of Babylon and the restoration of the Jewish exiles would not have a better" (*CP* 7:71). To locate a "centre-point" that gives meaning to history, to "ascertain the master-current" (3:107), is a constructive act, contingent upon one's education and purposes. Here, Babylon is conquered and the Jews restored from exile, but the Persian agents of these acts are suppressed (Arnold's "A Persian Passion Play" does not right the balance.) Even as Arnold gave critical voice to what was tacit in his culture, his tactic left certain areas intact, for "tact" judged them not worth pressing.

This discriminative cultural power, to which Arnold sacrificed himself and to which he gave direction, was overdetermined by three other powers: the power of the state's growing educational bureaucracy, the traditional power of the university, and the power of what Arnold called the "industrial and literary revolution" in publishing (*CP* 9:114). Let me detail these relations. Arnold joined many of his generation in the revulsion from electoral politics that followed soon after the 1832 Reform Bill. He functioned within the government not as an elective but as an administrative official, an inspector of schools. Yet even his contemporaries who knew his job allowed the stance of his writings to lead them into extraordinary confusions. The Cambridge utilitarian moral philosopher Henry Sidgwick, exasperated with the programmatic impracticality of "culture," burst out, "What does action, social action, really mean?" Not sweetness and light, but "losing oneself in a mass of disagreeable, hard, mechanical details, and trying to influence many dull or careless or bigoted people for the sake of ends that were at first of doubtful brilliancy, and are continually being dimmed and dwarfed by clouds of conflict" (Dawson and Pfordresher 227). Well, Arnold faced this all daily as an inspector, especially after 1862 when the Revised Code made the inspector into an examiner, who had to struggle in one visit to enter three bits of information about each of two hundred pupils, whom he had never seen before, and could barely see now through the crowds, and who would not speak up, and yet on the evaluation of their each and every performance rode the school's state educational grant. And he did not personally agree with this individualizing system of examination at all, but he argued against it and stuck it through, because the work in the schools was the practical base for the cultural elaborations of his larger program and polemic.

The extraordinary disciplinary responsibilities of school inspection make clear how enmeshed Arnold was in the practices of power his time offered, and he was well aware that such power was real and important: "He who administers, governs" (*CP* 2:6). For the first twenty years of his work, he covered a vast physical range, one-third of England, because as a nonclergyman he was restricted to schools not run by the Church of England that were nonetheless eligible for and willing to accept state aid. This fact may remind us that in the mid-nineteenth century the schools were an actively contested area of social power. (From Antonio Gramsci to William J. Bennett, many remind us that this remains true in the twentieth century.) No one doubted the importance of who was to form the minds of England's youth, and the Dissenters wanted to make certain that none of their taxes went to support the hegemony of a national church that had imprisoned and excluded their ancestors. Both practically and ideologically Arnold was in the midst of this resumption of hostilities from the seventeenth century. The growth of the government expenditures for grants and inspection is awe-inspiring, even for us who once were used to quick growth in social agency budgets. The Education Department was established in 1839, at the end of Arnold's schooldays at Rugby. According to R. H. Super, Arnold's modern editor, expenditure then was £20,000; by 1846, £100,000; by 1861, £750,000; by 1885, when Arnold was appointed to the honorary title of Chief Inspector, nearly £3,000,000. That was a growth of 150-fold in less than fifty years.

Arnold was involved with other powers as well. At Oxford he held the elective office of professor of poetry for ten years, which coincided with a major upturn in the quality and significance of Oxford intellectual life. His poetry provided him entry to the podium which then assured that his critical work would have some standing and win a hearing beyond the ordinary. But Arnold took a very important step on his own initiative to further assure the impact of what he said: he was the first professor of poetry to lecture in English rather than in Latin. Thus he defined his audience as reaching beyond the bounds of ancient erudition. He was, moreover, the first noncleric elected to the position. By the mid-nineteenth century the Church of England was in intellectual danger from the rise of modern, scientific criticism of the Bible and in political danger from the newly assured prominence of Dissenters, plus the reactionary turn taken by some of its own best minds and souls in the

"Oxford movement." These pressures on the church helped to open a space in which Arnold's criticism, and our discipline of criticism, became possible.

Yet the possibility of Arnold's critical disciplinary power depended as well upon his association with a third area, the "industrial and literary revolution" that made books and journals a vastly, and rapidly increasingly, greater part of English national life than they had ever been before. It would have done little good to lecture—even in English—to undergraduates, even at Oxford, unless there were some medium to spread the word beyond the university to the world at large. Some fifty years earlier, in the German system of education, Wolf's *Prolegomena ad Homerum* and the seminar at Halle in which he trained Ast and Boeckh set in motion the new disciplinary formation of *Altertumswissenschaft*, but not in Latin and not by direct pedagogy did Arnold effect his impact; rather through the proliferating public press.

Associated, then, with the power of the growing educational bureaucracy, the traditional university, and the new world of publishing, Arnold could feel confident that culture was a power. E. K. Brown remarked long ago on the strategic doubleness of Arnold's "Culture," in its contemplative commitment to "see things as they are" and its activist commitment to "make reason and the will of God prevail" (130). It is an agency of Enlightenment, like so many of the characteristic modes of power in its time and ours, and like the panoptic eye of Bentham, its vision is productive. Culture produces both the synoptically seen "tradition" and what Irving Babbitt called the "all-seeing, all-hearing gentleman" who is the subject of that tradition—that is, empowered to a certain vision by means of a certain blindness.

Let us look at one of Arnold's early poems, "The World and the Quietist: To Critias" (1849). We need not worry whether Critias is a mask for Arnold's friend Clough, but we should know that Critias tells Socrates the story of the lost continent of Atlantis and its ancient empire and unsuccessful war against Athens, and that he was a leader among the Thirty Tyrants:

> "Why, when the world's great mind
> Hath finally inclined,
> Why," you say, Critias, "be debating still?

> Why, with these mournful rhymes
> Learn'd in more languid climes,
> Blame our activity
> Who, with such passionate will,
> Are what we mean to be?"
>
> Critias, long since, I know
> (For Fate decreed it so),
> Long since the world hath set its heart to live;
> Long since, with credulous zeal
>   It turns life's mighty wheel,
> Still doth for labourers send
>   Who still their labour give,
> And still expects an end.
>
> Yet, as the wheel flies round,
> With no ungrateful sound
> Do adverse voices fall on the world's ear.
>   Deafen'd by his own stir
>   The rugged labourer
> Caught not till then a sense
> So glowing and so near
>   Of his omnipotence.
>
> So, when the feast grew loud
> In Susa's palace proud,
> A white-robed slave stole to the Great King's side
>   He spake—the Great King heard;
>   Felt the slow-rolling word
> Swell his attentive soul;
> Breathed deeply as it died,
>   And drain'd his mighty bowl.

In first setting a worldly affirmation of "passionate will" over "mournful rhymes," and then, by contrast, revising that passionate will into "credulous zeal," bound to the ceaseless turning of a "wheel," the poem repeated a romantic commonplace. This figure relating technological process to physical bondage and a diminished state of mind ran through Blake's "satanic mills," Schiller's image of modern humankind always hearing "the monotonous noise of the wheel" it turns (sixth letter on aesthetic education), Carlyle's invective against "machinery" in "Signs of the Times," and his adaptation in *Sartor Resartus* of Novalis' destructive "mill" of modern rationalism.

Set against this problem, there followed an equally romantic triumph. Just as the King's "soul" swelled at the slave's "word," so the laborer was enkindled with "a sense . . . of his omnipotence" that transcends his physical circumstances (recall Foucault on subjected sovereignty). "Sense" was the word on which many of Wordsworth's sublime moments hung, and this structure, in which the mind measured its infinite power precisely by its excess to any worldly condition, echoed a paradigm of the romantic sublime.

This reading takes the poem away from the quietist and gives it to the laborer and King, while the poem, however, in the third stanza greatly empowered the quietist. His "mournful rhymes" became "adverse voices," strong enough to define what Lionel Trilling later called an "adversary culture," carrying out the work that Arnold defined as Goethe's and Heine's "liberation war." These voices successfully reach the "world's ear," "deafen'd" though it had been. What sense of omnipotence did the laborer catch? A still, small voice that speaks against the world seems the voice of withdrawal, of what Lionel Trilling called "the opposing self," but Arnold judged that Wordsworth, by withdrawing into himself, had lost touch with the modern spirit and become only a "minor current." The message of the modern spirit was not individualism but "humanity" (*CP* 3:108–9, 121). The poet, quietistically, cares for the world.

What then of the fourth stanza, which diminished the quietist to a slave? It turns out that comprehending the poem depends not on our humanity but on our being initiated into a particular "education," to which Herodotus' *History* is second nature. Darius, the Great King of Persia, heard that the Athenians had helped burn one of his subject cities. He asked who they were, took an oath of vengeance, and ordered his servant at every meal to remind him of the Athenians. The Athenians marked a limit to the King's knowledge and power, and he intended to act against them. *We* it is who feel omnipotent because we know that the Athenians were not conquered by the Persians—their triumph shown in our possession of the knowledge that empowers us to understand the poem. To the degree that we are the subjects produced to read it, the Great King is marginal and the Athenians central. They, not he, carry the message of "humanity," and the slave speaks for them. The Athenians were the master current, and their opponents are fading into the oblivion of Atlantis. The all-seeing, all-hearing gentleman who determines the masterpieces of tradition can omit the Persians except as the failed oppressors of the Hellenes and the incidental agents by which the Hebrews were freed. Asceticism strengthens; history and power are on the side of the quietist; the world is not "finally inclined" the way Critias sees it. Well, the incline has tilted again. For us who are not at home with Herodotus, the poem no longer is "naturally" comprehensible but requires the violence of exegesis. Persia—Iran—has become a central concern for our world; the sense of political domination and concomitant cultural superiority, that particular center to which our education raised us, no longer holds.

Arnold worried over the social, political, ideological "machinery" (*CP* 4:96) Victorian England was producing and produced by. He revolted from Macaulay's praise of the mind, manners, and material achievement of the age, yet he never could join Ruskin's wholehearted denunciation of all that made this ugliness and joylessness and misery. He urged rather that "a tendency may be necessary, and even, as a preparation for something in the future, salutary, and yet . . . the generations or individuals who obey this tendency are sacrificed to it." We must therefore criticize the necessary and progressive tendency "lest it should take too firm a hold and last after it has served its purpose" (4:104). So we may grant the necessity of Arnold's mission against the Philistines, and yet we must critically question such reliance on biblical stereotypes in our world, whose politics demand rethinking the geographical and etymological carryover from Philistine to Palestine.

From the analysis of "The World and the Quietist," we have seen the sublimation of effects of force (the Greeks holding off the Persians; nineteenth-century European domination of the Middle East) into canons of judgment (Hellenic humanity, but not Eastern feasting, is part of the great tradition), as Nietzsche suggested in the first essay of the *Genealogy of Morals*. In the English domestic scene a comparable instance occurred. *Culture and Anarchy* arose out of Arnold's response to the "riots," in which the gates of Hyde Park were forced down by the pressure of massed bodies at a demonstration for the extension of the franchise. This was "anarchy," against which Arnold was offering culture. Yet his text defined the propitiousness of the moment for the advent of culture in these terms:

135

"The iron force of exclusion of all which is new has wonderfully yielded" (*CP* 4:92). In the yielding of iron without agency, his cultural position echoes that of the "rioters," even though such freedom for them is only "anarchy." This is a privilege of domination.

To reflect further on this sublimation of political struggle into cultural judgments, we might recall Arnold's comparison between his own major aim in writing and that of William Cobbett some fifty years earlier. Cobbett's constant concern was the "bad condition of the English labourer"; Arnold's the "bad civilisation of the English middle class" (*CP* 9:137). This suggests an important question regarding the function of criticism: must it always "rise above" material conditions, as in "The World and the Quietist" the condition of the laborer had its significance by figuring a spiritual state? It is tempting to think of Cobbett as "reformer," attacking institutional issues without caring to make ideological transformations, and of Arnold as "humanist," working only at the ideological but not at the institutional level. This would be fair to neither. In reducing the principles of the political parties from those of their "great statesmen" Pitt and Fox to "the principles of Pratt, the principles of Yorke" (two notorious party hacks), Cobbett worked hard at ideological subversion; and the politics of his publications, his constant need to find new ways to evade governmental restrictions, promoted a whole range of developments that opened a space for ideological polemic. Arnold, on the other hand, we have already noted as deeply involved in some of the major institutional transformations of his day. A more fruitful contrast between their positions might be that Cobbett spoke both to and for a large body of workers, while Arnold spoke against the philistine middle class. Arnold did not support the group to which he did belong, and he distrusted the role of advocacy for a group to which he did not belong. In explaining why he thought it proper to let agricultural laborers vote (despite their lack of property and education), he asserted that "it is well" for every social group "to be able to say for itself what it wants" (*CP* 9:140).

Then what is the legitimacy of the "adverse voice"? It is as himself a member of the middle class that Arnold claimed the right to try to tell the philistines what they should want—for that was precisely the issue. In looking to the greater amenity of life in France—the urban beauty, the restaurants—Arnold found evidence of the "immense middle class making the same sort of demands upon life which only a small upper class make elsewhere" (*CP* 8:361). What is the place and power of one who makes no such demands for himself but devotes his energies to trying to get others to make them, an ascetic agitator for hedonism? By submitting himself to "the severe discipline necessary for all real culture," could Arnold offer more than a new bondage to replace the "prison house" of Puritanism in which he believed the English middle class had locked itself (*CP* 3:121)?

Those who followed in his path believed that culture provided an alternative to the "prison-house." Leslie Stephen explained, "Your individualist only takes off the fetters so as to allow a free fight among the prisoners. The prophet of culture alone can enable us to get free from the prison-house itself" (Dawson and Pfordresher 418). Yet Arnold himself saw the triumph of culture in much more equivocal terms. Contrasting the England of the Hyde Park "riots" to the existing public order in France, Arnold suggested that the French Revolution had brought social, not just political, changes, and that therefore the relations of the classes were far more equitable in France than in England. An ordinary Frenchman, therefore, "feels that the power which represses him is the *State*, is *himself*." In England, however, one always felt that it was the Tories, or the landowners, or the factory bosses, or the church that was repressing one, and one therefore might resist—it was only their interest against yours, not a matter of common good.

Looking forward to the changes he wanted to see that would bring the unity and concord of culture, Arnold continued, "If there ever comes a more equal state of society in England, the power of the state for repression will be a thousand times stronger" (*CP* 5:385). This is an awesome spectacle, not a certain good, and yet Arnold looked, prophetically, to the future. Is it a promised land? If there is no "posterity," then this wilderness of bad choices and unsound causes is all we have. It seems to me more valuable to try to make possible a posterity, even at some cost, than to rejoice in the permanence of the wilderness, more salutary for the possibilities of choosing and acting. In recovering Arnold as critic and activist, I have tried to specify his goals and concerns enough to make evident that they are no more than partly ours. To accept the Arnoldian *definition* of criticism is only to prolong a dead yet dominant force. To accept the Arnoldian *challenge* for criticism requires both seeking different goals and finding different means.

Chapter 6
D. H. Lawrence and the
Modernist Sublime:
Stoning the Moon

IN FOCUSING CLOSELY on a passage from the "Moony" chapter of *Women in Love*, I aim to open for consideration a little-explored topic, that of a differentiated history of the sublime, which my initial discussion of Longinus and Bloom did not allow for. It has long been understood, of course, that the sublime analyzed and expounded by Longinus during the earlier Roman Empire differed considerably from what was inspired by Longinus' rediscovery, from the sixteenth through eighteenth centuries. In Burke and then in Kant, Schiller, and others, an aesthetic psychology replaced a literary rhetoric. Nonetheless, the most probing current critics and theorists of the sublime have tended to treat it typologically, as a set of qualities unrelated to history, while the most probing historians have often failed to connect their analyses to current concerns. While acknowledging the close relations between romanticism and modernism, I wish my reading of Lawrence to help pose the question of a possible negative relation between a romantic sublime exemplified by Coleridge and Lamb (whom I discuss in "The Media of Sublimity) and a modernist sublime exemplified by writers so different as Lawrence and T. S. Eliot.

It was a major event in the literary history of English romanticism that Coleridge captured crucial motifs of the sublime. Coleridge's theory of the symbol harnessed into a system of wholeness the moment of disruptive intensity that for Longinus had been the hallmark of sublimity. For Longinus, the sublime stood out against the "whole tissue of the composition"; it came with a "flash" which "scatters everything before it" (1.4). For Coleridge, the symbol shone with a steady "translucence" rather than fitfully for a moment, for it manifested the "Eternal" (*Collected Works* 6:30). Longinus sketched a process of transference in the relation between reader and text; we are "lifted up . . . as if we had ourselves produced" (7.2) what we hear or read. In contrast to this mobility of identity, by which through reading we become other, Coleridge devised a system which brought that movement to ultimate stability; against the alterity of allegory, Coleridge found the symbol "tautegoric," always saying the same. In Longinus, the sublime was the "echo" of a great soul (9.2). Coleridge transformed this motif in his decisively influential formulation of the imagination: the primary imagination was "a repetition in the finite mind of the eternal act of creation in the infinite I AM," and the secondary imagination was "an echo" of the primary (*Collected Works* 7.1:304). The Christian, monotheistic deity thus acted as a stopper, organizing and regulating the transformation that in Longinus operated more freely. The difference resembles that between Freudian primary process (in Longinus) and secondary process (in Coleridge). In modernism, that energy—of sublimity, of the primary process—was unbound, as in the shattering of identity in Eliot or in Lawrence. The internalized depth of character that Lamb found sublime in the experience of reading Shakespeare's *King Lear*, but not in the experience of seeing the role outwardly enacted on the stage, became an object of attack in much modernist work. The transsexual identification that Longinus offered to male readers in his response to Sappho's ode (10.1–3) became basic to Eliot's Tiresias in "The Waste Land" and to Lawrence's disruptions of the usual understandings of the masculine and the feminine. In scorning a "semi-ethical criterion of sublimity" in "Tradition and the Individual Talent," Eliot rejected the Victorian belletristic heritage from Lamb and Coleridge, but he, Lawrence, and others of their generation continued to energize their work through another mode of sublimity.

The romantic figure whose work most closely realized the elements of the sublime to which the modernists turned in opposing romanticism was Shelley, as we shall see. It fits perfectly the process Harold Bloom has characterized as "The Anxiety of Influence" that the essential strategic maneuver for Eliot should have involved not only denying Shelley (as immature) but also rediscovering Coleridge's theory of the imagination. On political and religious grounds, the positive relations between Eliot and Coleridge are clear, but poetically, and as a theorist of literary history, Shelley is much closer to the early Eliot than Coleridge is. Lawrence and Yeats, both of whom Eliot attacked in his "Primer of Modern Heresy," *After Strange Gods*, did not insist on denying Shelley, but such has been Eliot's influence that from Cleanth Brooks on Yeats to Sandra Gilbert on Lawrence (80) they have typically been read in terms of Coleridgean poetics.

Here, then, is the passage from which I shall proceed:

> He stood staring at the water. Then he stooped and picked up a stone, which he threw sharply at the pond. Ursula was aware of the bright moon leaping and swaying, all distorted, in her eyes. It seemed to shoot out arms of fire like a cuttlefish, like a luminous polyp, palpitating strongly before her.
>
> And his shadow on the border of the pond was watching for a few moments, then he stooped and groped on the ground. Then again there was a burst of sound, and a burst of brilliant light, the moon had exploded on the water and was flying asunder in flakes of white and dangerous fire. Rapidly, like white birds, the fires all broken rose across the pond, fleeing in clamorous confusion, battling with the flock of dark waves that were forcing their way in. The furthest waves of light, fleeing out, seemed to be clamouring against the shore for escape, the waves of darkness came in heavily, running under towards the centre. But at the centre, the heart of all was still a vivid, incandescent quivering of a white moon not quite destroyed, a white body of fire writhing and striving and not even now broken open, not yet violated. It seemed to be drawing itself together with strange, violent pangs, in blind effort. It was getting stronger, it was re-asserting itself, the inviolable moon. And the rays were hastening in in thin lines of light, to return to the strengthened moon, that shook upon the water in triumphant reassumption.
>
> Birkin stood and watched, motionless, till the pond was almost calm, the moon was almost serene. Then, satisfied of so much, he looked for more stones. She felt his invisible tenacity. And in a moment again, the broken lights scattered in explosion over her face, dazzling her; and then, almost immediately, came the second shot. The moon leapt up white and burst through the air. Darts of bright light shot asunder, darkness swept over the centre. There was no moon, only a battlefield of broken lights and shadows, running close together. Shadows, dark and heavy, struck again and again across the place where the heart of the moon had been, obliterating it altogether. The white fragments pulsed up and down, and could not find where to go, apart and brilliant on the water like the petals of a rose that a wind has blown far and wide.

Yet again, they were flickering their way to the centre, finding the path blindly, enviously. And again, all was still, as Birkin and Ursula watched. The waters were loud on the shore. He saw the moon regathering itself insidiously, saw the heart of the rose intertwining vigorously and blindly, calling back the scattered fragments, winning home the fragments, in a pulse and in effort of return.

And he was not satisfied. Like a madness, he must go on. He got large stones, and threw them, one after the other, at the white-burning centre of the moon, till there was nothing but a rocking of hollow noise, and a pond surged up, no moon any more, only a few broken flakes tangled and glittering broadcast in the darkness, without aim or meaning, a darkened confusion, like a black and white kaleidoscope tossed at random. The hollow night was rocking and crashing with noise, and from the sluice came sharp, regular flashes of sound. Flakes of light appeared here and there, glittering tormented among the shadows, far off, in strange places; among the dripping shadow of the willow on the island. Birkin stood and listened and was satisfied.

Ursula was dazed, her mind was all gone. She felt she had fallen to the ground and was spilled out, like water on the earth. Motionless and spent she remained in the gloom. Though even now she was aware, unseeing, that in the darkness was a little tumult of ebbing flakes of light, a cluster dancing secretly in a round, twining and coming steadily together. They were gathering a heart again, they were coming once more into being. Gradually the fragments caught together, re-united, heaving, rocking, dancing, falling back as in panic, but working their way home again persistently, making semblance of fleeing away when they had advanced, but always flickering nearer, a little closer to the mark, the cluster growing mysteriously larger and brighter, as gleam after gleam fell in with the whole, until a ragged rose, a distorted and frayed moon was shaking upon the waters again, re-asserted, renewed, trying to recover from its convulsion, to get over the disfigurement and the agitation, to be whole and composed, at peace. (Lawrence, *Women in Love* 239–40).

Take the moon conventionally for a moment as all that was vague, imprecise, dreamy, "romantic" in romanticism, and the characteristic modernist response to that understanding of romanticism was to stone the moon. More particularly, if the moon here figured the romantic theory of the symbol, elaborated by Coleridge, then Lawrence enacted thoroughgoing opposition to that symbolist aesthetic, especially in its metaphysical and political ramifications.

The Coleridgean symbol was a theological concept, transferred into aesthetics: "It always partakes of the Reality which it renders intelligible; and while it enunciates the whole, abides itself as a living part in that Unity, of which it is the representative" (*Collected Works* 6:30). In representing participation in a divinely founded universe, it enacted a closed economic system of return, of circulation from and back to a source: the "reconciling and mediatory power" of the imagination, by "incorporating the Reason in Images of the Sense, and organizing (as it were) the flux of the Senses by the permanence and self-circling energies of the Reason, gives birth to a system of symbols. . . . These are the *Wheels* which Ezekiel beheld, when the hand of the Lord was upon him" (6:29). The potential excess of that primary source (God, the father, the sun) was masked by mediation. As noted in the discussion of chapter 3, Coleridge's poetry characteristically built symbolic systems around the moon, deferring the sun's presence. The system thus operated through the rhetorical figure of synecdoche (as Paul de Man observed), displacing the whole with a part that represents it, allowing the human I AM of subjectivity to stand for the divine I AM to which it is subjected (in the terms of Foucault's analysis of "humanism").

Lawrence consistently and radically opposed the kind of romantic ontotheological aesthetic I have just sketched. Repeatedly he mocked the serpent of eternity with its tail in its mouth, one of Coleridge's favorite emblems for the "self-circling" energies of the symbolic system (e.g., "Him with His Tail in His Mouth," in *Reflections*, 127). In contrast to this system of return and closure, Lawrence valued "waste" and "excess" that transgressed the bounds of self-preservation (*Phoenix* 398–404). Turning away from dawn or sunset, the privileged cyclical moments of romantic poetry, Lawrence sought a poetry of the "immediate present." His terms for that poetry echoed what we have already read in the passage from "Moony": "Life . . . knows . . . no finished crystallization. The perfect rose is only a running flame. . . . We look at the very white quick of nascent creation. . . . The waters are shaking the moon. There is no round, consummate moon on the face of running water. . . . Don't give me the infinite or the eternal. . . . Give me the still white seething . . . the bubbling up of the spring" (*Phoenix* 219).

Despite the premise of unity in the Coleridgean symbol, Lawrence found all its manifestations in practice to be partial; what was supposed to be a totality proved exclusionary. In binding energy into an economic system, a fixation occurred, by which the part replaced

143

the whole it was to represent. Rhetorically, synecdoche reduced to metonymy; it lost what Coleridge called its "translucence" and became a wall, something that fills and blocks out perception. It became, that is, what Lawrence called a "vision." Lawrence strove always for a counterpoise that avoided exclusion by renouncing inclusion, that relied less on the translucency of the symbol than the opacity of the trace: "All vital truth contains the memory of all that for which it is not true" (*Letters* 2:247). In ways that Derrida has made familiar, such a structure, in leaving behind notions of an "outside" and "inside," through the permeability of its interior to what should be excluded, evaded the metaphysical closure of a false totality.

Consider the specific uses Lawrence made of the term "symbol" in the time of the project he called the *Sisters*, which led to both *The Rainbow* and *Women in Love*. Even where he used it positively, it was in a way that Coleridge could not have accepted: "I think there is the dual way of looking at things: our way, which is to say '*I* am all. All other things are but radiation out from me.'—The other way is to try to conceive the whole, to build up a whole by means of symbolism, because symbolism avoids the I and puts aside the egotist" (*Letters* 2:248). For Coleridge the world of the symbol had to begin from the I AM. The only alternative was the world of "It is," that of Spinozistic pantheism, which to Coleridge meant atheistic materialism. Lawrence thus repudiated what for Coleridge was the only possible ground of a symbolism. Even more striking is Lawrence's outright rejection of the symbol in a letter while composing *Women in Love*: "A symbol is something static, petrified, turning towards what has been, and crystallised against that which shall be" (*Letters* 2:633).

This tendentious interpretation of the Coleridgean symbol derives its interest from the century of history that elapsed between Coleridge's formulations and Lawrence's writings. For that interval revealed the effective meaning of the symbol as ideology. Consider the "Industrial Magnate" chapter in *Women in Love*, which shortly precedes "Moony" and is in implicit dialogue with it. The chapter concerns the history of Gerald's coal-mine-owning family, whose social and economic relations with the miners are implicated in the larger history of the Industrial Revolution, but I shall be exploring less these broad contours than some particular moments of language.

The decisive moment for Gerald came when there suddenly "crystallised" his vision of a new way to run things (*Women* 215). This word echoes that which negatively characterized the symbol in the letter just cited, and which in a passage from *Phoenix* was opposed to the values of the "immediate present." Central to this crystallization was Gerald's understanding of his hierarchically dominant position. He likened his place to that of the "sun" (219), and Lawrence showed the symbolic-synecdochic principle at work in his relation to his men: he "represented" them (221). The culminating passage that summarized his vision echoed the Coleridgean system of self-circling energies, based upon the human repetition of the divine, productive I AM: "He found his eternal and his infinite in the pure . . . principle of perfect co-ordination into one pure, complex, infinitely repeated motion, like the spinning of a wheel; but a productive spinning, a productive repetition through eternity" (220).

One crucial word was omitted from this passage. Lawrence calls Gerald's principle of coordination a "machine" principle, and no more than Lawrence could Coleridge have accepted that term as positive. But Lawrence's critical version of symbolism shows that Coleridgean principles, as ideology, served what Coleridge might have thought and hoped to oppose. For the secularization, the bringing down to earth, of Coleridge's theology yielded what Max Weber called routinization of charisma and bureaucratic rationalization. Coleridge's most famous statement on the imagination defined its power to "harmonize" (*Collected Works* 7.2:17), and I have cited earlier a passage on the symbol that hesitates over the word "organizing" by adding "(as it were)." The history encapsulated by this terminological waver Lawrence brilliantly sketched in describing Gerald's movement from philosophy to management, "translating the mystic word harmony into the practical word organisation" (220). Thus may an aesthetic be complicit with the technology of power. American critics will be sobered, if not dismayed, to recognize in Gerald's translation an act analogous to that which Lawrence's younger contemporary I. A. Richards performed in making Coleridge usable for the New Criticism, shifting Christian into utilitarian idiom. Lawrence's own excavation of his culture more closely resembled that of another younger contemporary, Martin Heidegger.

One further aspect of this sequence from the "Industrial Magnate" must be explored before returning to "Moony": the visual fixation, that process by which Gerald entered into his career as "God of the machine." It began with an image "impressed photographically on his consciousness," the recognition that the initials inscribed everywhere over the industrial landscape, the initials of the mining company, were "his own name written on the wall." It led to this result: "Now he had a vision of power" (214). It would be foolish to insist that for Lawrence power is always a good and not to be confused with the evils of will, but here at least it is less the "power" than the "vision" that does the damage. For as a good in Lawrence, power comes from "behind"; it is something given unexpectedly from unknown sources ("Blessed Are the Powerful," in *Reflections*, 146). But the vision places power before us, as known, defined, and limited, the wall blocking our way on which our name is inscribed.

The dangers Lawrence felt in "vision," the usurpations of the eye and i-dentity, further appear in a letter he wrote just as he was—he thought—about to leave England forever, for Florida. The letter caught with heartbreaking clarity the beauty of an English autumn, and Lawrence characterized it in this way: "So vivid a vision, everything so visually poignant, it is like that concentrated moment when a drowning man sees his past crystallised into one jewel of recollection" (*Letters* 2:459). Once more "crystallization" and "vision" are linked and associated with the deathly grip of the past. This vision must be rejected by the Lawrence who survives; it marked the end of one of the "several lives" he felt himself to have lived through: 'It is the vision of a drowning man, the vision of all I am, all I have become, and ceased to be. It is me, generations and generations of me. . . . And oh, my God, I cannot bear it. For it is not this me who am drowning swiftly under this last wave of time, this bursten flood" (*Letters* 2:460). "It is not this me who am"; that is, I is an other.

More programmatically, and at about the same time, Lawrence wrote to Bertrand Russell contrasting the "blood-consciousness," which defined itself through sexual connection, with "ordinary mental consciousness, which depends on the eye as its source or connector." Lawrence rejected the Platonic emphasis on light and the visual to insist on restoring the portion of our life "active in the darkness" (*Letters* 2:470).

For one who like Lawrence did not insist upon an exclusive and stabilized identity, the "bursten flood," however terrifying, might be valuable, but for Gerald, who was given exclusively to the power of vision, to lose that vision, to recognize it as an end and not as an eternity, was unbearable. Thus in contrast to Gerald's vision of power stands the ending of the "Industrial Magnate," in which he looked into the mirror and saw not his name but his face, which he feared was only a mask: "His eyes were blue and keen as ever, and as firm in their sockets. Yet he was not sure that they were not false blue bubbles that would burst in a moment," leaving Gerald himself "a purely meaningless babble lapping around a darkness" (224–25). The "burst" here echoes the "bursten flood" of drowning vision. The word "burst" rings through the next chapters of the novel, as Gerald's fear is variously enacted—by the outburst of Bismarck the rabbit (cf. 235) and in "Moony" by the "burst of sound and . . . burst of brilliant light" before the moon itself "burst through the air" (239). What Gerald feared for his eyes happened to the moon, and what he feared for himself happened too: "There was nothing but a rocking of hollow noise, and a pond surged up, no moon any more, only a few broken flakes tangled and glittering broadcast in the darkness, without aim or meaning" (240). Further terms associated with the outburst of Bismarck the rabbit, "to explode," "to writhe," terms that undid the firm boundaries of visualization, also persisted into the "Moony" sequence.

The end of fixity, the unbinding of the image, the destruction of vision that Gerald dreaded, we must find some way of wanting. This happened for Ursula in the opening of "Moony." Her hard, egoistic isolation as "a rock in a wash of flood-water," experiencing herself as the only real thing amidst the "nothingness" of the rest of the world, suddenly felt itself menaced by the "presence, watching her" of the moon, which in its isolation and completeness echoed her own: "And she wished for something else out of the night, she wanted another night, not this moon-brilliant hardness" (236–38). With all its pain and absurdity, this was what Birkin gave her when he stoned the moon.

Ursula's wish for a breakthrough repeats one of the most characteristic patterns in Lawrence, here as often closely modeled on the Platonic cave, an enactment of escape from enclosure within the unreal—that is, within something partial that becomes a lie by excluding the rest of its context. One psychological genealogy Lawrence offered of this process began with the formation of what he called a "symbol," to embody externally what we feel to be a deficiency within ourselves. This served as a "wall" against the "chaos" of lack surrounding us (*Phoenix* 446). Yet by the time he reached this analysis, Lawrence had already shown that the "little walled city," in which humankind enfolded itself against the "waste enormity" of the world, was stifling, and required bursting out (*Phoenix* 419). To break the wall, the symbol, is to contest our self-limitation, to tear down the wall with our name written on it.

At times the model seems very close to Plato's in imagery, as, for example, when in order to protect themselves from the "chaos" of reality, people form a "vision" as an "umbrella," or more precisely, as a "parasol" to keep out the "sun." This prosthesis, however, becomes ever more burdensome, a vault, a dome, until it too must be "burst" through (*Phoenix* 255–57). More typically, however, Lawrence's cave model was, paradoxically, anti-Platonic in intent. In contrast to the "darkness" that Western culture left behind with the Egyptians, there stood the Platonic path of the "Idea," of "vision" and the "sun," which led to the enclosure of our modern world of "Kodak" perception. We can imagine identity only as that which would be seen in a snapshot. Lawrence argued that with the advent of the "conscious ego," man "has learned to *see* himself," and we are now mechanically empowered to "see as the All-Seeing Eye sees, with the universal vision." It is worth noting the resemblance of this figure to Irving Babbitt's "all-seeing . . . gentleman" of "tradition," while also noting the radically different evaluation. As in his analysis of the "Industrial Magnate," Lawrence had an acute sense for the technological implications of secularization: "Because man, since he grew out of a personal God, has taken over to himself all the attributes of the personal Godhead. It is the all-seeing human eye which is now the eternal eye" (*Phoenix* 523–24). The exercise of technological power that severs things from context and represents them to us in abstraction is yet another of the disciplinings that Michel Foucault analyzed in his works of the 1970s on panopticism and the will to knowledge. Therefore, as Lawrence noted, all the moral weight of an outraged society fell upon someone like Cézanne, whose art dared to see an apple differently, for the limits of perception are integral to the technology of power.

Lawrence recognized the danger of being merely an anti-Platonist, the other half of a discredited, unacceptable opposition. He saw the damage, for instance, done to John Galsworthy, whose stance was still wholly bound by a "social" conception of life, varied but not significantly altered by frequently valuing the antisocial (see "John Galsworthy," in *Phoenix*). And in Cézanne, Lawrence noted the "repudiative" power with which he opposed cliché, and which "ec- stasizes the critics," but which for Lawrence was much less impor- tant than that new thing Cézanne wished to bring into our lives, to open our lives to, and which finally yielded only an apple (*Phoe- nix* 581). To bring to triumph the other half of a half truth is still to perish, and since every exclusive goal becomes a grave as soon as it is reached, the only path to life is to "side-step" (*Reflections* 132). Therefore Lawrence insisted that a work of art's greatness be measured by its capacity to include that which calls it most thor- oughly into question (*Phoenix* 476). Rather than an exclusive and dominant image of the moon, we want the state in which "there was no moon, only a battlefield of broken lights and shadows" (*Women* 239). As a reader, Lawrence performed a similar feat when he brought into emphasis the "background" Thomas Hardy's novels had thrust too far back. Lawrence read the fate of Hardy's characters in relation to that world of natural energies which their outburst- ings echo, rather than in terms of their limiting vision, the "map" of the enclosed social world that Hardy foregrounded (*Phoenix* 420).

Lawrence demonstrated an extraordinary, vigorous complexity in his deployment of dialectical terms, because he was aware of how rapidly a necessary overstatement became a crippling dogma. Note first how boldly he reversed the usual connotative association of certain images. In one of his most fascinating and bleak wartime letters, he argued that even having children is not a movement into new life but only a lapsing back into traditional patterns, fixed "symbols." What we must bring into the world is hope, but this may not come from physical generation. Thus, even while in this letter he continued to use the organic metaphor of a plant's growth to image his positive values, by his repudiation of the biological organic as it applied directly to the human, he emphasized that the "plant" was merely a figure for something unknown (*Letters* 2:633–36).

In the *Study of Thomas Hardy*, as he first introduced the polarity of male and female that figured so largely in the work, Lawrence defined the man as having to "clasp as a hub the woman who shall be the axle, compelling him to true motion" (*Phoenix* 444). The conventionally phallic axle and its compelling potency here was woman's, the passivity of clasping receptivity the man's. So too in "Moony" there was a fascinating interplay between the ritual stoning of the moon, associated with femininity, and the social destruction, later in the chapter, of the masculine image of paternal authority in Birkin's interview with Mr. Brangwen. Just as the integrity of the moon was shattered into conflicting components, so Brangwen's silly social fears, so little according with any real self that we might imagine for him, appeared to Birkin as a "patternless collection," a "roomful of old echoes" (*Women* 248–50).

The perversity of Lawrence's figures for the sexes in the *Study of Thomas Hardy* deserves further attention. For H. M. Daleski has used the *Study* as the ground for his important analysis of Lawrence's fundamental "dualism," remarking that "it is not the thought which is difficult but the terminology which is confusing" (25–26). Yet so long as writers write and people speak in words, matters of "terminology" must remain of the highest critical import. Daleski never considered that there may be a rhetorical energy displacing the terms whose mobility he grudgingly acknowledged. He invoked psychobiography to explain any anomalies, despite Lawrence's own preliminary remark that his whole polarization into male and female "is arbitrary, for the purpose of thought" (*Phoenix* 448). I would gloss this, for the purpose of aiding thought by showing the impossibility of maintaining confidence in the safe differentiation of arbitrary terms.

In the study of Hardy, two major oppositions operated, that of male and female and that of Law-Father-Flesh versus Love-Son-Spirit—that is, one biological (or perhaps "pagan") opposition and one Christian opposition. To each polarity accrued further associations until it finally became possible to read off equivalences from the one system to the other. So the body was associated with the female (conventionally enough), and the social principle, which was male, was associated with the Son (plausibly), but finally in the last pages of the work, Lawrence explicitly joined the Law complex with Woman, and the Love complex with Man (*Phoenix* 459, 487, 514). Remarkable consequences resulted from Lawrence's adding a female term to a Christian system that had originally excluded woman, for the final formula becomes Woman the Father and Man the Son. In relation to our usual gender stereotypes, we have reached the "meaningless babble lapping around a darkness," the "rocking of hollow noise when the moon has vanished and left only a few broken flakes tangled and glittering broadcast in the darkness without aim or meaning." Yet Martin Green's book on the von Richthofen sisters suggests that such transvaluations had a place in socially transformative movements in Germany associated with Bachofen's matriarchal arguments; and through attention to Edward Carpenter, Emile Delavenay has shown in the English scene some of the implications of such meddling with the ranks and lines among the sexes. Rhetorically to disrupt the logic of sexual differentiation shatters the vision of power that freezes technology into destructive shapes. This poses the question of the sublime in the whole range of our life activities, as Longinus adumbrates in the last remarks of his treatise.

After following Lawrence's dialectic so far, another twist still remains. For Frank Kermode and Raymond Williams, among others, have made clear that the modernists repeated the romantics at least as much as they rejected them. No matter how hard they threw stones, what remained was a "ragged rose, a distorted, frayed moon . . . shaking upon the waters again, reasserted, renewed, trying to recover from its convulsion, to get over the disfigurement and the agitation, to be whole and composed, at peace." *Romantic Image* and *Culture and Society* both linked romanticism to modernism through the problem of the isolation of the artist, even as that artist is guided by a motivating premise of inclusiveness. So in Ursula's initial confrontation with the moon in "Moony," the moon would figure "society," from which as an individual one stands apart, but with an impotence, and a violence, that only echoed what was most detestable within the society.

Under the pressure of the First World War, Lawrence felt a growing sense of isolation in 1915 and 1916 while writing *Women in Love*, turning from his fascination with schemes of new communities, however desperate, to an equally desperate and even bleaker position:

> The only thing now to be done is either to go down with the ship . . . or . . . *leave* the ship, and like a castaway live a life apart. As for me, I do not belong to the ship; I will not . . . sink with it. I will not live any more in this time. I know what it is. I reject it . . . I will stand outside this time. (*Letters* 2:528; the nautical metaphors are part of Lawrence's response to reading *Moby-Dick*, which he discussed in this letter)

Could Lawrence in turning away from his time avoid the consequences of the vision of power (which itself flees time for "eternality"), or was his flight doomed to echo merely, weakly, what he shunned? "I feel like an outlaw . . . quite anti-social, against this social whole as it exists. I wish one could be a pirate or highwayman in these days" (*Letters* 2:540). But one could only be an artist or robber baron, a captain of industry but not a Captain Macheath. Like the vision of power, the vision of impotence took consolation in the technical means at its disposal. "One can still write bombs," Lawrence reminded Russell, and he found satisfaction in his "way of shooting" people "with noiseless bullets that explode in their souls" (*Letters* 2:547, 540). Despite his wish to stand apart, Lawrence knew that there was no place for it. He wrote of *Women in Love*, "I know it is true. . . . And it is another world [such as he had once sought in communal undertaking] in which I can live apart from this foul world. . . . The world of my novel is big and fearless—yes, I love it. . . . It only seems to me horrible to have to publish it" (*Letters* 2:659). That is, to subject it to the stones that would be flung at it by the reviewers and other socially representative readers; yet he had to.

The paths of rejection lead to an impasse. One has no strength as an outsider, one loses any claim to moral superiority, and one cannot even maintain oneself apart. The will's "fearful resolve to find in itself alone the one absolute motive of action" Coleridge considered "sublimely embodied in the Satan of . . . *Paradise Lost*" (*Collected Works* 6:65), but he rejected this position and instead developed strategies of reinclusion. The romantics, however, offered another model of critical involvement different from that of Coleridge's, namely Shelley's. Like Lawrence, Shelley was an anti-Christian nonetheless saturated in the images and pathos of Christianity, and like Lawrence too, one who could not give his credence to Plato yet remained enmeshed in relation with him. One way out from mere anti-Platonism that Shelley found, and that Lawrence also used, was that of the imageless metaphor. So in one of Lawrence's most effective workings-through from the cave, when we finally gain contact with the world outside our enclosure, Lawrence emphasized not the Platonic-Coleridgean sun, but the "fresh air," like Shelley's "wind over a sea" (Shelley 504), something invisible with effects that can nonetheless be felt, and smelled. In "Moony" the satisfaction Birkin achieved with his stoning was not visual but auditory. In the initial sequence, the phrase "a burst of sound, and a burst of brilliant light" seemed to equate the two sensory modes in their disruption; finally, however, sound achieved the character of light: he "stood and listened" to the "flashes of sound" liberated by his stones.

(Here we arrive at a tangle too thick to more than indicate, that of the relations among the senses, their ideological valences, and their relations to the sublime. Derrida has made us acutely sensitive to the dangers of giving privilege to sound as authentic voice; more broadly, we could acknowledge that to oppose sound to sight will not offer any final escape from the entanglements among Hebrew [voice-oriented] and Hellene [sight-oriented] emphases sedimented within our culture. This all the more since that opposition already may be found between Socrates and Plato. Nonetheless, in reading the romantics, a distinction may be made that cuts across usual divisions to link the visual emphases of Blake and Coleridge against the Burkean imagelessness so important in Wordsworth and Shelley.)

As noted in chapter 4, Shelley's understanding of the temporal processes of art, language, and knowledge, like Lawrence's, involved a "bursting"; Shelley praised the prose of Francis Bacon because it "distends, and then bursts the circumference of the hearer's mind." One of Lawrence's most Shelleyan moments described how authentic poets write: "They blow bubbles of sound and image, which soon burst with the breath of longing for chaos, which fills them" (*Phoenix* 257). The history of poetry in Shelley entailed a sequence of competitive criticism, of which Longinus offered the first model by sketching Plato's relation to Homer and Harold Bloom offered the most prominent recent version. So in his "Ode to the West Wind," Shelley turned to his humanistic purposes the *terza rima* that Dante had invented for the Christian truth of his *Commedia*; in *Prometheus Unbound*, Shelley restored what history had denied us from Aeschylus, while at the same time within the play evoking and correcting the tragic despair of *King Lear*.

Lawrence was very close to Shelley in this area. He observed, for instance, how much it typified our culture that of Aeschylus' trilogy we have preserved only the *Prometheus Bound* (*Letters* 2:248), for, like Shelley, Lawrence saw tragedy, especially in the modern world, as all too likely to offer an anodyne, an acquiescence that kills whatever is most vital in us. Lawrence knew this temptation from experience. During the bleak days of his engagement with Louie Burrows and after his mother's death, Lawrence wrote, "Who can alter fate, and useless it is to rail against it. When I get sore, I always fly to the Greek tragedies; they make one feel sufficiently fatalistic. . . . These Greek tragedies make me quiet and indifferent" (*Letters* 1:235). This is the conventional, "semi-ethical" sublimity against which Eliot warned. But after Lawrence had met Frieda and taken on another of his "several lives" (*Letters* 1:554), his sense changed: "Tragedy ought really to be a great kick at misery," but "all the modern stuff since Flaubert . . . seems like an acceptance" (*Letters* 1:459). In his notable analyses of Dostoevsky, Tolstoy, Hardy, and Thomas Mann, Lawrence elaborated this verdict. In all these writers, he found an incapacity to maintain contact with vital transformative energies, not only in their plots, but also in "that craving for form in fiction," and in the marmoreal style which came from "that passionate desire for the mastery of the medium of narrative, that will of the writer to be greater than and undisputed lord over the stuff he writes" (*Phoenix* 308)—as Gerald is of his men and coal.

As a counterstatement to tragedy, *Women in Love* offered a revisionary rewriting of *The Idiot*, the novel of Dostoevsky's that Lawrence valued most highly and most fully used as a model for some of his own speculations. Just as he found *The Idiot* a novel that took one aspect of life as far as it could go, so *Women in Love* too was about a world at its end. Indeed, both novels are overtly saturated with apocalyptic language. Drawing from the comments Lawrence offered to Middleton Murry while Murry was writing a book on

Dostoevsky, we can say that Lawrence transformed Dostoevsky's "parable" into "art" by unlacing the moral scheme, for "people are not fallen angels." Dostoevsky's Rogozhin pursued "sensual ecstasy" to the murder of Nastasya, "*devouring* the other . . . like a tiger drinking blood," while the saintly Myshkin lapsed into "imbecility," and the novel's women served as "mere echoes and objectives of the men" (*Letters* 2:543–44). Against all this, Lawrence's Gerald was crippled in his pursuit of sensual reduction, so that he failed to kill the woman he loved but died instead; Birkin was fleshed out, overcoming the "saviour of the world" tendencies he shared with Myshkin and saving himself first; Gudrun and Ursula, meanwhile, became the book's titular, key figures, breaking free from the schemes even of their author.

But I must be cutting short what is an endless process. Lawrence always found the need to unhinge stability and set it into flow again. Therefore, the flower, the *flow*-er, was a privileged word for him (see *Phoenix* 442 for a relation between "overflowing" and "flower"). Likewise, our bodies are always in the sepulcher, needing to rise, and as an echo of their occasional success in having arisen, the *rose* serves as a recurrent emblem of passionate vitality. Yet look what happened in "Moony" to the term "rose." First it was part of the liberation of energy: "Rapidly, like white birds, the fires all broken *rose* across the pond" (my emphasis). But then, homophonically transformed from an action into a substantive, it became desolate: "The white fragments pulsed up and down . . . apart and brilliant on the water like the petals of a *rose* that the wind has blown far and wide" (my emphasis). Now the energy is in the wind, not the rose, but the next shift reenergized the rose—negatively— "intertwining vigorously and blindly, calling back the scattered fragments." Finally, a "ragged rose" is what endured of the moon after the stoning was over. What once rose comes down again; the risen body is buried again by the chapels and monuments built to it. Even in a work like *Women in Love*, where the images "shatter one another, line by line," some further source of power is needed to keep the work in motion. Writing solicits from us our interpretive power, the stones we critics and readers throw to shatter the old, fixed images and startle new life in again.

The sublime inheres not only in the text, but also in the reader's activity of fixing upon passages, highlighting them in ways that disrupt any equability of composition in favor of intensity of attention, the means by which literary history prolongs itself. Although my analysis has made use of Harold Bloom, no more here than in the first chapter do I accept Bloom's vision of inevitably triumphant poetic strength; instead, with Benjamin I emphasize a more contingent and risky readerly materiality. Before we can achieve the "constellation" which newly relates our present to a past urgently needed for a future we seek, first a process of destruction intervenes. Such alterations prevent stasis, yet they also disrupt any straightforward, cumulative progress; despite their concern for a future, they loop pastward. To conceptualize and figure such a process, without yielding to the despair in de Man's analysis of self-entanglement, is the work at hand.

Chapter 7
F. O. Matthiessen and American Studies: Authorizing a Renaissance

FOR DECADES SINCE his suicide in 1950, F. O. Matthiessen has exerted a compelling attraction. The documentation, analysis, and controversy around him bulk larger than for any other American literary scholar born in the twentieth century, and they grow.

There are at least three good reasons for this posthumous attention. First, Matthiessen played a decisive role in making possible the American academic study of American literature (for short, "American studies"). His major book, *American Renaissance* (1941), has given its name to courses taught at hundreds of institutions. More than any other single factor it enabled hundreds of Ph.D.'s in English to specialize in the American literature of the nineteenth century. Matthiessen himself, however, deplored the "barrenness" of what he termed the "now hopefully obsolescent practice of literary scholars' restricting themselves to the arbitrary confines of a single century in a single country" (*Responsibilities* 169).

Second, Matthiessen, both as a Harvard professor and as a private citizen, was widely and visibly active in left politics of the 1930s and 1940s. Although as a practicing Christian he was not a Communist and disavowed Marxism, he was considered a leading fellow-traveler. The clearest textual focus for this engagement is *From the Heart of Europe* (1948), a memoir of his time in Austria and Czechoslovakia in the months before the Czechoslovak coup of 1948.

Third, both as a teacher and friend, Matthiessen made an intense personal impression. A "collective portrait" by many hands was compiled soon after his death, but the most remarkable testimony came in *Rat and the Devil* (1978), a selection by their friend Louis

Hyde from the thousands of letters exchanged by Matthiessen and the painter Russell Cheney during the twenty years they shared their lives.

The interrelations among these three aspects of Matthiessen's career do not, however, offer an occasion for the rhetoric of "wholeness," even though that rhetoric was extremely important to Matthiessen himself. As a critic, for example, he concluded *American Renaissance* (henceforth abbreviated *AR* in references) by writing of Melville that he fulfilled "what Coleridge held to be the major function of the artist: he brought the whole soul of man into activity" (656). As a politically committed man, he began the book by subscribing to the test of "true scholarship," that it be "for the good and enlightenment of all the people, not for the pampering of a class" (xv). And as early as 1925, he wrote Cheney about their love: "In these last months I am a whole man for the first time: no more dodging or repressing for we gladly accept what we are. And sex now instead of being a nightmare is the most sacred, all embracing gift we have. Now I can see, as this morning, while riding along, a husky labouring feller asleep on a bank, one hand lying heavy across his thighs, and I can thrill at the deep earthiness and blood of him. For I know that I am of blood and earth too, as well as of brain and of soul, and that my whole self waits—and waits gladly—for you" (*Rat* 116).

Some problems about Matthiessen's "wholeness" emerge clearly in comparing the letters and *American Renaissance*. In the long section on Whitman, Matthiessen dispersed over sixty pages references to three topics—homosexuality (*AR* 585; cf. also 535), the "power of sex" (523), and transient "Good Moments" (541)—which are remarkably condensed in an early letter to Cheney. This letter narrated an encounter with a "workman—husky, broad-shouldered, forty" at Wells cathedral. Matthiessen began with a literary reference: this man was "the perfect Chaucerian yeoman," and he concluded by explaining that he wrote so much about the event "not because it is the least bit important, but because it was so natural, so like Walt Whitman." Such cultural awareness did not conflict with but rather enhanced erotic possibilities: "He caught my eye both as a magnificently built feller, and as fitting in so perfectly to the type of fourteenth century work man." He thus embodied the permanence of the people: "He might just as well have been build-

158

ing the original cathederal, as repairing it centuries later." For "about a quarter of a minute" they talked, allowing Matthiessen to note the man's "unusually gentle" voice and "dark full brown" eye. Then, as the man went off, Matthiessen "deliberately let my elbow rub against his belly," for he "wanted to feel the touch of his body as a passing gesture." He acknowledged that he was sexually excited, yet also that "there was no question of not wanting to keep myself for you." The "whole self" allows marginal responses to take on their wholeness: "It thrilled me, not only with sex, but with friendliness" (*Rat* 124).

The problems of temporality here merit further attention: the mythic co-presence of the fourteenth and twentieth centuries, set against its punctual disruption, the "passing gesture," the "good moment." What stands out now, however, is the difference between the sense of reading Whitman in Matthiessen's lively letter and in his monumental book. Between these two ways of reading, and ways of writing about reading, stands a long process of transformative discipline, closely related to issues addressed in the chapter on Arnold. The modern critical practice Leavis called the "discipline of letters" required abandoning the modes of "impressionist" reading, the orientation which M. H. Abrams has called "expressive," and the rhetoric of "flash" and fragment for which the classical antecedent is Longinus on the sublime. To create the centrally authoritative critical identity of *American Renaissance*, much had to be displaced or scattered or disavowed. Loose elbows had to be tucked in. T. S. Eliot's insistence on "form" and "impersonality" in poetry chastened Matthiessen's early commitment to the "human spirit," the "man himself," and the "flash of the spark of life" that reading sets off (*Rat* 102, 133).

Matthiessen joined his generation in sacrificing to modernist discipline a romantic theorist of the "spark," the politically and sexually revolutionary poet Shelley. Even a German left-wing modernist like Theodor Adorno (a year younger than Matthiessen) shared his derogation of Shelley, at least by the time he had emigrated to the United States. The first version of Walter Benjamin's essay on Baudelaire (the primary focus of the next chapter) cited a few lines from Shelley's "Peter Bell the Third" to contrast their "directness and harshness" (*Härte*, which may also be translated "rigor"!) to the obliquity with which Baudelaire represented Paris:

Hell is a city much like London,
A populous and smoky city;
There are all sorts of people undone,
And there is little or no fun done;
Small justice shown, and still less pity.
(lines 147–51; *Charles Baudelaire* 59)

In criticizing the essay, Adorno accused Benjamin of being fooled
by the "extraordinary" quality of the German translation of Shelley,
for "directness and harshness are as a rule not exactly his characteristics" (Benjamin, *Gesammelte Schriften*, 1:1112). Adorno no
doubt felt the odds were on his side, since the translation was by a
notoriously harsh and direct German poet—Brecht. In fact the
translation is lucidly literal although slightly less lapidary, and
without the savage comedy of the rhyme "undone / fun done":

Die Hölle ist eine Stadt, sehr ähnlich London—
Eine volkreiche und eine rauchige Stadt.
Dort gibt es alle Arten von ruinierten Leuten
Und dort ist wenig oder gar kein Spass
Wenig Gerechtigkeit und noch weniger Mitleid.
(Benjamin, *Gesammelte Schriften*, 1.2:562)

Brecht and Benjamin had been together in Denmark in 1938. While
Benjamin was drafting the essay, Brecht wrote one of his several
pieces against Lukács's conception of realism ("Weite"). This one
translated much of Shelley's "Mask of Anarchy" (which directly
precedes "Peter Bell the Third" in the Oxford Standard Authors edition to which Benjamin referred), to demonstrate that in his very
different way Shelley was as important a model for realism as Lukács's Balzac. It seems likely that Brecht did the "Peter Bell" translation for Benjamin, since it is not included in the standard edition
of his works, which, however, was completed before Benjamin's
essay reached publication.

Matthiessen's hostility to Shelley, then, was representative, but
it is especially significant because in the early letters, Matthiessen
was reading Shelley with positive engagement. At one point he even
archly identified himself with Shelley in their attachment to older
men (*Rat* 33, 78, 84). By *American Renaissance*, however, T. S.
Eliot's denigration of Shelley was in full force. Some half-dozen

times Shelley was evoked for predictable dismissals (*AR* 259, 311, 353, 388). Such gestures contributed to the critical authority of *American Renaissance* because they certified Matthiessen as emotionally "mature," and they distanced him from a figure whose philosophic, political, and literary activities can seem terribly unintegrated—in part, we have seen, because of his full commitment to both ends of polarities. Yet in the spread and energy of his own activism, Matthiessen more closely resembled Shelley than any of the antiselves he treated in *American Renaissance*.

These analyses suggest that the problem of the whole, the indivisible, the individual, requires attention to institutional circumstances. Can we make a whole without exclusion and divisiveness? Matthiessen joined Hawthorne in abjuring the "damned mob of scribbling women" (*AR* x); students ask me why Frederick Douglass showed insufficient "devotion to the possibilities of democracy" (*AR* ix) for Matthiessen even to mention him. These are matters of institutional power: in order to be a productive unit, a field must be marked off, delimited, defined—even if your commitment is to "all the people."

This kind of discrepancy is crucial to understanding the effects of Matthiessen's career. For Matthiessen's power to authorize an American Renaissance came from his mobilizing certain figures that were then appropriated in ways contrary to his intentions. Recall the irony that his work produced specialists of a sort which he himself considered "hopefully obsolescent." No less striking is the nationalist force achieved by Matthiessen's emphatically internal tional undertaking.

I want to explore in some detail Matthiessen's title: *American Renaissance: Art and Expression in the Age of Emerson and Whitman*. First off, it is significant to my institutional focus that the phrase which later American literary culture most closely identifies with Matthiessen was not originally his own, but provided by a younger colleague (Levin, preface to *Power*). It was important to Matthiessen that his work be collegial, based more broadly than in the solitary individual. Matthiessen acknowledged the oddity of considering the mid-nineteenth century a cultural "re-birth." He explained that "America's way of producing a renaissance" lay in

161

"affirming its rightful heritage in the whole expanse of art and culture" (*AR* vii). This still-cryptic clarification is better understood through a quotation from André Malraux cited a few pages later: "Every civilization is like the Renaissance, and creates its own heritage out of everything in the past that helps it to surpass itself" (xv n.). The theory of literary history adumbrated here deserves considerable attention, but for the moment note how obscure this line of intention has become; few can recall this logic for the title.

For "renaissance" has a force of its own. Ever since the historiographic notion was elaborated by Michelet and Burckhardt—in 1845 and 1860, exactly bracketing Matthiessen's period—"Renaissance" has carried a glamorous freight of secularism, progress, and preeminent individuality. All these values were in fact suspect to Matthiessen, but his title's figure translated "the Renaissance" westward to America just when the old, transatlantic Renaissance was being conservatively reevaluated in works like *The Allegory of Love* (C. S. Lewis, 1936) and *The Renaissance and English Humanism* (Douglas Bush, 1939). Matthiessen supported their claims for the medieval continuities of the Renaissance, emphasizing Christianity and traditional literary modes (cf. *AR* 246). But that was not how his figure worked.

What is the particular force of an "American" renaissance? As "American," it is new; more paradoxically, it is a repetition, a "renaissance of the Renaissance." It does for the Renaissance what the Renaissance had done for antiquity. Most important, however, it is *national*. People had long spoken of a Concord or Boston or New England "renaissance," but this was no longer local, regional, or sectional. It was shared among "all the people." Contrast Perry Miller's *The New England Mind* (1939), which not only sectionalized but also split off "mind" from the vigorous physical embodiment suggested by "Renaissance."

In emphasizing his focus on literature as "works of art" rather than as philosophical or social practice, Matthiessen imagined books that he might have written instead: *The Age of Swedenborg*, on transcendental thought; or *The Age of Fourier* on "radical movements" (*AR* vii–viii). The contrast of Emerson and Whitman with Swedenborg and Fourier strikes home. Emerson and Whitman are major, central, household words; Swedenborg and Fourier are minor, eccentric, obscure—and not even American. The literary and the American unite against the foreign, philosophical, and radical.

F. O. Matthiessen and American Studies

Matthiessen's title promoted a euphoria of America that gained power against the grain of his own methodological precepts and critical practice. From a review-essay of 1929 on the need to rewrite American literary history, to the lecture of 1949 on "The Responsibilities of the Critic," Matthiessen insisted on America's relation to "Europe" (which includes England) (*Responsibilities* 181, 12). His most important books before and after *American Renaissance* addressed T. S. Eliot and Henry James, the most notoriously transatlantic of America's great writers. In *American Renaissance* itself Shakespeare occupied more lines of the index than did Thoreau! Matthiessen conceived of his subject as essentially national *and* comparative. He taught courses on world drama, Shakespeare, and an introduction to major English poets. American studies has not followed Matthiessen's precept or practice, even while drawing its warrant to exist from him. His radical energies succeeded more in reinvigorating than in remaking culturally established figures.

In speaking of a "euphoria of America," I do not mean that Matthiessen was blind to social and political problems or that he didn't care about them. *American Renaissance* immediately proclaimed its solidarity with "those who believe now in the dynamic extension of democracy on economic as well as political levels" (4). But in writing about the social problems of America, Matthiessen failed to achieve specificity comparable to what he achieved in writing about the literary successes. Thus in Ahab he found an "ominous glimpse of what was to result when the Emersonian will to virtue became in less innocent natures the will to power and conquest." That will gave us the "empire-builders of the post–Civil War world," the "strong-willed individuals who seized the land and gutted the forests and built the railroads" (459). Matthiessen's rhetoric conflated the will with the deed, while introducing an oversharp chronological boundary. He failed to acknowledge that already in the 1850s, precisely in railroad building, not the tragic individual but the limited-liability corporation was the major agency, drawing capital from many sources, developing the techniques of bureaucratic management to organize the activities of its employees (the "hands" who executed the "will"), and even developing the ideology of free enterprise in order to get rid of existing government activities.

Matthiessen echoed the individualistic focus of Matthew Josephson's *The Robber Barons* (1934) but ignored the contrary perspective of Adolf Berle and Gardiner Means in *The Modern Corporation and*

Private Property (1933), which James Burnham brought to fruit in *The Managerial Revolution* (1941). Alfred Chandler's painstaking historical work on the "Visible Hand" of the "Managerial Revolution in American Business" postdates Matthiessen, but the classic work of Matthiessen's older contemporary George Rogers Taylor bears out my emphases on the connection of prewar to postwar (Taylor 101), the prevalence of corporate over individual enterprise (240–42), and the role of giant, bureaucratic corporations in fomenting the ideology of private enterprise (383). Instead of this analytic detail, Matthiessen's approach produced an abstract division from a willed unity. That is, his theology provided the human potential for evil (*AR* 180), and his intellectual history provided the rise of "individualism" in the American 1830s (*AR* 5–6). The two combined to produce the figure of the evil individuals who obstruct the common good of an otherwise united American People.

Throughout the 1930s, the negative term of "individualism" and the positive terms of the "community" or the "people" figured in the discourse of widely different American intellectuals (Pells 118). Matthiessen's use of such terms in *American Renaissance* had an important relation to the particular political and rhetorical strategy of the Popular Front (or "People's Front"), which from 1935 was the Communist party line. In contrast to the militantly divisive rhetoric of the "Third Period," which attacked even socialists as "social fascists," the Popular Front, in belated response to Hitler's success, emphasized a defensive policy of alliance building. The situation no longer promised imminent apocalypse, requiring radical separation of sheep from goats; now, rather, from liberals to communists all were sheep together, except for that wolf out there. This policy meant a changed stance toward America. In 1933 Granville Hicks published *The Great Tradition*, on American fiction after the Civil War. In reviewing it, Matthiessen shared its concern with "the class war which is becoming increasingly the central fact of American life" (*Responsibilities* 197). In 1938, still on the staff of the *New Masses*, Hicks published his next book, *I Like America*.

Matthiessen was not a Communist party member, he did not always follow party positions, but the strategy of the Popular Front clearly appealed to him. I have already noted his rhetoric of "all the people" and noted the absence of class analysis in *American Renaissance*. As opposed to earlier Communist emphasis on independent proletarian culture, the Popular Front emphasized defending the "cultural heritage," which included the masterpieces produced by the bourgeoisie. This project defined Georg Lukács's major studies of nineteenth-century realism as well as André Malraux's brilliant speech on "The Cultural Heritage" at the second congress of the International Association of Writers for the Defense of Culture, held in London in 1936 (see further my "Struggle for the Cultural Heritage"). This was the text Matthiessen quoted for its crucial assertion that every civilization is like the Renaissance.

To locate Matthiessen's rhetoric in relation to the Popular Front helps to clarify what I find *American Renaissance*'s most extraordinary idealization: the diminishment of the Civil War. The Civil War was not even indexed, although it was not literally absent from the book. It allowed for tragic poetry by Melville and Whitman, and it was mentioned again and again—as in the passage just cited on "empire builders"—as a marker, dividing the American Renaissance from an age of rampantly destructive individualism. But the war was not integrated into any understanding of the renaissance. Matthiessen demonstrated that his object of study, the literary, functioned for writers as an evasion, though not a complete disengagement, from a political life of which they did not wholeheartedly approve (e.g., *AR* 67). But his interpretations of this compromise failed to reckon with the affirmative support compromise still gave to dubious policies. It is both more understandable and less commendable than Matthiessen suggested that Hawthorne, despite his skeptical conservatism, supported the party of Jackson. For the Democratic party's commitment to slavery made "the Democracy" include much less than "all the people," as I detail in "The Politics of *The Scarlet Letter*." Rather than facing up to divisions within the renaissance, Matthiessen divided the renaissance from the war and segregated qualities "before" and "after." His wish for wholeness led to disconnection.

By splitting off the war, Matthiessen forestalled comparisons between the 1850s and 1930s that the Depression had provoked. Edmund Wilson's "An Appeal to Progressives" (1931), for example, defined the time as "one of the turning-points in our history, our first real crisis since the Civil War" (524–25). The comparison between the 1850s and 1930s was exciting for a militant strategy but embarrassing for a strategy of alliance and containment. If, as

Charles and Mary Beard argued in *The Rise of American Civilization* (1927), the Civil War had been "The Second American Revolution," then the analogy pointed to a class war that would make a third.

Yet to evade the analogy left a problem: what would mobilize change if "democracy" already existed and "class struggle" was forbidden? This impasse structured *American Renaissance*. Matthiessen was celebrating what he knew *must* be transformed. Renaissance yielded to Civil War, and the Popular Front too must yield to something else, but there was no acceptable image for that new state except an idealization of the present state. The result was an unhistorical freezing.

This conjunction between Matthiessen's cultural politics and those of the Popular Front has two consequences. First, it grants greater value and dignity to the cultural results of the Popular Front than they have been allowed in the most authoritative representations. Lionel Trilling devoted his career to portraying American "liberal" culture as so Stalinized as to make impossible any live or complex literary response. Such claims depend upon ignoring Matthiessen, as Trilling did, or considering his politics as unrelated to his critical accomplishments, as Irving Howe has done (*Margin* 156–58).

Lionel Trilling did not literally ignore Matthiessen. He reviewed Matthiessen's study of James, and the two appeared together on a panel (*Rat* 300, 333), yet the treatment of Matthiessen in Trilling's fundamental position paper, "Reality in America" (1950), is remarkable. The essay asserted that Parrington dominated "the college course in American literature" nationwide whenever it aimed to be "vigorous" rather than "genteel", an even stronger claim than Trilling had ventured in the essay's first version, "Parrington, Mr. Smith, and Reality" (1940). Yet according to Henry Nash Smith, also writing in 1950, Parrington's dominance in the thirties had yielded to *American Renaissance* in the forties. Trilling then spotlighted "the dark and bloody crossroads where literature and politics meet," that is, the choice between James and Dreiser. Having posed the inevitability of choice, Trilling then quoted Matthiessen's praise of Dreiser while remarking Matthiessen's admiration for James and criticism of Parrington, but he failed to notice the disruptive anomaly this introduced into his schematization (*Liberal Imagination* 1,

166

8, 12). Elsewhere in the volume Trilling repeated his claims for the divorce between "our liberal educated class and the best of the literary mind of our time" (94), i.e., Proust, Joyce, Lawrence, Eliot, and other modern masters. Again, Matthiessen's existence made nonsense of this claim, and he was ignored.

It is worth remarking the contrasted starting points Matthiessen and Trilling specified for their social thought about America. Matthiessen recalled the "comradeship" shared during college with older, foreign-born workers he helped to instruct in English, and he noted the self-awareness as an "American" provoked by his time in England as a Rhodes Scholar (*From the Heart* 72, 23). For Trilling, "America" only became "available" to his "imagination" through the "Jewish situation" (itself necessarily related to "social class") that he discovered working with the *Menorah Journal* in the late twenties (*Last Decade* 14–15). Matthiessen's national awakening obliterated class and ethnic divisions; Trilling's arose from them.

The second consequence of noting Matthiessen's relation to the Popular Front is to highlight the dangers of such a strategy of reconciliation, a special concern now when a renewed academic Marxism offers to embrace all other intellectual positions, a prospect to which the chapter on Jameson will return. Matthiessen's Popular Front figure of "America" suffered a sobering fate. The war (which, after all, did come) reconstellated American politics, and the figure of "America" that began as a Depression tactic of harmony became a postwar myth of empire. A mobilization intended as oppositional became incorporated hegemonically; American studies gained power by nationalistically appropriating Mattthiessen.

"Reconciliation" is not only a political strategy but also a well-known operation in literary theory. Having analyzed the discrepancy between Matthiessen's internationalism and the nationalist authority his work achieved, I want now to address another area of discrepancy: Matthiessen's attempt to use the politically conservative theory of the "symbol" in a critical discourse intended to be politically progressive.

American Renaissance made a major commitment to literary theory, both as views of the 1850s and as a current activity—"our own developing conceptions of literature" (*AR* vii). Matthiessen was alert to the significance of M. H. Abrams' work, citing the dissertation version of *The Mirror and the Lamp* (*AR* 261). Matthiessen related the theory and practice of his chosen writers to his own understanding of "the nature of literature" (xiii) on such topics as mode (myth), genre (tragedy), and figurative language (allegory and symbolism). Over the four decades of American studies, such theoretical engagement has not flourished, and where it has recently begun to emerge, it appears as an imported innovation rather than as reclaiming a founding heritage. The single theoretical topic that has become institutionally part of normal procedure is nationalistic: the question of "American romance"—a topic Matthiessen briefly highlighted but also seriously limited (*AR* 264ff.). Just as comparative literature became the subfield that kept alive Matthiessen's internationalism, New Criticism after the war became less a movement than a province, the subfield into which his theoretical commitments were segregated and developed.

Matthiessen's major theoretical resource was Coleridge, as elucidated by I. A. Richards in response to T. S. Eliot, but Matthiessen understood and emphasized that Coleridge's position made larger claims than Eliot or Richards or, as we have seen, Robert Penn Warren would accept. Eliot wished to separate poet from poem, and Richards used Coleridge in the service of utilitarian atheism, while Matthiessen proclaimed that "the transcendental theory of art is a theory of knowledge and religion as well" (*AR* 31).

The crucial passage in Coleridge has already been cited. In the fourteenth chapter of the *Biographia Literaria*, the poet, "described in *ideal* perfection, brings the whole soul of man into activity" through the "power" of "imagination," which "reveals itself in the balance or reconciliation of opposite or discordant qualities," such as general and concrete or individual and representative (*Collected Works* 7.2:15–16). From this passage, Richards in the chapter on "Imagination" in *Principles of Literary Criticism* elaborated a theory of tragedy as the most "inclusive" possible "attitude," which by contemplating the most extreme opposites—fear and pity— achieved a stable poise that he even called "invulnerable." Matthiessen drew also upon Coleridge's theory of the "symbol," which "enunciates the whole" yet "abides itself as a living part in that Unity, of which it is the representative" (*Collected Works* 6:30). Coleridge's image for this condition is "translucence," above all of

168

"the Eternal through and in the Temporal." This exposition of the symbol appeared in *The Statesman's Manual*, a theological guide to conservative politics for post-Napoleonic, early industrial England.

Matthiessen's aesthetics agreed with Coleridge's, as did his theology, but his politics, starting from a similar romantic anticapitalism, differed widely. Matthiessen identified himself with Hazlitt (*From the Heart* 83), who remained loyal to the revolutionary cause despite its horrors, rather than like Coleridge turning away in fright or revulsion. How could Matthiessen be a trinitarian formalist radical?

He could if radicalism meant reconciliation. The Popular Front enabled Matthiessen's criticism, his politics, and his religion to interact powerfully and positively. The strategy of alliance allowed these different elements to share the same discursive space. *The Achievement of T. S. Eliot*, written just before the Popular Front, is weaker than *American Renaissance* because Matthiessen's politics found no place in it. This is not to claim Matthiessen "followed" the line; rather, the line "released" him to bring together elements previously separated. But this is not to say either that they make a perfect whole.

Each of these three components had its own particular term for the fantasied unity, the figure of wholeness, that their interaction produced as "American Renaissance." For Matthiessen the political leftist, that term would be "all the people" in the People's Front. For Matthiessen the critical formalist, the ideal term of wholeness was "literature" itself. For the Christian, in a tradition that reached back into the seventeenth century and through Jonathan Edwards, as Richard Niebuhr and Sacvan Bercovitch have demonstrated, that term would be "America." Bercovitch has analyzed the "American Jeremiad" as provoking a sense of crisis that finally produces no fundamental change but reaffirms the existing "American" way. This logic I find operates like that of Coleridge's aesthetics or Popular Front politics—in Melville's phrase, "By their very contradictions they are made to coincide." This formula offers an American translation for the "reconciliation under duress" that Theodor Adorno criticized in Georg Lukács's Stalinist Hegelian realism.

The Jeremiad position is not easy or complacent; it is anguished and sincere, but it stands in a false position. Let me explain this through Matthiessen's reading of "The Try-Works." In this chapter from *Moby-Dick*, "Ahab's tyrannic will" is "symbolized," Matthiessen argued, through the process by which "the act of burning down the blubber on the ship's deck at night becomes, in its lurid flame, 'the material counterpart of her monomaniac commander's soul.'" From the spiritual symbolized in the physical, Matthiessen went on to read the representative from the individual: "It seemed then to Ishmael, in a rare symbol for individualistic recklessness—indeed for a whole era of American development—'that whatever swift, rushing thing I stood on was not so much bound to any haven ahead as rushing from all havens astern'" (*AR* 290). Matthiessen's exposition of the "symbol" here interacted with the motifs of America and individualism that I earlier analyzed. His trinitarian aesthetic highlighted the figure of embodiment ("material counterpart"), but in emphasizing the "will," Matthiessen's reading omitted the loose elbows, the actual bodies, the "Tartarean shapes of the pagan harpooneers," and the watch with "tawny features . . . begrimed with smoke and sweat, their matted beards, and the contrasting barbaric brilliancy of their teeth." In their racist demonization, these bodies did not represent "all the people."

As earlier "America" was idealized, here the literary was idealized as "symbol." So vivid was Melville's figure that Matthiessen took it as truth, embodying all that we need to know. Ishmael, however, went on to define his vision of "rushing from all havens astern" as a double error. He mistook his object, for it referred not to the try-works scene but his backward view; and he mistook himself—as his mind wandered, his body turned: "Lo! in my brief sleep I had turned myself about, and was fronting the ship's stern. . . . In an instant I faced back, just in time to prevent the vessel from flying up into the wind, and very probably capsizing her. How glad and how grateful the relief from this unnatural hallucination of the night." Not the demonic scene, but the observer's error posed the real threat: Ishmael neglected his responsibility as helmsman. Matthiessen, then, ignored literature's own recognition that it may err: "Wrapped, for that interval, in darkness myself, I but the better saw the redness, the madness, and the ghastliness of others." Thus, even at its most passionately intelligent and concerned, the stance of American studies cultural criticism has been misplaced, through a disorienting, self-involved detachment just at the moment it believed itself most perceptively involved with the way things are.

This danger threatens also the course of "detachment" Benjamin urged for historical materialism, yet despite the dangers these courses merit attention.

After treating the politics of America and of the theory of literature in Matthiessen's work, I want now to assess the possibilities for a new literary history in the practice of *American Renaissance*. These possibilities are still "new" after forty years not only because American studies failed to pick them up, but also because Matthiessen's own explicit theory of atemporal wholeness obscured his recurrent perception of transient, fragmentary moments.

I have mentioned the "freezing" of time and denial of history in Matthiessen's reading. Matthiessen used the term "structure" for the wholeness achieved by a successful symbol, a symbolic "form," when it reconciled the eternal and the temporal. His negative term for the failure of this process was "moments." Matthiessen most pointedly set these terms in opposition discussing D. H. Lawrence, that bogey of New Criticism (*AR* 313). Yet despite Lawrence's anti-Coleridgean emphases and his Shelleyan loyalties, he was quite important to Matthiessen, and Matthiessen's evaluation was more ambivalent than his theory. Indeed, when Melville himself reached the imaginative "level where both abstraction and concretion may have full play," Matthiessen did not emphasize symbolic stability; he observed instead that this was "not a level which . . . he can sustain for long—but rather, a precarious point of equilibrium between two opposed forces" (464). Melville could not "hold the wave at the crest" (408). Such evanescence resonates less with the New Critics' Coleridge than with the impressionists' Pater, who wrote: "This at least of flamelike our life has, that it is but the concurrence, renewed from moment to moment, of forces parting sooner or later" (*Renaissance* 187). Such a Paterian "tragic dividing of forces on their ways" rekindles autumnally what Emerson more buoyantly had asserted. Not an enduring "translucence" but the intermittent flare of moments proved in practice what Matthiessen found. Cleanth Brooks observed that Matthiessen's book on Eliot failed to offer a "complete, consecutive examination" of *The Waste Land* (*Modern Poetry* 136), and this remained true of *American Renaissance*. Matthiessen was typically a reader of passages, a judge of moments. The American Renaissance itself from the beginning stood as a moment: "The starting point for this book was my realization of how great a number of our past masterpieces were produced in one extraordinarily concentrated moment of expression" (*AR* vii).

As Aristotle is the exemplary structuralist, the great critic of the moment is Longinus on the sublime. Against structural unity, we have noted that the sublime is a "flash of lightning" that "scatters all before it." Longinus' discontinuous theory of influence—as the agonistic relation between two literary consciousnesses across a wide span of time, like that of Plato to Homer—offers the nearest precedent to Harold Bloom's "revisionary" theory of poetry. Bloom emphasized, however, the important precedent for his work in Emerson, and I would note that Matthiessen found it there: "Emerson knew that each age turns to particular authors of the past, not because of the authors but because of its own needs and preoccupations that those authors help make articulate" (*AR* 101–2). Thus, Melville achieved "his own full strength" through the "challenge" of Shakespeare (*AR* 424). Such a dynamic, recall, was also Malraux's claim in "The Cultural Heritage." In an italicized formulation that Matthiessen cited, "*A heritage is not transmitted, it must be conquered*" (xv n.). The energy of struggle, deflected by the Popular Front away from politics, reappears within culture.

Matthiessen understood that such claims violated established ways of conceiving and writing history, and he worried over historiographic method. He knew personally the painful struggle to possess a tradition. He wrote to Cheney in 1925: "This life of ours is entirely new—neither of us know of a parallel case. We stand in the middle of an uncharted, uninhabited country. That there have been other unions like ours is obvious, but we are unable to draw on their experience" (*Rat* 71). Against such blanking-out, Matthiessen found his own needs and preoccupations articulated in Whitman and in Proust. He accepted Richards' claim that great writing required "availability of experience" (*AR* 129).

For his own historical project Matthiessen rejected "the descriptive narrative of literary history" (*AR* vii). He was not alone in rejecting narrative. In 1929 there had appeared in England Namier's *The Structure of Politics at the Accession of George III* and in

172

France the first issue of the great journal *Annales*. Matthiessen, however, also rejected analytic history writing. Against scientific digging "into . . . the economic, social, and religious causes" (vii), Matthiessen chose Richards' analytic of experience. His project shared this ground with Walter Benjamin's essay on "The Story-teller" (1936) and Sartre's *Nausea* (1938), both of which lamented the unavailability of "experience" and marked a crisis of narrativity. Frank Kermode's *Romantic Image* studied Anglo-American modernist alternatives to this failure of narrative discourse.

Matthiessen evaded this crisis by studying the "fusions of form and content" that defined "*what* these books were as works of art" (vii). This aesthetic ontology projected a Coleridgean, "symbolic" history like that of Joyce's *Ulysses*. There one day's happenings come into contact with as much of the human cultural past as it could possibly evoke. Likewise, Matthiessen's "moment" focused centuries of American cultural history from the Puritans through James and Eliot. This mythic rhetoric leveled history into what Matthiessen quoted Thomas Mann as calling "recurrence, timelessness, a perpetual present" (*AR* 629), a relationship of temporality that was "continuous," as Matthiessen quoted Eliot on Joyce (630).

In *American Renaissance* there also operated, however, a temporal orientation that aimed not to perpetuate but to innovate, signaled by Matthiessen's sole positive citation of Nietzsche: "Only the supreme power of the present can interpret the past," and such power required the interpreter to be "architect of the future" (*AR* 629 n.). The urgency of relationship between this particular present moment and particular past moments contrasts both to the continuous linear sequence of traditional narrative time and to the equally continuous homogeneity of modernist myth. It produces a discontinuous, textured, historical temporality. One model for this could be found in Proust, whose correlation of moments through "involuntary memory" again highlighted Richards' problem of availability, which Matthiessen found as struggle in Malraux. During Matthiessen's work on *American Renaissance*, the critic most suggestively rethinking literary history—and working on Whitman's contemporary Baudelaire—was Walter Benjamin. (At one sole moment, Whitman occurs disruptively in Benjamin's "Central Park" notebook, 50.) It is worth noting that Malraux's original "Sur l'héritage culturel" referred to Benjamin's study of the artwork and mass reproduction (4), but that in translating and editing Malraux for the *New Republic*, Malcolm Cowley omitted that reference.

In his "Theses on the Philosophy of History," Benjamin characterized the relation between one historical moment and another as a "constellation" (*Illuminations* 263) and argued that "to articulate the past historically" meant to "seize hold of a memory as it flashes up at a moment of danger" (255)—as the French revolutionaries did with the Roman republic. This claim illuminates Matthiessen's conjunction of the 1850s and 1930s, his urgent sense that these were exactly the writers "all the people" needed at the moment of solidarity against the danger of fascism, disconnecting them from the Civil War in order to join them to "now."

Benjamin, however, opposed the Popular Front strategy. He deprecated the preservation of "cultural treasures," for they are tainted with "barbarism" (*Illuminations* 256) both in their origin and in their transmission. He urged instead "the fight for the oppressed past" (263), to redeem what was once stigmatized and suppressed as "minor" (254). Perhaps Matthiessen fulfilled this task, in rejecting the cultural treasures of Holmes, Longfellow, and Lowell to rescue once-marginal writers as Emerson, Thoreau, Hawthorne, Melville, and Whitman had been in their time. Matthiessen, however, disavowed any canon-shifting intervention, deferring to the judgment of "the successive generations of common readers" (*AR* xi) who selected the five authors. This version of the Popular Front he at once reconciled with the apparently contradictory claim by Ezra Pound that "the history of an art . . . is the history of masterwork" (xi).

Following Benjamin, I have tried both to specify the "barbarism" at work in Matthiessen's book and to "redeem" certain emphases and practices obscured through the representation of Matthiessen produced in American studies. Benjamin's concern with the cultural apparatus, his care for technical matters that relate the means chosen to the ends desired, leads me to a final question, which bears on Matthiessen's claims about his chosen writers, on his own project in his book, and on work any of us might do: can one espouse and further "all the people" by writing "masterwork"? *American Renaissance* achieved its masterful unity through the construction of figures that misrepresented Matthiessen's cherished values. Their effect was not a symbolic translucence but an allegorical alienation. He mobilized "America" on behalf of internationalism; he mobilized "renaissance" on behalf of communalism; he mobilized the theory of "structure" but actually elucidated "moments." The project of "wholeness" involved harmonizing, centralizing, normalizing, and "identifying." By tucking in elbows, Matthiessen empowered a particular self and work and nation and also rejected particular "other" identities, such as Shelley, and dispersed others, such as Whitman.

Near the end of his decade writing *American Renaissance*, Matthiessen suffered a psychic breakdown. While he was briefly hospitalized, Matthiessen posed as life-or-death choices the kind of issues that have concerned my analysis—Aristotle versus Longinus, structure versus moment. He asked, was it any reason to kill himself if his failure to accomplish this project proved to him that "I am an enthusiast trying to be a critic . . . a rhapsode trying to be an Aristotelian" (*Rat* 246)?

Matthiessen questioned the value for life of this discipline, this struggle of the will to define, formulate, mobilize, and authorize an American Renaissance. His question took its terms from a punning Latin phrase that evoked the extinction of democratic politics in ancient Rome and—as Cesare Borgia's motto—the assertion of identity in Renaissance Italy: "Must it be aut Caesar aut nullus?"—that is, is the only choice that between Caesar and utter nonentity? Only if we can define better alternatives for the intellectual career is there any chance to be of much use to "all the people."

Chapter 8
Walter Benjamin and Materialist Historiography: Romanticism, Experience, and the City

THIS CHAPTER JUXTAPOSES two explorations provoked by Walter Benjamin's large project on Baudelaire and Paris. In the first, Benjamin's work is used as if it gave the "hidden figure" (one of his favorite terms) with which to "constellate" (another of his terms) Wordsworth and Conrad anew in our literary-historical understanding. Implicitly, Benjamin himself becomes part of the tradition of urban writing that he analyzed but could not stand wholly apart from. He remains our contemporary insofar as his analytic modes still bring fresh results, and yet he belongs to a history that for us stands somewhat in the past. In the second exploration, Benjamin comes under more intensive scrutiny, for the apparent power of his insights to link so unusual a pair as Charles Baudelaire and Emily Dickinson raises questions about the precision of both his substantive claims and his theoretical perspectives regarding literary history.

WORDSWORTH AND CONRAD

This section tries to resituate the dilemma that Conrad continues to pose for literary history, exemplified in the opposed views held by two of his best critics. Ian Watt moved from a close analysis of the preface to *The Nigger of the "Narcissus"* to generalize: "Conrad represents the same central tradition of Romanticism of which

Wordsworth is perhaps the most representative figure. Both men were by nature antipathetic to the more extreme forms of romantic individualism; and Conrad's theory in the Preface implicitly denies the basic division between the artist and the general public which such writers as Byron, Baudelaire, or later the Symbolists and the Decadents had made essential to their theory and practice" ("Conrad's Preface" 105; Watt's *Conrad* moderated this position, briefly acknowledging the problems I emphasize [80–82]). In contrast, Edward W. Said began his survey of Conrad's *oeuvre* by announcing that the "irony" he found in Conrad "has a crucial place in the history of the duplicity of language which since Nietzsche, Marx, and Freud has made the study of the orders of language so focal" (*World* 90).

The line seems clearly drawn between the modernist Conrad and the romantic: Said's ironical Conrad and the Conrad of Watt and his follower David Thorburn, who saw Conrad's "decisive allegiances with the century of Wordsworth," especially in a passage from the preface that "emphasizes the . . . Romantic virtue of sincerity" (Thorburn 151–52). Yet the virtues that we, or even the romantics, profess and value are not always the ones that we practice. If it is good historiography to link writers on the basis of the values they share, it may be no less good to link writers through their common problems and the shifts by which they coped with these problems. Our "study of the orders of language" may begin in earnest with Marx, Nietzsche, and Freud, but the "duplicity of language" itself has no such recent beginning. Wordsworth's language was more duplicitous than Watt or Thorburn have acknowledged, as I have already argued at length in my reading of *The Prelude*. Wordsworth shared much not only with Conrad but also with Baudelaire, and their common strategies define a major strand in the literary history of the period from the French Revolution to the Great War. Against Watt's emphasis on a "central tradition," I find that Wordsworth and Conrad deploy what Walter Benjamin called, apropos of Baudelaire, "the art of being off center" (*die Kunst des Exzentriks*) (*Gesammelte Schriften* 1:632; *Illuminations* 176; henceforth abbreviated *GS* and *I*).

We may begin by examining more closely Watt's characterization of what Wordsworth and Conrad shared. Even if we grant that Wordsworth was "by nature antipathetic to the more extreme forms of Romantic individualism," nonetheless, his situation, the social order in which his language existed, what his culture allowed him to make of his nature, drove him to what some of his most astute and by no means unsympathetic contemporaries recognized as extreme individualism. To Keats it was Wordsworth, not as for Watt Byron, who represented the "egotistical sublime" (1:387). The "ballads" to which Wordsworth in 1800 wrote his great preface were "lyrical": that is, "the feeling therein developed gives importance to the action and situation, and not the action and situation to the feeling" (*Prose* 1:129). Of this aspect of Wordsworth's poetry Hazlitt observed, "He hardly ever avails himself of remarkable objects or situations, but, in general, rejects them as interfering with the workings of his own mind, as disturbing the smooth, deep, majestic current of his own feelings. . . . An intense intellectual egotism swallows up everything. . . . It is as if there were nothing but himself and the universe. . . . All other interests are absorbed in the deeper interests of his own thoughts" (4:112–13).

This egotism appears only to reflective, analytic inspection. Hazlitt recognized that it was no simple self-love: "His egotism is in some respects madness, for he scorns even the admiration of himself" (5:163). Hazlitt's repeated linkage of Wordsworth and Rousseau clarifies the problem. Both were theorists of community, solidarity, sincerity, out of want; all they really knew was the lack of community, the impossibility of public sincerity. So Raymond Williams described Wordsworth's play of feeling around the subject of "The Old Cumberland Beggar": "It is no longer from the practice of community, or from the spirit of protest at its inadequacy, but from

> this solitary being,
> This helpless wanderer

that the instinct of fellow-feeling is derived. Thus an isolation and silence and loneliness have become the only carriers of nature and community against . . . ordinary society. . . . The spirit of community has been dispossessed and isolated" (*Country* 131).

One might ground the claim that Wordsworth "denies the basic division between the artist and the general public" in his famous definition of the poet as "a man speaking to men" (*Prose* 1:138).

Yet the sincerity of this ideal was immediately compromised by its appearance on a page and by the printed, not spoken, poems it introduced. At this crucial point Wordsworth's writing, no less than Conrad's (when using Marlow) though in a different way, "tries . . . overtly to negate itself as *writing*" (Said, *World*, 130). Here Wordsworth appealed hopefully to a community of "men" (in discussing "Nutting" I have touched on the gender issues here), but at another moment in the preface he recognized that such a community did not exist. Even if it once existed for ballads, it must now, painfully, be recreated for lyrical ballads: "One request I must make of my reader, which is, that in judging these poems he would decide by his own feelings genuinely, and not by reflection upon what will probably be the judgment of others" (*Prose* 1:155). Such a request could be warranted only by the absence of any community of "feelings" (since such absence would make it impossible to predict "the judgment of others") or else by the presence of what Williams called "ordinary society"—what Wordsworth and Coleridge called "the public"—from whose bad consensus one must be torn away into true individuality, only then perhaps to rejoin "the people."

In the preface, Wordsworth himself analyzed the state of feeling in his day. It was an age of "gross and violent stimulants" that betrayed the "beauty and dignity" of the "human mind" and made "blunt" its "discriminating powers" (*Prose* 1:129). The "causes" of this process were "unknown to former times" and were "acting with a combined force"; they included especially "the great national events which are daily taking place, and the increasing accumulation of men in the cities, where the uniformity of their occupations produces a craving for extraordinary incident, which the rapid communication of intelligence hourly gratifies" (1:129). This passage specified the political agitation of the French Revolution and Napoleonic Wars, the growth of cities and new work routines, and the availability of quick news as the interacting determinants of this new state. Conurbation and mechanization created crowds, news then galvanized those crowds into mobs, and they performed the acts of agitation that provide the stuff for more news.

This destructive and absurd situation, in which "communication" served not a "community" but an "accumulation of men" and in which "intelligence" was no dignified power of mind but merely "information, news" (*OED*), he found intolerable. Wordsworth judged that it must be "systematically opposed" by new means that rely upon the power of mind and "the great and permanent objects that act upon it" (*Prose* 1:131). As Wordsworth escaped, in beginning *The Prelude*, from the discontent of "the vast city" to the "green fields" and "azure sky" and "gentle breeze" (1850 *Prelude* 1:1–7), so in the preface he turned from the city to the country as a counterstatement, a contrast. The very word "country" derives etymologically from Latin *contra*, "against." The negative marks left by his experience of revolutionary Paris and counterrevolutionary London helped to determine the positive character of Wordsworth's poetry. To understand Wordsworth's poetry requires awareness of the complex process that produced it: the pressures of what we have come to call mass society demand in response a strongly assertive formation of individuality. To adapt Jacques Derrida's analysis of *différance*: one defers to the community in principle but differs from it in fact and must defer its reality to the future.

Writing from Paris in the 1930s, and drawing upon his experience in Berlin earlier, Walter Benjamin argued that the conditions of urban mass society, which he characterized in terms remarkably similar to Wordsworth's, acted crucially on the poetic practice of Baudelaire. Benjamin began from a general sense of the psychological consequences of modern city and industrial life that corresponded to the analysis of Georg Simmel in "The Metropolis and Mental Life" (1900). Simmel charted the production of the urban "blasé" attitude (which for Wordsworth required "gross and violent stimulants" to move it) from the predominance of the head over the heart in a money economy. In his version of Marx's theory of commodity fetishism, Simmel argued that a money economy by establishing quantitative relations between things had "hollowed out their core" and floated them indiscriminately along, in contrast to the older ways of rooted growth in steady, unconscious rhythms. I need not belabor the close resemblance here between Simmel's analysis and Wordsworth's vision, in the "phantasma" of Bartholomew Fair, of the "epitome of what the mighty city is," a "perpetual whirl / Of trivial objects, melted and reduced / To one identity" (1850 *Prelude* 7:687, 722–27).

To investigate the artistic significance of this blasé condition, Benjamin took two concrete experiences as typical and formative of urban insensibility: the amorphous, irregular, constant jostle of the crowd that one undergoes as a walker in the city (*I* 165); the newspaper's barrage of information that is cut off from any lived experience of tradition (158–59).

Benjamin suggested that we learn to deal with the crowd in the same way as the newspaper deals with the events of public life: by anesthesia. The great danger of urban life is a sudden, overwhelming "shock," and we develop the defenses of consciousness to ward off such dangers, to ticket and categorize everything that happens in order to prevent its entering deeply and dangerously within us (160–62). Wordsworth similarly contrasted the degraded "intelligence" of news with the responsive "feeling" native to our mind's dignity. The Bartholomew Fair "lays . . . / The whole creative powers of man asleep!" because it is "a shock / For eyes and ears!" (1850 *Prelude* 7:681–86).

Benjamin built his case through a sharp distinction between two related German terms, both of which are usually translated "experience." *Erlebnis* (which characterizes city life) carries the further meanings of "event, occurrence, episode," that is of discontinuity and segmentation; *Erfahrung* (which the city threatens to annihilate and the poet must capture, preserve, and recreate) further connotes "practical knowledge," such as a traveler (way*far*er) or craftsman gains over a long period of time and can use in the future as part of a continuing life.

In Baudelaire's resistance to *Erlebnis* and insistence on *Erfahrung* Benjamin found an exemplary heroism. This process is imaged by Baudelaire (in "Le *Confiteor* de l'artiste") as "a duel in which the artist, just before being beaten, screams in fright" (*I* 163). Baudelaire let down some of his defenses, faced the city as an antagonist, allowed some of it to penetrate him so that it might return in memory and make possible the basis for a new art. Benjamin emphasized that Baudelaire overcame the undifferentiated chronology of clocks and news by creating a personal calendar of holidays, of commemorative poems built from "days of remembrance" (183–84). Wordsworth's theory of poetry's origin in emotion recollected and his poems of revisiting like "Tintern Abbey" and those like "Nutting," in which a past almost wholly washes over the present, make extensive comment superfluous. Wordsworth's struggle in *The Prelude* was not so obviously violent as Baudelaire's duel, but the energy

was no less powerful that summoned up the most disruptive moments of the past and tried to integrate them into a pattern of
growth, master them with commentary, and make them sources of
present strength.

I must emphasize, finally, that Benjamin considered crucial not
a specifically urban content but a particular form of experience. So
he argued that the eye's training in the city, in order to deal with
shifting crowds of people, underlay both the technique and the intelligibility of impressionist painting, even when the canvas portrayed country scenes (*I* 197). He argued further that, as in the case
of Bergson's philosophy, the structure of urban experience was clearest not when content is represented but as a negative "afterimage"
(157). So the "visionary dreariness" (1850 *Prelude* 12:256) of Wordsworth's significant moments in nature inverted the perceptual structure of reductive excitement in Bartholomew Fair.

Conrad addressed a comparable interrelation of city crowds,
news, and feelings in his essay "Autocracy and War" (1905). He
found the urban mass a social constant across the change in political
forms that marked the nineteenth century:

> An early Victorian . . . sentimentalist, looking out of an upstairs
> window . . . at a street . . . full of people, is reported, by an admiring
> friend, to have wept for joy at seeing so much life. . . . The psychology
> of individuals, even in the most extreme instances, reflects the general
> effects of the fears and hopes of its time. Wept for joy! I should think
> that now, after eighty years, the emotion would be . . . sterner. One
> could not imagine anyone shedding tears of joy at the sight of much
> life in a street, unless, perhaps, he were an enthusiastic . . . general
> . . . or a popular politician with a career yet to make. (*Notes* 84–85)

Conrad suggested here that however much sympathetic hope for
democracy might still have been possible before the first Reform Bill
(clearly the "eighty years" was more historically crucial for him
than the inaccurate "Victorian"), by the age of almost universal
male suffrage such hopes could only be manipulative. From the
revolutionary French *levée en masse*, crowds have served as shock
waves against the existing forms of national and international order. Conrad's explicit politics were more conservative than Benjamin's, but their frames of analysis are closely comparable.

The cultural correlate of the urban crowd for Conrad, as for

Wordsworth and Benjamin, was the mass-circulation newspaper, and Conrad's essay began in a somber meditation on the "cold, silent, colorless" journalistic reports that informed English readers of the carnage occurring in the Russo-Japanese War, in Manchuria, but could not make them feel its horrors. Journalism took from us, he argued, "both the power to reflect and the faculty of genuine feeling" and left only "the artificially created need of having something exciting to talk about." (Here he differs from both Wordsworth and Benjamin, who found specific historical causes for the "need" newspapers fill.) For Conrad, the page of a newspaper was a stimulating but unsatisfying "still uproar" (*Notes* 90). His meditation turned inward:

> Our imagination, luckily for our peace of mind, has remained a slumbering faculty. . . . Direct vision of the fact, or the stimulus of great art, can alone make it turn and open its eyes heavy with blessed sleep; and even there, as against the testimony of the senses and the stirring up of emotion, that saving callousness which reconciles us to the conditions of our existence, will assert itself under the guise of fatal necessity, or in the enthusiasm of a purely aesthetic admiration of the rendering. In this age of knowledge our sympathic imagination, to which alone we can look for the ultimate triumph of concord and justice, remains strangely impervious to information, however correctly and even picturesquely conveyed. (84)

These reflections demonstrate the full complexity of Conrad's position. They clearly link him with the Wordsworth of Watt and Thorburn in their eloquent appeal to the "sympathetic imagination" as the instrument of moral good and their defense of "great art" as the agency of awakening that imagination; and the danger Conrad suggested in the power of "purely aesthetic admiration" to deaden this freshly revived imagination is no less in this vein. Conrad here countered his own temptations to regard the universe as "purely spectacular" rather than "ethical" (*Personal Record* 92), a view that could lead to Wordsworth's dizzying "phantasma." The contrast of "knowledge" to "imagination" appears also to match the Wordsworthian distinction, noted by Watt in the preface to the *Nigger of the "Narcissus,"* between poetry and science.

Yet fundamental differences emerge. In this context, what Conrad meant by "knowledge" was clearly the "information" of news-

184

papers, the "intelligence" Wordsworth condemned in his mass society. The "saving callousness" Conrad ironically praised was the degrading failure of feeling deplored by Wordsworth, the blasé attitude noted by Simmel, the shock-defense Benjamin defined. The acts of imaginative recovery in Wordsworth bring joy or tranquillity, but for Conrad, to rouse the imagination from slumber was to disturb our "peace of mind": the "genuine feeling" at stake in this discussion was the full horror of the slaughter in Manchuria. The polemical, oppositional, antisocial force of "great art" as a substitute for "direct vision" opened to visibility a problem only implicit in Wordsworth and redefined the meaning of the artist's obligation to "make you see" in Conrad's earlier preface.

If the correct and even picturesque method of reportage fails to reach the imagination, then we may surmise—on the warrant of Conrad's practice as well—that art must follow a more indirect method, perhaps even like Marlow in *Heart of Darkness* abjure the journalistic "kernel" in favor of moonshiny "halos." Thus in *The Secret Agent* the newspaper account of Winnie Verloc's death was no "extraneous irony" arising from Conrad's mere dislike of the "yellow journalism of his time" (Widmer 139). Rather this "artistic displacement" calls into play our powers of imagination. To recognize the inadequacy of the news story, we must realize the meaning of Winnie's life as Conrad has offered it to us, the ways in which her life has been joined sympathetically with ours.

With an insight like Conrad's into the conditions of art in the nineteenth and twentieth centuries, Benjamin distinguished between "storytelling" and "information" as between *Erfahrung* and *Erlebnis*. Storytelling, indeed, is an instance of *Erfahrung*: "It sinks the thing into the life of the storyteller, in order to bring it out of him again. The traces of the storyteller cling to the story the way the handprints of the potter cling to the clay vessel" (*I* 91–92; cf. also 159). Like *Erlebnis*, "information" is discontinuous; its value "does not survive the moment in which it was new." In contrast, a story "does not expend itself. It preserves and concentrates its strength and is capable of releasing it even after a long time" (90). Conrad, by "negating his writing," aligned himself with storytelling against journalism. In the absence of the community of hearer and speaker that made traditional storytelling possible, a split opened up between the public and the writer.

Early in his career, Conrad felt such a split crippling his writing. He complained:

> I have to drag it all out of myself. Other writers have some starting-point. Something to catch hold of. . . . they lean on dialect or tradition—or on history—or on the prejudice or fad of the hour; they trade upon some tie or some conviction of their time—or upon the absence of those things—which they can abuse or praise. But at any rate they know something to begin with—while I don't. I have had some impressions, some sensations, in my time. . . . And it's all faded—my very being seems faded and thin. (*Letters from Conrad* 59)

For his writing Conrad could draw upon no shared intimacies of mother tongue ("dialect"), common cultural inheritance ("tradition"), or solidarity in doing and suffering ("history"). For Conrad, "my time" contained only evanescent "impressions" and "sensations," nothing so durable as the "tie" or "conviction" that linked other writers to "their time"; even if that time were only the "hour" of a "prejudice" or "fad," it was a shared time. They all seemed to Conrad fully present to each other, while he—a Pole in England, a sailor on land, a man of action become artist—felt barely present even to himself.

The author's note to *The Secret Agent* is a fascinating text, both in itself and in its relation to the novel and to Conrad's career, through which to investigate the problem of the artist's need to cope with the chaotic, shocking "experience" of mass society. The note itself (1920) exemplifies well the master of the simpler romantic decencies, the character of "Everyman's Favorite Old Novelist" that Conrad forged from the chaos of his earlier life and the agony of his earlier writing. The novel (1907) stands both in years and in volumes of literary production just about midway between the note and Conrad's beginnings as a writer, while the subject matter of the novel is intimately involved with those beginnings. *The Secret Agent* was Conrad's first extensive treatment of the city in which he had begun to write in 1889 and in which he had finished *Almayer's Folly* in 1894. In 1889 he started writing while a transient lodger like Verloc in the novel; over the next five years he carried his manuscript with him at sea and in Africa, leading a life as double as Verloc's; and in 1894, a month after leaving what proved to be his last maritime position, he learned in the same week of the death of his guardian uncle Bobrowski and of the Greenwich Bomb Out-rage—the attempt to blow up the observatory that marked zero meridian of longitude and zero hour of world time—which provided the subject for *The Secret Agent*. Two months later his first novel was completed.

For *The Secret Agent*, Conrad was blessed with a "starting-point." The "illuminating impression" (*Secret Agent* xi; henceforth abbreviated *SA*) that made the book possible, that allowed the outrage to "be laid hold of mentally" (*SA* x), was the odd fact about the victim's sister picked up by his "casual and omniscient" friend Ford Madox Ford out of urban oral tradition. Ford "was . . . a man who liked to talk with all sorts of people, and he may have gathered those illuminating facts at second hand or third hand, from a cross-ing-sweeper, from a retired police officer, from some vague man in his club, or even, perhaps, from a Minister of State met at some public or private reception" (*SA* x). Like the narrator of a novel by Dickens, Ford connected all strata of the city, and not from news-papers but from his acquaintance among diverse people he had the needful story. This story came upon Conrad like a shock: "Extreme surprise . . . kept me dumb" (*SA* x). When Ford changed the subject, Conrad didn't bring it up again, but the story stayed potent in him until a few weeks later, when it returned to combine in "crystalli-zation" (xi) with another impression.

While Conrad was writing, this almost archaic oral genesis com-bined with a more characteristically modern artistic experience. The germinative power of Ford's anecdote brought to life dormant parts of Conrad's past: "I had to fight hard to keep at arm's length the memories of my solitary and nocturnal walks all over London in my early days, lest they should rush in and overwhelm each page of the story." These memories provided necessary "hints" for the "surroundings" of Winnie Verloc (*SA* xiii) but like Baudelaire's dueler, Conrad had to struggle to keep the city from wholly triumph-ing over the space that he had cleared on his pages.

Even in memory, the shock of the city that has penetrated one's inner being may return overwhelmingly, just as the crowd threatens to overwhelm one in the street, as the revolutionary masses surge like a sea into formerly enclosed aristocratic precincts, as the jungle covers over the traces of settlement. The frame of experience in Conrad's writing may contain any setting. In the note he reflected on the relation between the London setting of *The Secret Agent* and the settings of the works that preceded it, *Nostromo* and *The Mirror of the Sea*:

> One fell to musing before the phenomenon—even of the past: of South America, a continent of crude sunshine and brutal revolutions, of the sea, a vast expanse of salt waters, the mirror of heaven's frowns and smiles, the reflector of the world's light. Then the vision of an enormous town presented itself, of a monstrous town more populous than some continents and its man-made might as if indifferent to heaven's frowns and smiles; a cruel devourer of the world's light. There was room enough to place any story, depth enough there for any passion, variety enough for any setting, darkness enough to bury five million lives. (*SA* xii)

The syntactically parallel "of" phrases and the repetitions of "continent," "heaven's frowns and smiles," and "world's light" establish the categorical identities within which occur the opposition of "world's light" to "man-made might" and the inversion from "reflector" to "devourer." "Room," "depth," "variety," and "darkness" are enough to constitute any Conradian narrative.

From the case of Conrad we may speculate that the urban experience of the writer—the fear defined in the city of the overwhelming shock that might flood over all defenses—underlay the characteristically romantic story of maritime trauma, of overwhelming experience in isolation, that ran from Oswald in Wordsworth's early tragedy *The Borderers* through to *Lord Jim*; this psychic knot ties the far-flung reaches of world trade and exploration to the urban political and economic centers that made such voyages possible and in turn were fed by them. Parts of this history include "The Rime of the Ancient Mariner" by Wordsworth's friend Coleridge, who was "reared in the great city" (1850 *Prelude* 2:451–52), and *The Narrative of Arthur Gordon Pym* by Poe, who wrote "The Man of the Crowd" and had so great an impact on Baudelaire. Prominent in this sequence also is *Moby-Dick*, which began from Ishmael's urban discontents, and Melville's next novel, *Pierre*, culminated in an infernal New York City. This speculation gains force if we consider that at least since the French Revolution—the historical experience that imprinted the urban crowd on all modern sensibilities—the city mass has been described in metaphors of the sea.

These stories of maritime adventure are also stories of the artist, for, as Georg Simmel argued, the adventurer and the artist share the same form of experience ("The Adventurer" 189). The adventurer brings a whole life to bear on the "island" of adventure, a spatial metaphor for privileged moments such as Benjamin found in Baudelaire's commemorations of "one evening" and Wordsworth found in "spots of time" (1850 *Prelude* 12:208). Like Baudelaire's duel, the adventure is a clearly defined, coherent structure with beginning and end—as is also a unit of assembly-line work—but it has been integrated into an individual life (as *Erhfahrung*) as no mechanical task can be. Such integration is also Conrad's task in taking that quintessential shock, the explosion at Greenwich, the annihilation of an individual for no reason that "could be laid hold of mentally," and doing his best, with the aid of oral tradition, to integrate it into motive and consequence and feeling.

This problem of integration and continuity brings us back to Conrad's note. In his early letters, Conrad had felt his "impressions" and "sensations" as "faded," his "opportunities" as "never finished" but "fizzled out" (*Letters from Conrad* 59, 80). In *The Secret Agent* his "starting-point" was emphatically "finished" with a bang, not a fizzle, but an explosion was still only a void, nothing one could stand on to push off from. So in the note, Conrad defined the book's "whole course" as "suggested and centered round the absurd cruelty of the . . . explosion" (*SA* xi). Standard usage dictates "centered *on*" or else "*circled* round," but this slip is symptomatically precise, for the center is absent. As Winnie argued against Verloc's wish to emigrate, she concentrated her thoughts on the welfare of Stevie, whom she did not mention while she "talk[ed] round that vital point" (*SA* 195–96). Yet that point no longer existed; she did not yet know that Stevie had been blown up; and the emptiness soon engulfed her in turn.

Conrad was not caught by surprise like Winnie; he knew his problem from the beginning. If her voice approached "absolute vehemence," and she went on "as if excited by the sound of her uncontradicted voice" (*SA* 196), she differed wholly from her author, who always had—to his pain and glory—a contradictory inner check to his voice. In his note, therefore, Conrad first placed his center in the explosion itself—the kernel—but at a metonymic remove from it, in the "absurd cruelty" that motivated it and emanated from it—the halo, its atmosphere. But then he described the work further as "the figures grouped about Mrs. Verloc" (*SA* xii), thus suggesting if not the impossibility of two centers, at least two focuses, as if the work were elliptically eccentric.

But treating the novel this way ignores Verloc, the "secret agent" himself, whose death is the only one of the three that wipe out his household which is directly reported in the book. At least one contemporary reviewer found the "absurd cruelty" displaced from Stevie's death to Verloc's. *Country Life*—a periodical whose very title suggests an antagonism to this work—found it "indecent" that "the whole inception, process, and accomplishment of a murder should have been planned . . . on the stage and in the sight of the spectators." It was as if, they thought, we were so barbaric as to put the butcher's "shambles in the public streets" (Watt, *Conrad: "Secret Agent,"* 31). This accusation raised a problem already familiar to Wordsworth and Baudelaire, that the modern artist is liable to duplicate in himself or herself the violence that the work exists to confront.

This review epitomizes the kind of reproach that Conrad wished to answer in the note. With an air of "sincerity," he adduced "the evidence of my general character" (*SA* viii) as testimony for the "decency" of his intentions; "those who have read so far" in his work may be trusted to credit him with the "tact" and "savoir-faire" that he confidently claimed in lieu of "modesty." He complicated his self-portrait by adding with an air of apology the quality of amiably moral, if possibly boring, eccentricity, his need to "justify" his works (viii). This move seems a heavy-handed irony. After all, why must he defend himself at all or apologize for his admirable morality? And how could he bore us? The very fact of the collected edition for which the note was written demonstrated that Conrad was a great author with a loyal audience. How could such a figure "commit a gratuitous outrage on the feelings of mankind" (xv)?

Yet the irony is subtler, for Conrad was innocent not of outrage but only of "gratuitous outrage"; the outrage was necessary. Here, as in "Autocracy and War," "great art" must arouse our "slumbering" imagination and defy our "saving callousness" in order to raise our level of experience from journalistic excitement and restore our

190

"power to reflect" and "faculty of genuine feeling." As *Erlebnis*, as information, the shock of the Greenwich outrage "could not be laid hold of mentally," but the story of the victim's sister, even though itself a further horror, permitted its integration into *Erfahrung*. The consequences alone, the explosion, were meaningless without motives.

In his self-justification of the note, Conrad repeated this pattern, if his book had not been understood by itself, he would tell readers how it came to be, even though "the world generally is not interested in the motives of any overt act but in its consequences." The world "loves the obvious," but Conrad "will go on" beyond and behind (*SA* viii). This concern with "motives" and "consequences" not only marked the genesis of the book and the note, it also appeared emphatically within the book, which a reviewer with journalistic love of the obvious called "a good story completely smothered by analysis" (Watt, *Conrad: "Secret Agent,"* 51).

Exemplary for Conrad's going-on is the presentation of Stevie's response to the cab driver's abusing his horse. The analysis begins from an implicit contrast between Winnie and the narrator (and his chosen reader). Her "constitutional indolence" kept her from seeking what was "fundamental" in Stevie's response; her muddling and pragmatic ways link her by a wrenching pun to all her fellow-Britons who believed themselves preserved from the need to think deeply by their revered political "constitution." Winnie, then, saw only consequences, "the signs of futile bodily agitation," and not the motives revealed by the narrator in their "twofold character," which allowed either "compassion" or "rage" to underlie the same physical signs (*SA* 169). Thus she was "in the dark as to the inwardness of the word 'Shame'" that Stevie uttered (171). Stevie himself "in his thoughts lacked clearness and precision" sufficient to know fully all that he meant by it. The narrator's analysis goes far beyond Stevie's self-consciousness. Nonetheless, Stevie is contrasted with Winnie and aligned with us and the narrator, for "he wished to go to the bottom of the matter." This motivation to seek a word "to fit . . . his sentiment in order to get some sort of corresponding idea" yielded his dictum "Bad world for poor people," which proved "familiar to him already in all its consequences" (171–72). The book's time-shift creates a situational irony here that once again separates us from Stevie. We already know, as he does

191

not, that one consequence of this passionate discovery is his death. For us this moment inserts that consequence into a chain of motivation that gives it meaning.

The failure of Winnie's "indolence" may awaken our "power to reflect" and spur us to give the ordinary institutions and expectations of our lives the "looking into" that she dreaded, yet Conrad's will to "go on" from the initial shock of the explosion led to our "genuine feeling" of horror at Verloc's murder and the desolation of Winnie's life. Stevie's wish "to go to the bottom" pushed him into the explosion. What, then, could tempt us into joining the quest for motives? As an inducement in the note, Conrad offered us a familiar and flattering companion. He took on the voice of Hamlet, alter ego for a century of romantics since Goethe and Coleridge: "Man may smile and smile, but he is not an investigating animal" (*SA* viii, echoing *Hamlet* 1.5.108: "One may smile, and smile, and be a villain"). Just as in the scene of the beating we shun Winnie's indolence and share the narrator's activity, so here the investigator, the motive-mongering Hamlet, wins our approval over the smiling villain Claudius, who has a guilty secret to hide. To avoid the thrust of the allusion, we join Conrad with Hamlet, over against Claudius and some imagined, morally compromised, and obtuse (no doubt mass) readership. As Hazlitt said, "It is *we* who are Hamlet" (4:232).

Yet who is this Hamlet who we are? He memorably professed the "romantic virtue of sincerity": "I know not seems" (1.2.76). Yet in his play, as in *The Secret Agent*, despite our humanistic pieties, it means death when people know each other. Verloc finally achieved a statement that "in sincerity of feeling and openness of statement . . . went far beyond anything that had ever been said in this home" (258). Next Winnie killed him. Hamlet's own path is socially disruptive. The inquiring revenger is parricide, regicide, and causes the death of his mother, his beloved, her father, and her brother. Like Oedipus, like Stevie, his investigations cause his own dreadful end.

Perhaps we would rather not be Hamlet, but for Conrad there was no question. His life was at any moment liable to be shattered by a ghost from his past, and as an author he ran the constant risk— fatal to Verloc—of not being "in accord with his audience" (250). Disguised in the author's note as Polonius rather than as a madman, this Hamlet assures all of us that his mousetrap, the display he's putting on before us, this story of death and treachery, has "no offence i'th' world" (*Hamlet* 3:2.245) in it, no "gratuitous outrage." As A. W. Schlegel observed, Hamlet "has a natural inclination for devious ways" (405). The drama of Hamlet shows us how costly, how dangerous and even compromising is the process of motivation and integration, of coming to terms with shock. No center holds, and the straight path becomes duplicitous, eccentric.

The role of Hamlet is especially suitable for the modern artist because the opposition of Hamlet and Claudius occurs within the similarity that Freud has made us recognize. In holding the mirror of his art up to nature, Hamlet was revealed in it as much as Claudius. Hamlet tried for an ironic superiority as he reassured the king, "Your majesty, and we that have free souls, it touches us not" (3.2.251–52). But Hamlet was obviously touched as strongly as Claudius, and in exposing Claudius he also uncovered himself. Hero and villain, hider and seeker, producer and audience, mirror each other as in the conclusion of Baudelaire's poem to his reader:

> Hypocrite lecteur—mon semblable—mon frère.

Reader and writer both see themselves in the work, but something nonetheless stands between them. If Conrad united numankind in a "fraternity" as Thorburn argued (151), this contestation of dueling doubles recalls Conrad's dismissal of "fraternity" as "the Cain-Abel business" (*Letters to Graham* 117). The romanticism I find in Conrad, even the Wordsworth I find through Conrad, must include this violence.

I conclude this section with an extravagant figure for the "art of being off center," which joins Wordsworth to Conrad as one devoted to "the way to do a thing" that involves the "most doing" (James 2:147). Wordsworth found that any "original Genius of a high order" confronted the necessity of "*creating* the taste" by which he was to be read. Despite the work of his predecessors, despite the literate community that revered them, he must make his way unaided against great obstacles: "For what is peculiarly his own . . . he will be in the condition of Hannibal among the Alps" (*Prose* 3:80). With his elephants, Hannibal was trying to reach Rome, that center to which all roads lead. Yet he followed an astonishingly eccentric path, employing grotesque means, for he came as an enemy. Wordsworth prefigured, as Harold Bloom emphasized, generations of belated romantics who have yearned for the unified culture, the order of tradition, that Rome represents, but who must seek their goal in the name of originality, as demonic adversaries, not as suppliants. When Wordsworth wrote, Napoleon's transalpine successes were fresh memories, but in reaching back to Napoleon's great precursor, Wordsworth chose a radically failed quester. Just when Hannibal was expected in Rome, he moved instead into the Campagna and never reached his goal. In trying to overgo Napoleon, romantic writers have repeatedly experienced the frustration of their "counterpolitical" strategies (Schorske 181–207). Instead of establishing a "central tradition," they have scattered the city's environs with memorials of heroism that remain, ironically, at a distance, marking what James, writing of Conrad, called a "special, eccentric and desperate course" (2:148).

CHARLES BAUDELAIRE AND EMILY DICKINSON

With the results in mind that Benjamin made possible for our thinking about Wordsworth and Conrad, I will sketch rapidly some more general orientations Benjamin offered for thinking about literary history. When we think of a "historical" curriculum in a literature department or of works of "literary history," our usual model, somewhat paradoxically, is synchronic, that of the period study, which tends to emphasize how things fit together within a limited span of years. Benjamin was very much oriented to this kind of work, as is clear from his working title *Charles Baudelaire: A Lyric Poet in the Era of High Capitalism* (GS 1:1086), and equally from a letter that described his plan to show Baudelaire as "embedded in the nineteenth century," like a "stone resting for decades on the floor of a forest" (1:1072). Benjamin was also very much interested in the process by which a work or author or event moves from one period to another; he considered "the analysis of the 'works' afterlife,' their 'fame,'" as "the basis of history itself" ("N" 5). As Hans Robert Jauss has acknowledged, Benjamin was a pioneer of reception studies. Moreover, he was committed to a version of diachronic history that denied continuity between the past and the present and em-

194

phasized "blasting out" ("N" 24 and *I* 261) pieces from the homogeneity of chronology. The juxtaposition of separated pieces released an energy like that of "splitting the atom," against the "narcotic" of orderly narrative ("N" 9). Even when imaging Baudelaire as a stone resting on the floor of the nineteenth century, he envisaged the critic's task as interpreting the shape of its impression, "after we have with . . . labor rolled it from its place." For Benjamin, the task of critical "construction" required first a "destruction" ("N" 17). As a critical historian, he demanded not "empathy" (1:1238), not "appreciation" or "apology," but a "rescue" that "includes the firm, apparently brutal grasp" ("N" 22). The negative element is never forgotten even in a history that has a "redemptive" goal, the "apocatastasis" (i.e., "the entry of all souls into Paradise"—*I* 103) of the whole past ("N" 4).

In orienting ourselves to Dickinson by these lines of thought, we recognize first that the very existence of her poems negates many of the most tempting generalizations about the period in which she lived. As we have already observed of Matthew Arnold's claim for the "wilderness" of his literary age, it was simply not true that the Civil War and the Gilded Age made impossible a lyric art of the most excruciating discrimination and passionate intensity, although such claims have often been made. The posthumous publication of her poems transposes the problem and requires new methods; as Benjamin urged, "the relationship of transmission and reproduction must be investigated" ("N" 16). The history of her reception has already received some attention. After seeming a rather naive, quaint verse maker when her work first appeared, Dickinson has emerged as ever more sophisticated and powerful, less a survivor of a transitional moment in the yielding of Puritanism to modernity than one who still heralds changes going on in our lives and times. Her case exemplifies what Benjamin meant by the particular urgency that certain moments from the past, threatened with loss, might hold in a particular present time.

There has been so much mystification and controversy around Benjamin that I want to lay out a few facts not readily available in one place in English. Of Benjamin's planned critical book on Baudelaire, only "On Some Motifs in Baudelaire" (1939) was published in his lifetime. It was the last major work Benjamin accomplished, but he had been involved with Baudelaire all his adult life. Beginning around 1914 or 1915, he was translating poems from Baudelaire's *Tableaux Parisiens*; in 1923 they were published, prefaced by his notable essay "On the Task of the Translator," on which both Paul de Man ("Conclusions") and Jacques Derrida ("Des Tours") have written. There was a hiatus of several years while Benjamin wrote the study on seventeenth-century *Trauerspiel* (1927), translated as *Origins of German Tragic Drama*. The methodological introduction of this book was decisive for Theodor Adorno's development, and its analysis of baroque allegory was taken up in the 1950s by Georg Lukács (in "The Ideology of Modernism") and in the 1960s by Paul de Man (in "The Rhetoric of Temporality").

In 1927 Benjamin began work on a project that occupied the rest of his life, although he did much else in those years also; this was the "Arcades" project, which took as its point of departure an architectural innovation, the passages of glassed-over ironwork that in the 1820s began to spring up as commercial centers in Paris. This book was to have been a cultural-historical collage of the nineteenth century, quite unlike any work of history that one can readily name (a partial analogue may be the documentary collages by Jay Leyda on Melville and Dickinson). Only in 1982 were the surviving one thousand-odd pages of notes for the "Arcades" published in German. The most purely speculative section, labeled "N," on "Theoretics of Knowledge and Theory of Progress," has been translated; there were also nearly two hundred pages of notes on Baudelaire, by far the single largest file. In 1935, Benjamin wrote up an abstract of the project, under the title "Paris—The Capital of the Nineteenth Century," and with this proposal won a promise of financial support from the Institute for Social Research, the "Frankfurt School." Only in 1955 was this published in German. Meanwhile in 1939, again seeking financing, he wrote up another prospectus, this time in French, which quite dramatically differs from the first, not least in its line on Baudelaire, but which was only first published in the 1982 German edition (*GS* 5:60–77) and has received almost no attention.

In 1937, Max Horkheimer from the institute suggested that their journal would most benefit from the Baudelaire section of the Arcades book; when Benjamin began serious work on it, he realized that it would become a book of its own, which he hoped would be a "miniature model" (*GS* 1:1073) of the whole project. The essay for the journal would be the middle one of three which together would comprise the book. Titled "The Paris of the Second Empire in Baudelaire," the essay was eagerly awaited by Horkheimer, Adorno, and others in exile in New York, but in the event they did not like it. (This was the essay that elicited Adorno's comments on Shelley mentioned in chapter 7.) It was published in parts from 1967 through 1969; it is now available in English, along with the 1935 "Paris—The Capital of the Nineteenth Century," some notes for an introduction, and "On Some Motifs in Baudelaire," under the title Benjamin envisaged for the whole book, *Charles Baudelaire: A Lyric Poet in the Era of High Capitalism*. Adorno's long, searching critique of "The Paris of the Second Empire" essay, along with Benjamin's reply, has been translated in *Aesthetics and Politics*. In reworking the essay, Benjamin set aside a special file of notes that bore especially on the projected first and third parts of the book; he called them "Central Park," anticipating his planned emigration to New York after he had completed his research in Paris. These were published in German in 1955 and English in 1985. The finally revised essay "On some Motifs in Baudelaire" was published in the journal of the Institute for Social Research in 1939 and translated for the 1968 *Illuminations*. In a letter about the revision, Benjamin noted that it differed from the first version by addressing issues from his great essays of 1936, "The Story Teller" and "The Work of Art in the Age of Mechanical Reproduction." Finally, in the frantic and desperate last months of his life, after the alliance between Nazi Germany and the Soviet Union and the start of the Second World War, he worked on what might have become the methodological introduction to the Baudelaire book (*GS* 1:1129) but which survives only as a series of "Theses on the Concept [or Philosophy] of History," published posthumously and included in *Illuminations*.

The special greatness Benjamin found in Baudelaire's poetry, we have seen, came from the genesis of that poetry in circumstances that threatened to make poetry impossible. The poetry was determined by the "decisive, unique experience" of being "jostled by the crowd" (*I* 193) of the great city of Paris, a place and time that made the masses of preeminent political and economical importance. Crucial to Benjamin's analytic mode was his insistence that the crowd appeared in Baudelaire not as subject matter, as direct object of representation, but rather as the condition of possibility of the poetry, only barely inferable between the lines or through the cracks, as a "hidden figure" (165). So in the exemplary sonnet "To a woman passing by" the noise of the street and the ineluctable passing by without chance for any turning back can only be accounted for by invoking the crowd that is neither named nor described, known only through its effects, "as the progress of a sailboat depends on the wind" (168).

This "decisive experience" of the crowd was part of an overall "change in the structure of . . . experience" (156), Benjamin argued: new circumstances produced an "isolation" of the "individual" (159). This individual was defined by a heightened consciousness that developed in order to ward off shock (an argument adapted from Freud in *Beyond the Pleasure Principle*) (I 161). This shock-defense of consciousness was needed above all to deal with the constant physical and psychological assaults deriving from all the other people one bumped up against in the city streets. This process of heightening individual isolation through consciousness applied particularly to the way time was transformed under these new conditions: "Every second finds consciousness ready to intercept its shock" (184). This readiness is the exacerbated awareness of time that Baudelaire's "Spleen" poems made the basis for a new poetry (which I study closely in "Charles Baudelaire"). The isolation of every second from every other Benjamin related to a widespread condition of "starting all over again" (179)—epitomized in our culture as the experience of the singles bar—that in his analysis marked not only the ever-renewed need for defense against the ever-renewed assaults of the crowd, but also structured elements of the age so diverse as gambling and industrial wage labor.

Three characteristics especially mark this critical procedure. First, it exemplified what Benjamin called "historical materialism" because it did not isolate literary history but instead integrated it with the whole life of the time, and in particular with changes in the structure of economic life, work, and the conditions of labor. It is engagingly materialistic in a further sense, since the direct documentable physical circumstances of Baudelaire's life are drawn upon. It's not that his mental activity was somehow like workers' physical activity, but rather that in his poetry he registered the

198

results of changes in the daily physical management of life that affected, although differently, both the poet and factory workers. Second, then, unlike most attempts to link poetry, or culture in general, with other areas of activity, it avoided any simple thematics because it depended on a process of discovery; its attention focused on what is not in the poem rather than what is directly there. Although it seemed liable to offer a second-level form of thematics by emphasizing "experience"—and we have seen previously that the argument as a whole depended on the discrimination between two modes of "experience"—its procedures proved very little biographical and rather more concerned with structural categories than with any "lived fullness." Third, although it was full of acute formal observations, it was by no means a formalism. All of these are very attractive in helping us toward a new literary history that is validated by its capacity to deliver a first-rate interpretation of one of the greatest figures of the period it is investigating.

I consider it embarrassing for the specificity of Benjamin's claims and damaging to their attractive materiality that it seems possible to transfer his insights about Baudelaire quite directly to the poetry of Emily Dickinson. For she lacked wholly the urban experience so fundamental to Benjamin's argument about Baudelaire. Indeed, the worlds of the poets, both biographical and imaginative, seem wholly different: against the city and its crowds, the isolation, the provinciality, the sheer availability of nature; against the satanic debaucheries, the ascetic renunciations.

Consider, however, Baudelaire's fourth "Spleen" and Dickinson's "I felt a Funeral." Baudelaire started, "When the sky, low and heavy, weighs like a lid on the groaning mind, long prey to troubles," and after further detail, moved toward the poem's end, "then bells suddenly strike furiously and hurl toward the sky an awful howl . . . and long hearses, without drums or music, file slowly by in my soul; Hope, defeated, weeps, and dreadful Anguish, like a tyrant, on my bent skull plants his black flag":

> Quand le ciel bas et lourd pèse comme un couvercle
> Sur l'esprit gémissant en proie aux longs ennuis,
>
> . . . .
> Des cloches tout à coup sautent avec furie

199

Et lancent vers le ciel un affreux hurlement,

. . . .

—Et de longs corbillards, sans tambours ni musique,
Défilent lentement dans mon âme; L'Espoir,
Vaincu, pleure, et l'Angoisse atroce, despotique,
Sur mon crâne incliné plante son drapeau noir

Dickinson began:

> I felt a Funeral, in my Brain,
> And Mourners to and fro
> Kept treading—treading—till it seemed
> That Sense was breaking through—
>
> And when they all were seated,
> A Service, like a Drum—
> Kept beating—beating—till I thought
> My mind was going numb—
>
> And then I heard them lift a Box
> And creak across my Soul
> With those same Boots of Lead, again,
> Then Space—began to toll,
>
> As all the Heavens were a Bell (#280)

The two poems immediately connect in their imagery, the funeral and the bells, but this would have little force were not these images also close in psychological feel and literary procedure: as allegories of depression. In both cases the intense focus on individual perception at once pained and numbed took place within a context that reached to the cosmic, the pressing round dome of the sky in Baudelaire, the bell of the heavens in Dickinson, while also evoking the grimly biological, the skull, the brain—both terms far removed from the sanctioned diction of lyric poetry. The new emotion for poetry that Baudelaire's "spleen" offered is remarkably close to what Dickinson called elsewhere the "bandaged moments" of the soul (#512). Particularly through the work of Wallace Stevens we are now relatively accustomed to poetry that can manifest imagination only in imagining the absence of imagination, the alienation of a mind that can display its powers but not take possession of them, or even fully recognize them as existing or as its own. Indeed, Benjamin suggested that Baudelaire registered powers that were not his own; he made himself a crossroads for the forces of his age to play themselves out on.

Baudelaire and Dickinson elaborated the poetry of spleen through what I will call images of "abandoned transport," especially at the endings of poems. These images at once abandoned the hope of any power to escape yet at the same moment were themselves abandoned to a sublime power that reached out to seize and communicate with their readers. In "Le goût du néant" (a title that itself deserves some attention—is it really "wish, longing, craving," or more something a little dandyish, the "tang" of nothingness, a "taste for" nothingness?) the last stanza began: "Moment by moment, Time sucks me in / Like a stiffening body in a giant snow":

> Et le Temps m'engloutit minute par minute,
> Comme la neige immense un corps pris de roideur.

Dickinson closely echoed this in "After Great Pain":

> This is the Hour of Lead—
> Remembered, if outlived,
> As Freezing persons, recollect the Snow—
> First—Chill—then Stupor—then the letting go (#341)

The letting go is an abandonment, a flight of the spirit, that gives up the hope of getting anywhere, yet there persists a hope for something that will end the ceaseless process of figurative transport that has continued to move the sensibility through the agonizing "round" of the poetic experience, a wish for some kind of grounding. Such grounding may itself be terrible as in the end of Baudelaire's poem: "I observe from above the globe in its roundness and don't even any longer look for the shelter of a hut. Avalanche, will you carry me down in your fall?"

201

Je contemple d'en haut le globe en sa rondeur,
Et je n'y cherche plus l'abri d'une cahute.

Avalanche, veux-tu m'emporter dans ta chute?

The poet is dangerously elevated, trapped in a condition of fatal exposure that cannot be integrated into the overall processes of life. (Only "redemptive criticism" can do that, but only at the cost of transforming the experience.) Freezing persons remember the snow with a memory that is not a totality but that has a hole in it; life may go on but its continuity is broken, again and again. Germane here is the great poem of failed apocalypse, "There came a Wind like a Bugle—"; after the shattering events, we are still left to make our lives again:

> How much can come
> And much can go,
> And yet abide the World! (#1593)

Benjamin analyzed the necessity of "starting all over again" in many sectors of nineteenth-century life, but Dickinson instanced that mode of repetition in yet a different sphere, that of "women's work."

> I tie my Hat—I crease my Shawl—
> Life's little duties do—precisely—
> As the very least
> Were infinite—to me—
>
> I put new Blossoms in the Glass—
> And throw the old—away—
> I push a petal from my Gown
> That anchored there—I weigh
> The time 'twill be till six o'clock
> I have so much do to—
>
> And yet—Existence—some way back—
> Stopped—struck—my ticking—through (#443)

The poem began as if to redeem the everyday through the house-keeper's intense care, "as if the very least were infinite to me": a Providence to her creation. But instead it moved into repetition so stale that time seemed stopped entirely: the burden of chores gave a fallen petal the mass of an anchor, the compression of obligation condensed the time until it could be weighed; discarded blossoms were replaced, but nothing grew or developed. This poem conveyed not the thrill of gambling, but the tedium of industrial work; neither romance nor career offered a structure to mobilize and shape time into larger units of eventfulness that might give life "reward."

Benjamin found in Poe a polarity crucial to Baudelaire's work: "the true connection between wildness and discipline" (*I* 176). In Dickinson we have seen much discipline, but even in poems that we have already touched on there is wildness too. In "The Soul has Bandaged moments," the moments of "freezing" are counterpoised to others:

> The soul has moments of Escape—
> When bursting all the doors
> She dances like a Bomb, abroad (#512)

In "I tie my Hat,"

> To simulate—is stinging work—
> To cover what we are
> From Science—and from Surgery—
> Too Telescopic Eyes
> To bear on us unshaded—
> For their—sake—not for Ours—
> 'Twould start them—
> We—could tremble—
> But since we got a Bomb—
> And held it in our Bosom—
> Nay—Hold it—it is calm— (#443)

The starkest contrast to the strategy of concealment in this poem, yet still within the same tension between wildness and discipline, is by now one of Dickinson's best-known poems, "My Life had stood—a Loaded Gun" (#754), where the explosive deadliness was subordinated to "The Owner," "My Master's" service. This poem intersects a related topic in Benjamin, the development in the nineteenth century, across a wide range of activities, of those processes where the flick of a hand, or switch, or trigger set going an elaborate

203

process, from the "lucifer" match to the camera's click to the telephone, and many more (*I* 174–75). Before the loaded gun, was there any form of "owned," "mastered" explosiveness? The most familiar poetic figures of lightning or volcanic eruption (which also occurs in this poem) are massive, natural, more phenomena than objects. And even the gun had only recently reached the technological condition in which the figure could make ready cultural sense. For until the development of percussion caps in the early nineteenth century made possible the sort of things that we call bullets, where the lead (like the "Boots of Lead" and the "Hour of Lead"?) and the powder are cased together in metal, guns could not stand long as loaded; soon enough the powder would lose its explosive potential. Not only do Dickinson's images, and structures of poetry and experience, bear close comparison with the Baudelaire of Benjamin's argument, but also Benjamin's overall analytic procedure proves helpful in thinking about Dickinson. Yet a problem lies at the core of this critical comparison. For despite sharing with Baudelaire "that precarious Gait / Some call Experience," Dickinson did not share with him "what only a city dweller experiences" (*I* 170), the bodily life of Paris or of any other great metropolis, which Benjamin found the indispensable precondition of Baudelaire's character as a poet.

I offer three lines of speculation for considering this problem, all of which bear mightily on the continuing attempt of critics in our time to find ways of writing literary history that reaches out to relate literature to more of life. In a nutshell, here are the three lines: first, perhaps Benjamin too little reckoned with the actual degree of literary autonomy; or second, perhaps my comparison has relied too much upon literary similarities while failing to account for the differences that the apparently "same" literary features possess when appearing in different historical and social contexts; or third, perhaps Benjamin was too specific in his argument, and that what he wanted to bring forward in Baudelaire should be related to much more abstract historical processes than those he emphasized.

It certainly is true that once we set the topic of comparing Baudelaire and Dickinson, the established data of traditional literary history provide a rich range of resources for carrying out the process. Both writers have been understood in their own national contexts as importantly postromantic, not just in chronology but in their attempt to make new space for themselves after the poetic terrain had been defined by the great romantic figures, Hugo for Baudelaire, Wordsworth and Emerson for Dickinson. And in this context, the poetic mode of spleen or bandaged moments clearly relates to the mode of "dejection" that Coleridge found a means for great poetry. Moreover, it has been widely recognized both for Baudelaire and Dickinson that in revising romanticism they drew intimately from the century centered on 1600. In that baroque age much in the literary procedures, the management of language, resembles those of romanticism rather more than it does those of the neoclassicism that intervened, yet the spiritual tenor is darker, though again perhaps "romantic" in its extremity as against the neoclassical ideal of just moderation. Similarly, the extensive exploration of Emily Dickinson's "Puritanism" parallels the studies of Baudelaire in relation to Pascal. Again, for both poets the relation to the seventeenth century provides a context for their shared recourse to allegory. Finally, it is well known that Baudelaire's work was profoundly influenced by his encounter with Edgar Allan Poe, who was an American of the generation immediately before Emily Dickinson, and whose work, if not certainly known to her ("Of Poe, I know too little to think," Dickinson wrote in 1879—Leyda, *Years*, 2:315), was well known to many of the magazine writers she is known to have admired; thus we have strong internal literary grounds for the "gothic" procedures that have been noted both in Baudelaire and Dickinson, as we might consider their uses of "skull" and "brain."

In adducing these critical observations, I hope to lend further weight to my own bringing together of the two poets, but for theoretical purposes, these observations do little. Even New Criticism reached out beyond literature in order to claim and explain literary value; Eliot's assessment (1930) of Baudelaire's residual Christianity (at least he possessed the consciousness of damnation, against the complacency of the bourgeoisie) in this respect parallels Allen Tate's placing of "Because I could not stop for death" in relation to the crisis of the New England theocracy (1932). As these instances suggest, "internal" literary history does not even wish to demonstrate that there is no further reason for the resemblances of the two poets; it has no means by which to prove that literature is radically (rather than relatively) autonomous from other areas of human activity. Moreover, to the extent that it does help to persuade us that there are real grounds for comparing two poets each of whom is so deeply idiosyncratic, it actually helps to undermine the myth of creative uniqueness that usually accompanies the claim of literary autonomy.

The second line of speculation is more truly critical, in the sense of discriminative, than the first. It suggests that even if literature and society are interrelated, this does not mean that the "same" literary features have the "same" meaning when they appear in different socio-historical circumstances. The clearest possible example of this somewhat unusual truism is Dickinson's own mode of literary production and inscription. To write by hand and to preserve manuscripts would be absolutely normal for a monastic poet of the Middle Ages; to circulate poetry in manuscript among a few chosen associates would be perfectly normal in a Renaissance court; but for Dickinson these modes were part of an unusual and painful strategy that signaled privacy and alienation rather than holiness or sociability. That she made great poetry in such conditions counts as an accomplishment in a way that would not have required attention if this were standard in her time and place. For the criticism of Dickinson, the overwhelming issue is that she was a woman, for a recurrent gesture in feminist criticism has been to demonstrate that what is unremarkable in men requires special attention in women; and furthermore, in our particular relation to Dickinson, the special force that binds our moment to hers, again the issues of women's lives are paramount.

I have already remarked on a subject important to Dickinson but alien to Baudelaire, that of everyday female domesticity (his poems about lesbians are of course equally female-oriented in subject matter and alien to Dickinson's work). Following Benjamin's analysis, we might argue that her apparently similar experience must have a different social meaning from Baudelaire's. Her world is that of the "interior," which Benjamin treated in section 4 of the 1935 prospectus for his book on Paris, followed by the contrasting section 5 on the *flâneur*, the stroller, exemplified by Baudelaire. Nonetheless, in exploring the social meaning of Baudelaire's sexual life, Benjamin linked Baudelaire's supposed impotence to the "paralysis of social fantasy" in a bourgeois class that could no longer form "images of the future" but preferred instead to enclose itself in the stuffing of Victorian "cosiness" ("Central Park" 37). This transsexually rejoined Baudelaire and Dickinson, but Benjamin's analysis of changes in the lives of women in the nineteenth century tended to separate them again. He emphasized only the tendency "to incorporate women wholesale into the process of commodity production" (39), which he connected to Baudelaire's particular concern with prostitution. What we know of life in the Dickinson household, however, shows the other side of this coin; life there shared in a historical process that had only recently made deep changes in the lives of "northern middle-class" American women (Douglas 49). For the home was no longer a center of economic activity as it had been on the frontier, and as it had also been in the traditional form of urban economic organization; and in Dickinson's class, her work was not necessary even for the processes of the household. If her father would eat only bread baked by her hands, this was a matter of luxurious affection, not economic necessity; the household had Irish "help" (see Leyda, "Miss Emily's Maggie"; Sewall 610, and the illustrations opposite). The terrible deadness of domestic time was an unproductive time, in contrast to that of the wage laborer in Benjamin's argument; yet it was also a time without financial waste, in contrast to that of the gambler; and yet again, a time of propriety, in contrast to that of Baudelaire's *femmes damnées*.

This cross-grained twisting of resemblance and difference only begins the activity Benjamin found most congenial; the most characteristic gestures of Benjamin's criticism are those which draw distinctions where the ordinary reader, teacher, or student would stop, content with having found similarity (precisely what then makes the new differentiations possible). This drive to difference operates crucially for the Baudelaire project as literary history. Benjamin did not want simply to repeat in his Baudelaire study the insights into allegory he had achieved in the book on seventeenth-century *Trauerspiel*. From the first his agenda required comparing "the function allegory possessed in the seventeenth and in the nineteenth centuries" (*GS* 1:1084). One challenging formulation bore on the kind of issue I have tried to elucidate with regard to Dickinson's mode of inscription:

The allegorical mode of seeing which shaped style in the seventeenth century no longer did so in the nineteenth. Baudelaire was isolated; as an allegorist his isolation was in certain respects that of a straggler [*Nachzügler*]. (His theories emphasize this belatedness [*Rückständigkeit*] sometimes in a provocative way.) If the style-shaping power of allegory in the nineteenth century was weak, so too was the seduction to routine which left so many traces in the poetry of the seventeenth. ("Central Park" 55)

When practiced by an occasional nineteenth-century poet, allegory meant and acted differently from when practiced as a major seventeenth-century mode; it involved more struggle and therefore more "destructive" power. If it could be maintained that "the allegorical mode of perception is always based on a devalued world of appearances," then it was still necessary to locate the "specific devaluation of the world of things" that was "the ground of Baudelaire's allegorical intention;" Benjamin argued that this was the degradation at stake in the "commodity" (a claim to which I shall return) (*GS* 1:1151). Therefore the historian's task would be to analyze "the refunctioning of allegory in the commodity economy" ("Central Park" 42).

It remains a matter for reconstructive interpretation just how Benjamin would have brought this scheme down to details, but it is significant that the scheme was important to him, and also that he worked at collecting details, at noting formulations that would help him define textually, not only conceptually, the differences between seventeenth-century allegory and that of the nineteenth century. "Central Park" suggested that "Baudelaire confronted modern life in a way comparable to that in which the seventeenth century confronted antiquity" (32); that "the fictitiousness (*Scheinbarkeit*) of the allegory is here no longer openly avowed, as it was in the Baroque" (33); that "Baroque allegory sees the corpse only from the outside. Baudelaire sees it also from the inside" (51); and, perhaps a gloss on that, "The key figure of the early allegory is the corpse. The key figure of the later allegory is the '*souvenir*' (*Andenken*)" (55).

All this is heartening to my present argumentative context, for it suggests the capacity of Benjamin to recognize the kind of resemblance I have been drawing but then to go ahead and make it a basis for further differentiations. It has even greater significance in our overall current considerations of literary history. For in the criticism associated with Paul de Man the discovery of tropological structures—often, precisely allegory—has typically been reckoned a stopper for historical criticism. It should be clear how much de Man's language in "Shelley Disfigured," discussed in chapter 4, draws from Benjamin's discursive orbit, but even more precisely the case may be made from de Man's critique of the "reception-historical" work of Hans Robert Jauss, where explicit mention is made of Benjamin and where the poem under discussion is Baudelaire's second "Spleen." De Man, claiming to have Benjamin on his side against Jauss, finds the poem's final image of a sphinx making the same point as Hegel's distinction between sign and symbol, and thus returning to the purely linguistic, over against inner "experience" and the historical, to forgetting rather than remembering. But de Man professed himself baffled why the Egyptian symbology should seem " 'right' in a lyrical poem as well as in a philosophical treatise" ("Lyrical Voice" 72). Based on my understanding of Benjamin, he would have quite readily grasped and used the kind of arguments Edward Said has made in *Orientalism*, "Egyptian Rites," and elsewhere for the particular imaginative roles that elements of the eastern Mediterranean cultures have been made to play by Western powers, and the relations of those roles to historical and political facts.

Benjamin here may give strength to those like Thomas Greene in *The Light from Troy* who have tried against de Man to argue for the historicity of tropes. The "same" trope may mean or function differently at different times and under different conditions. Something like this insight emerges also from Erich Auerbach's *Mimesis*. He defined "realism" in stylistic terms, capable of close rhetorical and grammatical specification, but most broadly as a "mixture" between stylistic "levels" that have themselves been established, by practice and precept over time, as separate. Such mixture occurred notably in Dante's *Divine Comedy* and Balzac's *Human Comedy*, and to deal with works nearly six hundred years apart, Auerbach developed quite different explanations (Christian figuralism in Dante; humanist historicism in Balzac). The "same" stylistic feature provided a challenge that required historically differential analysis. The contrast is very sharp with E. R. Curtius, who tried to reduce "realism" to nothing more than an always available stylistic option (e.g., *European Literature*, 387 n. 17). A related matter will be discussed in the last chapter, for in *The Order of Things* Foucault established differences between the functions of "representation" in the seventeenth century and in the twentieth. In that same book, Foucault also placed Mallarmé's mystique of "language" within historical limits that should give pause to current critics who consider it eternally self-evident that language is the privileged site of a negative ascesis.

After this long consideration of whether "similar" literary or linguistic figures require "different" contextual analyses, I now turn to my third speculative line. This starts in quite a different direction, but it will finally lead to another part of this same great interrogation chamber for our current theory and practice of literary history. This third line suggests that Benjamin may have overemphasized the specificity of a process that may better be understood more abstractly. This abstraction does not require that we abandon history for philosophy, but it changes the kind of history we practice. If we understand Benjamin's basic question as approximately "How did the full development of capitalism transform the psyche?" then the city may not be the only, or most, relevant mediation. Benjamin's overall project for the Baudelaire book, as we earlier glimpsed, indeed moved toward the abstraction of what I called a "scheme." The first section of that book was to focus on Baudelaire as an allegorist, isolated in his poetic practice; the second section (in the versions of both 1938 and 1939) was to place Baudelaire in his social relations; the third section aimed to solve the riddle posed by what preceded it by analyzing "The Commodity as Poetic Object" (*GS* 1:1091).

Thus Benjamin's overall line of thought in the Baudelaire project followed Georg Lukács in *History and Class Consciousness*, a book we know he had read and admired (e.g., *GS* 3:171). In the central essay of that book, "Reification and the Consciousness of the Proletariat," Lukács's resounding question had been "How far is commodity exchange together with its structural consequences able to influence the *total* outer and inner life of a society?" (84), and he had begun to develop an appropriately *total* answer, to which we can understand Benjamin's project as contributing. In criticizing Benjamin's first version of the Baudelaire essay, Theodor Adorno had objected in ways that are remarkable, given Adorno's current reputation as an unswerving critic of "totality." He wrote, "Let me

express myself in as simple and Hegelian a manner as possible. . . .
Your dialectic lacks one thing: mediation. Throughout your text
there is a tendency to relate the pragmatic contents of Baudelaire's
work directly to adjacent features in the social history of his time.
. . . Materialistic determination of cultural traits is only possible if
it is mediated through the *total social process*" (*Letters* 128–29). But
then Adorno greatly admired the revision in "Some Motifs in Baudelaire." How did it provide the missing "mediation" (*GS* 1:1120)?

When Walter Bagehot wrote about Emily Dickinson's favorite author, Charles Dickens, in 1858, he coined a brilliant simile: "London
is like a newspaper," because "everything is there, and everything
is disconnected" (176). For Benjamin, apparently unaware of Bagehot, this comparison suggested an important mediation. In first discussing the altered character of "experience" in the modern world,
Benjamin wrote at some length about newspapers both as examples
and as causes for this change (*I* 158–59); further on, in discussing
Baudelaire and the change in modalities of perception, he suggested
the equivalence of optical experiences between "the advertising
pages of a newspaper" and "the traffic of a big city" (175). This
possible equivalence offers a way of thinking about how Dickinson's
poetry came to resemble Baudelaire's. It's not just that both lived
in the era of high capitalism, but that some of the key mediations
by which commodity exchange affected perception were also shared
between Amherst and Paris. In both cases, the mosaic dispersion of
advertisements over the page offered a new field for perception arising from the great expansion of the market for commodities.

The United States was well known in the nineteenth century as
the most benewspapered of all world cultures; a recent study of the
city in the life of the American people argues that newspapers actively fostered "metropolism"—that is, they urbanized portions of
the United States that simply by their population and social and
economic character could not have been considered cities (Barth
25); and finally, we know that newspapers played an important role
in the Dickinson household. Her biographer Richard Sewall considers her reading the Springfield *Republican* a "daily ritual" (607); he
documents her exchange of clippings of bizarre *faits divers* with her
close friend Judge Lord (650 n.); and he even suggests that it provided her means of access to the poetry of the seventeenth century
(473)! In a letter from her early adulthood, Dickinson already

211

sounded like a thoroughly modern reader, wryly comic about her own love of sensation: "Who writes those funny accidents, where railroads meet each other unexpectedly, and gentlemen, in factories, get their heads cut off quite informally? Vinnie was disappointed tonight, that there were not more accidents" (598).

A strange nature poem of Dickinson's engaged the issue Benjamin and Lukács both highlighted for the transformation of consciousness under capitalism: a new sense of human time that changed our experience in the world. First, however, recall Dickinson's riddle poem about the railroad train, "I like to see it lap the miles" (#585). Her father Edward Dickinson's major role in bringing the railroad to Amherst tempts us to see in this poem a cutely filial act of mischievous piety; we are so bored by the banal naturalization of the machine as a pussycat that we miss the much bolder figure in the penultimate moment of the poem, when the train ended its trip, "punctual as a star." Time is the basis of a striking anecdote about Emily Dickinson's relation to her father (supposedly he tried to teach her to tell time, but she was so frightened that she could neither learn nor confess her ignorance for years afterward—Sewall 65), and we still have her watch (illustrated opposite Sewall 375), but my emphasis will be rhetorical and historical rather than biographical. For "punctual as a star" effected a powerful figurative transference: the stars, and the sun and moon, have been for almost all of human history the measure of time and therefore incapable themselves of being timed. We know we are punctual by the stars, rather than holding the watch to them. The term "punctual," as having to do with points, had been in the language for a long time, but in its current sense, "exactly observant of an appointed time," it dates only from 1675 (*OED*). That is, the term is contemporary with, and marks the impact of, the establishment of Newtonian, homogeneous space, the frame in which the new, empty time of modernity unrolls. Moreover, in 1675 there also was developed an accurate enough chronometer to provide "the material basis for what even we would consider punctuality" (as a modern historian has observed, without recourse to philology—Landes 128). This accuracy allowed marine navigators to ascertain longitude by reference to a fixed point. That point at Greenwich (where the observatory was established in 1675) became not only zero longitude but also time-giver for the globe when world time zones were es-

212

tablished. This followed the example of the United States, which introduced time zones in 1883, to permit standardized "railroad time" across a nation too large for a single hour-norm to prevail (Landes 286). (I leave readers to work out for themselves the reading of *The Secret Agent* that might interpose here.)

This mechanization of the world picture, in the context of the economic activities of overseas trade, the development of a full national market through railroad building, industrial transformation through precision metal tool design, and the scientific research on which they relied, all this in a household intimately involved with the railroad, the newspaper, and the scientific activities of Amherst College, a household in which a young woman lived who had many things to do, despite having servants also, all this I invoke to make something of a very small, light-toned poem, which domesticates nature, as Western humanity had been doing so assiduously for so long, and mimes the voice of reification in its arch personification:

> Lightly stepped a yellow star
> To its lofty place—
> Loosed the Moon her silver hat
> From her lustral Face—
> All of Evening softly lit
> As an astral Hall—
> Father, I observed to Heaven,
> You are punctual. (#1672)

In the least menacing way, a daughter puts father in his place, a woman puts heaven in its place and humankind puts nature in its place; now the latecomer sets the standards, blithely failing to recognize the authoritative relation by which the cosmos still marks time, instead reducing time to a matter of information, and of good form. At least this speaker still saw the heavens. Benjamin, however, noted the absence of stars in Baudelaire's poetry (e.g., *GS* 1:1152). He explained that absence by the gaslighting that made the Paris night sky starless and by Baudelaire's reluctance to represent the menacing crowd (here the crowd of stars), which figured the ever-same mass of commodities. Comparing Baudelaire and Dickinson thus yields the opposite from our previous line of speculation. In that line, similar figures might have different meanings; in this line, wholly different figures have the same meaning. The presence and the absence of stars both figure reification.

Comparing these two lines focuses a crucial issue for contemporary theory and practice of literary history. After the impasse I have defined in the 1970s' project of a new literary history, two major contrasting positions have made such a project once again attractive: the "new historicism" prominently represented in the Berkeley journal *Representations*, and much influenced by the French *Annales* school, as well as by the work of Michel Foucault; and the new Marxism for which Fredric Jameson is the most eminent figure. Foucault's immensely detailed work explicitly and polemically denied the idea of a social whole. In contrast Jameson, even when he draws on facts, resolutely holds aloof from any taint of "positivism" or "empiricism," and he continues to uphold Lukács's claims for totality and to insist, like Adorno against Benjamin, on "mediation" and "the whole social process." Benjamin's appeal for our time springs from his availability to both these positions. Yet my analysis has shown that he does not reconcile them so much as exacerbate their divergences. We reach back to rescue from the danger of oblivion a figure that inspires us but also threatens to embarrass us. We find ourselves in Benjamin as he found himself in Baudelaire. Unless we can also establish critical distance from Benjamin, as Benjamin did from Baudelaire, we can only play the farce to his tragedy. The problem area that I have sketched here will continue to figure in the remaining chapters.

PART THREE
HISTORY IN CONTEMPORARY CRITICAL PRACTICE

Chapter 9
Frank Kermode and Normal Criticism: History and Mystery

It is the text that saves us; the interlineary glosses, and the marginal notes, and the *variae lectiones*, controversies and perplexities, undo us.
— John Donne, quoted by Kermode in 1957 and 1973

FROM THE 1950s into the 1980s, Frank Kermode was one of the most interesting and admired critics writing in English, but his work attracted little specific discussion. For the purposes of my argument, his work complements that of M. H. Abrams in representing the best of what was seen as enhancing rather than challenging established understandings of literary history. Like Abrams, Kermode finally turned away from history, not toward the "spatial form" of which he had long been a leading opponent, but rather toward an emphasis on potentiality, what I call "mystery," that allied him with Geoffrey Hartman. Despite the great differences in rhetorical stance and explicit subject matter, both Kermode and Hartman turned to a hermeneutics descended from Arnold's rescue of the Bible from its historical referent. This rescue, for which Coleridge's theory of the symbol provided the theoretical underpinning in English-language culture, defines the new secular priesthood of literary interpreters that Arnold prophesied.

I argue that we can understand Kermode's critical career through following the interplay of history and mystery in his positions. *Romantic Image* (1957; henceforth abbreviated *RI*) banished mystery—the occult tradition of symbolism, the myth of the artist's specialness—and valued instead the flux of history, the linearity of discourse. *The Sense of an Ending* (1967; henceforth abbreviated *SE*) was less dismissive of mystery. It sympathetically probed our wish for some vertical elevation above existence on the plains of history, "in the middest"; yet it showed also the dangers of mystery, of myth, and emphasized that only in its coexistence with history can our life flourish. *The Classic* (1975; henceforth abbreviated *C*) showed how history breeds mystery: time and events drive us to seek new meanings in texts. Yet more than with either history or mystery, the book ended with a strange possibility of *mastery* through a structuralist literary science. The empty signifiers of structuralism, however, echo the symbolist temptation, the Paterian or Mallarméan art void of all meaning. Mechanism, Kermode had already seen in *Romantic Image*, was no liberation from the problems of organicism. *The Genesis of Secrecy* (1979; henceforth abbreviated *GS*) turned to hermeneutics to avoid the inhumanity of structuralism, to displace that mastery, but the humanity it found—the will to interpretive power—produced a history so bleak that it must be fled, and Kermode himself turned to mystery. This formed the background for his emergence in the 1980s as an elder statesman like Wayne Booth or M. H. Abrams.

This bare sketch cannot yet make clear why I am concerned with Kermode. Indeed, my project may seem strange. Kermode has not been much written about in books about criticism, beyond brief discussions by Graff and Lentricchia. Yet in the United States, he is surely the best-known English critic of the generation that began their careers just after the Second World War. Kermode's initial prominence—what established him in England—came with a rush, after the delays occasioned by military service. In his thirties, in the 1950s, he edited a textbook of *Renaissance Pastoral Poetry* and edited *The Tempest* in the distinguished Arden series; he wrote on seventeenth-century poetry both articles for scholarly journals and a handbook on John Donne; he published an innovative essay on "Richardson and Fielding"; he explored nineteenth- and twentieth-century poetry and criticism in *Romantic Image*; and he undertook extensive literary journalism, largely on contemporary fiction.

This was already an extraordinary range, both in its subject matter and in its audiences, and the next quarter-century amplified both. The audience grew particularly through Kermode's turn to America (which also provided a new subject matter, as he was the

218

first to write a book on Wallace Stevens). In journalism, Kermode became familiar to readers of the Sunday *New York Times* book section and of the *New York Review of Books*, while he also joined in founding the New York–sponsored *London Review of Books*. Academically he authored some half-dozen books. *The Sense of an Ending* embraced the history of Christian apocalyptic thought, Shakespearean tragedy, the novel, and existentialism. *The Classic* in 140 pages managed to say significant things about Vergil, Dante, Spenser, Milton, Marvell, Hawthorne, *Wuthering Heights*, T. S. Eliot, and Roland Barthes. *The Genesis of Secrecy* meditated continually on the Gospel of Mark, while drawing in analogous hermeneutic problems from Henry Green, Kafka, Joyce, Henry James, and Thomas Pynchon. *The Art of Telling* (1983; henceforth abbreviated *AT*) collected essays on fiction and interpretation, while *Forms of Attention* (1985) attempted a rounded statement on the hermeneutic issues at stake since *The Classic*, returning to the Renaissance grounds of *Hamlet* and Botticelli. For the classroom—beyond anthologies of criticism on Donne, metaphysical poetry, Shakespeare, and *King Lear* and texts of Spenser, Marvell, and T. S. Eliot—Kermode's journalistic expertise allowed him to edit the lively *Oxford Reader* with Richard Poirier, while his scholarly authority produced the *Oxford Anthology of English Literature* (which he edited with John Hollander, the two sharing specific responsibility for both the Renaissance and the twentieth century) and made him editor for the tragedies in the magisterial *Riverside Shakespeare*. Most extraordinary as a general cultural phenomenon was Kermode's editorship of the Modern Masters series, for which he wrote *D. H. Lawrence*. This series ran to some forty titles and would merit a separate study, from its pathbreaking currency around 1970 to the eighties, when it finally included books written by or about women.

I have listed all this to demonstrate Kermode's institutional prominence. Among his English age-mates the only possible equal is Raymond Williams (both are now retired from Cambridge professorships). Yet in the United States, which is my primary focus in this book, Williams is known almost exclusively through his books, lacking the classroom and journalistic resources Kermode deploys. Nonetheless, some comparison with Williams is to the point because of the striking relation between his first major book and Kermode's.

Romantic Image and *Culture and Society* came out within a year of each other. Each aimed to intervene in the current literary and cultural life of England through forging a chain of analysis that joined the romantics to the moderns; my own book follows late in their line. Critics more than a generation younger than the key modernists, and who had lived through another war, could finally see beyond the antiromanticism of the modernists to deeper continuities. Both Kermode and Williams focus on the isolation of the artist, and of art, from the ordinary involvements of life—a crucial event of the romantic period that we are still struggling to come to terms with, as I am in this book.

If from this close coincidence of starting points we consider the intellectual trajectory each has followed, we can define a crucial aspect of Kermode's American position: he stands as an alternative to Marxism. Kermode came to journalistic prominence in the later 1950s in the pages of the cold war *Encounter* and *Partisan Review* (whose editor William Phillips introduced *Puzzles and Epiphanies*, the first collection of Kermode's essays), and as recently as *The Genesis of Secrecy* Kermode remarked of Fredric Jameson that he put things "a shade too strongly . . . for he is a Marxist" (163). History was important to Kermode, but "tradition" (following Eliot) rather than "society" was the medium through which he felt history. Continuity and compromise rather than schism and conflict defined his historical thought and values. When horror does erupt, it results from "irrationalism" (*RI* 160), the predominance of mystery, rather than from anything more precisely specifiable. The brilliantly marshaled learning that did powerful historical analysis in several of his essays on Spenser diminished both in the work on more recent literature and in the more recent work.

To define further Kermode's interest for us, take another contemporary of his, also of transatlantic origin, who even after his death is still talked of wherever in the United States criticism is discussed: Paul de Man. Like Kermode's, de Man's early work concentrated on demystifying the romantic image, on replacing the fetishized symbol with a more discursive understanding of language. Between the time Kermode adumbrated his critique of "spatial form" in *Romantic Image* and elaborated it in *The Sense of an Ending*, there appeared Derrida's breakthrough essay "Force and Signification" (1963) and de Man's attack on spatial form in Joseph Frank and

Frank Kermode and Normal Criticism

Hillis Miller ("Spacecritics," 1964). Just as Kermode was criticizing prophets of crisis in *The Sense of an Ending*, de Man was working out his dialectic of "blindness" in "Criticism and Crisis." In that essay, de Man like Kermode worked the distinction of myth and fiction as a way of defending the cognitive value of literature while also vouching for its safety.

If, as we did with Williams, we compare de Man's later career with Kermode's, we can see that Kermode stands also as an alternative to deconstruction. Kermode's ethos is that of a man of light, not of the abyss, and he therefore associated himself with Jonathan Culler's early project for a theory of literary competence set within the limiting powers of an institution of literature. (As Kermode later remarked, this project seemed conservative in the United States but quite far out in Britain—*AT* 4–5.) Kermode learned the new moves, yet he remained safe. And in contrast to the science of any pure structuralism, he insisted upon and labored to demonstrate the irreducible complexity of literary works. As opposed, then, to the reductions of philosophy in de Man, of linguistics in structuralism, of social analysis in Williams, Kermode defended the literary object.

Kermode's special interest for us is that he represents "normal" criticism not only at its most intelligent and complex, but also at its most general—as opposed to Wayne Booth's identification with a particular school of "pluralism" or M. H. Abrams' powerful field identity as a romanticist. He is therefore extremely helpful to think about if we want to know where we are now. This question of "we" is hard, but I mean in the first place to acknowledge my own implication in the issues at stake in Kermode's work. Rereading Kermode makes clear to me the impossibility of standing cleanly away from him. To use history as a means for demystifying our reading without falling into platitude; to respect the complexity of textual practice without embracing the mysteries of negative theology— these are daunting, yet imperative, tasks for us to the extent that we remain literary critics, and among the current senior generation, Kermode has most fully tried to accomplish them.

It runs some risk to take Kermode to stand for so much and so many; but there is more use in the patient scrutiny of so reticent a figure than in the attempt to paint a composite, choosing as representative even smaller parts from more writers. And to examine

221

those less reticent than Kermode, those who avowedly represent the state of criticism, the more explicit generalizers, would lead me too quickly to dismay.

To write of "normal" criticism invokes Thomas Kuhn's notion of normal science in *The Structure of Scientific Revolutions*, that which goes on with whatever brilliance and resourcefulness within the established paradigm, the research consensus. This does not mean that there is no innovation in Kermode, only that he has not been an originary figure like I. A. Richards. In more precise local terms, Kermode's normality means that his essays appeared in *New Literary History* and *Critical Inquiry* but not in *Diacritics*, *Glyph*, or *boundary 2*. Nor have his works been reviewed in *Diacritics*, nor are they regular points of reference in the footnotes of these "advanced" journals. Furthermore, Kermode is not featured for attack in any of the hostile diagnoses of the current state of things. Whatever consensus exists, he falls within it.

This does not mean that Kermode's work has excited no controversy. Both Gerald Graff and E. D. Hirsch wrote combative reviews of *The Genesis of Secrecy*, but both treated the book as showing what was wrong inside the profession of literary study, thus as representative, not iconoclastic. I should add that Kermode himself in the last decade acknowledged institutional issues like those I have been raising. Indeed, Kermode developed codes of decorum that differentiated his discourse when he was speaking within the institution, to it, from when he was speaking from the institution, for it, to the laity. If Graff and Hirsch had reread the introductions to the *Oxford Anthology* and the *Riverside Shakespeare*, they would have worried less about the relativism they distrusted in Kermode. Only the smallest shadings of the uncertainties in Kermode's books mark these introductions. Kermode's own situation may echo one that fascinated him in both *The Sense of an Ending* and *The Classic*: the confrontation in the later Middle Ages between classical and Christian thought that led to the doctrine and the practice of "double truth." Professionals—lawyers specifically—operated from one perspective within their institution and from another outside it—one in the court, another "in the confessional" (*SE* 68; *C* 32).

To understand the direction Kermode took, we must define his initial situation. After the battles of the 1930s and 1940s between "the critics" and "the scholars," Kermode combined them with apparent ease, and this capacity to conjoin partial methods linked itself to his embrace—rare even in England and incredible in America—of both older and newer literature. Kermode's first major work—*Romantic Image* and the essays of *Puzzles and Epiphanies*—came from the interaction of three major areas, which can stand for the fruitful eclecticism Kermode achieved through omnivorous reading.

From the beginning, one strain was American: A. O. Lovejoy's history of ideas, particularly the idea of primitivism. This scholarly analysis of primitivism as an idea complemented Yvor Winters' critical analysis of its modern practice. Like Harold Bloom at the same time, Kermode found in Winters a way to link romantic and modern, and *Puzzles and Epiphanies* may be understood as a sketch in a Winters vein of the "Anatomy of Modern Primitivism," just as parts of *The Sense of an Ending* and associated essays in *Continuities* (1968) performed a "discrimination of modernisms" on the model of Lovejoy's essay discriminating romanticisms.

More important than the Americans for the future of Kermode's work, though not so predominant at first, was the harvest he reaped from the European intellectual emigration, especially the translation to England of the Warburg Institute. For Kermode, as a scholar of the Renaissance, this was the immediate point of impact. The Warburg emphasis on Neoplatonic magic and mythography marked Kermode's work. The occult tradition allowed him to build from the Renaissance to romanticism and then to modernism, both debunking Eliot's myth of "dissociation" and providing positive ground for the linkage of seventeenth-century poetry and modern symbolism. Furthermore, the Warburg work helped Kermode to recognize the fascination and importance of the history of scholarship and interpretation. Finally, the whole project of the Warburg might be defined as "The Survival of the Classic," to take the title of Kermode's essay (in *Shakespeare*) that most clearly marked the inflection of his work after *The Sense of an Ending*.

As a student not just of the Renaissance but of all Western literature, Kermode had most to learn from the magisterial works of E. R. Curtius and Erich Auerbach. Curtius' *European Literature and the Latin Middle Ages* made the earlier impression on him, and its method of analyzing topoi enabled Kermode's analysis of the figures of the dancer and the tree in *Romantic Image* (72). No less important was Curtius' attempt to set in historical perspective the whole issue of the canon, which had become such a modernist concern. In contrast to Curtius, Auerbach seemed to Kermode at first to fall into the camp of schismatics—antihistoric mystery mongers (*Puzzles* 32)—but Kermode's later work drew heavily from Auerbach's emphasis on the relations of realism to the Christian figural tradition, as focused through Dante, and from Auerbach's contrast between the uninterpretable world of the *Odyssey* and the end-determined world of the Bible that is therefore, paradoxically, open to reinterpretation (*SE* 5–6; *Continuities* 235–38).

Finally, I must sketch Kermode's relation to his native tradition. This included not only the great authors of the schools but also the personally discovered achievements of the early twentieth century: especially Yeats, Eliot, Forster, and Lawrence. Many of Kermode's own critical concerns emerged through these encounters, as, for instance, his own experience moved him to insist on the bafflement of reading as what provokes theory ("Novel and Narrative" 172). This personal relation to modernism proved important as well for Kermode's thought about the institutions of literature. The academic "routinization" of modernism he noted with dismay, even while having helped to make it possible (*Continuities* 84; *GS* 49).

As I have already suggested, the crucial idea that Kermode took from the moderns was Eliot's "tradition" (also important to Curtius). Kermode's scholarship allowed him to detail "tradition" in a freshly persuasive way, while his humanity committed him to trying to make it an instrument of life rather than of ossification. This meant for Kermode setting the tradition in history rather than making of it a myth; it meant defining the precise contexts in which a symbol functioned rather than committing the "typological fallacy" of taking tradition as a warehouse of pigeonholes, in each of which may be found the key to a particular mystery (*Continuities* 37).

Accordingly, *Romantic Image* fell into two parts. The first placed Yeats in a native English tradition of poetic concern and technique, complicated by the occult heritage. The chapter on what Kermode defined as Yeats' breakthrough into poetic maturity—"On the Death of Major Robert Gregory"—finely demonstrated Kermode's procedures, for Yeats' letters show that the poem from its inception was connected with the tradition of pastoral elegy that Kermode had studied in his early textbook. The second part of *Romantic Image* debunked schismatic writings that through their myths, pseudo-histories, attempt to deny tradition. The myths, Kermode argued, were both wrong and useless, but his greatest coup was to show that the claim of "our age" as radically cut off from the past is itself a traditional claim that ran from the early nineteenth century into the twentieth, an insight Harold Rosenberg formulated as "the tradition of the new." Thus Kermode's chapter on "Dissociation of Sensibility: Symbolist Theories of Literary History" saved Eliot from himself. In addition, it prefigured Kermode's battles with the schismatic historiography of the French avant-garde in his essays of the 1970s, and in its wider effect it helped to make possible a project like that which Paul Bové edited in *boundary 2* (1979) on "Revisions of the Anglo-American Tradition."

For a critic interested in the metaphysicals, Shakespeare, and the moderns and working in the 1940s and 1950s, Kermode remained remarkably aloof from New Criticism. This probably helped him to establish his authority while New Criticism was still controversial, and it helped his work retain its freshness as New Criticism aged. His distance from New Criticism was related to his perceiving its alliance with the symbolist occult, especially in accepting spatial form as a means of defeating history, and it was also related to his awareness that New Criticism was crucial in routinizing modernism. A recurrent early gesture of Kermode's was to refuse yet "another explication" (*RI* 83; *Wallace Stevens* 111). But beyond this, he took from the modernist writers themselves principles analogous to those of New Criticism, which he could therefore dispense with.

Thus, Lawrence's dictum to trust the tale not the artist, and its corollary that the critic's task was to save the tale from the artist, offered Kermode an anti-intentionalist position that de-authorizes the text (*Puzzles* 204). Consider his remarks on Lawrence himself: "The modernity of this master lies not in the metaphysic but in its transformation. He inherited a disposition to invent and to trust transcendent systems, but understood that the pluralities and ambiguities proper to art will not admit them" (*D. H. Lawrence* 28). Unlike the New Critics who therefore tended to ignore the metaphysic, Kermode attended scrupulously to it, took fierce, ingenious

225

pleasure in figuring it out and demonstrating just how much of the text it did account for, until its final defeat. This heritage from his work on Spenserian allegory and the willed obscurity of George Chapman informed Kermode's reading of twentieth-century texts. Moreover, when New Critics did attend to the "system," as in the exemplary readings by Cleanth Brooks of Yeats' *Vision* and Warren of Coleridge's "sober prose" along with the "Ancient Mariner," they showed the poetry as fitting, even if only through sleight of hand, while Kermode showed its discrepancy.

"Faking" is the crucial term Kermode adapted from E. M. Forster (*Puzzles* 81) for the process by which "vertical" dimensions of systematic consonance were added to the "horizontal" of the story line, a matter also at stake in *Mimesis* (as noted in chapter 1). Such faking was in Kermode's earlier work the writer's task, not the critic's. In his later work, concern with writing as itself an interpretive process made this distinction less tenable. This notion of Forster's, which has never been abandoned, caused Kermode trouble in another way as well. Kermode agreed with Forster that a novel did— "oh dear yes"—tell a story. Story was thus an atavism, responding to primitive needs (*Continuities* 150–51), but so also was the hermeneutic of "love" that performed "faking" by adding its verticals of consonance to "loveless sequence" (*Puzzles* 79). Thus both dimensions of novels proved "regressive" and implicated in myth and mystery. Such dilemmas arose from the very process of binary division, to which Kermode was from the first addicted, and they provoked many of the later twists to his work.

Let me return to the positive use Kermode made of modernist poetics. The position he had already established in the 1950s gave him a place to stand in the engagement, beginning from the later sixties, with French "structuralism." Kermode gained from this engagement technical specifications with which to elaborate his long preoccupations. For instance the polarity of metaphor and metonymy, drawn from Roman Jakobson, allowed his continuing to work with the two dimensions of "faking," while the Saussurean dispossession of the thinking subject from the system of language gave new force to Lawrentian anti-authorialism. Kermode once remarked that on the whole the English have always learned more from the French than the French from the English, although he did not endorse this situation (*Puzzles* 40). The native tradition of Empson and New Criticism, and before them Henry James, antedated the French discovery of plurality and ambiguity, while the French still suffered from the errors of schismatic historiography. (Kermode and de Man alike accuse Roland Barthes here.) Yet to give yourself, as Kermode did, even for a bewildering minute, to Roland Barthes will change you. For Kermode it opened the possibility of a "science of literature" apart from criticism.

Before I consider Kermode's quest for a literary science, however, I must address his most famous book, the work that made him a public and exemplary figure—*The Sense of an Ending: Studies in the Theory of Fiction*. This was Kermode's real book on Wallace Stevens, whose meditations on fiction figured in every chapter and whose words provided both the book's end and an epigraph for it. That epigraph was the same passage from "An Ordinary Evening in New Haven" with which Harold Bloom began his full-fledged revisionism in *The Anxiety of Influence*:

> a more severe,
> More harassing master would extemporize
> Subtler, more urgent proof that the theory
> Of poetry is the theory of life
> As it is, in the intricate evasions of as.

For Kermode, as for Bloom, Stevens provided a humane way of evading the impasse of modernism while remaining in touch with the greatest literature of our times. Yeats had been crucial in *Romantic Image*; here he was still important but was displaced by Stevens (as was Eliot, *Continuities* 76). Kermode noted in *The Sense of an Ending* that Yeats had claimed in *A Vision* to hold together "reality" and "justice" in a single thought, but Kermode argued that the system Yeats devised had no "reality" but was all "justice." It was "a plot, a purely human projection, though not more human than its apparent antithesis, reality, which is a human imagining of the inhuman" (105). Or, in Stevens' own words, "the absence of the imagination had itself to be imagined." This brilliant move set the stage for later problems with "reality" which complicated and confused Kermode's relation to history, but here it worked.

227

In *Romantic Image* Kermode had prophesied the end of Mallarméan "literature" and looked forward to a kind of writing that would acknowledge the discursive qualities of language, writing that would join human life instead of holding aloof in deathly indifference. Stevens' sense of "fiction" as a transient product of human need offered a bridge between myth and history that might function for us as *aevum* had for the Christian thinkers faced with Aristotle, in offering them an angelic time between human finitude and divine eternity. Kermode's recovery of *aevum* as a fiction of "complementarity" enabled him to achieve his most moving pages of criticism, on the sense of time in Shakespearean tragedy (*SE* 59, 67–74, 82–89).

The special success of *The Sense of an Ending* stemmed from its own "closure," achieved through the reconciling mediation of the concept of fiction. All of Kermode's books confronted a powerful ambivalence, like the "tension" he found in Edmund Wilson's *Axel's Castle* (*Puzzles* 60). In *Romantic Image* the object of ambivalence was Yeats himself; in *The Classic*, the myth of empire; in *The Genesis of Secrecy*, the division between insiders and outsiders; but only in *The Sense of an Ending* were both sides harmonized.

To grasp more concretely this harmony, or closure, take the original title of the lecture series on which the book was based: "The Long Perspectives." It immediately evoked one of Kermode's great virtues: his own willingness to take the long perspective. From the beginning he acknowledged in *Romantic Image* that this was "not . . . my 'period'" (vii); *The Sense of an Ending* took in all time, while *The Classic* and *The Genesis of Secrecy* spanned at least the whole of the common era, from the time of Vergil and Jesus to the present. Thus Kermode emulated the scope of Curtius and Auerbach. But this made Kermode himself a revisionist symbolist historian, despite his repeated, insistent opposition to notions of "crisis" that allowed a prophetic "Pisgah" sight, spatializing time (*Continuities* 45). When we recognize, however, the context from which Kermode drew the phrase "the long perspectives," all this turns around. The phrase came from Philip Larkin's poem "Reference Back" and thus reasserted Kermode's links with the modest poetry of the British "Movement" of the 1950s. In the poem the phrase works against the mastery that we have just associated with

Kermode's position, pushing us instead to his critique of the far-sighted:

> Truly, though our element is time,
> We are not suited to the long perspectives
> Open at each instant of our lives.
>   They link us to our losses.
>   (*SE* 179)

As perfectly as the key metaphor of a poem read New Critically, Larkin's phrase embodied the tension of Kermode's whole book and thus assured the work its unity.

After *The Sense of an Ending*, Stevens' direct presence diminished (though he yielded the epigraph to *Forms of Attention*). The imagination, that great reconciling term which links Stevens to the romantics and which literally had the last word in *The Sense of an Ending*, disappeared (as also from the work of Harold Bloom, as we have seen) in favor of linguistic and hermeneutic models of transformation. The existential pathos of death, or of "poverty," was no longer so emphasized. Yet Stevens' imperative "It must change" remained. Consider the subtitle of *The Classic: Literary Images of Permanence and Change*.

The major change I see between Kermode's earlier and more recent work began as a reversal, not a rupture. From focusing on the schismatic and the sectarian—the artist and symbol in isolation, apocalypticists—and bringing history, tradition, to bear on them, Kermode instead focused on the historical institution of tradition itself, the process of interpretive transformation in secular and Christian literature and within the academy.

In *The Sense of an Ending*, considering the irrationality that bred national socialism in Germany, Kermode believed that criticism had the responsibility to justify "ideas of order" (124), but the orders he found in *The Classic* and *The Genesis of Secrecy* were all too many and too strong. The values we seek may lie, after all, in disorder, in impropriety. How had this come about? History and myth, the dialectic opposites of the earlier work, collapsed into the single term

229

of fiction. What then could offer freedom from the institutions that constrain us, even while they empower us to produce and consume fiction? *Secrecy* became Kermode's positive answer, a term of mystery that replaced history as the positive; and secrecy was the benevolent dark complement of the institution itself—as in Shelley's *Prometheus Unbound* Demogorgon was to Jupiter. Kermode had begun to think about "secrets" in dialogue with the "hermeneutic code" of Roland Barthes' *S/Z* (*AT* 72ff.). Only in the last decade did he begin to take "hermeneutic" in a productive sense, rather than in the limiting senses of theorists otherwise so different as Barthes and E. D. Hirsch. In "Institutional Control of Interpretation" (*AT*) he emphasized limitation, in *The Genesis of Secrecy* production, while in "Can We Say Absolutely Anything We Like?" (*AT*) he referred to Foucault's work as a basis for limitation—although Foucault's work had by that time turned to emphasize productivity.

However vexed, the solution of "secrecy" only emerged after *The Classic*, which reached an impasse requiring a new departure. Following T. S. Eliot's line of inquiry, *The Classic* found Vergil "the type of all classics" and also "the classic of empire." The classic thus implied a central mastery, to which peripheral provinces must be subordinated, yet somehow there came to be a modern, vernacular classic that coexisted with linguistic and political dispersal. In one of his most illuminating historical inquiries, Kermode drew the line from Vergil to Eliot, showing how it happened that for Eliot the Mallarméan project of cleansing the tongue of the tribe was correlated to the divine right of kings. In the Middle Ages, "discrepancies" between the "mystique of Empire" and "the facts of imperial history" affected the fate of the classic. In a reading analogous to that in which he showed the disruption of metaphysics in Lawrence, Kermode dwelt on "the facts" and the concomitant theoretical-legal negotiations between the empire and the Papacy. Lawyers "emerged as philosophers of Empire" through developing a theory of "change," related to the system of "double truth." This analysis suggests a genealogy of the word *aevum*, the term that articulated so much of *The Sense of an Ending*: it is an imperial myth (*C* 17, 28, 32, 41). I would extend Kermode's insight to Coleridge's key term for the power of imagination: "co-adunation." The word first entered his writing (1802) to describe a goal of the Roman empire (*Collected Works* 3.1:319). Sublimated into aesthetics, it then participated in England's renewed imperial ambitions after Napoleon was defeated.

The next two chapters in *The Classic* traced the complex afterlife of the imperial concept in Milton and Marvell and then effected a translation further westward to America and Hawthorne, who offered a new, nonauthoritative classic that demanded—rather than merely allowing—the reader's participation. The dazzling wealth of philological insight in the Hawthorne chapter cannot hide the chapter's swerve from the political concerns so strong in the earlier chapters. But surely the replacement of empires by democracy should not eliminate the relevance of the political? (I have tried to give positive substance to this suggestion in "The Politics of *The Scarlet Letter*.") At whatever level of intention, Kermode's move echoed the American "end of ideology" theorists who are his contemporaries and who gained prominence in the pages of some of the same journals.

The book's last chapter, on *Wuthering Heights*, ignored the whole matter of history, except for the necessity that the work's original readers have died in order to free the text from its initial generic constraints and open it to us. As the weight of history lifted in these last two chapters, Kermode's book came itself to feel schismatic. Its final metaphor tried to bring the old imperial myth "down to earth," but the book was up in the air, resting only on the demonstration of structural properties in *Wuthering Heights* that allowed for a plurality of readings. M. H. Abrams had by this time in *Natural Supernaturalism* fully elaborated the Wordsworthian, Hegelian myth of secularization and internalization, but that myth, which had operated so effectively in *The Sense of an Ending*, remained in this case a futile gesture.

Kermode insisted that "accommodation," by which the classic for our purposes is "induced to signify what it cannot be said to have expressly stated," was preferable to the scholarly limitation of the text to what it *"meant"* (C 40). He insisted as well that this preference did not threaten "to beat history and sever our communications with the dead" (a phrasing drawn from Auden—*Shakespeare* 174). He emphasized, "It happens I set a high value on these and wish to preserve them. I think there is a substance that persists" (C 134–35). Yet the only reason Kermode offered for his belief was Barthes' "literary science," based on a system of "empty" signifiers that always maintain a surplus beyond whatever interest they serve. This promised a fecund permanence, while Jonathan Culler's theory of literary competence assured Kermode that there were limits to that fecundity. But Saussurean differential signifiers are not a "substance," however much we might wish them to be, and since the theory of competence was based on readers and not texts, I do not see that it promised anything for the identity of the text over time. Thus the metaphysical hopes of comfort ran to the ground, leaving the mechanisms of text and institution. Kermode himself did not confess the impasse I have here defined (although his "Reply" credited me with insight on this matter), but I offer two reasons for my claim. First, the extraordinarily meager response to *The Classic*, despite its author's eminence and the great merit in many of its parts, suggests that readers did not know what to make of it, sensing an incoherence. Second, positing this dilemma explains the new turn in Kermode's later work.

Resolutely, then, following out the path of his inquiry, Kermode turned to the institutions of reading themselves in *The Genesis of Secrecy*, but at one remove from literary study, examining instead the history and process of biblical interpretation. This swerve from literature deserves remark as a sign of the times. After the programmatic self-enclosure of New Criticism and long methodological indebtedness to linguistics, psychology, and anthropology, criticism had begun to enlarge its purview, to judge as well as learn from other disciplines. In this respect, Kermode's book resembled *Orientalism* (1978) by Edward W. Said, which likewise scrutinized a hitherto safe scholarly specialty. Yet there was also—ironically, perhaps timidly—in Kermode, as directly in Said, an element of institutional self-criticism. By looking at an adjacent field with the detachment of an outsider, Kermode was free to note facts and tendencies within the humanities that might be less easy to see or acknowledge in literary studies themselves, though no less present.

For *The Genesis of Secrecy* showed the horror of the historical institution of biblical interpretation. It was a genealogy of the way we read now, yet cast in a form whose displacement puzzled readers. Gerald Graff and E. D. Hirsch in simultaneous reviews said quite opposed things about what Kermode's position was, and I read it yet differently. Hirsch was wrong, I think, to believe that the book offered, even chimerically, the power of institutional control as a good thing ("Carnal Knowledge" 20). From the beginning, Kermode's stance was that of the outsider, beyond the institutional pale. He dedicated the book "to those outside" and then repeated it in Greek so that Greekless moderns would be sure to feel the pain and bafflement of exclusion. The readers he singled out for praise were those who contravened institutional norms. Take Kermode's third chapter: there, amid the ennui of routine Joyce scholarship based on the premise that everything Joyce wrote must have meaning, he credited Robert Martin Adams with a coup for claiming that the man in the macintosh in *Ulysses*, who appears at Paddy Dignam's funeral and is referred to several other times, meant nothing. By contrast, in the interpretation of Mark's Gospel, Austin Farrer won praise from Kermode for an elaborate typological exegesis that gave significance to the boy in a white shirt, who is mentioned only once as fleeing when Jesus was arrested. Farrer thus produced meaning where the institution had been content to see a mere historical detail. This praise of Farrer is especially telling because over the previous two decades Kermode had several times supported Helen Gardner's attack on Farrer, in which she charged Farrer's overingenuity with causing us to lose hold on the Gospel's "actuality" (*Puzzles* 32; *Shakespeare* 24; *SE* 48).

Why is it good to transgress "the institution's ideas of order"? Because the institutional will to power in interpretation had such disastrous consequences. In *The Sense of an Ending*, the ideology of the Third Reich, derived from the scriptural interpretations of Joachim da Fiore, could be safely segregated as a myth, but *The Genesis of Secrecy* recognized it as a fiction, and "fictions, wrongly or carnally read, may prey upon life" (72, 20). Yet institutional power builds walls, *making* outsiders, thus ensuring that reading will be carnal and, therefore, dangerous to life. Kermode described the force of institutions, and I think Gerald Graff was wrong to find Kermode transmuting this "fact into an imperative" (Review 29). For example, Kermode described the moment when a "hermeneutical fiat" (*GS* 18) created a previously nonexistent book, the "Old Testament," out of the Hebrew Bible and then found the Old Testament deafness, blindness, and forgetfulness except insofar as it prefigured Christianity. If this was a "model of our own procedures" (*GS* 20), as Kermode stated and as my earlier analysis of Matthew Arnold would underwrite, I take Kermode to mean so much the worse for us (he joins Harold Bloom against Northrop Frye). For we thereby assume complicity in activities like that by which Matthew imputed to the Jews guilt for the Crucifixion—a fiction Kermode mentioned in parallel with that of the Third Reich.

Another reason for thinking that Kermode did not recommend these procedures is that, as both Graff and Hirsch failed to emphasize, Kermode himself neither practiced nor prescribed interpretation: "My task is not so much to offer interpretations as to speak of their modes, their possibilities, and their disappointments" (*GS* 133). Kermode assumed a skeptical stance, as he had before. In *The Sense of an Ending*, skepticism meant a return from texts to reality, from myth to history—like Boswell's description of Samuel Johnson refuting Berkeley on the nonexistence of matter by "striking his foot with mighty force against a large stone, till he rebounded from it." In *The Genesis of Secrecy*, skepticism meant not kicking the stone but doubting the story, moving not from myth to history, but from interpretation to text, from history to mystery. By limiting his concern to "what is written" rather than "what . . . is written about" (*GS* 119), Kermode hoped to halt the rush to the referent that leads us to the insider's deluded hope for truth, on which are founded the murderous fictions of our history. Fredric Jameson, in contrast, prefers to replace the referent with an "absent cause."

What can you do then? In an examplary recent essay, "Secrets and Narrative Sequence" (*AT*), Kermode enacted in his procedure the model of Kafka's "Before the Law," which had served as his pivot from the insider to the outsider in *The Genesis of Secrecy*. He sits outside an open door, dimly sensing a radiance within. Were he within, his back would be to the radiance and he would only be a figure of malevolent exclusion, serving a light he could not see; but from the outside, the saving reserve of secrecy promises sense. "Secrets and Narrative Sequence" found in plot, the sequencing of a novel, a process of foregrounding that causes us not to read certain elements of the text, which become "background." Thus, much of "what is written" is excluded through our interpretive commitment to what has been "written about." By looking at the "background"—perhaps following Lawrence on Hardy—another plot, a secret plot, emerges, which cannot be mastered into integration—

or at least Kermode dismissed all the candidates for integration that he found. Thus the book was saved from being consumed.

Kermode once quoted a French sixteenth-century commentator on the Apocalypse, offering what we may take as an allegory of reading: the ungodly are "consumed," but the elect are "afflicted to their own profit: namely that they may be murthered into patience" (*Shakespeare* 172). By murdering, by molesting and afflicting the authority of the plot, by transgressing the institutional norms of interpretation and taking a stance outside them, writer and reader bring the work to patience. "Patience" throughout Kermode's work named the quality in literature that allowed it to bear interpretation. He took the term from a dictum of Alfred North Whitehead's: "Nature is patient of interpretation in terms of laws that interest us." Kermode cited this repeatedly over a period of twenty years, most recently altering it into "whatever" interests us, rather than "laws," perhaps because laws, ideas of order, had become less interesting (*Puzzles* 50; *Shakespeare* 158; *SE* 38; *GS* xi). What does interest Kermode is preserving the sense of literature as an ever-available second nature, maintaining an identity that was easily established for Pope thinking of Vergil imitating Homer ("Nature and Homer were the same"), but less easily in modern times.

It is as if there were an ecological crisis in literature, and Kermode feared texts' being used up—consumed as Roland Barthes in *S/Z* claimed that the "readerly" are—rather than remaining willing patients for our interpretive ministrations. The text's secrecy is what prevents its being consumed, for secrecy is *potential* for interpretation, an available reserve. Secrecy disappears when an interpretation is actually accomplished; the relation to Geoffrey Hartman's "hermeneutics of indeterminancy" is clear. A proliferation of interpretations threatens to foreground every element in the text, reducing it to a uniformly illuminated platitude: this would be the danger of sheer academic routinization in the service of actualizing pluralism. Marxism, however refined and complex its procedures, also risks that platitude by committing itself to an interpretation based on a particular wager about history. I have referred to Raymond Williams earlier, but Fredric Jameson has offered the most important current Marxist theory of interpretation. Deconstruction, in contrast to Kermode's model, refuses the dualism of light and dark or inside and outside; it distrusts any "grounding," whether "back-" or "fore-," and turns to ungrounded figures in Derrida's topology or de Man's tropology. Kermode is the alternative, but only at the cost of his both abandoning his concern with history and refusing the pleasuress and rigors alike of really reading. He alludes to the Derridian "supplement" as what his secret counterplot offers, but there is none of the reversal and more subtle osmotic leakage that in Derrida disrupts binary oppositions.

I find that Kermode abandoned history in at least two ways when in "Secrets and Narrative Sequence" he specified the secret counterplot of Conrad's *Under Western Eyes* in terms of a shiftily interrelated complex of unusual sensory modalities of hearing and seeing, along with a pneumatological world of phantoms, ghosts, spirits, and devils. First, he did not even allow into his essay the novel's culminating scene of suffering: Razumov is run down by a streetcar after being first deafened and then temporarily blinded. Thus Kermode's commentary truncated the plot—the history—of the work in order to enhance the mystery, lest the plot after all recuperate the secrets. Second, Kermode barely mentioned that what is at issue in *Under Western Eyes*—what is "written about"— is the world of revolutionary conspiracy in Geneva around 1900, with which Conrad had mixed echoes of the French revolutionary period as well as of the mid-century figures familiar to him from the Polish politics of his youth. Throughout the nineteenth-century literature of revolution within which Conrad inscribed his text there ran the language of the supernatural: "A spectre is haunting Europe," begins the Communist Manifesto. "Communication with the dead" occurs through politics as well as art: in their different ways Edmund Burke's *Reflections on the Revolution in France* and Marx's *Eighteenth Brumaire of Louis Bonaparte* insisted on this, as did a more recent retrospective fiction of politics in Conrad's period, John Berger's *G*. Such intertextual material has as much relevance to a reading of *Under Western Eyes*, even for its secrets, as do the wanderings of the term "type" in Kermode's exploration of Hawthorne. Yet to move in this direction would move toward interpretation, and that's the move Kermode wants to stop. There are, of course, problems in pursuing this course too, as chapter 11 finds with Fredric Jameson's interpretation of Conrad's *Nostromo*.

Kermode now values for their disruptive potential the very elements of the text that he once considered dangerous to its "actuality," the "vertical," "typological" elements he formerly associated with consonance, concord, and spatial form. We may sense here a wish to stare through the door and *know* the text's generative powers, a fascination comparable to the willed fixation in de Man's moment of rigor. Kermode has a loving eye for the quirk and oddity of Conrad's text, yet such textual eroticism may be no freer than the panopticism of spatial form, even while promising liberation. Choosing interpretation joins us to history; choosing secrecy opens the timeless, abstract potential of textual mystery: "it is the text that saves us."

Chapter 10
Paul de Man and Deconstruction:
Aesthetics, Rhetoric, History

FOR SOME FIFTEEN YEARS before his death in 1983, Paul de Man's writing and teaching led the American movement known as "deconstructive criticism." As already discussed in chapter 4, the fixity of death by no means assures that we can now understand his work with greater rigor. Influence may swell when its specific circumstances pass from consciousness under repression. So de Man argued from Nietzsche in "Literary History and Literary Modernity" (1970), the best brief elaboration of his theoretical starting point. Nonetheless, there is some use in trying to forestall myth by history, and here I essay this through a deliberately reductive strategy: setting de Man's major book, *Allegories of Reading* (1979; henceforth abbreviated *AR*), alongside the first book of a younger critic, *Nietzsche, Henry James, and the Artistic Will* (1978; henceforth abbreviated *NJ*) by Stephen Donadio. Donadio was more ambitious than most, placing himself in the lines of Lionel Trilling and Walter Kaufmann, yet compared with de Man, he exemplified recent "normal" American critical practice. The differences between de Man's position and Donadio's clarify the beginnings of de Man's work in countercommentary, more an intervention within criticism than a direct response to works of literature. Without the normal errors such as appear in Donadio, it seems that de Man might never have written, for his criticism was parasitic, belated, revisionary in presupposing a primary pattern of reading to work from. Almost always in de Man's essays, however, the primary pattern was assumed, merely alluded to or worked through so briefly that many readers did not grasp the point or else took it as a straw man. Donadio's book offers a usefully generous example. The contrast with Donadio, then, helps define the novelty of de Man's work in the arena of American criticism. Any similarities that remain between them emphasize all the more strikingly the defining traits of recent critical practice.

Nietzsche continues to puzzle us; reading him produces such divergent effects that even the limited discipline of literary criticism contains interpretations of Nietzsche which suggest wholly different ways of our living in the world. Stephen Donadio made art and the self his interlocked master term; reading and rhetoric were the key words for Paul de Man. The reality of literature for Donadio was aesthetic, for de Man linguistic. They agreed only in denigrating history. Nietzsche, however, did not compel us to consider writing as only a psychic event or only a verbal event. Nietzsche allowed us to understand writing as an event within a culture, among people, working from and toward social relations, between a past and a future, as I argue against Fredric Jameson in the next chapter. Yet after some attention to the cultural "air" of the later nineteenth century, Donadio left us stranded in the imagination, while de Man—for instance—found only "pseudo-historical arguments" (*AR* 117) in Nietzsche's specification of difference between Greek and German audiences.

The chapters on Nietzsche in *Allegories of Reading* followed initial chapters on great moderns—Yeats, Rilke, Proust—and preceded six chapters on Rousseau. In relating Nietzsche and his contemporary Henry James, Donadio looked forward to Yeats and modernism and backward to Emerson. The seriousness with which we take Nietzsche and his recognized extremity of mind and language allowed Donadio to treat James as the major figure he is, not as a provincial obsessed with "manners." These books thus suggest that recent literary studies share a canon. Both agreed on the appropriate context for Nietzsche: Yeats—who took so much from him and who still so defines our way of thinking about modern literary greatness; Rousseau, James, Proust—novelists of frustrated passion and passionate self-constructors. Beyond this canon, however, there seems no common ground. De Man attacked almost everything that Donadio relied on, for Donadio's book exemplifies the situation within American literary criticism that has made deconstruction flourish. An earlier chapter suggested a public, political context for the appeal of de Man's work; here the emphasis is more internal to the discipline.

From its preliminary remarks on Yeats to its concluding remarks on *The Golden Bowl*, Donadio's book strove to define a unity that reconciled opposites. Yeats wrote of two "pictures" in his memory. First, "I have climbed to the top of a tree by the edge of a playing field, and am looking at my school-fellows and am as proud of my-self as a March cock when it crows to its first sunrise." But then he recalled "a hotel sitting-room in the Strand, where a man is hunched up over a fire . . . a cousin who has speculated with an-other cousin's money and has fled from Ireland in danger of arrest." Each image "represents a fragment of the artist's experience," ar-gued Donadio, but together in "juxtaposition" they offered "simul-taneously and in a single plane" nothing less than "a complete account of the significance of the artistic enterprise" (*NJ* vii–viii). Donadio identified his juxtaposition of Nietzsche and James with the intention he discerned in Yeats. This was no modest gesture toward the necessary fictionalizing and wishfulness that accompany any critical project, for Donadio believed that such paradoxical totalizing actually worked. Witness his concluding observations on Maggie Verver in *The Golden Bowl*: her ultimate triumph he attrib-uted to "a fusion of contradictory qualities of personality" (*NJ* 244) that allowed her to live successfully through the "moral paradox" of the book and achieve within herself "aggressiveness" that was "reconciled" with "renunciation," bringing these "antithetical feel-ings" into a "tense equilibrium." Finally "self-interest and selfless-ness have fused, and the currency of worldly success has become interchangeable with that of spiritual nobility" (251).

This rhetoric was both critical and philosophical. It echoes phrases from Coleridge's *Biographia Literaria* that resound in T. S. Eliot, I. A. Richards, F. O. Matthiessen, Cleanth Brooks, and M. H. Abrams. The modulation within Western philosophy that helped make New Criticism possible and that continued to determine Do-nadio's project is "aesthetics." His work was continuously con-cerned with the "artistic will." To this end, he situated Nietzsche and James amid passages from Schiller's *Letters on the Aesthetic Education of Mankind*, Hegel's *Aesthetics*, and Oscar Wilde. A pas-sage he cited from Wilde gave Donadio's sense of this tradition: "From the high tower of Thought we can look out at the world. Calm, and self-centered, and complete, the aesthetic critic contemplates life." He "is safe" (*NJ* 55). Such distanced, secure overview Donadio defined as the goal both Nietzsche and James sought in the "central belief held increasingly by both" that "art" was "the sole means of ordering and justifying the chaos of our experience in the world . . . a means for the continual reassertion of personality and the mastery of experience" (16).

James demonstrated his mastery in the relation that he established to the "restless, chaotic, random world of experience." To that world, "he would have to yield . . . that portion of his life that was its due if only, ironically, to ensure that that area existing beyond his direct control would always remain available as the unfailing source of sustenance for his all-consuming art" (*NJ* 61). The only irony I find here is that of a sharp bargain. Yield a little to life, and you can make it yours to use forever.

Nietzsche's project was presented as much the same. He tried "to rescue values from the rush of time and to reestablish them—as Plato and his Christian followers also sought to do—on some secure, unchanging ground accessible to persons capable of detaching themselves from their immediate historical circumstances" (*NJ* 99). This read Nietzsche from the point of view of a humanities course surveying the Western tradition, for which Nietzsche had not even "reversed" let alone broken with metaphysics; he had merely recollected it.

To make up for thus diminishing Nietzsche's philosophical interest, Donadio did well to insist that James' concern with "point of view" requires serious philosophical attention. Early in his analysis, Donadio found the Jamesian "lucid reflector" a "simultaneous embodiment of ends and means" (125). This incarnation of reconciled opposites returned, at the climax of Donadio's analysis, as the figure demanded both by James' theories and by Nietzsche's "Use and Abuse of History":"an observer who stands at an ideal aesthetic distance from the experience he describes . . . [who] somehow remains above the experience without being altogether detached from it, a profoundly interested observer whose imagination is engaged" (141–42). Meditation on that "somehow" which made contradictories co-possible led Donadio to recognize "religious implications" (144), resulting in his final formulation: "To the extent that he succeeds, in James's terms, the novelist presents us with a complete and unobstructed vision of nothing less than the world as it is, the world as it would be perceived by the ultimate perceiver, God" (154). "God," however, was not one of "James's terms." It emerged from the logic, or rhetoric, of Donadio's inquiry.

This creation of God as a necessary consequence of an aesthetic position poses extremely serious questions. Where does Donadio stand? Was he showing James up by demonstrating that his position required an entity that it never acknowledged, just as Nietzsche too only echoed the religious "Platonism of the masses" that he thought he had seen through? Or was Donadio co-opting James and Nietzsche for a reconstruction of God to which he subscribes? Regardless of his stand, it is striking that Donadio arrived, quite independently, at Derrida's claim for a systematically coherent relation among art, the self, the symbol, the dialectic, and theology. If one cannot accept this package, if we think that there must be some other way to grasp our lives, must we discard Nietzsche and James?

I find much to suggest that on his own terms Donadio did not win his case. He idealized into a "center" what James called only the "effect of a center" (*NJ* 166) and ignored James' attention to the slippery "displacement" undergone by his makeshift centers (3:1299). I want to focus, however, on Donadio's assertion that Nietzsche and James found the transcendence of history necessary, lest the self be merely a passive product of its times.

Donadio based his claim on a long quotation from Leo Strauss on the function of "Jerusalem" and "Athens" in Nietzsche, from which he drew this lesson: "The distinction here between Jerusalem and Athens would seem to correspond in essence to James's distinction between 'Europe' and 'America'—if that distinction is seen as reflecting the contrast between 'historical' and 'inner' culture which we have already considered, and if it is noted that for James the transcendence of 'historical' culture and the attainment of 'inner' culture functions [*sic*] . . . as moral imperatives" (*NJ* 93). This analogical argument depends on a hall of mirrors, of "seem" and "is seen," correspondence and reflection. Even while emphasizing distinctions, it depends upon assimilation—as in the use of a singular verb for plural subjects. It parallels Athens and Jerusalem (which

Strauss claimed Nietzsche aimed to unite) with America and Europe (which Donadio claimed James aimed to separate).

The earlier links of the chain offer equally significant problems. The contrast of "inner" and "historical" culture came from Thomas Sergeant Perry's reading of Nietzsche (with no evidence offered either that James knew his friend's distinction or that it is a good reading of Nietzsche), and Donadio found in it a "resemblance" to James' "distinction between the culture of Europe and that of America." American culture "consists essentially in the cultivation of the self . . . while for the European [culture] suggests nothing so much as a passive relation—a veritable bondage—to the past." The European "is nothing in himself, but, like Madame Merle in *The Portrait of a Lady*, exists entirely in his 'relations'" (*NJ* 18–19). Madame Merle was the only reference this argument offered to any work of James', but she is an American: "Rarer even than to be French seemed it to be American on such interesting terms," thought Isabel Archer upon meeting Madame Merle (*Portrait* 1:246). She had to acquire her culture with all the avid self-fashioning of Isabel Archer or Henry James himself. So the opposition of Europe and America collapses into a split within "America." Moreover, this description of the European who "is nothing in himself" curiously echoes a great moment of American literature that Donadio later made much of. Emerson's revelation in *Nature*, "crossing a bare common, in snow puddles, at twilight, under a clouded sky," led him into a "passive relation": "I become a transparent eyeball; I am nothing; I see all; the currents of the Universal Being circulate through me" (*NJ* 163).

This Emersonian moment suggests that the problem of the self is more tangled than Donadio's argument allowed; another indication emerges in a passage from *The Portrait of a Lady* cited later. Madame Merle asked, "What shall we call our 'self'? Where does it begin? where does it end? It overflows into everything that belongs to us—and then it flows back again. . . . One's self—for other people—is one's expression of one's self" (*NJ* 80). Although Isabel Archer could not effectively answer Madame Merle, Donadio warned that "it is important not to be misled by James's irony," by which he meant not that we must recognize things are complicated, but that we must recognize Madame Merle as wrong. Yet Madame Merle saw the self as questionable, not as easily defined by conventional boundaries. She insisted only that external expression made one's self *for other people*. Whatever may remain hidden inside is not what we live in the world with.

Donadio rested his whole critical project upon a wager like Madame Merle's that by reading expression one may discover a self. For he characterized his book as entailing "what Nietzsche once described as 'those most difficult and captious of all deductions . . . the deduction which makes one infer something concerning the author from his work'" (x). I find that James also underwrote Madame Merle's stance, and not only in his own descriptive practice. When Isabel analyzed her errors in judging Osmond, she regretted having "mistaken a part for the whole," a synecdochic misinterpretation, but she neither wished nor judged that she could have avoided interpretation and gained immediate intuition of another self. Fully to explore this would involve the relation of James and Balzac, about which Donadio had nothing to say. Balzac was as important to Yeats as was Nietzsche, was as involved as Emerson in responding at once to Swedenborg and Cuvier, was for James the defining figure in the history of the novelistic enterprise to which he committed himself, and is the exemplary writer of the self within what Madame Merle called "the whole envelope of circumstances."

Consider further a letter of James' cited to show that his ambition far exceeded merely writing "novels of manners." Donadio claimed the letter based Americanness on "the assumption that it is possible to free oneself from the past" (*NJ* 75). Yet in the letter James hoped someday to "do for our dear old English letters and writers *something* of what Ste.-Beuve and the best French critics have done for theirs." To do something for old writers, to emulate great elders, was certainly not bondage, but it was hardly to be "free . . . from the past." The reference to Sainte-Beuve came early in the sequence, and Donadio hinted that it was left behind when James really got launched. In quoting about a page, Donadio omitted a few lines, including this sentence: "I feel that my only chance for success as a critic is to let all the breezes of the west blow through me at their will" (*Letters* 1:77). James had high ambitions, but they were attached to *critical* writing, including the critically self-conscious play with hyperbolic literary geography, the "western breezes" that had already for decades figured in American literary manifestos. James' freedom was not in a vacuum, but in refashioning a culture.

Donadio repressed James' wish to be a critic in order to emphasize the story of his creativeness; he emphasized Nietzsche's quest for transcendence but never mentioned the concern with "interpretation" so crucial to Nietzsche whether as philologist, genealogist, or Antichrist. To ignore criticism and interpretation was to ignore the attention both writers paid to reading, to language—both matters of relation to the past as well. One could not tell from Donadio's book that language was a major topic in Nietzsche's writing, nor could one guess the importance James placed in the preface to *The Golden Bowl* (the one novel Donadio read at all) on rereading as an activity continuously productive of differences (3:1330ff.). The New York Edition was James' greatest creation, and it was a historical act of revision.

De Man's work was an antidote for discontent with the James and Nietzsche produced by Donadio; it would have been even more useful for anyone happy with those figures, but happy people shun strong medicine. Just as Donadio expounded what de Man attacked, so he ignored what de Man expounded. Although neither author referred to the other, de Man often seems directly in dialogue with Donadio. Donadio began with the explication of a passage from Yeats, and the first work de Man read was "Among School Children." At the poem's end, de Man noted the modulation from the image of the chestnut tree to that of dancing and found that "synecdoche . . . the most seductive of metaphors" (*AR* 11) tempted us to answer with a happy totalization the question "How can we know the dancer from the dance?" De Man, however, wanted us to take that question very seriously, to feel dismay at the impossibility of separating what are nonetheless importantly distinct elements and thus of achieving knowledge. The problems that complicate the relation of knowledge and action, of any agent and action, are Nietzschean concerns that guided much of de Man's book and that first appeared here. Donadio took two disparate images from Yeats and claimed a unity for the totality they built; de Man took two closely related images, analyzed the temptation to unite them, and concluded that they must be placed firmly apart. In the rhetorical terminology so crucial in his book, and for which Nietzsche was the major explicit theoretical authority, de Man resisted the "seduction" of metaphor (including synecdoche) in order to create metonymies, reducing apparently necessary relations to relations that are merely contingent. De Man developed this basic argument as early as a dissertation chapter on "Image and Emblem in Yeats," first published in his posthumous collection, *The Rhetoric of Romanticism*. Several times there de Man cited Yeats' "How can we *know* the dancer from the dance?" as "How can we *tell* the dancer from the dance?" (both emphases mine), thereby emphasizing the metonymic process of reduction and separation over metaphoric (synecdochic) expression and identity.

De Man examined this pattern of metonymic reduction as it operated through all the texts he read, but one particular aspect of his inquiry opposed Donadio's most directly. De Man challenged the common judgment that after his early work on rhetoric as a professor, Nietzsche as philosopher "turned away from the problems of language to questions of the self" (*AR* 106). Donadio's book corresponded exactly to this commonplace in its lack of attention to language and its constant emphasis on the self as the supreme object of interest for Nietzsche and James.

De Man scrutinized writers' language, but he also showed the scrutiny to which writers' texts had already put language. He insisted that "discursive texts," those that we call nonfictional or philosophical, must be read just as attentively as we read fictional or literary texts. Both kinds of texts are difficult because "dialogical." Such a text "puts the truth or falsehood of its own statement in question." "Dialogical" texts are responsible in their assertions not by maintaining an inhibited equipoise, but, as in good dialogue, by making strong statements that are answered back, either explicitly in argument or implicitly through narrative or figure. As a result, we must interpret the whole text before we can know what to make of any part of it—that is, such texts "cannot be *quoted* without first having been *read*" (*AR* 226). This remark hit Donadio. Too often he quoted long passages as if their bearing were self-evident; too often the observations made on such quoted passages had no clear relation to what had been quoted and were clarified by no argument elucidating their relation to the work as a whole.

Because rhetorical language complicates the simple regularities of logic or grammar, because of the problematic relation between language in use and language as a tool of theory, de Man warned repeatedly against expecting to find a smooth continuity between a writer's "poetry and poetics" (*AR* 25). "Deconstruction" itself depends on discrepancies in this realm, for it does not work through a relation "between statements" as in logic or dialectic. Rather it "happens" between "metalinguistic statements about the rhetorical nature of language" and a "rhetorical praxis that puts these statements into . . . question" (98). Yet Donadio treated James for a whole book before finally offering a brief reading of one novel, and he gave no hint that the practice of James' fiction ever jarred with the theoretical statements about point of view in the prefaces to the New York Edition.

Donadio and de Man stood opposed on four issues then: should critics define unities, or specify the absence of unity? does language have priority over the self? may we quote without reading? can we trust that a writer's works embody his or her poetics? Taking de Man's side would give us a Nietzsche and James who do not aim to be God. But perhaps de Man was just the latest whitewash for literature, attempting to make it seem more responsible and harmless than it really is.

Such a suspicion is hard to avoid, and it can never be removed, for de Man's own position may have mistaken the effect of his readings. Yet the comparison with Donadio highlights those elements within de Man that most subdue this suspicion.

Allegories of Reading was a sustained polemic against the "aesthetic" as a category for criticism, however unavoidable it might be in life. Crucial to Donadio was Nietzsche's early statement that life found its justification only as an *"aesthetic phenomenon"* (*NJ* 196, 200). De Man remarked that for Nietzsche this was "an indictment of existence rather than a panegyric of art" (*AR* 93). Proust's writing, de Man argued, exposed "the metaphysical system that allows for the aesthetic to come into being as a category" (14). When de Man noted our neglect of the "dialogic" character of philosophic writing, he laid blame on "ideologies derived from the misuse of aesthetic categories" (226). Is there any proper use of the aesthetic? De Man's essay on Rilke stripped away all the reasons aesthetics ever offered for admiring great poetry, and Rousseau "never allows for a 'purely' aesthetic reading" of his novel *Julie*, for he

248

finds in "suspended meaning" not "disinterested play" but instead "always a threat or a challenge" (207–8). Rousseau therefore always acknowledged a referential dimension to his novel, as to the rest of his writings.

De Man followed Rousseau in elaborating this point. For Kant to "ground aesthetic judgment in nonreferentiality," de Man charged, was to make possible "semiological insight" but only "at the cost of a repression" with decisive consequences for literary criticism. For it turned "theoretical poetics," which is a "branch of applied linguistics," into "aesthetics," which is a "branch of applied psychology" (208). The rigor of de Man's disciplinary vision claimed to know precisely the proper scope and interrelations of our critical activities. So long as ordinary criticism prevails, the danger of rigorously reified categories may count for less than the reductive force of de Man's challenge. That challenge was to define our critical task as linguistic analysis, shunning aesthetics and the self, which are bound to each other in a metaphysical system of totalization that makes every writer and reader struggle to be God.

We might escape this totalizing temptation, this "seduction," only by recognizing the necessary referentiality of language, argued de Man. He did not, however, thereby return literature to the world. For referentiality he made a function of language quite independent of the real existence of its referents. Indeed, rhetorical analysis can show reference to be impossible. The nature of language is such, however, that, as my previous sentence exemplifies, "deconstruction states the fallacy of reference in a necessarily referential mode" (125). A fuller formulation of this principle summarized de Man's exploration of aesthetics and the self in Rousseau: "The discourse by which the figural structure of the self is asserted fails to escape from the categories it claims to deconstruct, and this remains true, of course, of any discourse which pretends to reinscribe in its turn the figure of this aporia. There can be no escape from the dialectical movement that produces the text" (187).

"Text" was de Man's most specific concern. In quiet polemic against the emphasis of Roland Barthes on the pleasurable "liberation of the signifier" (*AR* 114) and against the exhilaration that Derrida found warranted by Nietzsche, de Man insisted that textuality is terribly frustrating rather than gratifying. How *can* we know the dancer? He dwelt on, and in, this cognitive impasse. So he defined a *"text"* as a double bind, as "any entity that can be considered from [this] double perspective: as a generative, open-ended, non-referential grammatical system and as a figural system closed off by a transcendental signification that subverts the grammatical code to which the text owes its existence" (270).

A text can never "know" what it is doing; it has lost the privilege de Man once accorded to literature. *Blindness and Insight* argued that critics were caught in the strange logic of the title but that literary writing was free from it. In contrast to his interpreters, Rousseau had no blind spots. But in de Man's later work every text by definition had blind spots. Moreover, de Man abandoned the New-Critical and aesthetic terminology of "literary language," a crucially repeated term even in the latest essays of *Blindness and Insight* but virtually absent from *Allegories of Reading*. This trajectory of de Man's work hardly made him a defender of literature.

He stood rather with Rousseau and Plato, occupying and challenging the border between literature and philosophy by their willingness to name literature as "lie." Plato and Rousseau attacked literature by taking seriously its claims to truth—perhaps, readers have felt, because their own extreme susceptibility to literature kept them from heeding disclaimers that it need not be taken so seriously, no one believes it anyway. De Man wrote from the stance of one who had been betrayed by literature and was trying, gingerly, to discover what it was that had done this to him. His most common term for the effect of literature was "seduction" (e.g., *AR* ix, 11, 14, 15, 20–22, 24, 26, 35, 42, 45, 53, 55, 66, 67, 71, 93, 110, 114, 115, 119, 159, 169, 181, 184, 200, 205, 210, 262, 298). This was no happy eroticism, but a dangerous temptation that deconstruction existed to combat.

The function of this figure in de Man gains important illumination from the "Diary of the Seducer" in Kierkegaard's anatomy of the "aesthetic," *Either/Or*. The character A comments on the seducer, who may be himself:

> He knew how to excite a girl to the highest pitch, so . . . that she was ready to sacrifice everything. When the affair reached this point, he broke off without himself having made the slightest advances and without having let fall a single word of love, let alone a declaration, a promise. And still it had happened, and the consciousness of it was doubly bitter for the unhappy girl because there was not the slightest

250

thing to which she could appeal . . . since the relationship had had reality only in the figurative sense. . . . It was real, and yet, when she wished to speak of it, there was nothing to tell. (1:303)

In this model of the aesthetic text, its nonreferential, purely contemplative status produces a situation in which it seems that the victims seduce themselves. This for de Man was what we do in reading through the category of the aesthetic. Yet even to see that a text is referential, that it does make "promises" (*AR* 275–76), may lessen our guilt but in no way protects us from other pain. Such is our humanity that even when we have reduced the text to a "machine," its power remains and "seduces [us] into dangerously close contact" (298). Like Nietzsche, Rousseau, Proust, and James, de Man constantly rewrote a story of impossible, destructive passion.

In de Man's reading, Julie's insight into the blindness of her love for Saint-Preux (in Rousseau's *La Nouvelle Héloïse*) could not save her from repeating the error of love, with God as its object. In de Man's writing, his insight into the errors of metaphorical assimilation could not prevent him from repeating that gesture throughout his work. To write of rhetorical deconstruction necessitated de Man's stretching the senses of such rhetorical terms as chiasmus and anacoluthon, carrying them over from matters of word order and grammatical construction into semantics, thus himself leaping the gap he had so labored to establish between grammar and meaning. His most constant trope transferred consciousness and agency, such as we usually attribute to people, to language itself. We have already noticed "seduction"; "knowledge" also figured in this play. Thus he claimed, "Any speech act produces an excess of cognition, but it can never hope to know the process of its own production (the only thing worth knowing)" (*AR* 300). As if speech acts suffered from the Freudian family-romance syndrome!

De Man's practice undid his theoretical attempt to disrupt the categories of inner and outer (which allow for a transfer of properties leading to a synecdochic totalization). For to describe the process of deconstruction, he constructed metaphysical dualisms, the revelation of what was hidden, the discovery of reality beneath appearance. Thus he wrote, "A vast . . . network is revealed . . .

that remained invisible to a reader caught in naive metaphorical mystification" (*AR* 16); but this is only an example. (See also ix, 67, 72, 124, 212, 249.) Even to raise the question of "truth and error" and thus challenge the aesthetic, he appealed to a sense of "epistemology" that would offer philosophic "foundation" (245) for our beliefs. Yet Richard Rorty has argued at persuasive length, and de Man following Derrida elsewhere briefly suggested, that such a foundational epistemology is itself untenable.

All this is no more than de Man acknowledged; he claimed no freedom from the textual problematic that he elucidated. In his essay on Rousseau's *Narcissus*, for instance, he depicted a figure that many readers would take for his own ideal self-image: "No longer the dupe of his own wishes . . . he is as far beyond pleasure and pain as he is beyond good and evil. . . . His consciousness is neither happy nor unhappy, nor does he possess any power. He remains, however, a center of authority to the extent that the very destructiveness of his ascetic reading testifies to the validity of his interpretation" (173–74). The essay proceeded to dismantle this figure. The question remains, however, whether de Man's text can avoid establishing this "center of authority" and setting it to work. For in recent American criticism this figure, although an error, has had an extremely powerful effect. This mask walks among us, gives talks, writes dissertations, publishes, and its name is legion.

De Man's work has entered history, solving in practice the theoretical impasse from which *Allegories of Reading* began, when de Man found himself "unable to progress" (ix) from local reading to a broader history. His theory projects this case outward: history exists only as a repetition of that inability to progress, only in allegorizing the self-consuming tangle of textuality. If "necessity" is a mark of history, then history will always be a metaphorical fiction, but contrary to de Man's suggestion (289–90), there is no incompatibility between causality and contingency. He claimed that "the use of a vocabulary of contingency . . . within an argument of causality is arresting and disruptive" (288). But it is perfectly normal to say, "I was late because ⌊causality⌋ there happened [contingency] to be an accident blocking the way." Moreover, de Man linked contingency to metonymy, which most rhetorics link to causality. He derived metonymy as contingency from its accepted sense as "contiguity," and here too confusions arose, for at times he took contiguity as the "isolation" of one thing from another (145), at times as connection, continuity—or the surrealistically conflated "continguity" (14, 66). It would benefit us if de Man had read his own figures of history as attentively as he read the metaphorical seductions of the texts he scrutinized. For when de Man claimed that rhetoric had only the "appearance of a history" (131) or that "temporal sequence" was only a "semblance," these disjunctions, in abjuring history, reconstructed metaphysical duality.

Nietzsche, just where he most lent himself to de Man, offered also the possibility of another reading that enabled genealogical history. De Man quoted Nietzsche's famous answer to "What is truth?": "A moving army of metaphors [*sic*], metonymies and anthropomorphisms, in short a summa of human relationships that are being poetically and rhetorically sublimated, transposed, and beautified until, after long and repeated use, a people considers them as solid, canonical, and unavoidable" (*AR* 110–11; quoting from "On Truth and Lies in a Nonmoral Sense"). The "human relationships," the "people," and the "long use," however, de Man ignored. Yet these are the elements, no less than the figures, from which to construct a history of the contingencies that have put us in the odd place that we are.

I conclude with the rhetoric of several Jamesian topics that Donadio addressed. My own interest is in using such analysis to move toward a renewed sense of history, of "realism" even, rather than as an end in itself or in the service of Donadio's expressive aestheticism.

I have noted Donadio's reliance upon a rhetoric of reconciled opposites, which in Anglo-American criticism derives from Coleridge. Recall my earlier citations of Coleridge on the symbol as characterized "above all by the translucence of the Eternal in and through the Temporal. It always partakes of the Reality which it renders intelligible; and while it enunciates the whole, abides itself as a living part in that Unity, of which it is the representative" (*Collected Works* 6:30).

A moment from the grand party at Milly's palazzo in *The Wings of the Dove* demonstrates James' wary scrutiny of such rhetoric. Donadio took the novel as defined by Milly's point of view (*NJ* 130–

31), but James let us see Milly, and her effect, through others, dis-placing his center. Densher first sees Milly in romantic, symbolist terms, as "embodied poetry," but the scene moves toward acknowl-edging an arbitrary process of semiological construction rather than crediting a natural transparency that gives symbols their represen-tative power.

"But she's too nice," Kate returned with appreciation. "Everything suits her so—especially her pearls. They go so with her old lace. I'll trouble you really to look at them." Densher, though aware he had seen them before, had perhaps not "really" looked at them, and had thus not done justice to the embodied poetry—his mind, for Milly's aspects, kept coming back to that—which owed them part of its style. Kate's face, as she considered them, struck him: the long, priceless chain, wound twice round the neck, hung, heavy and pure, down the front of the wearer's breast—so far down that Milly's trick, evidently unconscious, of holding and vaguely fingering and entwining a part of it, conduced presumably to convenience. "She's a dove," Kate went on, "and one somehow doesn't think of doves as bejewelled. Yet they suit her down to the ground."

"Yes—down to the ground is the word." Densher saw now how they suited her, but was perhaps still more aware of something intense in his companion's feeling about them. Milly was indeed a dove; this was the figure, though it most applied to her spirit. Yet he knew in a moment that Kate was just now, for reasons hidden from him, exceptionally under the impression of that element of wealth in her which was a power, which was a great power, and which was dove-like only so far as one remembered that doves have wings and won-drous flights, have them as well as tender tints and soft sounds. It even came to him dimly that such wings could in a given case—*had*, truly, in the case with which he was concerned—spread themselves for protection. Hadn't they, for that matter, lately taken an inordi-nate reach, and weren't Kate and Mrs. Lowder, weren't Susan Shep-herd and he, wasn't *he* in particular, nestling under them to a great increase of immediate ease? All this was a brighter blur in the general light, out of which he heard Kate presently going on.

"Pearls have such a magic that they suit every one."

"They would uncommonly suit you," he frankly returned.

"Oh yes, I see myself!"

As she saw herself, suddenly, he saw her—she would have been splendid; and with it he felt more what she was thinking of. Milly's royal ornament had—under pressure now not wholly occult—taken on the character of a symbol of differences, differences of which the vision was actually in Kate's face. It might have been in her face too

that, well as she certainly would look in pearls, pearls were exactly
what Merton Densher would never be able to give her. Wasn't that
the great difference that Milly to-night symbolised?

(2:8.3)

The phrase "embodied poetry" suggests the inherence of Milly's
spiritual value within her physical body and echoes the infatuation
of symbolist critics from Coleridge to the present with Donne's
phrase "her body thought." But the passage dismembers that embodied poetry. Kate fixes Densher's attention on Milly's pearls, separating a part from the whole, destroying the totality, revealing
that Milly's embodied poetry owes its appeal to these jewels—un-
likely as that is for a "dove." Densher departs from Coleridgean
unity in seeing the pearls as the "symbol of differences," and then
comes a further shift. A moment later, Milly herself "symbolise[s]
. . . the great difference." She now stands for her pearls, rather than
their being part of a spiritual totality that she embodies. The thing
has taken over the person, as in Benjamin's analysis of Baudelaire's
commodified allegory.

Pearls, moreover, are not unique to Milly: "They suit every one."
They are detachable; Kate could wear them. They are arbitrarily
placed on Milly, like allegorical identifications, rather than inher-
ing naturally in her like symbols. The differences they symbolize
are not necessary to the nature of things but are contingent differences that money produces within human life histories in society.
Ordinarily we see the effects of money as if they were natural, but
at moments we recall that human activities are responsible for the
arbitrary distribution of wealth and its consequences, just as they
are for the rhetorical assignment of meanings to figures. Thus in
reducing the claims of symbol in this passage, James accomplished
a realistic function. In exposing the conventions of literature and
society alike, he reminded us that we might make things different.
The "will to power" is a Nietzschean concept, relevant here, that
de Man and Donadio ignored.

Consider in this context the metamorphoses of the figure of the
dove in the party scene. First the appropriateness of "dove" as a
figure for Milly is questioned: doves aren't usually bejeweled. Then
the symbolic force of the figure is recuperated through the natural
qualities of the dove, which has the power of flight and therefore

may properly represent the soaring splendor Milly manifests. The figure is no sooner naturalized, however, than it grotesquely exceeds nature. No dove is so large as to nestle in its wings a whole company of people, only a dove taken out of nature into an arbitrary system of signification. The other characters make Milly a dove, and her final triumph is to make their own figure return to haunt them.

The end of the book offers more specification of James' rhetorical concern. The dying Milly has sent Densher a note from Venice to London, which seems clearly intended to arrive on Christmas. Densher surmises that it must therefore inform him that he will inherit Milly's wealth. Profoundly moved by this act of generous forgiveness, he nonetheless brings the note unopened to Kate. Kate and Densher scrutinize the envelope. They marvel over its beautiful handwriting. Kate then takes the "sacred script" and throws it in the fire. They are sure of its intention. Why worry about how it is said? But as Densher later ponders the event, he reckons that in Milly's letter "the intention . . . would have been . . . the least part of it. The part of it missed forever was the turn she would have given" (*Wings* 2:10.6).

This "turn" that would have made all the difference translates Greek *tropos*, the general rhetorical term for figure of speech. Densher recognizes that a turn—a trope—is not just a means of expression; it is not necessarily at one with intention. The turn changes intention, for trope is interpretation, not transparency. So in *Pride and Prejudice* Bingley tells Lizzie Bennett that she has mistaken Darcy's comment: "You are giving it a turn which that gentleman did by no means intend," and thereby "converting" a sarcasm "into a compliment" (ch. 10).

"Converting," by its Latin etymology, involves the same semantic area as English "turn" and Greek *tropos*, and it operated powerfully within James' critical vocabulary. Donadio recognized the importance of the term, but he accorded it only psychological significance: "Alternating aspects of James' personality find their imaginative expression in his work, and . . . this book . . . attempts to trace that process of transformation (or 'conversion') by which one state of feeling reverses itself and becomes its opposite" (*NJ* 6–7). James used the term quite differently. In the early "Art of Fiction," the key term of "experience" was not a matter of feeling but an activity, an interpretive "power" that "converts the very pulses of the air into revelations" (2:52). The late "Lesson of Balzac" praises him for "converting . . . into history" so much (3:124).

"Conversion," this differential turning, was James' word for how an individual contributed to the making of culture, both works of art and the total human disposition toward society. It was not a smooth process of transmission. It produced a substitution, a difference made at some cost and loss, for the original was gone. As a writer, James' conversions involved the criticism of earlier modes of writing and their replacement by his own, and they involved equally the loss of any direct connection to a world outside his books. Representation is not transparent.

This position was elaborately articulated in a prefatory passage that itself transformed the "chemical" process of conversion into a "mystical" cooking: "We can surely account for nothing in the novelist's work that hasn't passed through the crucible of his imagination, hasn't in that perpetually simmering cauldron his intellectual *pot-au-feu* been reduced to savoury fusion. . . . It has entered . . . into new relations. . . . Its final savour has been constituted but its prime identity destroyed" (3:1236–37). James' figure makes clear that the process is not so reversible as Donadio wishes.

The value of conversions comes explicitly into question later in *The Wings of the Dove*. Densher has long been resisting any "turn"; he values his "straightness," and both as a matter of male sexuality and of general morality refuses to be "bent" by Kate's will. He seeks the straight path toward their sexual union and marriage and resents every "dodge" Kate finds to put him off (echoing a word James uses in the preface for his own compositional practice). Her "readiness" to love him is "the woman herself" (*Wings* 2:8.3), but the dodge, the turn, violates nature and its desirable straightness. Finally, however, at the book's end Densher tries to deny the passage of time and its consequences. He tries to re-establish his life with Kate "as we were" (2:10.6), bending time to his will through the rhetorical figure of metalepsis that replaces the present with past, wishfully substituting a far-distant cause for its no longer existent effect. If anything can protect against time, trope can, but nothing does: "We shall never be again as we were" are the book's last words.

The book's figures enact the transformation of "straightness" in Densher's awareness, and the turning point occurs in his reflections as the physician departs to confer with Milly about her disease (2:9.4). With a "cry" and a "swerve," the gondola suddenly vanishes from sight on its "short cut," and this "difference" suddenly evokes "the truth that was truest about Milly," that "great smudge of mortality" which speech refuses to "reflect." The passage makes us question with Densher: what is the value of "beautiful fictions," of the "aesthetic instinct" to avoid "outrage"? The line of feeling resonates with the traditional values of our culture. We believe in truth, disinterest, revelation, and not in "suppressions," and we therefore register deeply the difference between the two states evoked. Densher is facing the worst in the relation of art and life. Like Plato, Rousseau, de Man, he sees the baselessness of the aesthetic. But as he does so, the "fool's paradise" of art begins to turn to something else. In revising the first edition for the New York Edition, James made two crucial alterations at this point: for "had now come in" he wrote "had now crossed the threshold," and for "space" he rewrote "precinct." These changes suggest ritually sacred space, appropriately cut off (the etymological sense of "temple" and "precinct") from the rest of the world, and the physician becomes a mediating figure between the two realms. Like the "artist *in triumph*" (3:1118) James summons up in his prefaces, all we finally glimpse of the physician is his back, as he interposes his shoulders between us and the vision we are grateful to be spared. Through Densher, James here posed the fundamental critical question about his work: how do we appraise (or "appreciate") the losses exacted in making his kind of "beautiful fiction"?

Donadio made vivid to us the power of the aesthetic for James, for Nietzsche, and for himself. De Man placed the aesthetic in the "appearance" of history engendered by Kant's misreading of Rousseau. De Man's sexual figure here recurs frequently (e.g., *AR* 205, 272, 274). One instance makes clear its own place within a history of reading figures of history: "Texts engender texts" and "consist of a series of repetitive reversals that engenders the semblance of a temporal sequence" (*AR* 162). I take this sexual allegory as a transfer from Yeats: the swan "engenders . . . the broken wall, the burning roof and tower" through Leda's inevitable failure to gain Zeus' "knowledge with his power." The very conviction that temporal sequence is only semblance testifies to the transformation into de Man's theory of Goethe's final lyric from *Faust*: "Alles Vergängliche / Ist nur ein Gleichnis" (which in "Linguistics and Poetics" Roman Jakobson glossed, "Anything sequent is a simile").

Not only Nietzsche, however, but also, as we have seen, Matthew Arnold held that human history is real enough for our purposes, even if it is a history of error. If truth is not God's but a "mobile army of metaphors," their "long use" still makes one "people" different from another, or from itself over time. During the same years that de Man was working through his rhetorical alternative to the use of Nietzsche for American humanism, Michel Foucault turned Nietzsche's genealogical inquiries to use for antihumanist historiography. In the practice of Foucault's *Discipline and Punish* and *History of Sexuality*, genealogical history showed the creation and long use of the "delinquent," the "hysterical woman," the "pervert," in the war of "human relationships." Drawing upon the very passage from "On Truth and Lies in a Nonmoral Sense" that I have been discussing with regard to de Man, Edward Said in *Orientalism* showed the creation and long use of the "oriental" as some peoples' weapon against others. Without explicit reference to Nietzsche, the genealogical history of *The American Jeremiad* by Sacvan Bercovitch demonstrated the coercive power of the "American" to differentiate and mold a people. Daniel O'Hara's *Romance of Interpretation* and Paul Bové's *Intellectuals in Power* continue this genealogical project. The "aesthetic," then, is a lie that James and Nietzsche both dismantled, as Donadio overlooked, and a truth that both yielded to, as he saw and did likewise. Their struggle with the "aesthetic" formed part of the historical specificity of their writing, which de Man denied on behalf of an overall theory of textuality. De Man's vigilance preserves us from Donadio's error, but to preserve ourselves from de Man's, we must look elsewhere.

Chapter 11
Fredric Jameson and Marxism

AFTER THE POLITICAL TURMOIL of the 1960s, the next decade featured intellectual combat; established academic disciplines faced challenges from works like *Metahistory* by Hayden White and *Philosophy and the Mirror of Nature* by Richard Rorty. In literary studies, novel European theories preoccupied critics, whether primarily aesthetic and psychological like Geoffrey Hartman (*Beyond Formalism*, 1970; *Criticism in the Wilderness*, 1980) or historical and social like Fredric Jameson (*Marxism and Form*, 1971; *The Political Unconscious*, 1981, henceforth abbreviated *PU*). Jameson's accomplishments earned him a prominence unique among Marxist critics in America, and their stimulus provokes this meditation. For the brilliance of those accomplishments in *The Political Unconscious* cannot be separated from the deliberate scandal of Jameson's method. He took crucial arguments from the antihumanists Lacan and Althusser, while his fundamental understanding of modern capitalism was derived from Lukács' humanist critique of reification in *History and Class Consciousness*. With consistently triumphant dialectical vigor, he assimilated the work of structuralists like A. J. Greimas and Claude Lévi-Strauss, while overcoming structuralist ahistoricism in the service of his leitmotif, "Always historicize!"

No less remarkably, Jameson assimilated the hermeneutics of Paul Ricoeur and the analytics of Northrop Frye—both derived from theological and religious studies—in the service of a Marxist science. The proof of Jameson's successful totalization would seem to lie in this capacity to gather honey from every flower, like the early Christian exegete who could follow Augustine's principle of charity from *On Christian Doctrine* and turn to godly use the "Egyptian gold" of pagan literature. Jameson himself recognized and commented on the relation of his own project, which flies in the face of the typically postmodern stance "against interpretation," to the enterprise of Christian allegory. From the Christian example, Jameson argued that an effective interpretive stance requires a "genuine philosophy of history" (*PU* 18), and he therefore deprecated Althusser's "structural" strictures against "historicist" notions of "expressive causality." Such notions will involve "a vast interpretive allegory in which a sequence of historical events . . . is rewritten in terms of some deeper, underlying . . . allegorical master narrative" (28). Jameson found the Christian system of fourfold interpretation "particularly suggestive in the solution it provides" (31) for linking the privacy of individual experience to the communal history of humankind. Jameson's Marxist "social hermeneutic" thus managed to "keep faith" with its Christian "precursor" (74) both in evading the methodological limitations of Althusser and in reemphasizing the collective dimension, which Jameson considered that Frye neglected in his recasting of Christian allegory.

The novelty of Jameson's literary historicizing emerges in contrast to the historical monument of M. H. Abrams in *Natural Supernaturalism*, a more traditional work that shared Jameson's concern with the use we may find for Christian structures of thought. Jameson's work was the more explicitly theoretical. Abrams defended romanticism through an extraordinarily comprehensive and wideranging interpretation of one of its key texts; Jameson defended interpretation itself by the wide range of arguments to which his particular readings were always subordinated. Abrams practiced an Arnoldian discrimination that threatened to make his book seem all the same thing, Jameson an eclecticism that threatened to make his book seem everything. Yet both works were organized by a "secularization" thesis: they charted the interpretive reinvestment of Christian forms for purely human purposes. Jameson went a step beyond Abrams' humanism to claim an increasing scientification in the movement of culture from myth to magic to religion to ideology to Marxism, a sequence that paralleled Northrop Frye's literary "modes" in *Anatomy of Criticism* (myth to romance to high mimetic to low mimetic to irony). Just as Frye described a circularity by which irony returned to myth, so Jameson operated with a principle of dialectical reversal. For if each stage has the capacity to demystify the one that precedes it, thus to reduce it and bring it down to earth, there is also a continual gain in explanatory power, so that Marxism finally succeeds in delivering, as *valid*, an analysis so total that only myth had ever previously aspired to such grasp.

NIETZSCHE, THEOLOGY, THE POLITICAL UNCONSCIOUS

Against any such secularization thesis, Nietzsche remains the great opponent who wages unremitting warfare against the continued dominance from beyond the grave of a discredited Christianity. The battle against humanism in American criticism in the 1970s began with a Nietzschean attack on Abrams by J. Hillis Miller ("Tradition and Difference"). Jameson, however, seems safe against such a move by possible opponents, for he employed Nietzsche crucially within his own work. In this use of Nietzsche, I find both a symptom and a tactic. The tactic is not only defensive, but also diplomatic. The use of Nietzsche invited dialogue with those who pursue either of the neo-Nietzschean practices that shook the disciplines of history, philosophy, and criticism: the "deconstruction" associated with Jacques Derrida and the "genealogy" associated with Michel Foucault. Thus Jameson strove for an alliance between a possible political left and the intellectual left of the academy. When, on the other hand, I call the use of Nietzsche a symptom, I mean that it draws attention to an incoherence that it hopes to heal, or at least hide. Such incoherence, and the possibility that it may resist Jameson's dialectical sublation, is my target here.

First, however, I want to specify another area that, as globally as his secularization thesis, marks Jameson as anti-Nietzschean. This is the "repression" thesis contained in the very notion of the "political unconscious." This titular conception leads a strangely subdued existence throughout the book—receiving, for example, no entry in the index for either of its elements—but its function in the overall argument emerges from this reflection on Joseph Conrad's fiction:

> The perfected poetic apparatus of high modernism represses History just as successfully as the perfected narrative apparatus of high realism did the random heterogeneity of the as yet uncentered subject.

> At that point however, the political, no longer visible in high modernist texts, any more than in the everyday world of appearance of bourgeois life, and relentlessly driven underground by accumulated reification, has at last become a genuine unconscious. (*PU* 280)

The issue at stake here involves how a social totality is to be conceptualized. Is the whole implicit in each of its parts (a model like the rhetorical figure of synecdoche), or are the parts related to each other only by adjacency (a model like the rhetorical figure of metonymy)? Despite his use of Althusser's "structural causality," which followed the metonymic model, we have seen that Jameson also defended "expressive causality," which holds to synecdoche. If the whole is fully reflected in every part, then aspects of the whole not immediately visible in a part must be latent within it, repressed or unconscious within it.

The model of "production," however, may work better than the model of repression, as Michel Foucault's *History of Sexuality* notably argued with regard to its subject in the nineteenth century. Marx, for example, may be better understood as arguing that capitalism *produced* the proletariat than that it repressed it (except through a wordplay—a metaphor given literal force—that assimilates political domination to erasure from consciousness). In the middle of the nineteenth century "the dangerous classes" and in the later nineteenth century "the crowd" were produced as elements of bourgeois discourse that received great and anxious attention. What most strikes me in studying the century through which Jameson finds the repression of the "political" is rather the extreme visibility, even nakedness, of class conflict. (There is no indication that Jameson intended the "political" in the sense made prominent by Hannah Arendt, in which it is sharply distinguished from the "social.") If politics is so evident as I have claimed in "the everyday world of appearance," then where is it in the literature? In their different ways, both Foucault in *The Order of Things* and Raymond Williams in *Culture and Society* and *Marxism and Literature* studied the production of "literature" as a particular social and linguistic space in the nineteenth century, achieved through a series of separations and purifications. Their analyses confirm the arguments, which Jameson accepted, of Weber and Lukács for increasing differentiation of social functions. From this it would follow that literature and politics were not superposed, one upon the other ("politics relentlessly driven underground," as Jameson put it), but rather *juxtaposed* to each other. The political is not "below" but rather "beside" the literary text.

To conceptualize such affiliation does not, as Jameson feared, require us to "imagine" that "sheltered from the omnipresence of history and the implacable influences of the social, there already exists a realm of freedom" (*PU* 20). It does suggest, however, that the relations of literature and politics are different from what he conceived them to be. It also serves to disqualify the delving into literary texts as an authentically political activity—a sore matter for the conscience of the American academic on the left, who might sooner prefer to hold with Jameson that "everything is 'in the last analysis' political" (20). Against this metaphoric model of identification ("is"—like Frye's anagogic stage of the symbol) stands the metonymic model: "everything is *connected with* the political." These matters I pursue in "The Politics of *The Scarlet Letter*."

What has this to do with Nietzsche? Foucault's methodological reflections and his practice on these matters came from the understanding of Nietzsche that gave its title to Foucault's "Nietzsche, Genealogy, History," to which I allude in the title of this section. Foucault drew especially from the second essay in the *Genealogy of Morals*, which explored the production of "man" as "an animal *with the right to make promises*." Nietzsche's project was to understand how the force of remembering triumphed over the natural "forgetfulness," the "faculty of repression" (*Hemmungsvermögen*) that human beings share with animals (section 1). Thus Nietzsche stood at the other end from Jameson on this crucial matter Nietzsche's story was not of increasing repression, but of repression overcome.

We are now ready to ask after the particular use Jameson made of Nietzsche. At decisive moments in his remarkable chapter on romance (a masterpiece of condensed comparative reflection) and in his chapter on Conrad (the richest consideration of *Lord Jim* that I know), as well as in his conclusion (which radically revises our understanding of "ideological" criticism), Jameson drew on Nietzsche's attacks against ethics to make possible his own position. In the first instance Jameson used Nietzsche as a way of maintaining contact with contemporary poststructuralism, while shifting the grounds of argument. After Jameson had analytically demonstrated the fundamental function of "binary opposition" in romance, he then noted Derrida's critique of binary oppositions as metaphysical. He continued:

> To move from Derrida to Nietzsche is to glimpse the possibility of a rather different interpretation of the binary opposition, according to which its positive and negative terms are ultimately assimilated by the mind as a distinction between good and evil. Not metaphysics but ethics is the informing ideology of the binary opposition, and we have forgotten the thrust of Nietzsche's thought and lost everything scandalous and virulent about it if we cannot understand how it is ethics itself which is the ideological vehicle and legitimation of concrete structures of power and domination. (*PU* 114)

Jameson emphasized that for Nietzsche the concept of evil is "positional"; it is not absolute but coincides with the "categories of Otherness," of a "difference" that "*seems* to constitute a real and urgent threat to my existence" (115, my emphasis).

Now the interpretation of Nietzsche is extraordinarily vexatious, yet I do want to offer some fairly literal questionings of what Jameson attributes to Nietzsche. If the only result is that Jameson offers readings of Nietzsche to justify his claims, I will feel that some good has been done, for there are few sympathetic Marxist analyses of Nietzsche. Jameson, I argue, here neglected two aspects of Nietzsche's argument in the first essay of the *Genealogy of Morals*. First, even as a means of legitimating domination, ethics for Nietzsche was not imposed from above. Ethics, we recall, is a tool of the "slave," not of the "master," and it offered standards opposed to the masters'. Second, the positional analysis in the original situation did not for Nietzsche depend upon a fallacious "seems." In his view, the masters did unquestionably threaten the existence of the slaves, so he did not like Jameson insist on the element of fantasy.

In Jameson's analysis, as in Nietzsche's, the critique of the ethical was linked to the problem of the "individual subject":

> As Nietzsche taught us, the judgmental habit of ethical thinking, of ranging everything in the antagonistic categories of good and evil (or their other binary equivalents), is not merely an error but is objec-

tively rooted in the inevitable and inescapable centeredness of every individual consciousness or individual subjec.: what is good . . . belongs to me, what is bad belongs to the Other. (*PU* 234)

As opposed to what he claimed was Nietzsche's solution of this dilemma through the Eternal Return, Jameson found in Marxism "a rather different stance (this time outside the subject in the trans-individual, or in other words in History)" (235).

I find very odd Jameson's particular way of articulating the link of ethics to the subject. To begin with, the *Genealogy* did not like Jameson so blithely consider all binary oppositions ethical. The first essay set as its problem the *difference* between two binary systems, that of good/bad and that of good/evil. Only the latter was "ethical" in Jameson's sense. Both, however, were *class*-positional: "The protracted and domineering fundamental total feeling on the part of a higher ruling order in relation to a lower order . . . *that* is the origin of the antithesis 'good' and 'bad.'" In all such situations, "a concept denoting political superiority . . . resolves itself into a concept denoting superiority of soul" (*Genealogy* I,6). For Nietzsche, "good" was the affirmation of "we noble ones, we good, beautiful, happy ones!" (I, 10). Only "evil" in the alternative system of "slave" oppositions took its fundamental sense from comparison to an "Other." Moreover, these citations make clear that for Nietzsche both good/bad and good/evil were "political" notions, deriving from the domination or subjugation of one group by another. Ethics, in his analysis, the use of the opposition good/evil, is the particular class weapon of the "people," slaves or mob or herd, against the "noble ones."

Only as a by-product of this ethical class warfare did Nietzsche locate the production of the individual subject: "The 'doer' is merely a fiction added to the deed" (I,13). The notion of individual responsibility allowed for blame to be accorded to the activity of the strong and praise to the impotence of the weak: "The subject . . . has perhaps been believed in hitherto more firmly than anything else on earth because it makes possible to the majority of mortals, the weak and oppressed of every kind, the sublime self-deception that interprets weakness as freedom" (I,13). My reading of Nietzsche, then, moves in the opposite direction from Jameson's. Although Nietzsche's revulsion from the "herd," the "people," led

him to anticipate a positive revaluation of the subject that succeeded in going beyond ethics, nonetheless his genealogical analyses
demonstrated precisely the "transindividual" concerns desired by
Jameson. Where the "political" clearly existed in Nietzsche, Jameson repressed it, made it unconscious so that the dialectic could
gain credit by unveiling it.

It will not be possible to evaluate the function of Nietzsche within
Jameson's overall argument until we have examined the third locus
for his anti-ethical claim, in the conclusion. Here the liberation
from ethics was necessary for the "utopian" hermeneutics Jameson
proposed. By freeing ourselves from ethical dualities, we may give
positive value to strong class consciousness wherever in the past we
find it, even if manifested by "evil." In chapter 1 I made some use
of this perspective, for Jameson helps overcome that asceticism of
the left which refuses to traffic in effective means of mass organizing
because those means have been tainted by the villains who have
used them in the past (or are using them now). This capacity to
give positive, "anticipatory" value to what we otherwise critically
demystify as ideological promises a great gain. Major works of the
1970s like Foucault's *Discipline and Punish*, Raymond Williams' *The
Country and the City*, Sacvan Bercovitch's *The American Jeremiad*,
and Ann Douglas' *The Feminization of American Culture* all offered
pasts that cry out for condemnation. Yet one may find such con-
demnation insufficiently dialectical and may protest that if we are
to have any future at all, we need something in our past that we
can build from. Against these "affirmative" analyses of domination,
the "negative" analysis Jameson offered was alluring. Likewise his
notion of the "unconscious" appeals through promising a valuable
reserve of energy, which we can find with our "elaborate hermeneutic geiger counters" (*PU* 215). Yet for all this, I continue to find
problems at the level of practice—beyond the level of philology to
which I have thus far appealed in analyzing Nietzsche—with Jameson's attack on ethics.

First of all, I take seriously Nietzsche's demonstration that ethics
functioned in the service of the weak as a means of reversing the
relations of power in which they found themselves. Although he
attacked "slave morality," he could not deny its effectiveness. I
believe that ethics still works this way to some extent. At the very
least, I would like to see a much closer analysis than Jameson's

before I voluntarily gave up all the protections that justification may offer. At the worst, it might be suicidal for a small, weak left to urge the strong to act freely without check.

Second, Nietzsche, like most of us, closely associated the ethical with the keeping of promises (the first and second essays of the *Genealogy*). I agree with Jameson that an "alliance politics" (*PU* 54) is necessary for the American left, and I wonder in concrete terms how it will be possible for alliances to be made between the various groups in our national life and those who are known to hold an anti-ethical position. Charges that "Marxists" are unreliable allies because they aim at different goals and live by different codes from "Americans" have enough continuing force that I doubt it wise to strengthen such a position. We all know, moreover, that moral outrage against the brutal exercise of ruling power has helped cement valuable alliances. It is worth adding that for Jameson alliance politics fulfills in practice the theoretical goal of "totalization," that principle of Hegel and Lukács that has come under such attack from the French work of Althusser, Lacan, and others. Jameson argues that the force of French antitotalizers stems from their opposition to the oppressive monolith of the French Communist party, while in America, which has always lacked real organization on the left, the priorities, in theory and practice alike, must be different. If one accepts this strong argument, then Jameson's wish to use Nietzsche—a decisive figure for French antitotalizers—becomes even more puzzling. Granted that Nietzsche offers "dynamite" to blow up the conventional moral and psychological readings of academic literary criticism, there may be more lost in the explosion than is worthwhile. There may well be a valid left Nietzscheanism, but Jameson's particular use seems inconsistent with his goals.

Even Jameson's "anticipatory" readings worry me. In elaborating the utopian value of *any* class consciousness, Jameson established a "priority" of such consciousness over any "still limited by anarchist categories of the individual subject and individual experience" (*PU* 286). In the development of his analysis, such "anarchist categories" remained low on the scale, while fascism could have a high positive value (291). However much one may wish to combat cold war appropriations of anarchist values in Orwell and Camus, for example, one must also recognize that in the Spanish Civil War communists compromised the fight against fascism by violently suppressing antifascist anarchists. Can we desire a theory that makes such confusions programmatic?

This power of anticipatory reading to bring good from any evil, so long as it be strong enough, emerged proleptically in the last page of the first chapter, as Jameson addressed the sad historical spectacle of the "failure" of every revolution we know of. Applying the category of totality, he explained that every specific revolution must fail, for "socialist revolution can only be a total and worldwide process." But how could this worldwide totality become possible? Only through "the completion of the capitalist 'revolution' and of the process of commodification on a global scale" (*PU* 102). The element of traditional eschatology in such a vision of the last days— the reign of Antichrist reversed into the millennium—cannot be overlooked. Moreover, as Cornel West has argued, this is a particularly American version of the pattern, since the United States is the primary seat of the power that must triumph in order to bring on the end. We return, then, to the theological model for Jameson's work, and with Nietzsche we must ask whether such a theology is not more appropriate for consolation than for action. What can motivate anyone to struggle against a process that *must* triumph before any better world is possible? On the other hand, what use can such an apocalypse be to those actively engaged in local issues?

I will conclude this section by reflecting on the notions of narrative and the political unconscious that support the vision of history Jameson offered in the apocalyptic moment I just cited. For him the virtue of Marxism was that its theory and analysis made possible a sense that "the human adventure is one" and thus that everything that has ever happened, as well as all that is happening anywhere in the world, made "vital claims on us." Such potentially heterogeneous diversity could assume "urgency for us" only if told "within the unity of a single great collective story . . . sharing a single fundamental theme," namely, "the collective struggle to wrest a realm of Freedom from a realm of Necessity" (*PU* 19). Yet finally, the "form of Necessity" (101) is the effect, Jameson argued, of great historical narrative. I take this contradiction between a History of Liberation and the Form of Necessity in which it must be cast to be the same contradiction as that between the worldwide revolution and the total domination by capitalism that is its precondition. This dialectic of liberation and necessity ignores such a nonliberating contingency as nuclear war and offers instead a grim reassurance: "One does not have to argue the reality of history: necessity, like Dr. Johnson's stone, does that for us" (82). I find this sentence gives away too much human scope, for good and ill. Johnson could hardly have refuted Berkeley by saying, "Remember that stone I tripped over yesterday . . . ?" and for Boswell's readers before Jameson, the account of Johnson's demonstration has been understood rhetorically rather than ontologically. The stone *works* only by Dr. Johnson's kicking it at a certain moment; it is subordinated to his argument, which demands its presence. For Jameson, however, history is an "absent cause," and is "*not* a text, not a narrative, master or otherwise" (35).

I value immensely the seriousness of Jameson's undertaking. Its totalizing ambition provoked practical political questions about principles that within the limited disciplinary scope of reading romance, or Conrad, allowed him great advances over earlier work. Yet through unraveling the thread of Nietzsche in *The Political Unconscious*, I fear I have located an incoherence. Jameson needed Nietzsche to make possible his "utopian" hermeneutics and to meet the challenges to Marxism from deconstruction and genealogy; yet if taken seriously, Nietzsche disrupts every "totality" and dispels any hope of redemption through secular apocalypse. To protect his faith in the "fundamental reality one and indivisible" (*PU* 40) of social life, Jameson relied on the fiercest critic of such faith. This impasse, like that between Liberation and Necessity, or "collective story" and "absent cause," perhaps finally "represses history" (280) no less than did the masterpieces of high modernism (though one must also emphasize, no more: both repress history and both acknowledge it).

Recall in *Ulysses* the spectacle that confronted Bloom and Stephen as they emerged in the morning darkness from Bloom's house:

The heaventree of stars hung with humid nightblue fruit.

One of the most gorgeous sentences Joyce ever composed, it allegorized a realm of freedom, for it made beautiful, organic, and intimate the spectacle of cold, vast, distant indifference. Yet no sooner was the sentence out than the catechist of Ithaca began to interrogate it: "With what meditations did Bloom accompany his demonstration to his companions of various constellations?" The interplay of sounds in the earlier sentence made beauty; the jingle of "-ions," only the comedy of pompous cacophony. Bloom thinks of "evolution increasingly vaster," and amid the exotic appeal of stars' names the sheer grossness of numbers like 57,000,000,000,000 begins to dominate and make of "allotted human life" a "parenthesis of infinitesimal brevity." Another two pages in this vein lead to this thought about alternative possibilities for life: "An apogean humanity of beings created in various forms with finite differences resulting similar to the whole and to one another would probably there as here remain inalterably and inalienably attached to vanities, to vanities of vanities and all that is vanity." Yet another page leads to "Bloom's logical conclusion, having weighed the matter and allowing for possible error." Like Jameson, he has moved from the vision of desire—a single great collective story, a "heaventree"—to that of necessity—*not* a text, not a narrative. Dr. Johnson's stone has kicked him: "It was not a heaventree, not a heavengrot, not a heavenbeast, not a heavenman. . . . It was a Utopia, there being no known method from the known to the unknown" (698–701).

PROBLEMS OF POLITICAL CONSCIOUSNESS IN CONRAD AND HIS CRITICS

I should make clear that I do not believe Joyce's wisdom has revealed Jameson's utopian folly. I find ideology critique in both, and utopian projection in both, and value in both. I do, however, believe that it compromises Jameson's claims to find him operating so much in the same mode as a high modernist text of a sort that he has supposedly gone beyond. I turn now to think through another encounter between Jameson and modernism, here through his chosen ground of Conrad. I will compare Jameson's chapter on Conrad in *The Political Unconscious* with the chapter on Conrad in Irving Howe's *Politics and the Novel* (1957; henceforth abbreviated *PN*). This comparison will suggest changes over a quarter-century in the relations of left criticism to politics in the United States. I choose

272

Fredric Jameson and Marxism

Howe because the quality of his work is very high and because that work is ignored by Jameson in his "metacommentary" on the critical tradition around Conrad in the United States. Moreover, as I suggest further in the next chapter, the similarities and differences in the journals associated with each—*Dissent* for Howe and *Social Text* for Jameson—help illuminate the possibility for left intellectual culture in the United States in our time.

The first question, then, will be how to define the difference between Howe's criticism on Conrad and Jameson's. It's not simply that Howe addressed Conrad's political consciousness, Jameson the 'political unconscious." For Howe was sharply attentive to unconcious elements in Conrad's relations to politics. He noted conscious hostility to "the life of politics" (*PN* 79) and yet noted also ways in which Conrad's life, thought, and writing were determined by political elements so diverse as nationalism and the oppositely charged individualisms of conservatism and anarchism (86). These observations came to focus in an epigrammatic formula that related conscious to unconscious: "The Jamesian Conrad directs, the Dostoevskian Conrad erupts" (82). Yet Howe did choose for commentary the manifestly "political" works of Conrad, while Jameson devoted his major attention to *Lord Jim* (which is not manifestly political) and only treated *Nostromo* secondarily. For Jameson emphasized the "ideology of form," not elucidating political content. As a technical development within criticism, his work thus went far beyond Howe's. The contrast between the "Jamesian" and the "Dostoevskian" cited above, however, suggests that Howe did manage, using the traditional belletristic tokens of authors' names, to suggest correlations between Conrad's formal choices (and inadvertences) and ideological positions.

A difference remains, nonetheless, between the connections Howe drew and those with which Jameson was most concerned, which demand "elaborate hermeneutic geiger counters" (*PU* 215). Once having discovered the hidden energies of ideology, the critic's task for Jameson is to develop "mediations" that construct a bridge from an explicitly political realm of discourse to the facts of the literary work in which politics has been repressed. Howe had no theory for it, but in Jameson's terms, his procedure was indeed marked by an elaborate play of mediation, where apparently highly divergent discourses are intersected with Conrad's. Thus, *Nostromo* "verifies, in the limited way a novel can verify anything [this means, I take it, that even what it verifies a novel verifies only within limits; it does not mean that within limits anything at all can be verified by a novel], Leon Trotsky's theory of the 'permanent revolution'" (*PN* 103); and Howe went on to discuss that theory. In the same novel's treatment of "Montero, the Bonaparte of the Campo," Howe found "astonishing political insight," fully "as magnificent as Marx's analysis of Bonapartism in *The 18th Brumaire of Louis Napoleon*" (105); again, he went on to explain that analysis. Again in *Nostromo*, when Mrs. Gould lamented the "silent work of evil spirits" that "erected . . . a wall of silver bricks" between herself and her husband" (*PN* 111), Howe glossed this with Marx on the fetishism of commodities. Finally, in Mrs. Gould's vision of "the San Tomé mountain, hanging over the Campo, over the whole land, feared, hated, wealthy, more soulless than any tyrant, more pitiless and autocratic than the worst government, ready to crush innumerable lives in the expansion of its greatness," Howe found represented "nothing less than capitalism itself" (108). Howe's thematic concerns became the basis for considerable education of his readers in some of the most important arguments within Marxism. In contrast, Jameson defined his fundamental critical task as quite a different kind of education, meeting a test of prowess by "showing the capacity of Marxism to engage the most advanced currents of 'bourgeois' thinking" (Interview 73).

Jameson's orientation to the disciplinary concerns already in place within our academic culture pointed to a striking set of differences between his work and Howe's at the levels both of style and of overall discursive practice. Stylistically, Howe noted in a later preface that his book was marked by "tense verbal sequences" and "even occasional displays of bravura" (*PN* x–xi); he had come to prefer, however, "lucidity," even "a prose so direct, so clear, so transparent that it becomes virtually self-effacing." That is to say, Howe blamed himself for having verged on transgressing what Geoffrey Hartman, we have seen, called the "Arnoldian Concordat." Criticism has its place, which is subservient to the literature to which it submits itself. Even in the more self-displaying prose that actually still stands on the book's pages, the variation is only within the norms permitted to the "New York Intellectuals." Against these norms, Jameson stood as firmly as Hartman, but for quite different reasons:

> It is always surprising how many people in other disciplines still take a relatively belle-lettristic view of the problems of culture and make the assumption, which they would never make in the area of nuclear physics, linguistics, symbolic logic, or urbanism, that such problems can still be laid out with all the leisurely elegance of a coffee-table magazine. . . . But the problems of cultural theory—which address the relationship between, let's say, consciousness and representation, the unconscious, narrative, the social matrix, symbolic syntax and symbolic capital—why should there be any reason to feel that these problems are less complex than those of bio-chemistry? (Interview 88)

The issue, then, for Jameson was not criticism as art (Hartman's concern) but criticism as science, and in particular, as one scientific discipline among the many others of our age. In the terms Foucault suggested, Jameson stood within the limits of his practice as a "specific intellectual." Preferring to forge a technical language, with the risk of jargon, he gave to literature and literary study a greater relative autonomy than Howe's position would permit.

The problem Jameson left, and I shall return to it again in the conclusion, is how to relate such specialization to the claim that Marxism offers "the only living philosophy today which has a conception of the unity of knowledge and the unification of the 'disciplinary' fields" (Interview 89). The special danger of the "political unconscious" is to isolate the literary text just as classic psychoanalysis did the patient. Freud certainly at times knew better, and Jameson does too, but in teaching a method, what remains is the technique and not the unity. Given a literary discipline that already carries from New Criticism and from a certain understanding of deconstruction a commitment to the self-sufficiency of the text, there may be no effective critical edge in an approach that promises if you just peel down far enough, you'll find all that you need even for a Marxist reading. Jameson himself has read everything, but it's not clear that anyone could learn from *The Political Unconscious* what course of study might make a more learned Marxist.

To reformulate this issue is to ask: between the detailed techniques and the all-embracing claims, what gets left out? In *Nostromo*, I find that Jameson omitted the historical-political consciousness actually available in the work. Thus, his fundamental claim held that "*Nostromo* is . . . not really a novel about political upheaval"; instead, it is "a virtual textbook working-out of the structuralist dictum that all narrative enacts a passage from Nature to Culture." As evidence, he asserted that "the opening pages evoke the landscape of the gulf, a landscape without people" (*PU* 272). It would be onerous to develop a lengthy counterstatement, but let me cite the novel's first paragraph:

> In the time of Spanish rule, and for many years afterwards, the town of Sulaco—the luxuriant beauty of the orange-gardens bears witness to its antiquity—had never been anything more important than a coasting-port with a fairly large local trade in ox-hides and indigo. The clumsy deep-sea galleons of the conquerors that, needing a brisk gale to move at all, would lie becalmed, where your modern ship built on clipper lines forges ahead by the mere flapping of her sails, had been barred out of Sulaco by the prevailing calms of its vast gulf. Some harbours of the earth are made difficult of access by the treachery of sunken rocks and the tempests of their shores. Sulaco had found an inviolable sanctuary from the temptations of a trading world in the solemn hush of the deep Golfo Placido as if within an enormous semi-circular and unroofed temple open to the ocean, with its walls of lofty mountains hung with the mourning draperies of cloud.

I find in this paragraph a constant mingling of nature and culture; within its prose, the "passage" has always already occurred. If there are literally no individual "people," their traces are everywhere. From the first sentence we already have a "town," long-cultivated "gardens," "trade" in products that arise from human labor transforming nature, and above all a system of political domination with a history: the "Spanish rule" of "the conquerors" at one "time" and something else "afterwards." The "gulf" does indeed play a climactic role in the extraordinarily contorted second sentence: it is responsible for barring the galleons, but they are cast as the subject of the sentence, and the whole syntax is disrupted by the comparison between nautical technology then and now (or almost now—steamships are omitted from consideration). I take this construction as further intermingling, and in particular I think that this emerges because the obstacle to the galleons was no action ("treachery" or

276

"tempests") of the gulf but its "calms." From the beginning technology supplements natural absences. The last sentence carries the
mingling of the human and natural back to the archaic, as even
before the town, the gulf itself is cast as a "temple," its mountains
as "walls," and in wordplay that carries through the point, the
natural time of "morning" is blurred with the human ritual of
"mourning." I find here a historical consciousness wholly suppressed by Jameson's reading.

It is fundamental to Jameson's understanding of Marxism that it
portrays history, the realm of necessity as we have earlier discussed,
as a "nightmare" (deliberately echoing Joyce). As opposed to the
traditions of historicism, "for which the human past and the immense variety of human cultures was (within their libraries) an
invigorating and exhilarating perspective," this past "cannot be
confronted without nausea" (echoing Sartre?). This is related to
Benjamin's "Theses," which have been important to my own arguments in this book, but the question here is how it relates to
Conrad's novel and what Jameson attended to in it. The primary
horror of history is sheer labor, "mindless alienated work" ("Marxism and Historicism" 56). Jameson's reading of *Nostromo*, however,
said nothing about this matter, I take it, because attention to the
manifest surface of the text is not sufficiently taxing to display
Marxism's engagement with the most advanced bourgeois thought.
For Conrad puts on the surface as nauseating a portrayal as anyone
could want, or stand, of how money is made:

> Mrs. Gould knew the history of the San Tomé mine. Worked in the
> early days mostly by means of lashes on the backs of slaves, its yield
> had been paid for in its own weight of human bones. Whole tribes of
> Indians had perished in this exploitation; and then the mine was
> abandoned, since with this primitive method it had ceased to make
> a profitable return, no matter how many corpses were thrown into
> its maw. (*Nostromo* 52).

Or again, when Mrs. Gould sees the countryside under the guidance
of Don Pépé, "The heavy stonework of bridges and churches left by
the conquerors proclaimed the disregard of human labour, the trib-
ute-labour of vanished nations." Even though "the power of king
and church was gone . . . at the sight of some heavy ruinous pile

277

overtopping from a knoll the low mud walls of a village" (89), Don Pépé would cry out in lament.

Social injustice stands legible in the physical disproportion of the built landscape not only in Conrad's fictional Costaguana, but also in Raymond Williams' Britain. Williams devoted a memorable page to the "visible stamping of power" in "the great iron gates and the guardian lodges" of the eighteenth-century "great" houses that transformed the countryside by their "barbarous disproportion of scale":

> People still pass from village to village, guidebook in hand . . . to look at the stones and the furniture. But stand at any point and look at the land. Look at what those fields, those streams, those woods even today produce. Think it through as labour and see how long and systematic the exploitation and seizure must have been, to rear that many houses, on that scale. . . . The working farms and cottages are so small beside them. (*Country* 105–6)

It would be important for Jameson's purpose to discriminate Williams' Marxist analysis from what we find in Conrad. Certainly Conrad is not offering bourgeois historicism, but what is it? Howe tried harder than Jameson to answer this question.

As part of his analysis of Conrad's strategies of "containment" (*PU* 242), the fundamental ideological activity performed by literary form, Jameson brilliantly explored the role of sound in the novel, but he took sound as pure sensuality, not at all "conceptual" (212) but rather hallucinatory. One of the most extraordinary passages in the novel dealing with sound evokes the railroad train, like a "shrieking ghost" (*Nostromo* 172) that first "rolled lightly" with "no rumble of the wheels, no tremor on the ground," until it entered the yards, and then, "when the ear-splitting screech of the steam-whistle for the brakes had stopped, a series of hard, battering shocks, mingled with the clanking of chain-couplings, made a tumult of blows and shaken fetters under the vault of the gate." This ends one chapter, and then in the next chapter, Decoud goes on to "read" the history of his land and his people in the repetition of metallic clamor: "This sound puts a new edge on a very old truth." For "there used to be in the old days the sound of trumpets outside that gate" (173–74) when the English "adventurers" like Drake had come up to the town. From those days of galleons to these days of modern technology, one constant remains: "'In those days this town was full of wealth. Those men came to take it. Now the whole land is like a treasure-house, all these people are breaking into it, while we are cutting each other's throats. . . . It has always been our fate to be'—he did not say 'robbed,' but added, after a pause—'exploited!'"

Finally, I note Hirsch as the figure of the book wholly omitted from Jameson's account, even from the elaborate schematization of characters in the "structural" relations of meaning that emerged from his procedure. This is the one figure of whom Howe asserted, "He has a sense of history" (*PN* 114). In accord with one understanding of history, he mars the symmetry of a structural pattern: for in Jameson's reading, the basis of the fundamental myth of the book was "the expedition of Decoud and Nostromo to the Great Isabel" (*PU* 272), but in fact Hirsch, in hiding, made a third person. He was a trader in ox hides, which links him to the earliest economic activities of the region, as evoked in the book's first paragraph, and in the key period of historical transition that occupies much of the book's middle, his screams and his silences alike are foregrounded by the narrative. That is to say, he is everywhere in Jameson's patterns but nowhere in his text. As I suggested earlier in the argument concerning Nietzsche, Jameson must hide the political in order then to find it elsewhere.

Yet this problem I find with Jameson's reading is very close to the problem that I found in Kermode's reading of *Under Western Eyes*. The technical requirements of brilliant innovation in reading performance overwhelm the explicit materials at issue in the book. A Marxist understanding of *Nostromo* has as great a responsibility to these passages of political consciousness as a proper narrative account has to the materials of the plot that Kermode excluded. I have learned much that I find intensely useful from Jameson, but the method he teaches will never do more than extend the already prevailing lines of formalist technicism unless it extends itself to account for what everyone can find in the novel, not just what is available to "elaborate hermeneutic geiger counters." The wager of *The Political Unconscious* was to win a hearing for Marxism among literary critics by showing that Marxism could support literary skills equal to any; the danger was that it would only subordinate Marxism to the production of readings as usual, rather than making possible new grounds for literary history.

Chapter 12
Postmodernism, Politics, and the
Impasse of the New York Intellectuals

IN THE TWO DECADES since it first consciously began to define itself, postmodern criticism has chosen to be worldly. Not that it is urbane; this is not a world in which one can or should too easily be at home. Yet the struggle against received forms of reading, writing, and public discourse has not been mundane either. Philosophy, and its difficulties, served a necessary function in countering the technicist emphases of New Criticism and structuralism alike, as well as in marking the difference between a simple quest for relevance and a movement that was willing to wield the weapons of criticism in all their cultural elaboration. Then, in the seventies, postmodernism experienced an exhilarating but unsettling confluence with poststructuralism, the critique of method, the philosophic cure, that sprang up athwart structuralism. Now that the sixties have faded emphatically into a past, the radical social and political activities, the urgency of questioning that formed the atmosphere from which postmodernism condensed, no longer define our immediate world. They must not be repressed, however; we must solicit the uncanny without becoming somnambulists. This need locates the dialogue between postmodern criticism and the Anglo-American renewal of Marxism that is itself a product of the sixties. This new Marxism and postmodernism share the conviction that literature and theory and criticism are not only contemplative, not mere superstructure, but active; they share commitments to human life in history.

It would be foolish, however, to suggest that this beginning heralds the dawn of a new day. Irving Howe recently looked back to the founding of *Dissent* in 1954 and ruefully explained its premise: "We were saying . . . that socialism in America had to be seen mostly as an intellectual problem before it could even hope to become a viable movement" (*Margin* 236). At about the same time as Howe's explanation, Fredric Jameson similarly summarized his own current theoretical concerns and the project of *Social Text*: "No real systemic change in this country will be possible without the minimal first step of the achievement of a social democratic movement [but] that first step will not be possible without two other preconditions . . . the creation of a Marxist intelligentsia, and that of a Marxist culture" (Interview 73). The congruence of analysis is striking, and the endurance of the problem is dismaying.

The bar between culture and politics in the United States that seems to be marked here has stood at least since the first great American novel appeared. Hawthorne set "The Prison Door" as the title of his first chapter. It stands between the "official," political life of "The Custom House" and the passionate, artistic representation of "The Scarlet Letter," and it blocks the passage from one to the other. Of these two unequal parts that together make up *The Scarlet Letter*, each may be read as the source of the other, yet each is unconscious of the other. The marks that trace their relations remain to be produced through our reading, beyond which lies a task of historical interpretation to revise our sense of politics in the American life of letters.

BOUNDARY 2 AND THE WIDER DEBATE

The preceding remarks define one of this book's major claims, but when first written, they introduced a special issue of *boundary 2* on "Postmodernism and Politics." The history of *boundary 2* therefore forms an important context for understanding them. When it was founded in the early 1970s, *boundary 2* projected a clear sense of the "postmodern"; as a university-based intervention in the world of literature, it stood against the classics of modernism as they had been interpreted and institutionalized by the New Criticism. A Sartrean, existential concern for the engagements of worldly life opposed New-Critical emphasis on "impersonality" in its many forms, whether distance through myth, hardness through image, or lucidity through point of view. The journal's roots in phenomenology reached back from Sartre to Heidegger, toward a sense of temporality against New-Critical modernist spatialization; and beyond Heidegger to Kierkegaard, who offered an understanding of irony quite different from that which was popularized by Robert Penn Warren and Cleanth Brooks. This renewed sense of irony enabled *boundary 2* critics to elaborate postmodern interpretations of Eliot, Joyce, Yeats, Conrad, and other modernist classics. Much in the previous chapters carries on such a project. The "postmodern" thus proved not straightforwardly chronological. It partook of a more complex hermeneutical temporality, as the journal uncovered an ever-receding history of postmodernism through unsettling received New-Critical interpretations over the whole of Western literature.

A further complication in the position of *boundary 2* emerged over time in its relation to issues of political and social life. Although conceived from the beginning as oppositional, its concerns might at first have seemed those of a "personal" individualism, which, however full-bodied in comparison with New Criticism, would remain no more than an alternative aestheticism. Already by the middle of the 1940s, however, Sartre had visibly begun his own turn to politics, and Lucien Goldmann had offered the suggestion that Heidegger's existential phenomenology took its point of departure from the critique of "reification" by Georg Lukács in *History and Class Consciousness* (1923), to which *Being and Time* (1927) offered an ontological rather than historical analysis. Since, moreover, *boundary 2* had been founded in part as an attempt to prolong the energies of the 1960s, both its situation and its intellectual genealogy pointed toward what in fact occurred: postmodernism and politics came together in the journal's agenda. Yet Lukács' insistence on "totality" seemed suspiciously like that of the New Critics on the "tradition" or on the work as "icon." In confluence with contemporary revisions of Heidegger in France, the politics of *boundary 2* proved "deconstructive" like Derrida; like Foucault more concerned with the fields of "micropolitics." This acknowledgment of the micropolitical allowed *boundary 2* to take seriously its location as an academic journal, rather than yearning nostalgically for the days of the independent man of letters and looking only with disabling self-contempt at the current place of literary intellectuals.

The postmodernism of *boundary 2* is only one of many varieties. The discussion of postmodernism has been most notable for its international and interdisciplinary extent, running from architecture through the visual arts and music, through literature and history, to the social and natural sciences, while bringing in contributions from several cultures beyond the anglophone world. A sampling of significant positions in the overall debate would include those of the English historian Perry Anderson, who was long editor of *New Left Review*; the Harvard sociologist Daniel Bell, whose collaboration with Irving Kristol on *The Public Interest* led to his characterization as a "neoconservative"; the German social philosopher Jürgen Habermas, who is often treated as the heir of Frankfurt School critical theory; Fredric Jameson, who revitalized American Marxist cultural studies while professor of French at Yale amid the controversy over deconstruction; Jean-François Lyotard, a French philosopher and former independent socialist activist, long involved with the critique of Stalinism; Richard Rorty, whose renewal of American pragmatism led him out of Princeton's philosophy department and into the pages of general literary and cultural journals.

Using even this limited group as a field for comparison, it becomes obvious how little the debate has reached clarity. To begin with, the debate is motivated by evaluative differences. The first significant literary discussions of the "postmodern" at the end of the 1950s by Irving Howe and Harry Levin established a clear negative stance: the postmodern was a weak successor to the vigorous glory of literary modernism, brought about because mass society had eroded the artist's vital distance. During the sixties, a more complex attention to new modes of mass media in work by Leslie Fiedler, Susan Sontag, Richard Poirier, and above all Ihab Hassan helped to establish the context within which *boundary* 2 appeared. In recent years, however, the initial hostility, exacerbated by a sense of beleaguerment, has fueled new antipostmodern projects like that of Hilton Kramer's *New Criterion*. So it remains even now typically the case that to "have a position" on postmodernism means not just to offer an analysis of its genesis and contours but to let the world know whether you are for it or against it, and in fairly bald terms. Thus Anderson, Bell, and Habermas all treat postmodernism as something that we could be spared if only people would trade excessive rhetoric for sensible analysis (at just these moments, however, their own rhetoric swells); Lyotard and Rorty, on the other hand, urge us to adopt postmodern positions. Jameson argues that postmodernism necessarily includes both positive and negative aspects, but that the notion helps us to make sense of our times and therefore should be used; to all who oppose the postmodern, however, this can seem no more than disguised advocacy.

It remains wholly unsettled whether the relation of the "postmodern" to the "modern" is more a break or a continuity. Anderson finds "modern" and "postmodern" alike terms which mask more important facts about the times they purport to describe; Bell finds the postmodern acting out principles that were already dangerous within modernism; while Lyotard finds in the postmodern a sublime potentiality that is realized in the modern, unsettling our usual conception of sequence. Habermas, Jameson, and Rorty agree in finding a significant break between the modern and the postmodern, but there is no consensus as to where the break falls. Jameson, perhaps because he is a professional student of literature, roughly identifies the modern with the first half of the twentieth century and the postmodern with what has come later. Habermas, perhaps because professionally a student of social philosophy, identifies the modern with the still-unfulfilled project of the eighteenth-century Enlightenment, while the postmodern remains a threatening shadow rather than something that has quite occurred. Rorty, perhaps because his defining professional engagement was with the analytic epistemological tradition, locates the modern with Descartes and finds the major contours of the postmodern already visible in Hegel. These disagreements help to explain why my situating of postmodern literary studies reaches back to the nineteenth and earlier twentieth centuries.

In their methods of analysis, these figures fall into yet further combinations. Habermas, Lyotard, and Rorty all employ versions of "thin" or "philosophical" history to establish their points; in contrast, Anderson, Bell, and Jameson, even though also writing relatively brief treatments, draw upon a much wider range of empirical materials. On the other hand, Bell joins Lyotard and Rorty in de-emphasizing "totalizing" modes of description and explanation. Among these three, however, further splits appear.

Against attempts to ground Value in Humanity, Nature, or Reason, Rorty insists on the local contingencies of values, approaching a position like that of current literary theory on "interpretive communities." Yet Rorty still relies upon the integrity of his local units. He therefore warns "the intellectual" not to become separated from "the social needs of his community" ("Habermas" 175), for he fears that American intellectuals' response to the Vietnam war acted "to separate the intellectuals from the moral consensus of the nation" ("Postmodernist" 588). Lyotard's overall position seems to agree with Rorty's; Lyotard contrasts the *"grands récits"* (perhaps best translated "tall tales") that unify human history in the name of Emancipation (the French Revolution) or Speculation (the German university) or both (Marxism) with the language games of *"petits récits"* ("white lies") that operate over smaller units both conceptually and demographically. Yet in exploring "the differend" (dispute, conflict, difference), Lyotard looks to situations where power and language intersect to victimize minorities wrongly treated as if they were members of a community from which they actually differ in ways that are "not presentable under the rules of knowledge" ("Differend" 14). As against Rorty, Lyotard does not trust the integrity of "communities" any more than of "totality."

In a mode that he might blush to find Lyotard characterizing as postmodern, Daniel Bell insists against both functionalists and Marxists that there is no integral entity called "society"; between the separate realms of the polity, the economy, and the culture "disjunction" prevails. Bell can therefore assert, in a statement that would seem to be so scandalous that his critics in the debate do not even comment upon it, that he is "a socialist in economics, a liberal in politics, and a conservative in culture" ("Modernism" 206). This takes to an extreme a notion like that of the "relative autonomy" with which Althusser made possible fresh Marxist thought regarding questions of the state and of culture, and which remains crucial in the attempts by Anderson and Jameson at a "totalizing" frame of argument. Habermas, while insisting on Weber's neo-Kantian separation of rationality into separate spheres of knowledge, morality, and taste (corresponding to science, social organization, and art), tries to establish a new, if reduced, totality of "everyday life," which in order to flourish must be kept in contact with the results of all three spheres.

It might be thought that the question of art's autonomy would only be a special case of "totality," but in fact yet different alignments emerge on this issue, which has been crucial, as we already noted, since the beginning of the postmodernism debate. In Anderson's argument, surprisingly close to traditional Marxist "reflection" theory, the possibilities of art are determined by social conditions but art does not have the power to alter those conditions; for Lyotard, art's value depends upon its maintaining itself as a separate "language game," distinct from the discourses of power. On the other side, Rorty's pragmatic anti-Kantianism grants, and encourages, that art and criticism may intervene in speculation and debate on issues that would traditionally have been reserved for natural or moral philosophy; Bell, however, is distressed at the incursion achieved by cultural values into the separate realms of politics and, especially, economics. Habermas and Jameson stand as if explicitly opposed to each other. For Habermas, the postmodern is the threat, carried on from surrealism, to de-autonomize art, freeing its energies for use in all of life, but he claims that this is based upon a misunderstanding, for "when the containers of an autonomously developed cultural space are shattered, the contents get dispersed. Nothing remains from a desublimated meaning or a destructured form" ("Modernity" 11). Jameson argues that capitalist reification has already destroyed any cultural autonomy, but that cultural modes and practices are now spread throughout the fabric of social life by a process of "acculturation" ("Periodizing" 201). What remains, therefore, are opportunities for cultural production and criticism much more significant than had existed under earlier conditions. The struggle over what Antonio Gramsci called "hegemony" (see Williams, "Base and Superstructure," and Buttigieg) in everyday life becomes a significantly political activity once there is no longer a decisive separation of the cultural sphere. The example of Latin American liberation theology powerfully exemplifies the political potential of cultural issues, and the example of Matthew Arnold testifies that the connection is not brand new.

This survey of some exemplary positions in the postmodernism debate makes it painfully plain that a great deal of the controversy depends upon misunderstandings, not at all surprising across so wide a range of disciplinary and national traditions, which obstruct significant direct engagement with the arguments, motives, and implications of the various positions. To elucidate several problem areas, I shall first examine one of the most important essays in the debate, and I shall then turn to one of the most important issues associated with the debate as it has been conducted within the profession of literary study in the United States.

AN EXEMPLARY ESSAY: HABERMAS ON MODERNITY

Jürgen Habermas' "Modernity Versus Postmodernity" brought the discussion of postmodernism into its current phase. Originally an address upon receiving the Theodor W. Adorno prize from the city of Frankfurt in 1980, it was subsequently delivered at New York University, translated as the lead article with a notable response by Andreas Huyssen in *New German Critique*, and republished as the first essay in the excellent reader on postmodernism *The Anti-Aesthetic* (under the title "Modernity—an Incomplete Project"). It provoked responses in the French journal *Critique* by Lyotard and Rorty. Lyotard's reply has appeared in English both in a collection edited by Ihab Hassan and as a supplement to his earlier *Postmodern Condition*. Rorty's response to Habermas and Lyotard has been published in English both by *Praxis International* and in Bernstein's *Habermas and Modernity*, which includes Habermas' response to the controversy. The significance of Habermas' "Modernity Versus Postmodernity" is manifold. It attempted to reassert a reasoned commitment to the Enlightenment while speaking under the auspices of Adorno, who in *Dialectic of Enlightenment* had found contemporary totalitarianism prepared for by the Enlightenment ideal of dominating nature. It participates in Habermas' "reconstruction of historical materialism," which draws upon all the intellectual resources of the twentieth century in order to redeem the nineteenth-century Marxist science of society. Habermas' essay thus stands for a left-wing progressive view of world history, underwritten by his extraordinary erudition and seriousness and projected in his thousand-page *Theory of Communicative Action*. Yet in making his case, Habermas rapidly dismissed competing political and theoretical positions with an inaccuracy, a failure of understanding, that is shocking in one whose best work so depends on probingly sympathetic critique of others, and whose long-standing ethical norm has been the transcendence of "systematically distorted communication." (His full book on modernity, *Der philosophische Diskurs der Moderne*, appeared only after this book was written.)

Habermas honored Daniel Bell as the "most brilliant of the American neoconservatives," and he rightly recognized Bell's concern with the "dissolution" of the Protestant ethic that had long dominated American values and with the aftermath of that dissolution: the "adversary culture" of "modernism" that now seems to reign, despite the exhaustion of its own original impulses, "dominant but dead," transformed into postmodernism. Habermas went on to charge that in Bell's analysis, "neoconservatism shifts onto cultural modernism the uncomfortable burdens of a more or less successful capitalist modernization of the economy and society." Habermas then summarized Bell's prescription: "What new norm will put a brake on the levelling caused by the social welfare state, so that the virtues of individual competition can again dominate? Bell sees a religious revival as the only solution" ("Modernity" 6–7). I know no treatment of Habermas that challenges these claims (although Habermas himself moderated them, without acknowledging the change ["Neoconservative Culture Criticism" 82]); we all are grateful for the rhetorical vigor that sweeps away the threat of neoconservatism. Yet these claims do no justice to Bell's arguments, however frustrating we may sometimes find his loose, repetitive, and not wholly consistent exposition.

Bell's major work addressed by Habermas is *The Cultural Contradictions of Capitalism* (1976), successor to *The Coming of Post-Industrial Society* (1973). In keeping with Bell's emphasis on the "disjunction" of polity, economy, and culture, the later book emphasized the cultural as the earlier had the economic. Yet Bell understood that his different realms interact with each other, with effects that include both reinforcement and hindrance. Let me try to sketch Bell's argument as clearly as possible while still acknowledging its blurriness. Some five centuries ago, "modernity" produced two new figures, the "bourgeois entrepreneur" and the "independent artist" (freed by the market from patronage) (*Cultural Contradictions* 16). Similar in their origins, these two figures diverged: "Radical in economics, the bourgeoisie became conservative in morals and cultural taste" (17), that is to say, developed the Protestant ethic character structure. During the "early development of capitalism," the radical "unrestrained economic impulse" was held back by this character structure, but in later capitalist development "the Protestant Ethic was undermined not by [cultural] modernism but by capitalism itself": "The greatest single engine in the destruction of the Protestant Ethic was the invention of the installment plan" (21). Bell concluded: "The breakup of the traditional bourgeois value system, in fact, was brought about by the bourgeois economic system—by the free market, to be precise. This is the source of the contradiction of capitalism in American life" (55). Thus he found that "the erosion of traditional American values took place on two levels": in the "realm of culture and ideas," to be sure, "but a more fundamental transformation was occurring in the social structure itself: the change in the motivations and rewards of the economic system" (74).

More recently Bell summarized this topic:

> Bourgeois capitalism, as the sociological form of the modern economy, and avant-garde modernism, as the victorious feature of the culture, had common roots in their repudiation of the past, in their dynamism, in the search for novelty and sanction of change. Yet, inevitably, the different axial principles of these realms (the techno-economic realm segmenting a person into "roles," the culture emphasizing the achievement of the whole person) brought the bourgeois economic system into sharp conflict with the modernist culture. . . . Thus are discerned contradictions in the fundamental structures of modern society [that is, *between* realms]. Within the realms, other contradictions have developed. . . . From the 1920s modern corporate capitalism, being geared to mass production and consumption, has promoted a hedonism that has undercut the Protestant Ethic which was the initial motivation or legitimation for individuals in bourgeois society. (*Winding Passage* xv)

Bell does not blame modernism for the damage done by capitalism; instead he analyzes the "cultural contradiction of capitalism" as precisely its own power to undermine the human basis on which its success had depended. As one who is a "socialist in economics," Bell has no reason to reject social welfare or to require "individual competition" once more to dominate. He does not believe that the political liberties he values depend upon capitalism, and his notion of the "public household" seeks "to detach political liberalism from bourgeois society," for they are only "associated by origin, but not actually interdependent" (*Cultural Contradictions* 26). It is true that he looks to a religious revival, but this is part of being a "conservative in culture," not in economics or politics. In the realm of culture "modernism has been the seducer" (19) by undoing "the hold of restraint" and urging "the acceptance of impulse" (18).

To be a cultural conservative for Bell cannot mean merely preferring Mann to Barth, Beethoven to Boulez, or Shakespeare to Woody Allen, because in his historical scheme every one of these figures has worked along the axial principle of the self. No less than Fredric Jameson or Perry Anderson, Bell if taken seriously would have us imagine a new art that responded not to the self, rather to communal norms known in the past as religion but that we must invent anew for our future. (I regret Bell takes no interest in the unselving energies of such a postmodern work as Thomas Pynchon's *Gravity's Rainbow*, which follows Slothrop from the uniquely determining perversion of his Pavlovian youth along an anti-oedipal path until he finally becomes "a crossroads, a living intersection," [625] renewing one of Longinus' tropes for sublime mobility of identity.) In the meantime, however, Bell adapts Gramsci's analysis of hegemony ("Modernism and Capitalism" 216) to suggest that after many centuries in which bourgeois principles dominated culture, especially in religion and education, there is now a "radical disjunction" between cultural and social values, and that "such disjunctions . . . historically have paved the way for more direct social revolutions" (*Cultural Contradictions* 53). That is to say, precisely because it is now commodified as postmodernism and no longer at its former distance, the antihegemonic force of modernism can now more effectively undo capitalism.

Just as Habermas wished at the beginning of his essay to sweep away American "neoconservatism," which I have tried to suggest as hardly the best way of categorizing Bell, so he also at the end turned against what he considered the self-contradictory "anti-modernism" based on "modernistic attitudes" of the French "young conservatives" from "Georges Bataille via Michel Foucault to Jacques Derrida" ("Modernity" 14). I had earlier contrasted Foucault favorably to Habermas (in "The Function of Foucault"), and others have defended him against Habermas. Nonetheless, there are so many who echo Habermas, ranging from Jameson ("Postmodernism" 57) and the British sociologist Anthony Giddens (224–25) to Rorty, that it is worth devoting a little more attention to the problem. The fundamental objection offered to Foucault (and with little change to Derrida, but often by different critics) is that his work saps the basis for social action.

For one who has so chided our nostalgic wish for grounding as Rorty has, it is remarkable that this becomes the basis for his criticism of Foucault: "Foucault affects to write from a point of view light-years away from the problems of contemporary society. His own efforts at social reform (e.g., of prisons) seem to have no connection with his exhibition of the way in which the 'humane' approach to penal reform tied in with the needs of the modern state" ("Habermas" 171–72). Rorty has forgotten here that the purpose of Foucault's prison work was not humane reform (that is to say, providing a new representation of prisoners by which they could be better known) but to facilitate prisoners' attempts at representing themselves. Moreover, Rorty does not consider that in defining the project of *Discipline and Punish* as "writing the history of the present" (31), Foucault allied himself with Nietzschean genealogy. This genealogical practice transforms history from a judgment on the past in the name of a present truth to a "counter-memory" that combats our current modes of truth and justice, helping us to understand and change the present by placing it in a new relation to the past (*Language* 160, 163–64). Instead Rorty cites "writing the history of the present" as evidence of a "remoteness" that arrogates "the eye of a future historian." Rorty therefore concludes that "there is no 'we' to be found in Foucault's writings," but surely a pragmatist can acknowledge that making a "we" is up to us as well as to the author we read. Foucault often claimed that his works were offered as tools; we join him then by using them, and enough of us have done so over the last decade that it should by this time be clear: those who claim that his work depresses are only saying that they have no use for it (although it has evidently energized them at least to rejection; only putative "others" are wholly paralyzed by its torpedo charms).

For the reader at home in the Anglo-American traditions of literary study, probably the strangest moment in Habermas' essay comes in his discussion of the need to maintain an autonomous sphere of art, while also allowing everyday life access to that sphere:

Albrecht Wellmer has drawn my attention to one way that an aesthetic experience which is not framed around the experts' critical judgments of taste can have its significance altered: as soon as such an experience is used to illuminate the life-historical situation and is related to life problems, it enters into a language game which is no longer that of the aesthetic critic. The aesthetic experience then not only renews the interpretation of our needs in whose light we perceive the world. It permeates as well our cognitive significations and our normative expectations and changes the manner in which all these moments refer to one another. ("Modernity" 13)

What is strange is not the set of connections made, but the idea that without Albrecht Wellmer's inspired suggestion, Habermas would never have thought of the relations between art and life that are the basis of Wordsworth's and Coleridge's poetics, of Emerson's writing, of Arnold's criticism, of Lawrence's "art for *my* sake," of Lionel Trilling's teaching career, and Leavis' belief that close literary analysis was "the discovery and animation of central human values" and therefore in our world "involved you in an assault on a whole system of social and cultural and academic values" (Williams, *Writing*, 185).

Perhaps no one formed in the American literary academy can really understand what the meaning of art's autonomy has been in philosophic aesthetics (one reason for Richard Rorty's importance is his ability to speak for literature to philosophy). Addressing "The Crisis in Culture" as long ago as 1960, Hannah Arendt observed, "The great works of art are no less misused when they serve purposes of self-education or self-cultivation than when they serve any other purposes; it may be as useful and legitimate to look at a picture in order to perfect one's knowledge of a given period as it is useful and legitimate to use a painting in order to hide a hole in the wall" (203). Yet in those same years, Lionel Trilling taught *Heart of Darkness* and *Death in Venice* explicitly as "background" for his course in modern literature. Following the analysis but not the evaluation of Peter Bürger's brilliant *Theory of the Avant-Garde*, Habermas located the programmatic, antimodernist "negation of culture" among the surrealists, as one of their "two mistakes" ("Modernity" 10–11). Trilling, however, found the essential note of all modern literature the "disenchantment of our culture with culture itself," its "hostility to civilization" (*Beyond* 3).

The power of modern literature, for Trilling, was its uniquely "personal" appeal, its capacity to shake our beliefs about all aspects of our life that had been settled by society, tradition, or habit, and his essay "On the Teaching of Modern Literature" became what it described. Moving from Trilling's own "personal experience" (*Beyond* 3) as a teacher, the essay ironically stripped away the pieties of literary study by charting the diminishment effected upon both our literary masterpieces and our selves by their academic institutionalization: "More and more, as the universities liberalize themselves and turn their beneficent imperialistic gaze upon what is called Life Itself, the feeling grows among our educated classes that little can be experienced unless it is validated by some established intellectual discipline, with the result that experience loses much of its personal immediacy for us and becomes part of an accredited societal activity" (10). Habermas would condemn Trilling's view as antimodernism for its distrust of liberal rationalization, and Bell would condemn it as modernism for its prime emphasis on experience (he drew the notion of "adversary culture" from the preface to the book in which this essay appears), while in the critique of a "beneficent imperialistic gaze," Foucault might have found some interesting resonances with his own genealogy of panoptical disciplines.

AN EXEMPLARY ISSUE: REPRESENTATION

I cannot resolve the misunderstandings that I have been exposing, but I think that the debate over postmodernism will benefit from this preliminary attempt at clarifying some problems in one of its most important statements. By the same token, I wish to offer a preliminary inquiry into one of the most vexed areas in contemporary theory, that of representation. Here I shall advance a hypothesis of my own about some relations of modern and postmodern.

It would be fruitless to detail all the critics and theorists who have helped to establish "the so-called critique of representation" as a major "form of what must be called postmodernism generally" (Jameson, "Periodizing," 194). This discussion ranges over the history of philosophy, bearing particularly on epistemology; the theory of history, whether as concept, practice of writing, or course of actions; debates over politics, whether Marxist attacks on liberalism or libertarian attacks on Marxism; and the history and future of literature, as the question of "realism" and the larger issue of "narrative" overall. Jacques Derrida ironically notes the consensus among critics that postmodern theorists, especially the French figures associated with poststructuralism, hold one simple view: "representation is bad" ("Sending" 304); critics as diverse as the DDR Marxist Robert Weimann (in much the richest engagement), the American neorealist Gerald Graff, the English semiotic materialists Rosalind Coward and John Ellis, and the late deconstructive Romanist Eugenio Donato, among many others, can all agree. I disagree, and I am happy to find myself accompanied by several contributions to *The Anti-Aesthetic*, as well as by Fredric Jameson and Edward Said in much of their recent work. Nonetheless, it remains worth trying to spell out the contours of the problem, in the hope of changing the consensus.

A residual modernist problematic obstructs our understanding on issues of representation. This problematic contrasts an antirepresentational antihumanism against humanist defenders of representation—across so wide and distinguished a spectrum as that from E. H. Gombrich to Erich Auerbach to Georg Lukács. But current advanced theory crosses these lines: it is antihumanist, but it acknowledges—critically—our enmeshment in representation. This change may be related to changes in dominant modes of cultural practice, from easel paintings and novels to films and electronic media, and these in turn to the transformation from national to global modes of social and economic relations.

The received belief that "advanced" theorists are "against" representation has two damaging consequences. On the one hand it seems to require us to discard the concerns and results of much postmodern inquiry if we are to pursue the play of representations in the world, where the power of representation is something sought, indeed passionately struggled for, by groups that consider themselves dominated by alien and alienating representations (see, for example, Said, "Permission to Narrate"). On the other hand, however, it encourages an ultraleftist avant-gardism which assumes that any critic seriously willing to work with "representation" and its inevitably associated notions of "narrative" and "history" must be dismissed as a reactionary hierarchalist. Both of these positions deprive us of valuable critical resources; both tend to paralyze our critical enterprise into internecine warfare—the further spinning of "theory" without any concrete engagement.

I cannot present the details of how this particular belief has become established within the American academy. I shall only try to demonstrate that much crucial postmodern theory is not against representation and to sketch the recent history of the confused transition from modern to postmodern views on representation. As with the discussion in chapter 4, I shall not try to define representation; we know well enough the different things we mean by it. People do it all the time, and the crucial issue is by what means, to what purpose, with what effect—pragmatic questions rather than the essentialist fuss whether we have finally found something that will not prove after all just to be representation again. I will venture to represent the history of representation in a particular narrative, which follows.

The tangled historicity of "representation" offers no convenient place to start. Plato, Aristotle, and Descartes are particularly instructive because they mark the major line of Western metaphysics, yet each strove to reject his predecessor. Plato wished to banish the poets for their practice of mimesis, but to Aristotle mimesis guaranteed the value of poetry. Descartes helped overthrow both Aristotelian physics and Platonic epistemology; knowledge itself became a matter of representation—the tradition Rorty swerved from in *Philosophy and the Mirror of Nature*.

For the modernist case against representation, Virginia Woolf is exemplary. *To the Lighthouse* holds an especially privileged place in discussions of representation because of the analysis Erich Auerbach devoted to it in the final chapter of *Mimesis*. There he found that Woolf challenged the very premises of order on which the Western representational tradition had depended, even as at the same time she culminated that tradition through her work's unremitting attention to the most mundane of everyday details, rendered with the richest existential seriousness. If Woolf's overall practice, then, stood as part of the modernist case against representation, that case was rendered significantly visible at memorable moments of the novel. The philosophical impasse of Mr. Ramsay—his inability to move from Q in the alphabet of thought on to R—humorously imaged that of the whole tradition in which he stood (part of the

296

tangled heritage of Descartes) through the anecdotal figure of fat David Hume, stuck in a bog and depending on the help of a woman of the people, who required him to say the Lord's Prayer.

Lily Briscoe's painting has clear analogies to Woolf's own project of writing. In a remarkable moment, Woolf followed the consciousness of Mrs. Ramsay as she dissolved into a "wedge-shaped core of darkness" (95), but that moment was prefigured in Lily's pictorial treatment. Mr. Bankes asked Lily, "What did she wish to indicate by the triangular purple shape, 'just there'?"

> It was Mrs. Ramsay reading to James, she said. She knew his objection—that no one could tell it for a human shape. But she had made no attempt at likeness, she said. . . . If there, in that corner, it was bright, here, in this, she felt the need of darkness. . . . Mr. Bankes was interested. Mother and child, then—objects of universal veneration, and in this case the mother was famous for her beauty—might be reduced, he pondered, to a purple shadow without irreverence.
> But the picture was not of them, she said. (81)

This sequence exemplifies what the modernist philosopher Ortega y Gasset was calling the "dehumanization of art," yet Woolf also exposed women's "humanity" as no more than objectification in a man's gaze, even of "veneration" (same root as Venus and venereal).

My own language here, when I write of rendering and prefiguring and exemplifying, exploits the resources of representation in order to discuss what I claim is antirepresentational. But to take a stand against representation is not in fact to escape it; by and large modernist polemic does not succeed, and confusion has come from taking its claims for results.

Another crucial aspect of the modernist case against representation involved Marxist politics. Georg Lukács was both the most important Marxist literary theorist of our century and also closely involved with the institutional dimensions of revolutionary culture; from the 1920s through the 1960s he defended the tradition of critical realism, always associated with representation. Since Lukács was identified with representation, with realism, with humanism, and also with Stalinism (if for no other reason than his survival in Moscow during the purge trials), antirepresentationalism became not only a defense of modernism, but also a declaration of anti-Stalinism. Popular Front aesthetics in the United States provided a similar target against which the *Partisan Review* critics could stand for modernism and against Stalinism. I do not think representation is Stalinist (for all its complexities, the case of Solzhenitsyn clearly shows the techniques of realist representation used to criticize Stalinism, as Lukács was quick to observe), but we cannot understand antirepresentationalism in our time without understanding this linkage. From the point of view I am developing here, even so notable an advocate of postmodernism as Lyotard echoes the modernist position when he deplores claims for "realism" as "desire for a return of terror, for the realization of the fantasy to seize reality," and urges instead, "Let us wage war on totality" ("What Is Postmodernism?" 81).

The major recent anti-Lukácsian Marxist theorist—Althusser—also rested immense weight upon the term "representation." For Althusser ideology "represents the imaginary relationship of individuals to their real conditions of existence" ("Ideology" 162), and by the psychoanalytic premises that support this view, even in communist society ideology will persist, and therefore also representation. In *Reading Capital*, a German term for representation, *Darstellung* (29), named the "structural causality" (188) that operates through overdetermination and that Marx showed but never named as such. To produce this absent concept, and in language like that of Derrida's contemporaneous essays, Althusser looked to those moments when Marx represented the capitalist system as "mechanism, a machinery, a machine, a construction" (192). And this is *Darstellung*:

> the very existence of this machinery in its effects: the mode of existence of the stage direction (*mise en scène*) [= *Darstellung*] of the theater which is simultaneously its own stage, its own script, its own actors, the theater whose spectators can, on occasion, be spectators only because they are first of all forced to be its actors, caught by the constraints of a script and parts whose authors they cannot be, since it is in essence *an authorless theater*. (193)

The language of such an anti-*auteur* theory points toward a third aspect of the modernist case against representation, which involves the context of mass culture. For plot was the basis of Aristotelian mimesis, and plot has also been understood as the backbone of mass

298

cultural appeal, so that high culture retreated from plot, and neo-platonic arguments against plot's seductive power have been re-newed. Indeed, in my elementary class on literary theory, students confronted with Aristotle's one-hundred-word summary of the ac-tion of the *Odyssey*—a decisive moment in the history of Western thinking about literature, a demonstration of the analytic power to achieve over a thousandfold reduction, the capacity to perform what the *Ion* suggests neither Socrates nor anyone else in his culture could accomplish—and asked to try a similar exercise on some work that they know and admire, regularly complain that in its plot, the admired work is indistinguishable from something they value so little as a Harlequin romance. Postmodern inquiry has renewed the attempts of Bertolt Brecht and Walter Benjamin to achieve a posi-tive use of mass culture, but modernist hostility to mass culture has ranged from the economic determinism of the Frankfurt School be-lief that its place in "the culture industry" necessarily dooms a work to cooperate with the system of domination, to the formalist con-viction that particular signifying practices in themselves are polit-ically reactionary (if realist) or progressive.

The immediate horizon for current debate about representation is "French theory" from the 1960s. My focus now is restricted to a particular institutionalization that this body of work has undergone in America: the view that as a whole it is against representation, and that in particular Derrida is. Such a view prevails in the im-portant University of Minnesota Press series Theory and History of Literature. In *The Structural Allegory*, John Fekete refers to Derri-da's "rejection of representation" and specifies that Derrida's "at-tack on representation" strives to undermine the "structure of representation" because that is the "epistemological foundation" of structuralism (235). Jochen Schulte-Sasse, coeditor of the series, in introducing Peter Bürger's *Theory of the Avant-Garde*, claims that Derrida "subjects to thorough critique the notion of representation" as a part of his attack against "epistemological closures." Schulte-Sasse finds Derrida guilty of employing "the same suspect strategies of exclusion" as does the metaphysics he is deconstructing, a "clear and neat oppositional structure" (xxi, xxv).

I find several problems here. It colonizes Derrida all too easily within institutional Anglo-Saxon philosophy to consider him an epistemologist, even an anti-epistemologist; as might be expected of a Heideggerian, he is far more an ontologist than an epistemologist. Rorty, whose work influences those I have been citing, himself knows better in his direct discussions of Derrida, but this mistake (facilitated by the predominance of the term "representation" in Rorty's critique of foundational epistemology and the term's undeniable prominence in Derrida's work) is part of what has endeared his work to the literary academy. Even more important, however, is that Derrida simply does not attack representation; even where he may be quoted to this effect, he has more to say on the matter.

Derrida's *Speech and Phenomena* argued that what Husserl thought could be treated as "immediate" was instead always already mediated by representation. The inescapability of representation was Derrida's deconstructive point against the metaphysical fantasy of pure presence. Derrida defined the "prime intention" and "ultimate scope" of the book as "affirming *Perception does not exist* or that what is called perception is not primordial, that somehow everything 'begins' by re-presentation" (45 n.) The key term "trace" entered the book in order to elucidate the "re" of representation as part of the most fundamental structure of repetition that was "more 'primordial' than what is phenomenologically primordial" (67).

In *Of Grammatology* it was Rousseau (not Derrida) whose praise of the assembled people was "always a critique of representation" (296). On the other hand, in unraveling the strange graphic of supplementarity, Derrida was perfectly clear that he was following the thread of representation. The design that traced the relation of forces between the two movements of the text, Derrida wrote, "seems to us to be represented in the handling of the concept of the supplement" (163). This claim inaugurated his reading, and at its end Derrida hauntingly concatenated the "entire series of supplementary significations" that he had teased out from Rousseau: "the North, winter, death, imagination, representation, the arousal of desires" (309).

Speech and Phenomena featured Derrida's claim that Husserl's *"phenomenological reduction is a scene, a theater stage"* (86). His whole early essay on Freud operated by staging, as a *mise en scène*, a *Darstellung*, a representation, two series of metaphors in Freud, both of which Freud represented in terms of further instruments of representation: "Psychical *content* will be *represented* by a text whose essence is irreducibly graphic. The *structure* of the psychical *apparatus* will be *represented* by a writing machine" (*Writing* 199). The layered repetitions of representation here may evoke the passage from Husserl that Derrida quoted epigraphically and then again at the end of *Speech and Phenomena*: "A name on being mentioned reminds us of the Dresden gallery . . . we wander through the rooms and stop in front of a painting by Teniers which represents a gallery of paintings. Let us further suppose that the paintings of this gallery would represent in their turn paintings, which, on their part, exhibit readable inscriptions and so forth" (*Speech* 1, 104). Derrida's conclusion in the Freud essay echoed his reading of Husserl, while archly underwriting Freud's pansexualism: "Everything begins with reproduction" (*Writing* 211). Here again the connection to issues of technical reproducibility in mass culture is clear.

From the two essays on Artaud that Schulte-Sasse made his prime examples of Derrida's inadequacies, I can offer only two representative citations. Derrida asked whether Artaud would have "refused the name *representation* for the theater of cruelty." He answered:

> No, provided that we clarify the difficult and equivocal meaning of this notion. Here we would have to be able to play upon all the German words that we indistinctly translate with the unique word representation. The stage, certainly, *will no longer represent*, since it will not operate as an addition, as the sensory illustration of a text already written, thought, or lived outside the stage. . . . The stage will no longer operate as the repetition of a *present*, will no longer *re*-present a present that would exist elsewhere and prior to it. . . . It will not even offer the representation of a present, if present signifies that which is maintained in *front* of me. Cruel representation must permeate me. And nonrepresentation is, thus, original representation, if representation signifies also, the unfolding of a volume, a multidimensional milieu, an experience which produces its own space. *Spacing* . . . (*Writing* 237)

And here Derrida moved on to the play of trace and *différance* that introduces a self-disarticulating distance into what had been credited as immediacy.

I have cited this passage to show that Derrida did not *simply* place Artaud against representation. The next passage I cite to establish that Derrida did not *simply* take any side with regard to representation. Derrida's practice resembles that of novelists. The dream of metaphysics, blind to mortality, sees a world of enchanted giants.

Representation, however, is the windmill in which the quest always gets tangled up. The history of metaphysics, our reality, is both the dream and its disabuse, and to gain any glimpse of a different horizon, we must stage this as a process, not state it as a position.

Here, then, Derrida summarized his first essay on Artaud:

> One entire side of his discourse destroys a tradition which lives *within* difference, alienation, and negativity without seeing their origin and necessity. To reawaken this tradition, Artuad . . . recalls it to its own motifs: self-presence, unity . . . etc. In this sense, Artaud . . . fulfills the most profound and permanent ambition of western metaphysics. But through another twist of his text . . . Artaud affirms the . . . law of difference. . . . This duplicity of Artaud's text . . . has unceasingly obligated us to pass over to the other side of the limit, thereby to demonstrate the closure of the presence within which he had to enclose himself . . . To an inexpert scrutiny, we could appear to be criticizing Artaud's metaphysics from the standpoint of metaphysics itself, when we are actually delimiting . . . a necessary dependency of all destructive discourses: they must inhabit the structures they demolish. (*Writing* 194)

Or as Derrida made the same point in *Speech and Phenomena*: "What we are describing as primordial representation can be provisionally designated with this term only within the closure whose limits we are seeking to transgress by setting down and demonstrating various contradictory or untenable propositions within it, attempting thereby to institute a kind of insecurity and open it up to the outside. This can only be done from a certain inside" (57).

No less than Althusser and Derrida, Michel Foucault devoted crucial work to representation. *The Order of Things* constantly focused on representation, from its opening pages on Velázquez, but at the same time the book argued for radical historical discontinuity. Representation, therefore, cannot be the same across time. From the Cartesian, classical point of view, there is a problem in the relation of the modern human sciences to representation. For even though the human sciences understand "*man*" precisely as "that living being who . . . constitutes representations by which he lives, and on the basis of which he possesses that strange capacity of being able to represent to himself precisely that life" (352), the human sciences look to "unconscious mechanisms" (356) rather than to the clearly illuminated conscious space of classical representation.

302

Against this classical objection, Foucault emphasized that "representation is not consciousness," and "this bringing to light of elements or structures that are never present to consciousness" does not "enable . . . the human sciences to escape the law of representation" (361). There exists, then, a resemblance *but without filiation* between the human sciences and classical philosophy, which produces a recurrent anachronistic effect: "Every time one tries to use the human sciences to philosophize . . . one finds oneself imitating the philosophical posture of the eighteenth century" (363–64). This was Foucault's riposte to Lévi-Strauss' Rousseauism, the vestigial homologue to Derrida's many pages on Lévi-Strauss and Rousseau.

Foucault posed a telling formulation of the dilemma of Derrida's that we have encountered—the Samsonic position of the "destructive" intellectual, inhabiting the edifice he is pulling down—but he construed it as part of our historical moment rather than as an inherent necessity of thought or discourse:

> The human sciences, when dealing with what is representation (in either conscious or unconscious form), find themselves treating as their object what is in fact their condition of possibility. They are always animated, therefore, by a . . . transcendental mobility. They never cease to exercise a critical examination of themselves. They proceed from that which is given to representation to that which renders representation possible, but which is still representation. So [they are] constantly demystifying themselves . . . unveiling . . . the non-conscious. (363–64)

For Foucault at this point in his career, no less than for Derrida, there was nothing to do within the enclosure except glimpse the change that would transform everything—in this case the end of "*man*" and a return to the "power of discourse" (310). Foucault's later work, however, did much to give that formulation specificity and helped to make possible the deep concern with the mechanisms of representational power that mobilizes so many interesting current projects.

I conclude this section with Heidegger's essay "The Age of the World View" both because Derrida discussed it in an essay on representation ("Sending") and because it allows us to consider anew the historical dimensions of the issue. "The Age of the World View" supports Lucien Goldmann's thesis that Heidegger tried to account ontologically for the features of modern life that Lukács defined through the Marxist problematic of reification. Heidegger began the essay with the dual constitution of subject and object through Descartes' analysis of knowledge as representation, and he then defined "the basic process of modern times" as "the conquest of the world as picture" (353)—which involves politics and technology.

Heidegger updated Lukács' focus in *History and Class Consciousness.* Lukács had followed the line explored in chapter 8, analyzing the characteristically nineteenth-century mode of newspaper journalism; Heidegger cited new mass media, "the unlimited power of representing foreign and remote worlds, made present through the turn of a hand, through the radio" (354). Heidegger neither gloried in this new political technology of global representation, nor did he simply stand against it. With astonishing relevance to current debates over education in the United States, this most conservative of modern thinkers, who more than anyone else in the twentieth century remade our intellectual life through engagement with ancient Greece, warned that in the face of our historical situation, the "flight to tradition" offered only a mixture of "humility and arrogance," a "blindness and self-deception" that would not enable us to deal with our current needs (354).

Heidegger also cut closer to where many of us live. For in defining the new forms of knowledge in our time, he emphasized its "institutionalization" in a new "business character." The new dealer in knowledge "does business at meetings and gets information at congresses. He contracts to work for publishers, who [thereby] now help to determine what books must be written." Moreover, part of the new structure Heidegger isolated is something that many of us may value because we believe it challenges the usual business of our departmental structures, namely "the greatest possible ability to . . . switch research," a "regulated mobility of transference and integration of activities with respect to whatever tasks happen to be of paramount importance" (347–48). This is a chilling warning, set in a lecture from Germany in 1938. Does it have the same force now? Postmodern thinking about the responsibility of intellectuals has had to acknowledge that most critics and artists alike are now institutionally located within the university, another loss of the distance that modernists found a guarantee of independence. This

304

essay of Heidegger's helps clarify the interdependence of representation not only with history and narrative, but also with professionalism and questions of intellectuals as the "new class." On all these matters, it is no longer possible *simply* to take sides. By analyzing some of the confusions that have attended recent talk about representation, I hope to have helped make possible more lucid political analyses of the postmodern situation.

POLITICS: OUR CURRENT DEBATES IN THEORY AND HISTORY

Political lucidity requires some sense of what we m¯an by politics at all, and there has been no easy understanding here, either conceptually or historically. More than twenty years ago Peter Sedgwick charged that the "sociocultural" emphasis of such British "New Left" figures as Stuart Hall, E. P. Thompson, and Raymond Williams was "subversive of political activism" (138); yet without shifting his emphasis, Thompson has put aside historiography for an important role in nuclear disarmament agitation. In recent statements that appeared within a few months of each other, Edward Said and Fredric Jameson offered perspectives that show how wide the range of uncertainty can be even among figures, both on the left, who urge that we renew our practices of narrative representation. As part of the "separation of fields" that weakens American intellectual and academic life, Said pointed out "literary Marxists who write for literary Marxists, who are in a cloistral seclusion from the world of real politics." As a consequence, "both 'literature' and 'Marxism' are thereby confirmed in their apolitical content and methodology: literary criticism is still 'only' literary criticism, Marxism only Marxism, and politics is mainly what the literary critic talks about longingly and hopelessly" ("Audiences" 149). Said might also be contesting Foucault's claim that the role of the "universal intellectual" from Voltaire to Sartre has been exhausted and replaced by that of the "specific intellectual," working to change the practices of truth within particular disciplines ("Truth and Power" 126–33).

This issue of totalization versus localization links Paul de Man's practices to those of critics more evidently concerned with social issues. For de Man's challenge—his rhetorical reductions of synecdoche to metonymy, within the proper disciplinary bounds of linguistic analysis—exemplified the strengths and weaknesses of a "specific" intellectual's work no less than the work of the Marxists Said criticized.

As if directly responding to Said's concern over "separation of fields," Jameson insisted, "As far as 'the political' is concerned, any single-slot, single-function definition of it is worse than misleading, it is paralyzing," for the following reasons:

> We are, after all, fragmented beings, living in a host of separate reality-compartments simultaneously; in *each one of those* a certain kind of politics is possible, and if we have enough energy, it would be desirable to conduct all those forms of political activity simultaneously. So the "metaphysical" question: what is politics . . . is worthwhile only when it leads to enumeration of all the possible options, and not when it lures you into following the mirage of the single great strategic idea. (Interview 75)

Since, however, the limitations of discourse necessitate "that we talk about each of these forms of political intervention separately," we must beware of the "supreme misunderstanding," that is, "the misconception that when one modestly outlines a certain form of political activity—such as that which intellectuals in the university can engage in—this 'program' is meant to suggest that this is the *only* kind of politics one should do" (75).

Perhaps Jameson here neglected an aspect of "relative autonomy": the "political" does exist as a realm of state and law. For example, we can speak literally of a "politics of reproduction" because of the battles over the legality of abortion; a "politics of sexuality" because laws forbid certain practices or fail to ensure equal protection to those who engage in them; a "politics of gender" because women have turned to courts and legislatures in attempting to gain equal access to jobs and equal pay within them. One reason the personal has become the political is because of the agitation for public remedies in areas long considered private, including a professor's expectation that a secretary will make coffee, or that a student will tolerate an unwelcome pat. Jameson does not in fact exclude these concerns, but his conceptualization tends to elide their political specificity.

Jameson's understanding of "reification" (like Bell's "axial principle" of role segmentation in economics) recognizes the actual fragmentation of intellectual and political life, while his commitment to "totality" (like Bell's "axial principle" of the "whole person" in culture) insists that these parts be understood in relation to a global context. Many developments in twentieth-century Marxism help to elucidate his position. Gramsci's analysis of "hegemony" laid the basis for understanding the cultural sphere (especially education and religion) as not merely a reflection of social and economic relations but as also a means by which those relations may be enforced, amplified, or contested. (Arnold's career demonstrates this process, but he did not raise it to conceptualization.) The Frankfurt School critique of the "culture industry" gave new insight into culture as a means of domination, and if modified by the ideas of Brecht and Benjamin on "refunctioning," suggested the possibility of the mass media as an arena for political contest. Althusser's conception of "ideological state apparatuses" helped to make clear how even if politics may ultimately mean smashing the state, or taking over the state, or forming a new state, nonetheless activity in the area of culture may be understood in relation to those ultimates.

In Said's terms, then, it is probable that a Marxist "reading" of a "canonical" work is in and of itself no more significant a political challenge than a deconstructive reading, an archetypal reading, or any other "approach"; all alike contribute to legitimating the academic literary institution as autonomous. If, however, Marxist literary critics make part of their argument a challenge to the idea of "literary criticism" itself, demonstrating and challenging the social uses which such an idea has served, we may move toward the political. The crucial contemporary agenda is elaborating the relations that join the nexus of classroom, discipline, and profession to such political areas as those of gender, race, and class, as well as nation.

The current movement from "literary" to "cultural" studies, from "literary criticism" to "criticism," shows this direction, as was ironically, sadly, but accurately understood by Harry Levin as early as 1960. He observed then of the separation of the sphere of high culture, "The thought that a man of letters should consider himself a

307

practitioner of the fine arts, or that he should be designated professionally as an artist, is a legacy from Flaubert's generation which
is not likely to outlast Joyce's by long" (*Refractions* 291). Like Habermas now, Levin then valued the process of separation understood
by both as part of the Enlightenment's heritage (271), but Levin saw
it as already past: "Instead of a tension between the uncompre-
hending majority and the saving remnant . . . there has been a *dé-
tente*, a relaxation, and a collaboration for mutual profit. . . . But
this is a subject notoriously better appreciated by professors of sociology and experts on mass communication than it is by old-fash-
ioned scholars and modernist critics" (293). Postmodern critics,
new-fashioned scholars, can carry on a significant political activity
by relating the concerns once enclosed within "literature" to a
broader cultural sphere that is itself related to, although not identical with, the larger concerns of the state and economy.

At best, however, the idea of "cultural politics" must remain
vexed. The history of cultural opposition movements in the United
States helps to specify some of this discomfort. The 1930s is our usual
point of reference, but already then there was a previous history.
Malcolm Cowley's work for the *New Republic* in the thirties was
closely sympathetic to the conjunction of cultural and political radicalism, coming close to fellow-traveling with communism. He had
already lived through both Greenwich Village bohemianism and
aesthetic expatriation, as he described in *Exile's Return*, published
in 1934, the year *Partisan Review* was founded as an organ of the
John Reed Club. That memoir both illuminates Daniel Bell's arguments about the erosion of the "Protestant Ethic" and shows that
concerns about the "co-optation" of the avant-garde are no longer
novel.

In discussing the "ideas" characteristic of Greenwich Village's
bohemian ways of living around 1920, Cowley emphasized that
"from the standpoint of the business-Christian ethic then represented by the *Saturday Evening Post*," they were "corrupt." For
"this older ethic . . . was a *production* ethic"; its "great virtues"
included "industry, foresight, thrift, and personal initiative."
Against this, however, there emerged "a new ethic that encouraged
people to buy, a *consumption* ethic":

Many of the Greenwich Village ideas proved useful in the altered

308

situation. Thus, *self-expression* and *paganism* encouraged demand for all sorts of products—modern furniture, beach pajamas, cosmetics, colored bathrooms with toilet paper to match. *Living for the moment* meant buying an automobile, radio or house, using it now and paying for it tomorrow. *Female equality* was capable of doubling the consumption of products—cigarettes, for example—that had formerly been used by men alone. Even *changing place* would help to stimulate business in the country from which the artist was being expatriated. The exiles of art were also trade missionaries: involuntarily they increased the foreign demand for fountain pens, silk stockings, grapefruit and portable typewriters. (61–62)

The socially serious 1930s, then, found the preceding generation, which we link with modernism at its height, already liable to the charges that critics urge against postmodernism. Located halfway between, echoing Cowley's language of 1934 and prefiguring that of Charles Newman in 1984, Harry Levin wrote in 1960 of postmodernism: "This is reproduction, not production; we are mainly consumers rather than producers of art. We are readers of reprints and connoisseurs of high fidelity, even as we are gourmets by virtue of the expense account and the credit card. For our wide diffusion of culture is geared to the standardizations of our economy, and is peculiarly susceptible to inflationary trends. . . . The independence of our practitioners, when they are not domesticated by institutions of learning, is compromised more insidiously by the circumstances that make art a business" (*Refractions* 279). Taken further, such analysis leads to the important contemporary topic of intellectuals as a "new class," a group fully interested in social struggles, rather than independent of them.

Independence is difficult to analyze. At one extreme, independence is merely isolation, irrelevance. Independence is valuable only as a relation to that from which, or perhaps by means of which, one is independent, but this opens a further danger of purely reactive independence. For the most influential American cultural intellectuals to emerge from the thirties, these problems were posed not only in terms of the dominant institutions of life in the United States, but most particularly in terms of "Stalinism." They live in history, by their own repeated choice, as the "anti-Stalinist" intellectuals, and this chosen negative independence continually acted to restrict their positive independence. Nathan Glazer offers an analysis, which I find chilling, of how this particular small group "bec[a]me *the* American intellectuals." Although in the thirties their "politics" had usually not even involved voting, let alone the give and take of "who gets what," but instead "positions on . . . great historical issues," when the postwar years brought to sudden dominance a concern with the relations between the United States and the Soviet Union, "the one thing they knew became important." Their unique knowledge was "that the Soviet Union represented a radical threat to freedom, and that variations in its leadership and policies scarcely affected in any significant way the unyielding nature of this threat," and they knew this not even directly from the USSR but because their American "experiences . . . had taught them how different Communists, and Communism, were" (34–35). The exemplary case of Lionel Trilling suggests that their independence from Stalinism came only at the price of their integration into the cold war, as their independent literary views prepared them for authority in the postwar institutionalization of modernism.

If "the two M's" of "Marxism in politics and Modernism in art" were the foci that guided the course of the refounded *Partisan Review* from 1937 according to William Barrett's memoir (11), Irving Howe's retrospect found instead a fundamental split between "radicalism" and modernism as a distinctive American experience of this period (*Decline* 218). In using modernism to criticize the "liberal imagination" from the later thirties into the seventies, Lionel Trilling was combating what he considered "the liberal intellectual middle-class acceptance of Stalinist doctrine in all aspects of life" (*Last Decade* 240). (Trilling held this view despite what seems to a later generation overwhelming evidence to the contrary, such as the debacle of the Wallace campaign in 1948 and the failure of anything like a renewal of the Popular Front in the Waldorf conference of 1949, the expulsion of communists from the labor unions and their prohibition from the newly founded Americans for Democratic Action, all this even before McCarthyism.) To Howe, Trilling's critique "eased a turning away from all politics" (*Margin* 231), yet the point for Trilling had been precisely that it was Stalinists who were not really political. For by refusing to consider any facts that "refuted" their central dogma ("that the Soviet Union had resolved all social and political contradictions and was well on the

310

way toward realizing the highest possibilities of human life"), Stalinists revealed a "disgust" with the substance of real politics: "contingency, vigilance, and effort," which in a remarkable idealization Trilling associated with "such energies of the human spirit as are marked by spontaneity, complexity, and variety" (*Last Decade* 140–41).

Trilling admitted that, for himself and his associates, "Stalinist" was purely a "pejorative designation" that they used against others: "No one, of course, called himself a Stalinist" (*Last Decade* 140). (In fact documents cited for other purposes by Howe and Coser [171] and by Klehr [171, 415] incidentally reveal that "Stalinist" was sometimes used as a self-designation.) Working with such a definition of "Stalinism," which depended neither on what people called themselves nor on their actions but rather on the cast of temperament they displayed, Trilling could not grant that a novel he admired for its bright, comic spirit, *The Unpossessed* (1934) by his friend Tess Slesinger, might be a Communist satire on half-hearted intellectual leftists, even though he acknowledged that after she left New York for Hollywood she "g[a]ve her assent" to "the Party" (*Last Decade* 19). (He himself in 1934 had with others only just left "the Stalinist intellectual camp" [Howe and Coser 299–300] after involvement in a planned collaborative book on Marxism and American life [Klehr 79–80, 427 n.25]. The editors of this project, Newton Arvin, Granville Hicks, and Bernard Smith, were all close to the Communist party, and a few years later Smith's *Forces in American Criticism* [1939] provoked the first version of Trilling's manifesto, "Reality in America," called "Parrington, Mr. Smith, and Reality.") Slesinger's novel does not portray the Communist party as the "rather comical remote abstraction" (*Last Decade* 19) Trilling claimed; on the contrary, the party is sought but remains rigorously offstage, a source of value in the absence of which only silly velleities are possible. Trilling here may have failed in his own appreciation for the complex variety of views. So too his opposition to "Stalinist" principles of art led him to exclude from serious consideration certain modes of writing, to downgrade realism, and in the effect of his own authority become to a younger generation "the mirror image of Zhdanov" (Aronowitz 248), independent only in relation to his chosen opponent.

We lack the history of American intellectuals from the thirties through the sixties that will allow us fully to make sense out of these crossings back and forth, yet they continue to haunt our current situation. It is in principle well known that Habermas' extreme sensitivity to the political dangers of what he reckons antimodernism can be understood in relation to the history of Germany in the twentieth century, for in the two decades before the Nazis came to power, the German academy was full of antimodernist polemic, transmitted from the intellectual concerns of teachers to the agitational concerns of students (Ringer 252). It is less generally known that at the time of the Moscow purge trials, Delmore Schwartz cried out, "If there were no such thing as an objective world, the Stalinists would have their way. But I think there is such a world. If subjective idealism were correct, the Stalinists would be in the right, and we would be lost" (Abel 63). Yet once known, this moment is obviously relevant to current concerns over the "arbitrariness" of meaning or reference, as in the work of Gerald Graff.

It is important that American academics involved in the study of current "theory" be aware of such contexts, here as well as abroad, yet even this is not enough. For Habermas' sensitivity to antimodernism forgets that in the 1920s, it was the modernizing wing in the academy that set in motion the rhetoric of "crisis"; this rhetoric was seized by the antimodernists for their own purposes, which they made prevail (Ringer 351). Those who join Schwartz in embracing the rock of reality against the Stalinists forget that Stalinism saw *its* opponents as idealists, subjectivists who ignored the plain lessons of objective truth. (Rorty has valuably criticized the "silly relativism" ["Texts and Lumps"] of those who believe epistemology necessary to underwrite choice.) Trilling's definition of Stalinism forgot that the German academic mandarins of the 1920s were "apolitical" in considering that the "details of everyday politics were ethically as well as intellectually beneath the notice of the cultivated man" (Ringer 121), in their "dream of a total escape from interest politics," and in their yearning to "transcend the political mechanism in terms of some idealistic absolute" (446). That is, they correspond to what Trilling called Stalinist, but they were in historical fact precursors of fascism. Coming from this German experience, Adorno and others of the Frankfurt School found in the American "culture industry" signs of incipient fascism, seizing on some of the same elements ("the amiable fumblings of the 'little man'") that to

Howe and Coser defined the residue of the Stalinist Popular Front (366). Theories of "totalitarianism" appealed to the 1950s by promising to resolve these inconsistencies, eliminating the differences between Nazis and Communists, but it is now generally conceded that in offering a typology of deviation such theories overlooked too much history.

The lesson of history is that we must know both our history and our difference from our history. In 1937, when William Phillips and Philip Rahv of *Partisan Review* proclaimed that the existing contradiction between Marxism and American traditions required a "Europeanization" of American culture if Marxism were to flourish here (J. Gilbert 147), who would have imagined that the heirs of the "New York intellectuals" would so firmly oppose the recent excitement over "European theory"? When a young lifetime later in 1974, Warren Susman echoed in a new key Henry James' litany of American absences, "Why have we . . . no Luxemburg, no Gramsci, no Lukács, no Gorz, no Althusser?" (84), who would have imagined the "arresting historical change" Perry Anderson proclaimed in 1984: for Marxist theory, "today the *predominant* centres of intellectual production . . . lie in the English-speaking world" (*Tracks* 24).

The key figure in this change was Raymond Williams, born in Wales, not New York, as a contemporary of Daniel Bell and Irving Howe. Like them, he early found the communism of the 1930s "an impasse" (*Politics* 52) and later suffered painful exchanges with the new radicalism of the late sixties and its aftermath. Yet his work has inspired rather than obstructed the conjunction of postmodernism and politics. The shocks that defined the British New Left after 1956—de-Stalinization, Suez, Hungary (a time memorably captured in Doris Lessing's *The Golden Notebook*)—did not lead Williams to a "post-Marxism" as the shaking loose of the sixties did so many French intellectuals and as later developments have done in America. If Marxism in the 1930s gave Williams no resources with which to hold his own against conventional scholarship in a Cambridge English tutorial, by the time he was again willing to identify himself as a Marxist in the 1970s, he had developed critical resources for understanding the politics of culture that went beyond anything else in the anglophone world. While moving out from the exclusive literary canon of Eliot and Leavis to study a wider range of writing, and a wider range of media from theater to television to communications in general, Williams maintained and developed a sympathetic concern for the democratic and radical potential of such work. Moreover, his studies of the conceptual and institutional apparatus of culture have powerfully complemented the "genealogical" research of Foucault.

Yet Williams' work also testifies to the continuing power of humanist figures of thought. After the challenges poststructuralism has posed, is there not something that remains, which may be very different from the *Erlebnis* of German *Lebensphilosophie* or the "experience" which seemed so self-evident to Leavis, and yet which it is still worthwhile to call, explore, and even rely on as "experience"? For Trilling, the great danger of the current institutionalization of learning was its threat to the real individuality of "experience." He noted the shift from Matthew Arnold's exigent question (echoed from Goethe) "Is it true? Is it true for me?" to what he considered the rather slacker "Is it true for us?" (*Beyond* xvi). Benjamin, however, in lamenting the decline of "experience" that had made storytelling no longer possible, argued that collective sharing was essential to experience.

The great impasse against which Trilling's generation and their inheritors struggled could be put this way: rejecting the false experience of Stalinism in the thirties seemed only to yield the false experience of conformity in the fifties. In certain respects we are better positioned. Let us grant that they eradicated from American culture the dangers of Stalinism; now that it is gone, we are again free to explore possibilities on the left. The debates over new developments in theory have allowed fresh perspectives on many of the shibboleths in American cultural-political discourse and given a philosophic vigor not often seen in this country before. Mass culture is our element, neither a sudden and welcome liberation from a worn-out high culture, nor the threat to corrupt all that we most treasure. Since we come late enough not to confuse ourselves with the modernists, we can accept our condition as postmodern. No doubt this was not the name one might have independently chosen; as we have seen, it was originally a pejorative from those who attributed to others a belatedness that was also their own. Finding ourselves, as if from birth, in the academy, we can work there without the shame of ivory tower isolation or the euphoria of being at the nerve center of a brave new world. We will not transform American life today, or tomorrow, but what we do to change our academic habits and disciplines, the questions we dare to ask or allow our students to pursue, these are political and make a difference too, for the academy itself is in the world.

WORKS CITED

Aaron, Daniel et al. "Symposium: Thirty Years Later: Memories of the First American Writers Congress." In *American Scholar* (1966), 35:495–516.

Abel, Lionel. *The Intellectual Follies.* New York: Norton, 1984.

Abrams, M. H. "English Romanticism: The Spirit of the Age." In Northrop Frye, ed., *Romanticism Reconsidered*, pp. 26–72. New York: Columbia University Press, 1963.

—— "How to Do Things with Texts." In *Partisan Review* (1979), 46:566–88.

—— "Introduction: Two Roads to Wordsworth." In *Wordsworth: A Collection of Critical Essays*, pp. 1–11. Englewood Cliffs, N.J.: Prentice-Hall, 1972.

—— *The Mirror and the Lamp: Romantic Theory and the Critical Tradition* (1953). New York: Norton, 1958.

—— *Natural Supernaturalism: Tradition and Revolution in Romantic Literature.* New York: Norton, 1971.

—— "Rationality and Imagination in Cultural History." In *Critical Inquiry* (1976), 2:447–64.

Adorno, Theodor. Letters to Walter Benjamin. Harry Zohn, tr. In Bloch et al., *Aesthetics and Politics*, pp. 110–33.

—— *Minima Moralia.* E. F. N. Jephcott, tr. London: NLB, 1974.

—— "Reconciliation under Duress." Rodney Livingstone, tr. In Bloch et al., *Aesthetics and Politics*, pp. 151–76.

Adorno, Theodor W. and Max Horkheimer. "The Culture Industry." In *Dialectic of Enlightenment* (1947), John Cumming, tr., pp. 120–67. New York: Seabury, 1972.

Alpers, Svetlana. *The Art of Describing.* Chicago: University of Chicago Press, 1983.

Althusser, Louis. "Ideology and Ideological State Apparatuses" (1970). Ben Brewster, tr. In *Lenin and Philosophy*, pp. 127–86. New York and London: Monthly Review Press, 1971.

—— *Reading Capital* (1965). Ben Brewster, tr. New York: Pantheon, 1970.

Anderson, Perry. *In the Tracks of Historical Materialism.* Chicago: University of Chicago Press, 1984.

—— "Modernity and Revolution." In *New Left Review* (1984), no. 144, pp. 96–113.

Arac, Jonathan. "Charles Baudelaire." In George Stade, ed., *European Writers: The Romantic Century*, pp. 1323–48. New York: Scribner, 1985.

—— *Commissioned Spirits: The Shaping of Social Motion in Dickens, Carlyle, Melville, and Hawthorne.* New Brunswick, N.J.: Rutgers University Press, 1979.

—— "The Function of Foucault at the Present Time." In *Humanities in Society* (1980), 3:73–86.

—— "The Media of Sublimity: Johnson and Lamb on *King Lear.*" In *Studies in Romanticism* (1987), forthcoming.

—— "The Politics of *The Scarlet Letter.*" In Sacvan Bercovitch and Myra Jehlen, eds., *Ideology and Classic American Literature*, pp. 247–66. Cambridge: Cambridge University Press, 1986.

—— "Rhetoric and Realism in Nineteenth-Century Fiction: Hyperbole in *The Mill on the Floss.*" ELH (1979), 46:673–92.

—— "The Struggle for the Cultural Heritage: Christina Stead Refunctions Charles Dickens and Mark Twain." In *Cultural Critique* (1985–86), no. 2, pp. 171–89.

Arendt, Hannah. "The Crisis in Culture: Its Social and Political Significance" (1960). In *Between Past and Future* (1961), pp. 197–226. Cleveland and New York: World, 1963.

Arnold, Matthew. *Complete Prose Works.* R. H. Super, ed. 11 vols. Ann Arbor: University of Michigan Press, 1960–1977.

—— *The Poems of Matthew Arnold.* Kenneth Allott, ed. London: Longmans, 1965.

Aronowitz, Stanley. *The Crisis in Historical Materialism.* New York: Praeger, 1981.

Auerbach, Erich. "Epilegomena zu *Mimesis.*" *Romanische Forschungen* (1953), 65:1–18.

—— *Literary Language and Its Public in Late Latin Antiquity and in the Middle Ages* (1958). Ralph Manheim, tr. New York: Random House, 1965.

318

Works Cited

—— *Mimesis* (1946). Willard Trask, tr. Princeton: Princeton University Press, 1953.

—— Reviews of Curtius, *Europäische Literatur und lateinisches Mittelalter. Romanische Forschungen* (1950), 62:237–45 and *MLN* (1950), 65:348–56.

Austin, J. A. *How to Do Things with Words*. Cambridge: Harvard University Press, 1962.

Averill, James H. *Wordsworth and the Poetry of Human Suffering*. Ithaca: Cornell University Press, 1980.

Babbitt, Irving. *Literature and the American College*. Boston: Houghton Mifflin, 1908.

Bagehot, Walter. "Charles Dickens" (1858). In *Literary Studies*, 2:164–97. London: Dent, 1911.

Bakhtin, M[ikhail] M. *The Dialogic Imagination*. Michael Holquist, ed. Caryl Emerson and Michael Holquist, trs. Austin: University of Texas Press, 1981.

Barrett, William. *The Truants*. New York: Doubleday, 1982.

Barth, Gunther. *City People: The Rise of Modern City Culture in Nineteenth-Century America*. New York: Oxford Univ. Press, 1980.

Bate, Walter Jackson. *The Burden of the Past and the English Poet*. Cambridge: Harvard University Press, 1970.

—— *John Keats*. Cambridge: Harvard University Press, 1963.

Bateson, F. W. *Wordsworth: A Re-Interpretation*. 2d ed. London: Longmans, 1956.

Baudelaire, Charles. *Oeuvres complètes*. Yves-Gérard le Dantec, ed. Paris: Gallimard, 1954.

Bell, Daniel. *The Cultural Contradictions of Capitalism*. New York: Basic Books, 1976.

—— "Modernism and Capitalism." In *Partisan Review* (1978), 46:206–26. Reprinted as introduction to 1978 paperback edition of *The Cultural Contradictions of Capitalism*.

—— *The Winding Passage*. New York: Basic Books, 1980.

Benjamin, Walter. "The Author as Producer" (1934). Anna Bostock, tr. In *Understanding Brecht*, pp. 85–103. London: NLB, 1977.

—— "Central Park." Lloyd Spencer, tr. In *New German Critique* (1985), no. 34, pp. 32–58.

—— *Charles Baudelaire: A Lyric Poet in the Era of High Capitalism*. Harry Zohn, tr. London: NLB, 1973.

—— *Gesammelte Schriften*. Rolf Tiedemann and Hermann Schweppenhäuser, eds. 6 vols. to date. Frankfurt: Suhrkamp, 1974–.

—— *Illuminations* (1968). Harry Zohn, tr. New York: Schocken, 1969.

—— "N [Theoretics of Knowledge; Theory of Progress]." Leigh Hafrey and Richard Sieburth, trs. In *Philosophical Forum* (1985), 15:1–40.

—— *The Origin of German Tragic Drama* (1927). John Osborne, tr. London: NLB, 1977.

Bercovitch, Sacvan. *The American Jeremiad*. Madison: University of Wisconsin Press, 1978.

Bernstein, Richard J., ed. *Habermas and Modernity*. Cambridge: MIT Press, 1985.

Bloch, Ernst et al. *Aesthetics and Politics*. London: NLB, 1977.

Bloom, Harold. *The Anxiety of Influence: A Theory of Poetry*. New York: Oxford University Press, 1973.

—— *Blake's Apocalypse: A Study in Poetic Argument*. Garden City, N.Y.: Doubleday, 1963.

—— *Figures of Capable Imagination*. New York: Seabury Press, 1976.

—— "Freud and the Sublime." In *Agon: Towards a Theory of Revisionism*, pp. 91–118. New York: Oxford University Press, 1982.

—— *Kabbalah and Criticism*. New York: Seabury Press, 1975.

—— *A Map of Misreading*. New York: Oxford University Press, 1975.

—— *Poetry and Repression: Revisionism from Blake to Stevens*. New Haven: Yale University Press, 1976.

—— *The Ringers in the Tower: Studies in Romantic Tradition*. Chicago: University of Chicago Press, 1971.

—— *Shelley's Mythmaking* (1959). Ithaca: Cornell University Press, 1969.

—— *The Visionary Company: A Reading of English Romantic Poetry* (1961). Garden City, N.Y.: Doubleday, 1963.

—— *Wallace Stevens: The Poems of Our Climate*. Ithaca: Cornell University Press, 1977.

—— *Yeats*. New York: Oxford University Press, 1970.

Bloom, Harold et al. *Deconstruction and Criticism*. New York: Seabury Press, 1979.

Bloomfield, Morton W. and Leonard Newmark. *A Linguistic Introduction to the History of English*. New York: Knopf, 1967.

Works Cited

Bové, Paul A. *Destructive Poetics: Heidegger and Modern American Poetry*. New York: Columbia University Press, 1980.

—— *Intellectuals in Power: A Genealogy of Critical Humanism*. New York: Columbia University Press, 1986.

Bradley, A. C. "Wordsworth." In *Oxford Lectures on Poetry* (1909), pp. 99–148. Bloomington: Indiana University Press, 1961.

Brecht, Bertolt. "Weite und Vielfalt der realistischen Schreibweise." In *Schriften zur Literatur und Kunst*, 2:162–73. Frankfurt: Suhrkamp, 1967.

Brisman, Leslie. *Romantic Origins*. Ithaca: Cornell University Press, 1978.

Bromwich, David. *Hazlitt: The Mind of a Critic*. New York: Oxford University Press, 1983.

Brooks, Cleanth. *Modern Poetry and the Tradition* (1939). New York: Oxford University Press, 1967.

—— *The Well Wrought Urn*. New York: Harcourt, Brace, 1947.

Brooks, Cleanth and Robert Penn Warren. *Understanding Poetry: An Anthology for College Students*. New York: Holt, 1938.

Brooks, Cleanth and William K. Wimsatt. *Literary Criticism: A Short History*. New York: Knopf, 1957.

Brower, Reuben A. *Alexander Pope: The Poetry of Allusion*. Oxford: Clarendon Press, 1959.

—— *Hero and Saint: Shakespeare and the Greco-Roman Heroic Tradition*. New York: Oxford University Press, 1970.

Brown, E. K. *Matthew Arnold: A Study in Conflict*. Chicago: University of Chicago Press, 1948.

Bürger, Peter. *Theory of the Avant-Garde* (2d ed., 1980). Michael Shaw, tr. Minneapolis: University of Minnesota Press, 1984.

Burke, Kenneth. "The Philosophy of Literary Form." In *The Philosophy of Literary Form*. Baton Rouge: Louisiana State University Press, 1941, 1–137.

Butler, Marilyn. *Romantics, Rebels and Reactionaries: English Literature and its Background 1760–1830*. Oxford: Oxford University Press, 1981.

Buttigieg, Joseph A. "The Exemplary Worldliness of Antonio Gramsci's Literary Criticism." In *boundary 2* (1982–83), 11(1–2):21–39.

Carlyle, Thomas. *Complete Works: Centenary Edition* (1896–99). H. D. Traill, ed. 30 vols. New York: AMS, 1969.

Chandler, Alfred D. *The Visible Hand: The Managerial Revolution in American Business.* Cambridge: Harvard University Press, Belknap Press, 1977.

Chandler, James K. *Wordsworth's Second Nature: A Study of the Poetry and Politics.* Chicago: University of Chicago Press, 1984.

Coleridge, Samuel Taylor. *Collected Letters.* Earl Leslie Griggs, ed. 6 vols. Oxford: Clarendon Press, 1956–1971.

—— *Collected Works.* Kathleen Coburn, ed. 10 vols. to date. Princeton: Princeton University Press, 1969–.

—— *Complete Works.* W. G. T. Shedd, ed. 7 vols. New York: Harper, 1853.

—— *Notebooks.* Kathleen Coburn, ed. 3 vols. to date. Princeton: Princeton University Press, 1957–.

—— *Poems.* Ernest Hartley Coleridge, ed. London: Oxford University Press, 1912.

Conrad, Joseph. *Letters from Joseph Conrad* (1928). Edward Garnett, ed. Indianapolis: Bobbs-Merrill, 1962.

—— *Letters to R. B. Cunninghame Graham.* C. T. Watts, ed. Cambridge: Cambridge University Press, 1969.

—— *Nostromo* (1904). Garden City, N.Y.: Doubleday, 1921.

—— *Notes on Life and Letters* (1921). Garden City, N.Y.: Doubleday, 1924.

—— *A Personal Record* (1912). London: Dent, 1923.

—— *The Secret Agent* (1907). Garden City, N.Y.: Doubleday, 1924.

Courthope, W. J. "Modern Culture." In *Quarterly Review* (1874), 37:389–415.

Coward, Rosalind and John Ellis. *Language and Materialism.* London: Routledge and Kegan Paul, 1977.

Cowley, Malcolm. *Exile's Return* (1934). New York: Viking, 1956.

Crane, R. S., ed. *Critics and Criticism.* Chicago: University of Chicago Press, 1952.

Crews, Frederick. "Analysis Terminable." In *Commentary* (1980), 70:25–34.

Culler, Jonathan. *Structuralist Poetics.* Ithaca: Cornell University Press, 1975.

Curtius, Ernst Robert. *Essays on European Literature.* Michael Kowal, tr. Princeton: Princeton University Press, 1973.

—— *European Literature and the Latin Middle Ages* (1948). Willard R. Trask (1953), tr. New York: Harper, 1953.

Works Cited

—— "Die Lehre von den drei Stilen in Altertum und Mittelalter." In *Romanische Forschungen* (1952), 64:57–70.

Daleski, H. M. *The Forked Flame: A Study of D. H. Lawrence.* Evanston: Northwestern University Press, 1965.

Dawson, Carl and John Pfordresher, eds. *Matthew Arnold: The Critical Heritage: Prose Writings.* London: Routledge and Kegan Paul, 1979.

DeLaura, David J. "Arnold and Literary Criticism (i): Critical Ideas." In Kenneth Allott, ed., *Matthew Arnold: Writer and Background*, pp. 118–48. London: Bell, 1975.

Delavenay, Emile. *D. H. Lawrence and Edward Carpenter: A Study in Edwardian Transition.* London: Heinemann, 1971.

de Man, Paul. *Allegories of Reading: Figural Language in Rousseau, Nietzsche, Rilke, and Proust.* New Haven: Yale University Press, 1979.

—— *Blindness and Insight: Essays in the Rhetoric of Contemporary Criticism.* 2d ed., enl. Minneapolis: University of Minnesota Press, 1983.

—— "Conclusions: Walter Benjamin's 'The Task of the Translator.'" In *Yale French Studies* (1985), no. 69, pp. 26–46.

—— "Lyrical Voice in Contemporary Theory." In Chaviva Hošek and Patricia Parker, eds., *Lyric Poetry: Beyond New Criticism*, pp. 55–72. Ithaca: Cornell University Press, 1985.

—— "A New Vitalism." Review of Bloom, *The Visionary Company.* In *Massachusetts Review* (1962), 3:618–23.

—— *The Rhetoric of Romanticism.* New York: Columbia University Press, 1984.—

—— "Spacecritics." In *Partisan Review* (1964), 31:640–50.

Derrida, Jacques. "Des Tours de Babel." In Joseph F. Graham, ed., *Difference in Translation*, pp. 165–207. Ithaca: Cornell University Press, 1985.

—— *Of Grammatology* (1967). Gayatri Chakravorty Spivak, tr. Baltimore: Johns Hopkins University Press, 1976.

—— "Sending: On Representation." Peter and Mary Ann Caws, trs. In *Social Research* (1982), 49:294–326.

—— "Signature Event Context" (1971). Samuel Weber and Jeffrey Mehlman, trs. In *Glyph* (1977), no. 1, pp. 172–97.

—— *Speech and Phenomena* (1967). David B. Allison, tr. Evanston: Northwestern University Press, 1973.

—— "The Supplement of Copula." In Harari, ed., *Textual Strategies*, pp. 82–120.

—— "White Mythology: Metaphor in the Text of Philosophy." F. C. Moore, tr. *New Literary History* (1974), 6:5–74.

—— *Writing and Difference* (1967). Alan Bass, tr. Chicago: University of Chicago Press, 1978.

Dickinson, Emily. *Poems.* Thomas H. Johnson, ed. 3 vols. Cambridge: Harvard University Press, Belknap Press, 1958.

Donadio, Stephen. *Nietzsche, Henry James, and the Aesthetic Will.* New York: Oxford University Press, 1978.

Donato, Eugenio. "The Museum's Furnace." In Harari, ed. *Textual Strategies*, 213–38.

Douglas, Ann. *The Feminization of American Culture.* New York: Knopf, 1977.

Eagleton, Terry. *The Function of Criticism: From the "Spectator" to Post-Structuralism.* London: Verso, 1984.

Eliot T[homas] S[tearns]. *Selected Prose.* Frank Kermode, ed. New York: Harcourt Brace Jovanovich and Farrar, Straus and Giroux, 1975.

Emerson, Ralph Waldo. *Essays and Lectures.* New York: Library of America, 1983.

Empson, William. "'Sense' in *The Prelude*." In *The Structure of Complex Words* (1951), pp. 289–305. Ann Arbor: University of Michigan Press, 1967.

—— *Seven Types of Ambiguity* (1930). 3d ed. New York: New Directions, n.d.

Fekete, John. "Modernity in the Literary Institution." In John Fekete, ed., *The Structural Allegory*, pp. 228–47. Minneapolis: University of Minnesota Press, 1984.

Ferry, David. *The Limits of Mortality.* Middletown, Conn.: Wesleyan University Press, 1959.

Fitzgerald, Robert. *Enlarging the Change: The Princeton Seminars in Literary Criticism, 1949–51.* Boston: Northeastern University Press, 1985.

Foerster, Norman, ed. *Humanism and America.* New York: Farrar and Rinehart, 1930.

Foster, Hal, ed. *The Anti-Aesthetic: Essays on Postmodern Culture.* Port Townsend, Wash.: Bay Press, 1983.

Works Cited

Foucault, Michel. *Discipline and Punish* (1975). Alan Sheridan, tr. New York: Pantheon, 1977.

—— *The History of Sexuality* (vol. 1). Robert Hurley, tr. New York: Pantheon, 1977.

—— *Language, Counter-Memory, Practice*. Donald F. Bouchard, ed. Donald F. Bouchard and Sherry Simon, trs. Ithaca: Cornell University Press, 1977.

—— "My Body, This Paper, This Fire" (1972). Geoff Bennington, tr. In *Oxford Literary Review* (1979), 4(1):9–28.

—— *The Order of Things* (1966). No translator named. New York: Random House, 1973.

—— "Truth and Power" (1977). Colin Gordon, tr. In *Power/Knowledge*, pp. 109–33. New York: Pantheon, 1980.

Frank, Joseph. "Spatial Form: An Answer to Critics." In *Critical Inquiry* (1977), 4:231–52.

Freud, Sigmund. *Standard Edition of the Complete Psychological Works*. James Strachey, ed. and tr. 24 vols. London: Hogarth Press, 1953–1974.

Fried, Michael. *Absorption and Theatricality*. Berkeley and Los Angeles: University of California Press, 1980.

Fry, Paul H. *The Reach of Criticism: Method and Perception in Literary Theory*. New Haven: Yale University Press, 1983.

Frye, Northrop. *Anatomy of Criticism: Four Essays*. Princeton: Princeton University Press, 1957.

—— *Fables of Identity: Studies in Poetic Mythology*. New York: Harcourt, Brace and World, 1963.

—— *Fearful Symmetry: A Study of William Blake* (1947). Boston: Beacon Press, 1962.

Gasché, Rodolphe. "Deconstruction as Criticism." In *Glyph* (1979), no. 6, pp. 177–215.

Giddens, Anthony. "From Marx to Nietzsche? Neo-Conservatism, Foucault, and Problems in Contemporary Political Theory." In *Profiles and Critiques in Social Theory*, pp. 215–30. Berkeley and Los Angeles: University of California Press, 1982.

Gilbert, James Burkhart. *Writers and Partisans*. New York: Wiley, 1968.

Gilbert, Sandra. *Acts of Attention: The Poetry of D. H. Lawrence*. Ithaca: Cornell University Press, 1972.

Glazer, Nathan. "New York Intellectuals—Up from Revolution." In *New York Times Book Review*, February 26, 1984, pp. 1, 34–35.

Goldmann, Lucien. *Lukács and Heidegger* (1973). William Q. Boelhower, tr. London: Routledge and Kegan Paul, 1977.

Graff, Gerald. *Professing Literature: An Institutional History*. Chicago: University of Chicago Press, 1987.

—— *Literature Against Itself*. Chicago: University of Chicago Press, 1979.

—— Review of Kermode, *Genesis of Secrecy*. *New Republic*, June 9, 1979, pp. 27–32.

—— "Who Killed Criticism?" In *American Scholar* (1980), 49:337–55.

Grattan, C. Hartley, ed. *Critique of Humanism* (1930). Port Washington, N.Y.: Kennikat, 1968.

Green, Martin. *The Von Richthofen Sisters*. New York: Basic Books, 1974.

Greenblatt, Stephen. *Renaissance Self-Fashioning*. Chicago: University of Chicago Press, 1980.

Greene, Thomas. *The Light from Troy*. New Haven: Yale University Press, 1982.

Habermas, Jürgen. "Modernity—An Incomplete Project" (1980). Seyla Ben-Habib, tr. In Foster, ed., *The Anti-Aesthetic*, pp. 3–15.

—— "Neoconservative Culture Criticism in the United States and West Germany: An Intellectual Movement in Two Political Cultures" (1983). Russell A. Berman, tr. In Bernstein, ed., *Habermas and Modernity*, pp. 78–94.

—— *Der philosophische Diskurs der Moderne*. Frankfurt: Suhrkamp, 1985.

—— "Questions and Counterquestions" (1984). James Bohman, tr. In Bernstein, ed., *Habermas and Modernity*, pp. 192–216.

Hacking, Ian. *Why Does Language Matter to Philosophy?* Cambridge: Cambridge University Press, 1975.

Harari, Josué V., ed. *Textual Strategies: Perspectives in Post-Structuralist Criticism*. Ithaca: Cornell University Press, 1979.

Hartman, Geoffrey H. *Beyond Formalism: Literary Essays, 1958–1970*. New Haven: Yale University Press, 1970.

—— *Criticism in the Wilderness: Literary Study Today*. New Haven: Yale University Press, 1980.

Works Cited

—— *The Fate of Reading and Other Essays.* Chicago: University of Chicago Press, 1975.

—— "Preface." In Bloom et al., *Deconstruction and Criticism,* pp. vii–ix.

—— *Saving the Text: Literature/Derrida/Philosophy.* Baltimore: Johns Hopkins University Press, 1981.

—— "A Touching Compulsion: Wordsworth and the Problem of Literary Representation." in *Georgia Review* (1977), 31:345–61.

—— *Wordsworth's Poetry, 1787–1814.* New Haven: Yale University Press, 1964.

Hassan, Ihab. "Postface 1982: Toward a Concept of Postmodernism." In *The Dismemberment of Orpheus: Toward a Postmodern Literature* (1971), 2d ed., pp. 259–71. Madison: University of Wisconsin Press, 1982.

—— "POSTmodernISM" (1971). In *Paracriticisms,* pp. 39–59. Urbana: University of Illinois Press, 1975.

Hassan, Ihab and Sally Hassan, eds. *Innovation/Renovation.* Madison: University of Wisconsin Press, 1983.

Hazlitt, William. *Complete Works.* P. P. Howe, ed. 21 vols. London: Dent, 1930.

Heidegger, Martin. "The Age of the World View." Marjorie Grene, tr. In *boundary 2* (1976), 4(2):341–55.

Hirsch, E. D. "Carnal Knowledge." In *New York Review of Books,* June 14, 1979, pp. 18–20.

—— *Validity in Interpretation.* New Haven: Yale University Press, 1967.

Hodgson, John A. *Wordsworth's Philosophical Poetry, 1797–1814.* Lincoln: University of Nebraska Press, 1980.

Hogle, Jerrold E. "Shelley's Poetics: The Power as Metaphor." In *Keats-Shelley Journal* (1982), 31:159–97.

Homans, Margaret. *Women Writers and Poetic Identity: Dorothy Wordsworth, Emily Brontë, Emily Dickinson.* Princeton: Princeton University Press, 1980.

Holloway, John. *The Victorian Sage.* London: Macmillan, 1953.

Howe, Irving. *The Decline of the New.* New York: Harcourt Brace Jovanovich, 1970.

—— *A Margin of Hope.* New York: Harcourt Brace Jovanovich, 1982.

—— "Modern Criticism: Privileges and Perils." In Irving Howe, ed., *Modern Literary Criticism*, pp. 1–37. Boston: Beacon Press, 1958.

—— *Politics and the Novel* (1957). Greenwich, Conn.: Fawcett, 1967.

Howe, Irving and Lewis Coser. *The American Communist Party: A Critical History (1919–1957)*. Boston: Beacon Press, 1957.

Huyssen, Andreas. "The Search for Tradition: Avant-Garde and Postmodernism in the 1970s." In *New German Critique* (1982), no. 26, pp. 23–40.

Jakobson, Roman. "Linguistics and Poetics." In Thomas A. Sebeok, ed., *Style in Language*, pp. 350–77. Cambridge, Mass.: MIT Press, 1960.

—— "The Metaphoric and Metonymic Poles." In *Fundamentals of Language*, ch. 5. The Hague: Mouton, 1956.

James, Henry. *Henry James*. 3 vols. to date. New York: Library of America, 1983.

—— *Letters*. Leon Edel, ed. 4 vols. Cambridge: Harvard University Press, 1974–1984.

—— *The Portrait of a Lady*. New York: Scribner, 1907.

—— *The Wings of the Dove*. New York: Scribner, 1909.

Jameson, Fredric. Interview. In *Diacritics* (1982), 12(3):72–91.

—— *Marxism and Form: Twentieth-Century Dialectical Theories of Literature*. Princeton: Princeton University Press, 1971.

—— "Marxism and Historicism." In *New Literary History* (1979), 11:41–73.

—— "Periodizing the 60s." In Sohnya Sayres et al., eds., *The 60s without Apology*, pp. 178–209. Minneapolis: University of Minnesota Press, 1984.

—— *The Political Unconscious: Narrative as a Socially Symbolic Act*. Ithaca: Cornell University Press, 1981.

—— "Postmodernism, or The Cultural Logic of Late Capitalism." In *New Left Review* (1984), no. 146, pp. 53–92.

Jarrell, Randall. "The Age of Criticism." In *Poetry and the Age*, pp. 70–95. New York: Knopf, 1953.

Joyce, James. *Ulysses* (1922). New York: Modern Library, 1961.

Kay, Carol. "Canon and Ideology: Mary Wollstonecraft's Critique of Adam Smith." In *New Political Science* (1986), no. 15, pp. 63–76.

Works Cited

Keats, John. *Letters*. Hyder Edward Rollins, ed. 2 vols. Cambridge: Harvard University Press, 1958.

Kermode, Frank. *The Art of Telling: Essays on Fiction*. Cambridge: Harvard University Press, 1983.

—— *The Classic: Literary Images of Permanence and Change*. New York: Viking, 1975.

—— *Continuities*. New York: Random House, 1968.

—— *D. H. Lawrence*. New York: Viking, 1973.

—— *Forms of Attention*. Chicago: University of Chicago Press, 1985.

—— *The Genesis of Secrecy: On the Interpretation of Narrative*. Cambridge: Harvard University Press, 1979.

—— "Novel and Narrative." In John Halperin, ed., *The Theory of the Novel*, pp. 155–74. New York: Oxford University Press, 1974.

—— *Puzzles and Epiphanies: Essays and Reviews, 1958–61*. New York: Chilmark Press, 1962.

—— "Reply to Jonathan Arac." In *Salmagundi* (1982), no. 55, pp. 156–62.

—— *Romantic Image* (1957). New York: Random House, 1964.

—— *The Sense of an Ending: Studies in the Theory of Fiction*. New York: Oxford University Press, 1967.

—— *Shakespeare, Spenser, Donne: Renaissance Essays*. New York: Viking, 1971.

—— *Wallace Stevens*. Edinburgh and London: Oliver and Boyd, 1960.

Kierkegaard, Søren. *Either/Or*. David F. Swenson and Lillian Marvin Swenson, trs., rev. Howard A. Johnson. Princeton: Princeton University Press.

Klehr, Harvey. *The Heyday of American Communism*. New York: Basic Books, 1984.

Knight, G. Wilson. *The Starlit Dome* (1941). London: Oxford University Press, 1971.

Kristeller, Paul O. "The Modern System of the Arts." In *Journal of the History of Ideas* (1951–1952), 12:496–527; 13:17–46.

Kristeva, Julia. *La Révolution du langage poétique*. Paris: Seuil, 1974.

Kuhn, Thomas S. *The Structure of Scientific Revolutions*. Chicago: University of Chicago Press, 1962.

LaCapra, Dominick. *History and Criticism*. Ithaca: Cornell University Press, 1985.

Lamb, Charles. *The Letters of Charles and Mary Anne Lamb*. Edwin W. Marrs, Jr., ed. Ithaca and London: Cornell University Press, 1975.

Landes, David S. *Revolution in Time: Clocks and the Making of the Modern World*. Cambridge: Harvard University Press, Belknap Press, 1983.

Lawrence, D[avid] H[erbert]. *Letters*. James T. Boulton, ed. 3 vols. to date. Cambridge: Cambridge University Press, 1979–.

—— *Phoenix* (1936). New York: Viking, 1968.

—— *Reflections on the Death of a Porcupine* (1925). Bloomington: Indiana University Press, 1963.

—— *Women in Love* (1920). New York: Viking, 1960.

Leavis, F. R. "Wordsworth." In *Revaluation*, pp. 154–202. London: Chatto and Windus, 1936.

Lentricchia, Frank. *After the New Criticism*. Chicago: University of Chicago Press, 1980.

Levin, Harry. *The Power of Blackness*. New York: Knopf, 1958.

—— *Refractions*. New York: Oxford University Press, 1966.

Leyda, Jay. "Miss Emily's Maggie." In *New World Writing: Third Mentor Selection*, pp. 255–67. New York: New American Library, 1953.

—— *The Years and Hours of Emily Dickinson*. 2 vols. New Haven: Yale University Press, 1960.

Lindenberger, Herbert. *On Wordsworth's "Prelude."* Princeton: Princeton University Press, 1963.

Lipking, Lawrence. "The Marginal Gloss." In *Critical Inquiry* (1977), 3:609–55.

Litz, A. Walton. "Literary Criticism." In Daniel Hoffmann, ed., *Harvard Guide to Contemporary American Writing*, pp. 51–83. Cambridge: Harvard University Press, 1979.

Longinus. *On the Sublime*. D. A. Russell, ed. Oxford: Clarendon Press, 1964.

Lovejoy, A[rthur] O. *Essays in the History of Ideas* (1948). New York: Putnam, 1960.

—— *The Great Chain of Being*. Cambridge: Harvard University Press, 1936.

Lukács, Georg. *History and Class Consciousness: Studies in Marxist Dialectics* (1923). Rodney Livingstone, tr. Cambridge: MIT Press, 1971.

Works Cited

—— "The Ideology of Modernism" (1957). In *The Meaning of Contemporary Realism*, John and Necke Mander, trs., pp. 17–46. London: Merlin, 1963.

—— "On the Nature and Form of the Essay." In *Soul and Form*, Anna Bostock, tr., pp. 1–18. Cambridge: MIT Press, 1974.

—— *Solzhenitsyn* (1970). William David Graf, tr. Cambridge: MIT Press, 1971.

Lyotard, Jean-François. "Answering the Question: What Is Postmodernism?" (1982). Régis Durand, tr. In *The Postmodern Condition*, pp. 71–82.

—— "The Differend, the Referent, and the Proper Name." Georges Van Den Abbeele, tr. In *Diacritics* (1984), 14(3):4–14.

—— *The Postmodern Condition* (1979). Geoff Bennington and Brian Massumi, trs. Minneapolis: University of Minnesota Press, 1984.

McGann, Jerome J. *A Critique of Modern Textual Criticism*. Chicago: University of Chicago Press, 1983.

—— *The Romantic Ideology: A Critical Investigation*. Chicago: University of Chicago Press, 1983.

MacIntyre, Alasdair. *After Virtue*. Notre Dame, Ind.: Notre Dame University Press, 1981.

Malraux, André. "The Cultural Heritage." Abridged and translated by Malcolm Cowley. In *New Republic* (1936), 88:315–17.

—— "Sur l'héritage culturel." In *Commune* (September 1936), no. 37, pp. 1–9.

Martz, Louis L[ohr]. *The Poetry of Meditation*. New Haven: Yale University Press, 1954.

Matthiessen, F[rancis] O[tto]. *American Renaissance: Art and Expression in the Age of Emerson and Whitman*. New York: Oxford University Press, 1941.

—— *From the Heart of Europe*. New York: Oxford University Press, 1948.

—— *The Responsibilities of the Critic*. John Rackliffe, ed. New York: Oxford University Press, 1952.

Matthiessen, F. O. and Russell Cheney. *Rat and the Devil: Journal Letters*. Louis Hyde, ed. Hamden, Conn.: Archon, 1978.

Miles, Josephine. *Eras and Modes in English Poetry*. 2d ed., rev. and enl. Berkeley and Los Angeles: University of California Press, 1964.

Miller, J. Hillis. "The Critic as Host." in Bloom et al., *Deconstruction and Criticism*, pp. 217–53.

— *The Disappearance of God.* Cambridge: Harvard University Press, 1963.

— "The Fiction of Realism." In Ada Nisbet and Blake Nevius, eds., *Dickens Centennial Essays*, pp. 85–153. Berkeley and Los Angeles: University of California Press, 1971.

— "Narrative and History." In *ELH* (1974), 41:455–73.

— "Tradition and Difference." In *Diacritics* (1972), 2(4):6–13.

Newman, Charles. "The Post-Modern Aura: The Act of Fiction in an Age of Inflation." In *Salmagundi* (1984), nos. 63–64, pp. 3–199.

Niebuhr, H[elmut] Richard. *The Kingdom of God in America* (1935). Hamden, Conn.: Shoe String Press, 1956.

Nietzsche, Friedrich. *The Antichrist.* Walter Kaufmann, tr. In *The Portable Nietzsche.* New York: Viking, 1954.

— *The Genealogy of Morals.* Walter Kaufmann, tr. In *The Basic Nietzsche.* New York: Modern Library, 1968.

— *The Will to Power.* Walter Kaufmann and R. J. Hollingdale, trs. New York: Random House, 1968.

O'Connor, William Van. *An Age of Criticism, 1900–1950* (1952). Chicago: Regnery, 1966.

O'Hara, Daniel T. *The Romance of Interpretation: Visionary Criticism from Pater to de Man.* New York: Columbia University Press, 1985.

Ohmann, Richard. *English in America: A Radical View of the Profession.* New York: Oxford University Press, 1976.

Olson, Elder. "A Symbolic Reading of the *Ancient Mariner.*" In Crane, ed., *Critics and Criticism*, pp. 138–44.

Ortega y Gasset, José. *The Dehumanization of Art, and Notes on the Novel.* Helene Weyl, tr. Princeton: Princeton University Press, 1948.

Orwell, George. *Collected Essays, Journalism, and Letters* (1968). 4 vols. Harmondsworth: Penguin, 1970.

Panofsky, Erwin. *Idea.* Leipzig and Berlin: Teubner, 1924.

Parrish, Stephen, ed. *The Prelude, 1798–1799.* By William Wordsworth. Ithaca: Cornell University Press, 1977.

Pater, Walter. *Appreciations* (1889). London and New York: Macmillan, 1897.

Works Cited

—— *The Renaissance* (1873, 4th ed. 1893). Donald L. Hill, ed. Berkeley and Los Angeles: University of California Press, 1980.

Pells, Richard H. *Radical Visions and American Dreams*. New York: Harper and Row, 1973.

Perkins, David. *The Quest for Permanence*. Cambridge: Harvard University Press, 1959.

—— *Wordsworth and the Poetry of Sincerity*. Cambridge: Harvard University Press, 1964.

Pulos, C. E. *The Deep Truth: A Study of Shelley's Scepticism*. Lincoln: University of Nebraska Press, 1954.

Pynchon, Thomas. *Gravity's Rainbow*. New York: Viking, 1973.

Raleigh, John Henry. *Matthew Arnold in America*. Berkeley and Los Angeles: University of California Press, 1957.

Richards, I[vor] A[rmstrong]. *Principles of Literary Criticism* (1924). New York: Harcourt, n.d.

Ringer, Fritz. *The Decline of the German Mandarins: The German Academic Community, 1890–1933*. Cambridge: Harvard University Press, 1969.

Rogin, Michael Paul. *Subversive Genealogy: The Politics and Art of Herman Melville*. New York: Knopf, 1983.

Rorty, Richard. *Consequences of Pragmatism*. Minneapolis: University of Minnesota Press, 1982.

—— "Habermas and Lyotard on Postmodernity" (1984). In Bernstein, ed., *Habermas and Modernity*, pp. 161–75.

—— *Philosophy and the Mirror of Nature*. Princeton: Princeton University Press, 1979.

—— "Postmodernist Bourgeois Liberalism." In *Journal of Philosophy* (1983), 80:583–89.

—— "Texts and Lumps." In *New Literary History* (1985), 17:1–17.

Rosenberg, Harold. *The Tradition of the New*. New York: Horizon, 1959.

Said, Edward W. "Audiences, Opponents, Constituencies, and Community" (1982). In Foster, ed., *The Anti-Aesthetic*, pp. 135–59.

—— *Beginnings*. New York: Basic Books, 1975.

—— "Egyptian Rites." In *Village Voice*, Aug. 30, 1983, pp. 43–46.

—— *Orientalism*. New York: Pantheon, 1978.

—— "Permission to Narrate." In *London Review of Books* (1984), 6(3):13–17.

—— *The World, the Text, and the Critic*. Cambridge: Harvard University Press, 1983.

Sartre, Jean-Paul. *L'Idiot de la famille*. 3 vols. Paris: Gallimard, 1971–72.

Schlegel, A. W. *A Course of Lectures on Dramatic Art and Literature* (1811). John Black, tr., rev. A. J. W. Morrison. London: Bohn, 1846.

Schorske, Carl E. *Fin-de-Siècle Vienna*. New York: Knopf, 1980.

Schulte-Sasse, Jochen. "Foreword: Theory of Modernism versus Theory of the Avant-Garde." In Bürger, *Theory of the Avant-Garde*, pp. vii–xlvii.

Sedgwick, Peter. "The Two New Lefts" (1964). In David Widgery, ed., *The Left in Britain, 1956–1968*, pp. 131–53. Harmondsworth: Penguin, 1976.

Selincourt, Ernest de, ed. *The Prelude or Growth of a Poet's Mind*. By William Wordsworth. 2d ed. Rev. Helen Darbishire. Oxford: Clarendon Press, 1959.

Sewall, Richard B. *The Life of Emily Dickinson* (1974). New York: Farrar, Straus and Giroux, 1980.

Shaver, Chester and Alice C. Shaver. *Wordsworth's Library: A Catalogue*. New York: Garland, 1979.

Shelley, Percy Bysshe. *Shelley's Poetry and Prose*. Donald H. Reiman and Sharon B. Powers, eds. New York: Norton, 1977.

Simmel, Georg. "The Adventurer." In Donald N. Levine, ed., *Georg Simmel on Individuality and Social Forms*, pp. 187–98. Chicago: University of Chicago Press, 1971.

—— "The Metropolis and Mental Life." In *The Sociology of Georg Simmel* (1950), Kurt H. Wolff, ed., pp. 409–24. New York: Free Press, 1964.

Smith, James. "Wordsworth: A Preliminary Survey" (1938). In F. R. Leavis, ed. *A Selection from "Scrutiny"*, 2:137–56. Cambridge: Cambridge University Press, 1969.

Spanos, William V. "Modern Literary Criticism and the Spatialization of Time: An Existential Critique." In *Journal of Aesthetics and Art Criticism* (1970), 29:87–104.

Susman, Warren I. "Socialism and Americanism" (1974). In *Culture as History*, pp. 75–85. New York: Pantheon, 1984.

Tate, Allen. "Emily Dickinson" (1932). In *The Man of Letters in the Modern World*, pp. 211–26. New York: Meridian, 1955.

Works Cited

Taylor, George Rogers. *The Transportation Revolution*. New York: Holt, Rinehart and Winston, 1951.

Thompson, E[dward] P[almer]. *The Making of the English Working Class*. New York: Random House, 1964.

Thorburn, David. *Conrad's Romanticism*. New Haven: Yale University Press, 1974.

Trelawny, Edward John. *Recollections of the Last Days of Shelley and Byron*. Boston: Ticknor and Fields, 1858.

Trilling, Lionel. *Beyond Culture*. New York: Viking, 1965.

—— "Introduction." In *The Portable Matthew Arnold*, pp. 1–36. New York: Viking, 1949.

—— *The Last Decade*. New York: Harcourt Brace Jovanovich, 1979.

—— *The Liberal Imagination*. New York: Viking, 1950.

—— *Matthew Arnold* (1939). Cleveland: World, 1955.

—— "Parrington, Mr. Smith, and Reality." *Partisan Review* (1940), 7:24–40.

Tuve, Rosemund. *Renaissance and Metaphysical Imagery*. Chicago: University of Chicago Press, 1947.

Warren, Robert Penn. *Selected Essays* (1958). New York: Random House, 1966.

Wasserman, Earl R. *The Finer Tone: Keats's Major Poems*. Baltimore: Johns Hopkins University Press, 1953.

—— Review of Bloom, *Shelley's Mythmaking*. In *Yale Review* (1959), 48:609–12.

—— *Shelley: A Critical Reading*. Baltimore: Johns Hopkins University Press, 1971.

Watt, Ian. *Conrad in the Nineteenth Century*. Berkeley and Los Angeles: University of California Press, 1979.

—— "Conrad's Preface to *The Nigger of the 'Narcissus'*." In *Novel* (1974), 7:101–16.

Watt, Ian, ed. *Conrad: "The Secret Agent": A Casebook*. London: Macmillan, 1973.

Webster, Grant. *Republic of Letters: A History of Postwar American Literary Opinion*. Baltimore: Johns Hopkins University Press, 1979.

Weimann, Robert. "Text and History: Epilogue, 1984." In *Structure and Society in Literary History: Studies in the Theory and History of Historical Criticism* (1976), expanded ed., pp. 267–323. Baltimore: Johns Hopkins University Press, 1984.

Wellek, René. *A History of Modern Criticism, 1750–1950*. 6 vols. to date. New Haven: Yale University Press, 1955–.

Wellek, René and Austin Warren. *Theory of Literature*. New York: Harcourt, Brace, 1949.

West, Cornel. "Ethics and Action in Fredric Jameson's Marxist Hermeneutics." In Jonathan Arac, ed., *Postmodernism and Politics*, pp. 123–44. Minneapolis: University of Minnesota Press, 1986.

White, Hayden V. *Metahistory*. Baltimore: Johns Hopkins University Press, 1973.

Widmer, Kingsley. "Conrad's Pyrrhonistic Conservatism." In *Novel* (1974), 7:133–42.

Williams, Raymond. "Base and Superstructure in Marxist Cultural Theory" (1973). In *Problems in Materialism and Culture*, pp. 31–49. London: NLB, 1980.

—— *The Country and the City*. New York: Oxford University Press, 1973.

—— *Culture and Society, 1780–1950*. New York: Columbia University Press, 1958.

—— *Politics and Letters*. London: NLB, 1979.

—— *Writing in Society*. London: Verso, 1984.

Wilson, Edmund. "An Appeal to Progressives" (1931). In *The Shores of Light* (1952), pp. 518–33. New York: Random House, 1961.

Wilt, Judith. *Secret Leaves: The Novels of Walter Scott*. Chicago: University of Chicago Press, 1985.

Winters, Yvor. *Primitivism and Decadence: A Study of American Experimental Poetry* (1937). New York: Haskell House, 1969.

Woolf, Virginia. *To the Lighthouse*. New York: Harcourt, Brace and World, 1927.

Wordsworth, William. *The Letters of William and Dorothy Wordsworth: The Early Years, 1787–1805*. Ernest de Selincourt, ed. 2d ed. Rev. Chester Shaver. Oxford: Clarendon Press, 1967.

—— *The Poems*. John O. Hayden, ed. 2 vols. Harmondsworth: Penguin, 1977.

—— *The Poetical Works of William Wordsworth*. Ernest de Selincourt and Helen Darbishire, eds. 5 vols. Oxford: Clarendon Press, 1949.

—— *The Prelude, 1799, 1805, 1850*. Jonathan Wordsworth, M. H. Abrams, and Stephen Gill, eds. New York: Norton, 1979.

—— *The Prose Works of William Wordsworth*. W. J. B. Owen and

336

Works Cited

Jane Worthington Smyser, eds. 3 vols. Oxford: Clarendon Press, 1974.

—— *"The Ruined Cottage" and "The Pedlar"*. James Butler, ed. Ithaca: Cornell University Press, 1979.

Young, Edward. *Conjectures on Original Composition* (1759). In *Literary Criticism in England: 1660–1800*, pp. 359–72. Gerald Wester Chapman, ed. New York: Knopf, 1966.

Zabel, Morton Dauwen. *Literary Opinion in America*. 3d ed., rev. New York: Harper and Row, 1962.

Zeitlin, Froma I. "The Dynamics of Misogyny: Myth and Myth-making in the *Oresteia*." In *Arethusa* (1978), 11(1–2):149–84.

Index

Abrams, M. H., 3, 4; and Aristotle, 59; and Arnold, 71–72, 125; and Auerbach, 71, 75; and Benjamin, 79–80; and Bloom, 141; and Booth, 77; and Coleridge, 241; and Curtius, 75; and deconstruction, 77; and Hartman, 25, 27; and heterocosm, 14, 59; and Harvard, 77–80; and history, 76–80; and institution, 77–80; and Jameson, 262; and Kermode, 217, 218, 221, 231; and Matthiessen, 168; and Miller, 263; *The Mirror and the Lamp*, 12, 59, 77–79; *Natural Supernaturalism*, 23, 25, 27, 59–60, 70–71, 75, 77–79, 231, 262; and New Criticism, 75, 77–78; and *The Prelude*, 79; and romanticism, 14; and tact, 123; and tradition, 77–78; and Wordsworth, 59–60, 64–65, 67, 70–74, 100

Adorno, Theodor: and America, 312–13; and Benjamin, 159–60, 196, 197, 210–11; and Habermas, 288; and Lukács, 169; and Shelley, 159–60; and tact, 123; and totality, 214

Aesthetics: and America, 293; and Bloom, 23; and Coleridge, 84; and de Man, 108; and Donadio, 241; German, 293; and James, 258–59; and Matthiessen, 173; and New Criticism, 205–6; and Nietzsche, 259; and postmodernism, 286–87, 307–8; and power, 145; and *The Prelude*, 65–66; and rigor, 108; and theology, 243; and Warren, 84; and Wordsworth, 45, 49

Allegory: and Baudelaire, 200, 205, 207–8; and Benjamin, 207–8, 255; Christian, 261–62; and de Man, 24, 209; and Dickinson, 200, 205; and Jameson, 261–62; and Matthiessen, 175;

and novel, 73; and representation, 45; and symbol, 140; *see also* Rhetoric

Allen, Woody, 13, 291

Althusser, Louis, 5; and *Darstellung*, 298; and Foucault, 302; and ideology, 54, 307; and Jameson, 261–62, 264; and representation, 298

America: and cultural opposition, 308–15; culture and politics in, 282; and Jameson, 270; socialism in, 281–2

Anderson, Perry, 284–87, 291, 313

Arendt, Hannah, 293

Aristotle, 5, 17, 59, 175, 296, 298–99

Arnold, Matthew, 3, 4, 5, 6, 8, 115–36; and Abrams, 262; and academic liberalism, 123–24; and Bible, 124–25, 217, 233; and Bloom, 11, 15–17, 27; and canon, 118, 129; and Cobbett, 136; critical career of, 16; and culture, 132, 137; and current criticism, 121–25; and de Man, 82, 105; and Dickinson, 195; and discipline, 117, 129, 137; and Frye, 20; and Habermas, 293; and Hartman, 27, 29, 31; and hegemony, 287, 307; and history, 129–30, 134–37, 259; and humanism, 126; and irony, 126, 128; and judgment, 120; and Kermode, 217; and Matthiessen, 159; modernist reception of, 117–21; and New Criticism, 82; and Nietzsche, 124–25, 126; and novel, 119; and pedagogy, 118–19; and Persia, 129–30, 134–35; and power, 124, 130–37; and prophecy, 119–20; and publishing, 130, 132; and rhetoric, 124–25; and Said, 82; and state, 130–31; style of, 127–30; and subject, 124, 125–26; and tact, 123–24, 130; and touchstones, 118; and Trilling, 314; and university,

Index

Index

284–87; and representation, 295; and
repression thesis, 263–65; and socialism, 282; and sound, 278–79; and textualism, 82; and totality, 214, 305–7
Johnson, Samuel, 8; and Arnold, 120,
129; refutes Berkeley, 234, 271; refutes
Bloom, 272
Joyce, James: and Curtius, 74–75; and
Jameson, 277; and Kermode, 233; and
postmodernism, 283; and Trilling,
167; *Ulysses*, 173, 271–72

Kay, Carol, 45, 51
Keats, John: and American academic
criticism, 100; and Arnold, 118, 120;
and avant-garde, 32; and Bloom, 13,
14; and Hartman, 31; and Hazlitt, 33;
and Wasserman, 103–4; and Wordsworth, 179
Kermode, Frank, 3, 5, 6, 217–37; and aevum, 228, 230; and Bible, 20; career
of, 218–21, 229; and Conrad, 236–37,
279; and deconstruction, 221; and
de Man, 220–21; and double truth,
222, 230; and Hartman, 33; and history, 217–18, 227, 229–31, 234–37; and
institution, 222, 224, 229, 232–35; and
interpretation, 231–37; and Jameson,
220, 279; and literary science, 231–32;
and Marxism, 220; and modernism,
24; and mystery, 217–18; and New
Criticism, 225; and normal criticism,
221–22; and patience, 235–36; and secrecy, 230; and spatial form, 70, 225;
and Williams, 219–20
——Works: *The Classic*, 218, 219, 222,
228, 230–32; *The Genesis of Secrecy*,
119, 218, 219, 222, 228, 229, 232–34;
Romantic Image, 151, 173, 217, 218,
220, 223, 224–25, 228; "Secrets and
Narrative Sequence," 234–37; *The
Sense of an Ending*, 218, 219, 220,
222, 227–29, 231, 233, 234
Kierkegaard, Søren, 283; *Either/Or*, 250–
51
Kristeva, Julia, 45, 48
Kuhn, Thomas, 2–3; *The Structure of
Scientific Revolutions*, 222

Lacan, Jacques, 23, 45, 261, 269

Lamb, Charles, 69, 139–40
Larkin, Philip, 228–29
Lawrence, D. H., 4, 5, 139–55; and
Bloom, 15; and Coleridge, 88, 142–45,
171; and dialectic, 149–51; and Dostoevsky, 154–55; and flower, 155; and
gender issues, 150–51; and Habermas,
293; and imagelessness, 153; and Kermode, 224, 225, 230, 234; and Matthiessen, 171; and moon, 142–43, 149;
and Plato, 147–49, 153; and public,
151–53; and rose, 155; and Shelley,
153–54, 171; and the sublime, 139–40;
and sun, 148; and symbol, 142–45,
148; and tragedy, 154–55; and Trilling, 167; and vision, 146–49, 151, 152;
Study of Thomas Hardy, 150–51;
Women in Love, 139–47, 154–55
Leavis, F. R.: and Arnold, 119; and
Bloom, 20; and experience, 314; and
Habermas, 293; and Matthiessen, 159;
and media, 34; and Williams, 313;
and Wordsworth, 26, 71
Lentricchia, Frank, 3, 11, 218
Lessing, Doris, *The Golden Notebook*,
313
Levin, Harry, 284, 307–8, 309
Lindenberger, Herbert, 70–74
Literature, as institution, *see* Institu-
tion
Longinus, *see* Sublime
Lovejoy, A. O., 223; *The Great Chain of
Being*, 78
Lukács, Georg, 5; and Benjamin, 196,
210; and Hartman, 27, 29, 31; and
Heidegger, 283, 304; *History and Class
Consciousness*, 210, 283, 304; and
Jameson, 214, 261, 264, 269; and Mat-
thiessen, 169; and popular front, 165;
and realism, 160; and representation,
295, 297–98; and time, 212
Lyotard, Jean-François, 284–88, 298

Malraux, André, 162, 165, 172, 173–74
Marx, Karl, 5; and Althusser, 298; and
Arnold, 117; and Bloom, 23; and
Howe, 274; and language, 178; and
Simmel, 181; *18th Brumaire of Louis
Bonaparte*, 236, 274; and production
model, 264

Index

347

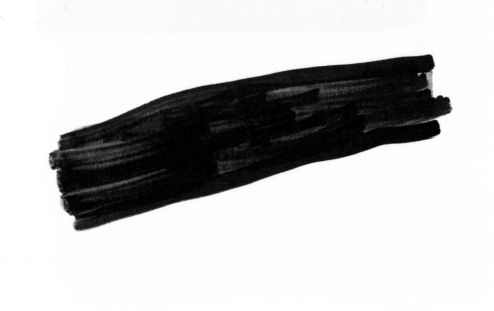